Role Playing
in the Curriculum

SECOND EDITION

Role Playing in the Curriculum

Fannie R. Shaftel
Professor Emerita
Stanford University

George Shaftel

Prentice-Hall, Inc.
Englewood Cliffs, New Jersey 07632

Library of Congress Cataloging in Publication Data

SHAFTEL, FANNIE R.
  Role playing in the curriculum.

  First ed. published in 1967 as: Role-playing
for social values.
    Bibliography: p.
    Includes index.
    1. Social sciences—Study and teaching
(Elementary)   2. Role playing.   3. Social values.
I. Shaftel, George Armin.   II. Title.
LB1584.S47 1982   372.8'3   81-7342
ISBN   0-13-782482-3   AACR2

*Editorial/production supervision and interior
  design by Linda Schuman
Cover design by Zimmerman/Foyster
Manufacturing buyer: Edmund W. Leone*

Printed in the United States of America

10 9 8 7 6 5 4 3 2 1

PRENTICE-HALL INTERNATIONAL, INC., *London*
PRENTICE-HALL of AUSTRALIA PTY. LIMITED, *Sydney*
PRENTICE-HALL of CANADA, LTD., *Toronto*
PRENTICE-HALL of INDIA PRIVATE LIMITED, *New Delhi*
PRENTICE-HALL of JAPAN, INC., *Tokyo*
PRENTICE-HALL of SOUTHEAST ASIA PTE. LTD., *Singapore*
WHITEHALL BOOKS LIMITED, *Wellington, New Zealand*

For
DAVID
HARRIET
   Douglas
   Matthew
   Rebecca

Contents

Table of Problem Stories   xi
Preface   xiii
Acknowledgments   xvii

ONE
THEORY AND METHODOLOGY

1
Role Playing in the Curriculum   3

*Moral and ethical development   5   Language arts   8
Human relations   9   Citizenship   9   History   9
Guidance and counseling   10   Futures studies   10
Conclusions   10*

2
What Is Role Playing?
Some Basic Assumptions   12

*Role playing: A group problem-solving method   12
The process is transactional   13   The self as source   13
A more profound concept of individuality   14
Content is as important as process   15*

3
Education for Citizenship   17

*Educational implications   17   The "open person"   18
Tasks   22   Conclusions   34*

4
Some Guidance Functions of Role Playing   35

The teacher as supportive adult   35
Children's opinions of themselves   36
Improving the emotional climate of the classroom   39
The feelings class   40   Helping a troubled second grader   41
Role playing with mentally retarded children   44
Easing out-of-school problems through role playing   45
Conclusions   47

5
Role Playing: The Process   48

Essential steps   48
Fifth graders role-play "The Clubhouse Boat"   49   Conclusions   64

6
Guiding Role Playing   65

Establishing a climate   66   Leading role playing   71
Conclusions   80

7
Dramatic Play: Groundwork for Role Playing in Social Studies   85

Learning the play way   86   Organization and procedures   89
Sociodrama: An extension of dramatic play   96

8
Extended Role Playing   97

Thematic sequence in role playing   97   Conclusions   104

TWO
PREPARING TEACHERS TO LEAD ROLE PLAYING

9
Training Teachers to Lead Role Playing   107

Training   108   A new dimension   113
Conclusions   117

10
Materials for Learning by Doing   118

Materials for role playing   118   Humorous dilemmas   119
Dilemmas of tact   136   A serious dilemma   141
Dilemma exercises for teachers   143

11
Role Playing in the Preservice and Inservice Training of Teachers   145

Situations for use in teacher education   147

THREE
CURRICULUM MATERIALS FOR ROLE PLAYING

12
Moral Development   153

Honesty   153   Responsibility for others   168
Integrity in friendship relations   187
The "Getting Even" series: Being fair   198

13
Social Studies   213

Teaching citizenship   213   Teaching history   232
Decision crises in United States history   235
Teaming history and language arts   261

14
Interpersonal and Intergroup Relations   270

Sensitivity to others' feelings   270
Surmounting prejudice   274

15
Guidance   283

Self-acceptance   283   Practice sessions   303
Accepting others: The deviant   304

16
Role Playing and Language Arts   317

Feelings are important content   318
Using dilemma stories to motivate composition   319
Using role playing to motivate reading   331
Using role playing for speech improvement   332
Exercises   335
Improvisation for understanding literature   341

Appendix
Materials for Role Playing   348

Bibliography   350

Index   356

Table of Problem Stories

The Weight Watcher 119
Dinner Date 120
The Helpful Wife 122
A Good Impression 123
Welcome to Our City 125
The Windfall Syndrome 127
The Mess 137
Listen, Doctor 138
Advice and Dissent 139
Paper Drive 141
The Clubhouse Boat 153
Finders Weepers 157
Boy Out on a Limb 159
Little Echo 164
Trick or Treat 168
Blind Fish 171
Frogman 175
Rocket Shoot 181
Heavy, Heavy Hangs Over Your Head 183
The Apple Orchard 186
Birthday Present 187
Lost Ball 193
Money for Marty 199
Tell-Tale 199
Eyewitness 202

You're Not Invited 206
Mr. Even Steven 209
The Menace in the Tree 215
The Junior Cavemen 218
Shutter-Bug 222
The Un-Invitation 224
Sacrifice Hit 226
A Long Nose Has a Short Life 229
King Ferdinand Decides 237
The Exiles Decide 238
The Iroquois Dilemma 240
Redcoats against Minutemen 241
Union—or No Union? 243
What Shall Thomas Jefferson Decide? 245
Captain's Choice 246
Rivals for Empire 248
Who Can Vote? 250
Mr. Jensen Decides 251
Fugitive 253
A President on Trial 254
Shall We Go on Strike? 255
The Battleship Maine—257
Pass a Literacy Test? 258
Humankind's Most Powerful Weapon 259
But Names Will Never Hurt Me? 271

Eeny-Meeny-Miney-Mo 272
Seed of Distrust 273
Second Prize 274
Josefina 279
Fast Ball 285
The Big Comic 287
Big Shot 291
Judy Miller 294
Johnny Kotowski 296
Jimmy Garrett 297

Bandit Cave 304
The Squawk Box 310
Your Turn Next 327
Mind Your Own Business 328
The Wrong Mrs. Smith 336
The Accuser 338
Hijacker 339
Where There's Smoke 340
Bus Fare 340

Preface

When the first edition of this work was published, the use of role playing in classrooms was a fairly new procedure. Although it was already in wide use in industry and in mental health programs, it was not yet recognized as a significant educational process. Since then, however, role playing has become broadly accepted and used in education.

As we worked on this revision, we asked ourselves, Who is using role playing? And why? A thorough investigation would require a lot of time, money, and organization. However, a brisk survey of the field can be made simply by looking at the articles on role playing in the education journals of recent years. Accordingly, with the help of a skillful librarian at the School of Education at Stanford University, we obtained a computer printout of abstracts of articles on role playing from a wide variety of journals. In all, there were over three hundred titles.

We studied these abstracts to learn how teachers are using role playing. A gross evaluation of the results showed:

22 percent of the articles focused on the use of role playing in teacher education.

20 percent focused on role playing in teaching language arts.

15 percent focused on the use of role playing in developing values (ethics, social values, moral education, and moral values).

10 percent focused on career education.

10 percent focused on guidance and counseling.

10 percent focused on citizenship.

6 percent focused on intergroup education.

6 percent focused on teaching history.

1 percent focused on teaching science.

These divisions, of course, are not absolute: The areas of concern overlap. Moreover, citizenship, values education, history, and intergroup education might all be listed under social studies; however, listing these areas separately provides a clearer picture of the uses to which teachers put role playing.

The category "teacher education" is so broad that it, too, needs further analysis. Here it refers to a whole grab bag of functions. Role playing in teacher education refers, first of all, to articles that focus on helping teachers to "learn by doing"—that is, preparing them in the methodology of role playing by doing role playing, which is the thrust of this book. Other articles discuss preparing teachers to use role playing for other specific functions such as teaching language arts, history, moral education, and so on. Still other articles focus on using role playing as a way of practicing skills and confronting teaching situations in preservice teacher education.

In the first edition, our main emphases were on citizenship education and on improving interpersonal and intergroup relations. Our aim was to provide teachers with classroom materials and procedures that would help young people explore the personal and interpersonal dilemmas that are part of the human experience of growing up; in addition, these materials would help them acquire problem-solving skills for resolving ethical conflicts.

Today, children have an even greater need than before to learn to cope with the ambivalences and confusions of contemporary life. Our complex society confronts young people with many choices and shifting values. In addition to the conventional areas of the curriculum, schooling must provide students with experiences in values clarification and problem solving and, especially, opportunity for moral development.

Originally, we saw role playing to be most useful in social studies and guidance. Now, as a glance at the educational index reveals, role playing is used in many other curriculum areas: in language arts, science and ecology courses, vocational education, urban studies, futurological studies, as well as history, interpersonal relations, and citizenship education.

Accordingly, in this new edition, we have greatly broadened the range of our materials. For one thing, the book now contains a large section on preparing teachers to lead role playing. This body of methodology is the fruit of many years of experience in instructing both preservice and inservice teachers, in classes and workshops, on the "how-to-do" aspects of role playing for the classroom. This methods section includes an abundance of story materials for role playing by adults at the training level, materials that vary from humorous warm-ups to serious dilemmas.

In addition, the materials sections include sociodramas for teaching history and citizenship and sociodramas for language arts: reading, speech improvement, English as a second language, and—especially—composition. In addition, we have included more materials on guidance and counseling and for improving interpersonal and intergroup relations. Most particularly, there is new material on ethical development that comes under the labels "moral behavior" or "moral education," which the vast majority of parents now wish schools to provide for their children.

The title of the first edition of this book was *Role-Playing for Social Values*. Because we have expanded the application of the role-playing process to many other areas of the curriculum, we have retitled the work *Role Playing in the Curriculum*.

FANNIE R. SHAFTEL
GEORGE SHAFTEL

Acknowledgments

Many teachers and colleagues have helped us prepare the materials for this book. To all of them the authors are sincerely grateful. To the following we wish to express specific appreciation:

To Lois Meek Stolz, Professor of Psychology Emerita, Stanford University, for her early and continued support in the development of this book. To Pauline S. Sears, Professor of Education Emerita, Stanford University, for her encouragement through the years. To Jean Grambs, Professor of Human Development, University of Maryland, who helped us in writing *Role-Playing the Problem Story* and who gave us a detailed critical examination of the first edition and has continued to be helpful.

To Mary Wilcox, Jane Stallings, Sister Mary Peter Traviss, and Leonard Davidman for their extensive use of our materials and their insightful aid.

To the many graduate students in our classes in sociodrama and related classroom procedures who contributed richly to our knowledge as they role-played our problem stories, wrote and shared their own materials, and brought the living dilemmas of their own students to our class sessions.

And to Barbara Celse Hunt, gifted leader of role playing, to whom we are much indebted for her sensitive use of our stories. Her unusually fine skill in leading role playing helped us refine our procedures.

We are indebted to Harcourt Brace Jovanovich for permission to reprint the following stories by George Shaftel: "Spelling Bee" and "Finders Weepers," from John Warriner, John H. Treanor, and Norman H. Naas, *Warriner's English Grammar and Composition 7, Teacher's Manual*, pages 126 and 128; and "Trick or Treat," from John Warriner, John H. Treanor, and

Norman H. Naas, *Warriner's English Grammar and Composition 8, Teacher's Manual,* page 136.

The story "George Wanted In" by Marie Zimmerman Solt, *Childhood Education*, 38, No. 8 (April 1962), is reprinted by permissions of the Association for Childhood Education International, 3615 Wisconsin Ave. N.W., Washington, D.C.

Role Playing
in the Curriculum

PART ONE

Theory

and

Methodology

1

Role Playing
in the Curriculum

The school curriculum today competes with the attractions of the mass media and a faster, more dramatic pace of life. Young people, and adults, often settle for instant knowledge, however superficial.

The uncertainties of the social-political scene and rapidly changing life styles and values all contribute to the ambivalence and confused motivation of youth. Many young people today are rejecting traditional values; others are searching for a way of life that promises personal fulfillment in a world of uncertain futures.

The conventional curriculum often seems irrelevant, nonfunctional, and obsolete to youth. Facing this challenge, curriculum planners are developing many new programs. They have, for example, devised Law in Society programs that present the dilemmas of citizens as they face complex social problems. Such programs serve to guide children and young people in developing an understanding of the role of law in society and how citizens can shape the laws so urgently needed. Urban studies programs present housing problems, redevelopment programs, designs for better living in cities. Biological science and social studies programs are increasingly concerned with human circumstance, with ecological considerations, and with the promotion of future-oriented thinking and planning. Ethnic studies have attempted to enhance pride in one's roots and respect for the contributions of the many groups in our multicultural society.

The task undertaken by forward-looking curriculum planners has several vital goals: to develop programs that make sense to young people, that are relevant to life as they know it, that are people-centered, and that deal honestly with issues, conflicts, and dilemmas.

Such emphases are based upon a recognition that we live in a complex, problem-ridden world. We are members of "Spaceship Earth." What happens across the world affects us in the United States directly.

The ability to identify such events, to analyze them critically, and to relate empathically to the people who are affected demands a teaching-learning process in which students move from personal concerns to personal-social concerns, in which significant curricular experiences are presented in problem-solving, inquiry settings.

A significant curriculum must deal, in appropriate ways, with such critical concerns as how to cope with our energy problems, how to share on a worldwide basis both renewable and nonrenewable resources, and how to define—and act on—the interdependence that is necessary to the world in the nuclear age.

On a more immediate, community level, we have many other problems of living to resolve: air and noise pollution, litter; the need for responsible behavior to make life safe and positive for all; the need to develop citizen behavior that means more involvement for everyone.

Young people face conflicts that have very personal impact. Peer pressure to use drugs and alcohol threaten children and youth with demands they are often unable to handle. Students want more rights, responsibility, and power in their schools and need guidance in dealing with these tasks constructively. And, always, there are ethical issues to resolve, value-laden decisions to make: What is right, fair, and decent versus the expedient and opportunistic.

A most serious problem in developing curricula that attempt to enter these arenas is the lack of communication between adults and young people in our society. Teachers need to establish real communication with children and teen-agers. They must win recognition as persons who care about the concerns of their students. This requires a climate of trust in which teachers "listen" intently to students, demonstrating their respect for the capacities of young people and their belief that given the opportunity to explore feelings and ideas carefully, young people can come to sound conclusions. To achieve such a climate of trust requires a nonjudgmental stance on the part of teachers, an honest facing of issues, and problem-solving skills. Only in such a teaching-learning setting can teachers win the serious attention and application of youth to the challenges involved in living in today's world and in preparing for the future.

Role playing is a potent tool for this undertaking. It permits teachers to use the present and past experience of students as resources in solving personal and social problems. It promotes problem-solving thinking as students explore such issues as how to cope with demands by peers that they experiment with drugs or how to make decisions involving the redevelopment of their neighborhood or what they would do if they were members of a United Nations commission attempting to resolve an international incident.

Role playing enables students to respond spontaneously, even emotionally at first, and then gradually, through many enactments, to consider in depth the data needed, the consequences to be faced, the value decisions to be made. This process permits both affective and cognitive aspects of a problem to be developed in ways that make sense to the students as they formulate a decision.

Role playing is a problem-solving procedure and a communication process. John Flavell makes the point that in order to communicate with another "the subject seeks out the other's role attributes, not to *play* out his role, but to *understand* it—and understand it from his own, still active role position *vis-à-vis* the other."[1] He asserts that effective communication is based upon the extent to which an individual can take an accurate measure of another's role attributes. Jean Piaget points out that intellectual egocentrism is fundamentally an inability to take roles, an inability to search out the role attributes of others, compare them with one's own, and make effective use of the comparison in any of a variety of adaptations. Flavell states that "social interaction is the principal liberating factor, particularly of social interaction with peers. In the course of his contacts (and especially his conflicts and arguments) with other children, the child increasingly finds himself forced to reexamine his own percepts and concepts in the light of those of others, and by so doing, gradually rids himself of cognitive egocentrism."[2]

Role playing permits one to put oneself in the other's shoes, to decenter, step out of one's own view, momentarily, and see things from another person's viewpoint. Thus role playing helps young people overcome their own egocentrism.

Role playing is an empathy process. By placing oneself in the role of another, we are often enabled to feel what it is like to be in the other's situation.

Role playing is also a skills tool. It enables us to practice many skills: how to apply for a job, how to be a spokesperson for a group, how to introduce people.

Role playing lends itself most powerfully to moral development and ethical education.[3] As such, it is a much needed aid to developing awareness of one's responsibilities as a citizen.

All of the above points are made in order to emphasize the possible wide-ranging uses of role playing in the curriculum.

MORAL AND ETHICAL DEVELOPMENT

A recent Gallup poll reported that 84 percent of parents of children in public schools and 85 percent of parents of children in parochial schools wish schools to give instruction in moral behavior. A general view of how

[1]John H. Flavell, *The Development of Role-Taking and Communication Skills in Children* (New York: John Wiley and Sons, Inc., 1968).
[2]John H. Flavell, *The Developmental Psychology of Jean Piaget* (Princeton, N. J.: Van Nostrand, 1963), p. 279.
[3]Sister Mary Peter Traviss, *The Growth of Moral Judgment of Fifth-Grade Children through Role Playing* (Unpublished dissertation, Stanford University, May 1974).

children acquire their codes of conduct would probably hold that they accept, first of all, the values of those nearest and dearest to them: their parents. This means home influence—the precepts and example of immediate family. Next in influence upon children are the values of their peers. Indeed, at times (as in adolescence) peer values seem to outweigh those of parents. Third is the combination of school, church, and media.

It seems sensible to conclude that our children develop their codes of conduct from the modeling of peers and adults who are loved and admired and from the influence of church, media, and school (classroom and playground). We all have sets of values, however mixed their source. Most of us, when we "do wrong," feel pangs of guilt. The stories of people who, late in life, repay money they had stolen when young are familiar features in newspapers. Children, discussing their own behavior, often attest to such feelings. One boy, in a discussion following a reading of "Clubhouse Boat" (see p. 153), commented that after he had committed a series of petty thefts he felt as if he "had been stuffed in a bottle and the top clamped on." Such feelings are truly real and motivating. The insightful person will often reject a course of action that may be momentarily advantageous but will have an aftermath of remorse. ("How could I live with myself if I did that!")

In any event, young people *do* acquire sets of values, and schools do contribute to their moral development. Most parents wish schools to enlarge their contribution, to focus more clearly and emphatically on helping young people develop far clearer, keener, stronger, and more humane inner guides to conduct. Schools are aware of this urgency. It puts pressure upon classroom instructors and the traditional curriculum already imposes a heavy workload. Nevertheless, many educators are trying to meet the needs of children as they and the parents perceive them.

Educators have long been interested in moral education. In the early part of this century there was a strong character education movement in schools which resulted in the National Religious Education Association combining with the National Education Association in promoting the famous Hartshorne and May *Studies in the Nature of Character*.[4]

In recent years Jean Piaget, Lawrence Kohlberg, and others have focused on the development of moral judgment. These researchers see a sequential development of the ability to make such judgments. Kohlberg sees this development as consisting of invariant stages through which children pass in their moral growth. While other theorists take slightly different views, there is a general agreement that children take an active, spontaneous part in their own moral development rather than being passive recipients of external influences and teachings. "It suggests that children spontaneously formulate moral ideas that form organized patterns of thought, that these patterns go through a series of qualitative transformations as the child develops."[5]

Kohlberg identifies three levels of development, with stages within

[4]H. Hartshorne, and M. May, *Studies in the Nature of Character*, 3 Vols. (New York: Macmillan, 1928–1930).
[5]Sister Mary Peter Traviss, op. cit.

each level.[6] He proposes a program that identifies where each child is on this developmental sequence, then presents groups of students with situational materials that offer a "mismatch"—that is, one level above the level that the student is on. He has an elaborate discussion technique that is designed to challenge the student, to stretch his or her thinking as a stimulus for progress to the next stage. He has also designed pre- and posttests to measure growth after such treatment. His procedures require intensive training for the persons who administer these programs.

Sister Mary Peter Traviss, in her doctoral work at Stanford University, undertook a comparison of the effects of Kohlberg's procedures with those of role-playing problem stories involving moral issues.[7] As part of her preparation she trained under Lawrence Kohlberg at Harvard University. She also trained with this author at Stanford in the theory and methodology of role playing. Using an experimental design, Sister Mary Peter used classes of fifth-grade boys and girls in the Catholic schools of the San Francisco Bay Area. The children were given the Kohlberg pretest. They were then divided into experimental and control groups. The treatments were role-playing sessions for the experimental groups and no role playing for the control groups. In her summary of findings, Sister Mary Peter concludes:

> The classroom technique, role playing, used as the independent variable in this study, was found to promote moral development, as defined by Kohlberg, among middle-grade children in a significant way. That is, when subjects participated in role-playing sessions, over a period of three months, their growth in moral judgment, according to the Kohlberg scale, was significantly greater than the growth in judgment of those children who had no role-playing experience.

She concludes that role playing is a classroom technique that is readily available to the practitioner and that while the Kohlberg methods appear to promote faster growth (one stage in three months compared to one-half stage in role playing) the techniques required to lead role playing are more readily available to the classroom teacher than the elaborate training skills required by the Kohlberg procedures. She suggests that through role playing the teacher can help the student to

1. Focus on genuine moral conflicts (those having meaning in the life-space of the child)
2. Think about the reasoning used in solving such conflicts
3. See inconsistencies and inadequacies in his or her thinking
4. Find ways of resolving such inconsistencies and inadequacies.

Other interesting researches are under way in the field of moral education. In Great Britain, John Wilson, Lecturer and Tutor in the Department of Education Studies, Oxford University, is Director of Research for the

---

[6]"Moral and Religious Education in the Public Schools: A Developmental View" in T. Sizer, ed., *Religious and Public Education* (Boston: Houghton Mifflin, 1967).

[7]Sister Mary Peter Traviss, op. cit.

Warborough Trust. He emphasizes that moral education requires a nonpartisan approach and a grasp of moral methodology: We are to show young people *how to get* the right answers, not to give the answers to them.[8]

Robert Hogan hypothesizes that moral behavior can be explained and moral character can be described by using five social and psychological dimensions: moral knowledge, socialization, empathy, autonomy, and moral judgment. He challenges the progression of preset stage theorists. He emphasizes that moral character and moral behavior can be predicted by means of the interrelationships of the five dimensions. For example, high socialization and high empathy in conjunction with autonomy produce moral maturity; whereas low socialization and low empathy in conjunction with autonomy tend to produce "strong, effective, resolute, unyielding scoundrels"; low empathy and high socialization combined with autonomy describe a "stern patriarchal moralist."[9]

Peter M. Nardi reviews Hogan's work and questions some of his research procedures. Nardi comments that although the efficacy of Hogan's theory needs to be assessed, he finds it provocative as a viable alternative to other theories. Nardi concludes:

> Moral education has largely been viewed as a matter of stimulating the development of moral judgment to higher stages of reasoning. Since this paper suggests that moral character plays an important role in determining moral conduct, programmes in moral judgment development might be fruitfully integrated with an approach to character development based on Hogan's theory. For example, attempts to raise individual levels of empathy could be designed as part of a values clarification programme in schools. *Role-taking and role-playing exercises could easily be developed and implemented.* (Italics added.)[10]

Throughout the professional literature on moral education there is discussion of the need for a child to develop autonomy in moral judgments, to develop empathy for other people, to develop what Piaget calls "respect" and "reciprocity," and to develop the ability to use reason in the solution of human problems. In this book we emphasize the fact that the role-playing process, with the use of appropriate classroom materials, provides a powerful technique for use in moral education.

LANGUAGE ARTS

Many recent articles on role playing in the professional journals stress the use of role playing and drama materials in language arts classes. Dilemma stories can provide strong motivation for composition, for speech improve-

---

[8]John Wilson, "Moral Education: Retrospect and Prospect," *Journal of Moral Education,* 9 (1979): 3–9.

[9]Robert Hogan, "Moral Development and the Structure of Personality," in D. De Palma and J. Foley, eds., *Moral Development: Current Theory and Research* (Hillsdale, N.J.: Lawrence Erlbaum Associates, 1975).

[10]Peter M. Nardi, "Moral Socialization: An Empirical Analysis of the Hogan Model," in *Moral Education Forum* (New York: Hunter College, City University of New York, 1979), pp. 153–67.

ment, and for creating interest in reading. A number of reports stress the value of role playing in facilitating children's language development and suggest strategies for its use in primary and intermediate classrooms. Role playing has the special quality of capturing children's interest so that they listen intently to peer talk and are impelled to use language in realistic and spontaneous response. Drama has proved particularly stimulating to students learning English as a second language and to English-speaking students learning another language.

HUMAN RELATIONS

Many teachers use role playing to work on problems of interpersonal and intergroup relations. This concern is, of course, closely related to values education—the intelligent concern for the rights and welfare of others. In exploring the dilemmas of human interaction, it is often easier for children to solve their problems if they can stand off and look at them through the eyes of someone else. Role playing provides an opportunity for children to experiment with a variety of ways for dealing with sensitive situations and thereby discern what ways are better than others.

In the *How to Do It Series* of the National Council for the Social Studies, a bulletin titled "Perspectives on Aging"[11] discusses negative attitudes toward the aging process and aged persons. This thoughtful guide uses simulations, case studies, and role playing to help young people develop empathy for aged people.

Articles in other publications deal with dissent and disruption in secondary schools, providing thoughtful studies of the role of racism in such incidents. Other social problems—the draft, poverty, political power inequities—that contribute to student-school conflict come under analysis through role playing to heighten students' understanding and broaden their perspectives on issues that cause much trauma in human relations.

CITIZENSHIP

Articles on young people's relations with the law, such as an experimental unit on "Police," provide students with role-playing experiences that help them develop insight into the role of citizens who make a conscientious and responsible effort to uphold our laws. Such experiences help young people realize that observing the law is enlightened self-interest and not mere subservience. They are also helped to realize that when circumstances necessitate a change in the law, it shows wisdom to observe democratic process.

HISTORY

Many teachers use role playing as a very rewarding method of recreating historical crises. Children, by assuming roles of individuals in historic set-

---

[11]"Perspectives on Aging," *How to Do It Series*, Series 2, No. 6 (Washington, D.C.: National Council for the Social Studies, 1978).

tings, step into the shoes of people who had to make difficult choices at critical times in human affairs; they thereby achieve a deeper understanding of the emotional impact of such historical demands upon people.

GUIDANCE AND COUNSELING

A number of teaching guides explore the possibilities of "spontaneous drama" in invoking the life experiences of students as the basis for reflection, decision making, and attitudinal change. Some of these guides suggest applications to literature and guidance for use in school settings.

FUTURES STUDIES

Numerous articles and guides concerned with the quality of life in the future suggest role playing as a means of exposing students to alternative viewpoints and to intensive experience in envisioning possible and probable consequences: Full exploitation of resources in the present—with exhaustion of resources in the future? Overpopulation—and its stresses? Controls—or no controls? Facing such general issues in realistic detail enables students to focus sharply on dilemmas that can form the basis for decision making and attitudinal change.

CONCLUSIONS

Role playing is a process for problem solving, critical thinking, and transactional experience and a tool for exploring content areas in the curriculum. As a methodology it can be used to

Initiate a study—as a means for immediate involvement.

Delineate a problem—which then demands a follow-up of data collecting, reorganization of information, a testing of ideas. In this way students can be inducted into in-depth studies.

Develop empathy—help students in any study to involve themselves in the affective as well as the cognitive aspects of an area through exploration of specific people in delineated situations. For example, how it would feel to indenture yourself for seven years to an unknown master in order to get passage on a boat to the New World?

Stimulate communication—between students and between students and teachers. It is easier to express ideas in the safe environment of role playing than to risk yourself in the arena of abstract ideas. Opinions flow freely from discussions of enactments during the role-playing sequence.

Motivate writing—as students respond in action to a situation, both the affective and cognitive aspects of writing are involved.

Create awareness of the need for skills—as students are confronted with situations (how to interview an expert, for example), the need for specific skills training becomes immediately apparent.

Teach elements of problem solving—when first confronted with a problem situation, students tend to reach for simplistic solutions. As the teacher encourages alternative proposals for resolving a difficulty, the complexity of situations is revealed, the need for alternative thinking emerges, consequential analysis is encouraged, and students can be inducted into problem solving *in action.*

Stimulate moral development—as students face moral and ethical dilemmas, the problem-solving process of role playing, *with focus on who is involved, how the decisions proposed affect each person, how each one feels,* helps the participants achieve growth in moral development.

Stimulate the decision-making process—as personal-social dilemmas are presented, or community action situations delineated, students engage in decision making at a level that is meaningful to them.

Perhaps the most significant feature of role playing is that it is a transactional process. It thus stimulates both the emotive and analytic aspects of thinking as students learn to express ideas spontaneously, to listen to the ideas of others, and to develop respect for themselves and others.

For the teacher, role playing is not only a teaching tool, it is a *teaching stance.* The teacher who learns to use role-playing strategies listens to students' ideas and expressions of feeling, utilizes their experiences, and encourages the exchange of perceptions and opinions.

Role playing is one of many teaching procedures the skilled teacher uses in developing his or her curriculum. Sometimes it is completely effective in a particular lesson and needs no other follow-up. But most often it will be one of a variety of teaching components: sometimes introducing an area of study, sometimes illuminating an aspect of a larger project, sometimes a way of exploring final views at the end of a study. In human relations work and in moral development programs or values education, role playing can provide the basic process for a series of experiences.

In other chapters of this book, role-playing techniques are presented along with analysis of curriculum treatment for various content areas as well as materials for working for better interpersonal relations and for moral and ethical development.

2

What Is Role Playing?
Some Basic Assumptions

ROLE PLAYING:
A GROUP PROBLEM-SOLVING METHOD

Role playing can be described as a group problem-solving method that enables young people to explore human problems in spontaneous enactments followed by guided discussion.

Usually, a role-playing session consists of an incident or problem situation which involves two or more people in which some decision must be made to solve the difficulty. A role-playing "problem story" is usually open-ended—that is, the human situation is a dilemma. No solution is offered to the group. The story stops at the dilemma point. The young people involved must analyze what is happening and make proposals for possible action that might solve the problem.

Typically, in real life, when we confront such circumstances, we *feel*, we *act*, then we *think* (and often, afterward, we wish we had chosen to act differently). Young people need to be taught to feel, to think ("What will happen if . . .") and *then* act—that is, to make decisions in the light of probable consequences. This is the essential goal of the whole process: to make decisions in the light of probable consequences.

The great blessing of role playing lies in that fact that it is a rehearsal of behavior: It is a reality practice that permits young people to explore life situations in a "safe" environment wherein feelings can be expressed, ideas of reality can be explored in action, and likely consequences can be delineated. In role playing, there is always another chance to try out new ideas. One can learn from mistakes.

THE PROCESS IS TRANSACTIONAL

One of the unique elements of role playing, which makes it more powerful than discussion alone, is that when a person gets up to act out a proposed line of behavior—with other players in other roles—the situation is not entirely within that person's control. *It has become transactional.* Ideas are complicated by the often unexpected responses of others in the situation. As is true of life itself, actions bring responses, some expected, some unforeseen, to which the person must then react. Spontaneity is basic to role playing. In human interaction, the unpredictable is ever-present. An individual acts; people involved with him or her react; the situation changes as consequences occur. The interchange heats up. A planned decision may be moulded into something different by the variety of pressures brought to bear. Instead of a rigid scenario, role playing provides the fluidity of life to decision making.

THE SELF AS SOURCE

Students' own perceptions are revealed in enactments; their own life experiences are a resource for use. As an individual offers his or her idea of what is happening in a problem that is being role-played, the group becomes aware that different people see different things in a commonly experienced event. The many perceptions revealed serve to widen the awareness of each participant.

In a skillfully led role-playing session, beliefs are challenged. The variety of ways in which an incident is experienced enables each participant, no matter what his or her own experiential background is, to contribute to the situation. The result is that students learn to respect and value a variety of interpretations of social realities. The following classroom episode is illustrative.

> Several ten-year-olds are discussing ways to get money they badly need for a project.
>
> MARY: Well, if I ask my father and he says no, I ask my mother.
>
> RICK: But it's Tommy's own money. He has a right to spend it any way he wants.
>
> JASON: There's another way. You go to your father and tell him you need a microscope. He'll give you money for that. Then you pay your club and borrow a friend's microscope to show your dad.
>
> TEACHER: People have many different ways of trying to solve a problem like this. I wonder what would happen if we try each way.
>
> The children then enact the behaviors they think will work for them. At the end of each enactment, the class discussion offers a range of insights into the consequences of the offered solution. Expediency, such as Jason's, may be explored and found wanting. Some child may say, "You might get away with that, but if it was me, I wouldn't feel so good inside." The sensitive teacher may say, "Sometimes we're pressed to use solutions that aren't easy to live with." In this way she opens the door to safe but honest discussion. New proposals may offer the children a range of resources that gives them more productive ways to solve the problem.

Going through this process, the children learn with the support and opposition of their age-mates. The teacher contributes by asking facilitating or clarifying questions, such as "How will Tommy (or Jason) feel if we do this?" or "What will happen now?"

A MORE PROFOUND CONCEPT
OF INDIVIDUALITY

There has been a strong tendency in our society to interpret individualization as "doing your own thing" and going at your own pace in order to achieve more sooner. Role playing can provide a more profound concept of individuality.[1] The teacher in role-playing groups works for a climate in which it is safe to try out all ideas, even those that are expedient and not socially acceptable or are even antisocial. Each is a reality to be actually tested in a public arena (the enactment). *The focus is not on right answers but on open inquiry.* Both teacher and group "listen" to each other with full attention. The teacher models this behavior by probing with such questions as "If I understand you, you are saying that . . ." And a child can say, "Yes, that's what I mean" or "No, I mean . . ." The observing class is asked to listen and watch carefully so as to be able to respond to a proposal in terms of *How are people feeling? Who is affected? Could this really happen? What will happen now?*

Instead of a competition in which each student is trying to display a better idea, the group is guided to give full support to the exploration of Debby's idea, for example, before going on to the next student's proposal. This cooperative process can build a cohesive group in which individuals learn to like one another, respect each other's thinking, and support variability. Such a group can become a "community" in which children develop the courage of their convictions and can both support group efforts and oppose them. It is in such groups that children learn who they are, what they believe, and what they value.

Kenneth Benne has said eloquently:

> Self emerges originally in the process of interaction and interchange with others. . . . If . . . the standards of the group elicit and reward honest, individual self-expression and self-searching by its members and meaningful encounters and conflicts among members, its effect upon those to whom the group is important will be to support their quest for identity."[2]

The teacher who is unafraid to say, "You two seem to have opposing ideas of what has happened (or what will work), can we explore these differences and try to understand how each of you has come to your opinions?" is guiding students to respect individuality.

---

[1] Kenneth D. Benne, *Education in the Quest for Identity and Community* (Columbus: Ohio State University College of Education, 1962), pp. 39–40.
[2] Ibid.

CONTENT IS AS IMPORTANT AS PROCESS

As children learn to consider consequences by taking roles and learning how it feels to be on the receiving end of an action, the *content of life* that they explore is of vital importance. Children make decisions every day that both shape and reflect their values. In these daily life encounters, they can learn to care about others or to use others for their own selfish purposes. They may decide to go ahead with their crowd when a cruel prank is planned rather than risk ostracism. They may stand by, mute, while a friend is teased or rejected. Sometimes a child stands against the group and follows his or her own convictions—a difficult task.

Children need help in confronting such dilemmas. They can be helped to seek socially productive solutions that consider the welfare of others as well as themselves. Such early learning becomes a basis for the development of caring, humane individuals.

It is futile to present the larger critical problems of society to children who have not yet learned to relate empathically to others. Significant social learning starts with children's own deeply felt experiences. When they explore through a social process like role playing how it feels to be left out or to be discriminated against, what it means to be a friend, and whether it is worth the price to just go along with the crowd, they gradually make explicit the values which influence their decisions. In the context of role playing, they can reconsider values in the light of the clarification that comes from the group controversy. When a child says, "I had to snitch something from the dime store to join the gang," and the teacher asks, "What happened?" and the child answers, "Nothing. I only took an eraser, but it bothered me," the way has been opened to candid discussion of pressures, feelings, and social consequences. Thus, children can conclude, after a number of enactments and discussions, that friends who have to be won by going along with vandalism may not be friends one wants after all.

For very young children, problem situations may center around such developmental problems as how to shift to the role of brother or sister when the new baby comes, how to defend their rights on the playground, or how to cope with property damage. Through role playing children can gradually learn to accept their feelings, to begin to think in terms of consequences. A simple and effective way to present problems to children is through the use of problem pictures or the narration of a brief problem story. Many situations emerge naturally out of the daily living on the playground and in the classroom.

Today older elementary-school children are increasingly exposed to pressures to try drugs, to participate in vandalism, and to show bravado in petty thievery. How can they be helped to resist such pressures? A role-playing curriculum can present life situations that range from the less threatening problems such as how to reconcile loyalty to a new friend with the counter demands of a group, to such antisocial ones as what to do when the club says you have to earn membership by stealing something from the supermarket.

When children feel free to explore candidly such situations in the role-playing community they can share their fears or admit their desire to please or be liked; they can accept their impulsive or expedient solutions as ideas to be explored in public and perhaps modified by the group discussion that role playing generates.

A teacher who has learned to be nonjudgmental, to accept all ideas as worthy of exploration, is in a position to help children clarify values and learn from experience. Pupils can be helped to realize that people usually cannot solve all their problems. We often must give up one "good" for another. As children recognize this fact of life and struggle to decide which object or goal to give up, they steadily grow in their capacity to choose that good that does the least harm.

Underlying successful guidance of role playing is the belief that individuals have the ability to cope with their own life situations. When they are helped to be honestly in touch with their innermost feelings and can explore them in a supportive group, they and their group become capable of creating more humane and enduring solutions to social problems. Role-playing work with children supports this view over and over again. Social life will be filled with controversy in the years ahead. Young people need to learn early to confront problems with a measure of skill and confidence. They should be encouraged to welcome intellectual conflict as evidence of ideas passionately held, to explore divergent ideas with interest and compassion. Through this process they will be helped to grow up as rational, caring human beings.

3

Education
for Citizenship

EDUCATIONAL IMPLICATIONS

A democratic society rests on the base of an educated, concerned citizenry. As society becomes more complex and interdependent, citizens are asked to make judgments on social policies that demand information, participation skills, clearly defined values, and commitments far beyond those that sufficed in the past.

Such intelligent participation is greatly complicated by rapid changes in social conditions and technological and scientific developments that demand consequential thinking and the breakup of traditional ways as societies move into the modern postindustrial world.

Here in America the multicultural and pluralistic value orientation of different groups creates great ambivalence and confusion in young people. Different voices have different definitions of the rights of individuals, of the functions of government, of social—policy making. There is a confusion of perceptions of responsible behavior. Seekers of a more open society assert their varying definitions of the "good life." The focus on individualization and self-realization has often led to a preoccupation with "doing your own thing." To an alarming degree many persons have become anomic, have withdrawn from responsibility for participation in the improvement of group life, and have, instead, focused all their energies on a so-called inner life. Another response is that of alienation. Angry, cynical, and frustrated young people turn against society and express their anger in lawless behavior.

As a result, many concerned citizens are expressing a renewed interest in "citizen education." Educators have always had as a major goal the preparation of young people for responsible participation in public life. There have been periodic attempts at redefining citizenship education. In 1979 a new effort was launched to try to define citizenship:

> Citizenship comprises the rights, responsibilities, and tasks associated with the governance of the various groups to which a person belongs. These include families, churches, labor unions, schools, and community organizations as well as cities, states, nations and global systems. As members of such groups, young people as well as adults are involved—directly or indirectly, knowingly or unknowingly—in citizenship problems and tasks. . . .
>
> Citizenship competence, the goal of citizenship education, refers to the quality of a person's participation in civic and public life. Competent citizens make thoughtful decisions. They communicate effectively with others. Competent citizens promote and protect their interests as members of groups in responsible ways.[1]

The project lists seven basic competencies which research and theory indicate individuals need to discharge responsibilities and protect their interests. These are (1) acquiring and using information, (2) assessing involvement, (3) making decisions, (4) making judgments, (5) communicating, (6) cooperating, and (7) promoting interests.

Underlying these competencies is another basic consideration: *The way in which children and young people are socialized in our society will determine the way information is perceived, the kinds of assessments, decisions, and judgments that will be made and the quality of communication and cooperation that will occur.*

Kenneth Benne has expressed his conviction that human beings achieve their identity in community and that only as the individual is afforded the experience of being a member of caring, concerned groups does he or she forge individual integrity and group responsibility. According to Benne, "If . . . the standards of a group elicit and reward honest individual self-expression and self-searching by its members, its effect upon those to whom the group is important will be to support their quest for identity."[2]

Citizenship education must be based in a careful reconsideration of group life in schools and emphasis upon the teaching-learning processes that encourage understandings, sensitivities, and skills that come from exploring conflicting views and confrontations. It means facing value difficulties along with the need for facts in the choices made by groups.

What does this commitment imply in the way of tasks?

The knowledge we now have of the dynamics of human behavior imply a number of major emphases.

THE "OPEN PERSON"

We must guide the experiences of children and youth so that, as a result of the inner security that comes of successfully meeting their developmental

---

[1]Richard C. Remy, *The Basic Citizenship Competencies Project* (Columbus and Boulder: Mershon Center at Ohio State University and Social Science Education Consortium, 1979), pp. 1, 2.

[2]Kenneth D. Benne, "Education in the Quest for Identity and Community," Bode Memorial Lectures (Columbus: Ohio State University, Department of Education, 1961).

tasks, they are "open" to new experiences. They can relinquish learned ways of behavior that are no longer appropriate, can tolerate the ambiguity of changing situations, and can be challenged by the unknown and unresolved in the situations that confront them.

Inner Directedness

As children face the many situations in their lives that demand action and choice, they need to be helped to become conscious of the values that guide their behavior, and *to learn to criticize those values in terms of their consequences to themselves and other people*. Inherent in this process, if it is to be more than *self*-centered, is the development of a sensitivity to the feelings and welfare of others. Individuals who clarify their values and beliefs are less likely to be swayed by others, or to be victims of "unconscious" values.

Young children entering school build self-concepts based on their past experiences and their evolving relations with others in their immediate life-space. If the adults in their early life have helped them negotiate each crucial transition successfully, they build a self-confidence that enhances their growing ego. They feel adequate and competent; they are able, they can do things! If their experiences with parents, teachers, and friends have been positive and supportive, their self-concepts are strengthened; they gain an inner security that enables them both to "be for themselves" and to relate well to others.

It is out of healthy self-concept development and the gradual clarification of values that the quality of inner directedness emerges: the ability of individuals to act, despite outside pressures, in the light of ideas they respect.

A Problem-Solving Orientation

Highly related to an "openness" to new experience is the development of a problem-solving orientation. Ideally, not only should one be "open" to the new, but one should also acquire attitudes and specific skills for tackling problem situations. A *problem* has been defined as a situation in which old responses cannot be applied routinely, in which new elements demand definition, rethinking, and often call for creative responses.

Role Behavior

Children and youth need guidance in learning appropriate behavior in a great variety of social and work situations. Never before in our history have families moved so often. Mobility is a reality of contemporary life. Never before have so many of us encountered such a broad range of social and work demands as we move from one community to another, as we improve in our jobs and professions or learn new work skills and take on heavier responsibilities. As job requirements change swiftly because of automation and industrial rationalization, more and more of us become students and trainees again, or teachers and supervisors. Competence in a wide variety of roles requires flexibility, and flexibility in adapting to new roles is related both to openness and to practicing a wide range of different roles.

Young people who have the chance to *practice* many roles, to face the demands of new situations under conditions that maximize learning, will be better prepared for the demands of change in later life. Role playing can provide such practice.

Cross-Cultural Perceptions

Perhaps one of the most crucial needs of our time is keen sensitivity to the feelings and perceptions of others. The ability to "be someone else" and to sense how he sees the world and how he feels is a preliminary condition to the ability to sympathize with members of a subculture or national culture other than one's own.

As children explore open-ended situations and specific roles, they tend to respond to them in terms of their own cultural experiences. Thus a child playing a mother role in a story will reveal by her behavior the values and role definitions of her own family group. Occasionally, children demonstrate a knowledge of other subcultural definitions of such roles. Usually, however, children express their own cultural experiences.

The realization that each one of us defines what is real and good in terms of our individual cultural perceptions is basic to communication across cultures. It is only as we understand the other person's (or nation's) perceptions and assumptions that we are in a position to come to mutually acceptable solutions of problems. Such an understanding does not necessarily require us to abdicate our own cultural values; it means, rather, that we enter another person's frame of reference in order to think with him. It makes possible real communication about differences.

In discovering how individuals of different cultural backgrounds think and feel, young people will realize that there are many different—and acceptable—cultural solutions to common human problems.

Only if we develop empathic cross-cultural communication can we evolve some generalized ideals that rise above cultural differences and enable us to create a genuine world community.

The emphases outlined above are fundamental orientations to learning and action that demand a comprehensive program. They require teachers who are committed to the values and insights underlying such conceptions as "openness," "problem solving," "respect and concern for others," and "cross-cultural perceptions."

Developmental Considerations

All children learn their way into the culture into which they are born. In the process they build self-concepts that, to a great extent, are a product of how others react to their efforts to meet their own needs. Teachers play crucial roles in this process. The ways in which children come to terms with many developmental tasks go far to determine whether they become cooperating members of society or hostile individuals; teachers can do much to help shape the kind of people they eventually become.

The Peer Culture

The groups of which a young person is a member exert a tremendous influence. They are central in shaping self-concepts; they influence motivation and values; they even assign roles.

The group may decide that Johnny is "funny," a clown, that Elizabeth is a " 'fraidy-cat," or that Tim is the willing dupe onto whom the tedious jobs can be dumped. Often a group will glorify a popular leader and choose him or her over and over again for leadership roles even though that child is not qualified by skill or merit for the allotted positions. Ronald Lippitt and his associates have found that once a child has acquired a certain reputation within the group, the introduction of new data that should change their view is resisted (Lippitt and Gold, 1963). It is difficult for a young person to change the roles and esteem (or lack of it) that is acquired early in his or her relationships with a group—difficult, but not impossible.

Children are keenly aware of the power of the various groups in their life-space. They know who is influential and work very hard at winning their way into certain groups and maintaining a status in a group or clique. Individuals may even accept rather ignominious roles, such as scapegoat or the butt of jokes, just to be "in" with an admired group. And, having won their way into a favored group, young people who are especially anxious and insecure will conform doggedly to the group code, even at times when such conformity means violating parental regulations. Some children, having achieved a comfortable place in a group, may lose their individuality. Other children, it is true, reject groups; rather than submit to group requirements, they become hostile and withdrawn.

A few children do not need groups. They are content with close affiliation with a single friend, or, being blessed with consuming interests, they prefer to go off on their own explorations.

In American culture, where adult social life is usually separate from that of children, the child culture becomes more potent in young people's lives than in those cultures where large kinship families include children in adult activities. As a result, for most children, the values and codes of the peer culture tend to dominate their outlook and shape their actions. This results in the immature leading the immature! This condition is revealed in the sometimes dangerous and often cruel demands made by the group on its individual members.

A great need exists for constructive guidance of groups. *They need to be helped to an awareness of the consequences of their codes, their exclusion devices, their demands for blind conformity, their intolerance of deviant behavior.*

Just as the individual needs to be helped to sensitivity and concern for others, the group needs to be guided to concern for the individual. Ronald Lippitt speaks of the *cohesive group*—a group in which the individuals like one another and will support variability among members. Such groups are sensitive to the ways in which their actions may affect others. When people work, live, or play together, there are times when teamwork is necessary, and other times when divergence of opinion makes the difference between wisdom and folly. (When a popular leader suggests a rash or inconsiderate act, the member of the group with sounder judgment must feel secure enough to suggest cautioning second thoughts with force and confidence; when the imaginative member of the group suggests a plan involving effort and departure from cherished group plans, the group must feel that he deserves a hearing, however impractical his suggestions may seem at first glance.)

Such group attitudes must be systematically cultivated; we cannot depend upon their spontaneous emergence.

Studies in group climates (the emotional stress and harmony between members of a group) suggest that educators need to plan specific experiences for the promotion of the kind of group climate in which the members respect and like and support one another. Children need help in realizing how their decisions affect both members of their group and people outside their groups. They need to be encouraged to lend support to individuals who differ from the majority. This is a goal that role-playing procedures are uniquely productive in helping to achieve.

Values

One of the great sources of stress and confusion in modern society is the fact that people act upon the basis of unconsciously held values. As a result, they are often the victims of their impulses and fears. They need to make their values conscious so as to be aware of what values they act upon. Once values are out in the open, they can be looked at, considered, compared with alternative values. Only then can people criticize, evaluate, deny, confirm, or reconstruct their value system.

Children can be helped to face up to the decisions they make, analyze why they made them, and develop an explicit set of values. In group discussions, in role-playing enactments, in individual writing, they can explore their values and learn the process of criticizing and reconstructing them in the light of tested experience. (It is within such a process, under skillful guidance, that young people can develop a sense of responsibility for others as well as develop a core of values that becomes the basis for personal integrity.)

TASKS

To use role playing most effectively for teaching citizen behavior, one must be aware of the purposes for which role playing is especially helpful. Some of these purposes are described in the following sections.

To Help Children Understand That Behavior Is Caused

When young people explore in action the consequences of choices they have made, they can more easily see causal relationships. In the discussions that follow enactments of alternative proposals for solving a problem there is opportunity, under guidance, for a classroom group to explore such questions as, "Why did they behave that way?" or "Why do mothers (or teachers) feel this way?" In such analyses, children can be helped to see the relationships in a group problem and to become increasingly sensitive to why individuals respond the way they do. Young people are in this way helped to move from a surface approach to explaining behavior to an approach that takes into account the basic, less obvious, dynamics of human behavior.

Children can be helped to see that (1) behavior is caused, (2) it occurs in a setting, (3) there are usually multiple causes for behavior, and (4) behavior is usually not wholly "good" or wholly "bad" but just the best that the individual can manage at the time. (The consequences may be "good" or "bad"—for individuals or for society—but childish behavior needs to be viewed as efforts to be adequate in meeting the demands of circumstances.)

To Develop Sensitivity to the Feelings of Others

The egocentric young child is intensely involved with her own feelings. Gradually, as she interacts with others, she begins to relate to them. As she senses how they feel, she is enabled to step out of her own shoes into theirs and to begin to feel with others. This capacity to imagine how another person feels—to "get inside his skin and move around"—needs to be nurtured.

To Release Tensions and Feelings

Teachers are not therapists, and most are not sophisticated in the clinical aspects of catharsis. They can, however, help children release their tensions and express their feelings, even if this means providing a quarter-hour for folk dancing on a rainy afternoon. Children experience many frustrations in the process of socialization. One aspect of growing up is learning to deny some immediate, personal urges because the culture does not permit their expression or demands other forms of behavior. Young people need an opportunity to release the tensions built up by such restrictions.

It is a great relief to act out your feelings toward younger brothers (whom, you are continually told, you must love—not beat) and to find out that others experience the same feelings. It is "safe" to role-play an angry or bitter response, and then go on to explore other, more socially acceptable solutions. How much better to siphon off the anger in role playing than to have it find expression in making a scapegoat of some vulnerable child on the playground!

To Diagnose the Needs of Children

There is a growing body of procedures, in addition to conventional test materials, to diagnose human relations needs. Role playing is a potent member of this group of procedures; or rather, it is an especially fruitful and revelatory cluster of mutually energizing procedures.

As children portray roles and react to the enactments of others in discussion, they tell us much about themselves. One child always chooses to play dominant roles, another displays an obsessive awareness of antisocial solutions to human difficulties, and still another is invariably punitive when he enacts adult roles; still others display strong impulsive trends. While teachers should not jump to conclusions, they should always consider that children are showing possible symptoms. Such symptoms can be followed up with further study through other diagnostic procedures. And, when serious difficulties are suspected, the help of guidance personnel and clinical psychologists can be enlisted.

To Improve the Child's Self-Concept

Every child must, of necessity, learn his or her way into the culture in which he is born. In the process he builds a picture of himself, of who he is and what he is good for: he develops a self-concept. This image of himself is to a great extent a product of how people—adults and children—react to his efforts to meet his needs in the cultural environment. True, the self-concept is also a product of his innate abilities; but the environment permits or blocks his efforts to realize those capacities. If he has the good fortune to experience much loving support from the adults who surround him in infancy and early childhood, he explores the world with confidence and eagerness. If he is helped to be successful in negotiating the cultural learnings required of him at each stage of his development, he builds a strong ego and has faith in his ability to face and cope with new tasks. In this process, his age mates play a powerful role. If they accept him as a person and support his efforts at learning, whether on the playground, in the street, or in the classroom, they reinforce his perceptions of himself as an adequate person. As a result, he likes himself; and this self-esteem in turn frees him from preoccupation with self and enables him more easily to relate to others. Such a child can afford to be "open" to new experiences; he is not threatened by his environment.

Teachers play a key role in this process. They must be sensitive to the crucial transition points in the growth sequence of each child and provide the necessary support as a child comes to terms with new demands in the environment. They must so arrange the teaching-learning situation that children can be successful and, savoring the mastery that comes with honestly earned success, be eager for more learning. In addition, teachers need to be highly alert to the interpersonal relations among children and plan situations which will teach children in their group life—on the playground, in the classroom, in their out-of-school group—to support each other positively. An increasing number of studies find that a child's success in school work, as well as his success as a social person, reflects the state of his self-concept.

The growing child faces many developmental tasks that are a product of his biological needs and the cultural demands of his environment. Coping with these tasks, he becomes a member of society. This membership can be positive or negative. Because of loving help and adult and peer acceptance, he may become a "character-conditioned" friendly person; or lacking such experiences, he can become a hostile person—one who never develops "trust" but always expects the worst from others.

These socializing experiences shape his attitudes toward authority. Being sure of his own worth, successful in his efforts to learn his way into the culture, he can accept authority, he can accept guidance by adults, he can accept necessary restrictions; if hostile, however, he begins to view authority as something to be circumvented.

Such attitudes powerfully influence his relationships within groups. If he is insecure and unsure of who he is, his anxiety may lead him to curry favor, to please the powerful children in groups he encounters. He becomes an "other-directed" conformist who follows the crowd or submits to the powerful and influential. In the more exceptional cases, he will become a rebel. If he is developing into a hostile personality, his conditioning may take the form of defiance that eventually leads to delinquency. If he has a strong, healthy self-concept, his rebellion may reflect a kind of independence and integrity that enable him to go against the group when necessary.

The child with a healthy self-concept can become an inner-directed person. He can conform appropriately—that is, order his behavior to meet the demands and sanctions of his cultural group when he wishes to do so; but he has built an inner core of personal values that enables him to stand for his beliefs, even against the pressure of the group, if necessary, because he is secure in his ego strength and can be himself.

A Child's Self-Concept Can Be Improved

As we have noted, a child sees himself or herself to a large extent through the reflected perceptions of the people around him, especially his peers. In some cases, age mates provide strong support for a child; in many cases, they arbitrarily assign him a demeaning and belittling role. As a result, some youngsters—because they are labeled weak or timid or stupid or unco-operative—never have a chance to exhibit their actual capabilities to their peers.

Role playing, used in a planned sequence, can do much to help change such an individual's underappreciated status in his group. The teacher can give such an individual opportunities to play roles quite different from the ones assigned him by his peers—roles in which he can demonstrate a wider range of skills and perceptions and qualities than the group ever permitted him to exhibit. In this process, not only is his status among his age mates changed but, if he receives recognition and status from the group, his self-concept also is altered for the better. Some evidence supports the belief that the teacher, by carefully selecting roles for an underappreciated individual to play in a sequence of role-playing sessions, can do much to help him win respect and sometimes even admiration from the classroom group, and thereby help him acquire a higher degree of self-respect and confidence.

A frequent concomitant is an improvement in classwork (Sears, 1963). The more serene child usually works more effectively. Pauline Sears has studied the strong influence opinions of teachers and peers have on the learning of less able children. She observes that these children are the ones who are least likely to find inherent satisfaction in their schooling and will be most likely to drop out of high school. If self-esteem is associated significantly with the warmth with which children are regarded by teachers and classmates, then opportunities for maximizing these personal relations should be provided.

Another important consideration is the fact that as the individual is helped, the *group* is being helped to develop appreciation for individual differences in talents, in ordinary abilities, in ways of perceiving problems and interpreting data. Here again, we can encourage independent thinking and, along with it, a respect for the "odd-ball" ideas that may be the creative aspects of problem solving in emergent situations.

In addition, individuals and groups can be helped, through the use of problem stories, to explore their own feelings about themselves—to face up to and accept their limitations and explore their strengths. In the stories we have tried to show how a poor self-concept causes children to "over-read" others' responses and, in their anxiety, accept defeat or anticipate failure unnecessarily.

To Explore Roles

Each child, in the process of growing up, learns many roles and discovers as he tries out various behaviors what is permitted and sanctioned by the culture and, especially, the subculture in which he lives. He is a son, perhaps an eldest son (with responsibility for younger siblings), a grandson, a brother, a pupil in school, a member of a gang on the playground, the captain of his baseball team at school, a newspaper delivery boy (with customers he must please and a boss to whom he must account)—and so on. In each of these roles he is expected to behave in certain accepted ways, to live up to culturally sanctioned demands. In certain subcultures, for example, the eldest son is expected to start to work at an early age and to give his earnings to his parents; in other subcultures, he is expected to finish high school, go to college, and then to professional school while his parents expect to support him all the way.

As our lives become more complex and varied, the range of our roles becomes wider. In addition, as life circumstances change, we are often required to take on new roles.

The city child, when his father starts earning more money and moves the family to a suburb, has to win his way into new groups, often in new subcultures. Not only does he have to learn the role behavior that is acceptable in this new subculture, he may also be assigned a role in the new peer group different from the one he held in his city play group. Thus Tom, who was leader of his gang on the big city street by virtue of being a good fighter, may discover that if he wishes to be respected or a leader in the suburb he must be skilled in soccer. He may even have to struggle against the reputation he has acquired as a fighter and attempt to win the admiration of a group who value "interesting things to do."

Children need opportunity to practice the many roles which they must assume in the process of growing up. They also need help in exploring and defining appropriate role behavior for different situations. Frequently a child experiences rejection or failure in social situations simply because he is not able to differentiate among the role behavior expectations of several quite different situations.

Groups also need help in order to become supportive of individuals as they seek new roles. Too often the group quickly assigns a reputation to a child and blocks his or her efforts to try new roles.

Role playing can also give children the opportunity to practice roles they would *like* to acquire, such as being the leader in a group or the expert who teaches others a skill. Furthermore, they can have the benefit of seeing numerous responses to the role as different members of the class demonstrate their ideas of how such roles are performed. The boy who is going to be master-of-ceremonies for a Boy Scout program, the girl who is going to teach clay modeling or folk dancing to small children in summer camp, can benefit from practicing the job ahead of time.

To Explore the Core Values
of American Culture

Young people growing up in a culture must, of course, learn the ways of that culture. They learn what is sanctioned and acceptable by imitation, by trial and error, and by instruction. In the multicultured American society, this task is most complex. Children learn some behaviors that are generalized as "American," and they learn subcultural behavior, which may be ethnic (Italian, for example), regional (e.g., "Southern"), local ("our town"), or family (the Browns).

Teachers serve as mediators between children and the culture or cultures in which they are growing up. Teachers help children learn what is both negatively and positively sanctioned and, thereby, to acquire the core values of their culture. Teachers can also help the group (class) to accept subcultural differences and value their positive qualities in American life.

To Learn More about the Functioning
of Various Subcultures

As children explore open-ended situations and specific roles, they tend to respond to them in terms of their own cultural conditioning. Thus a child playing the mother role in a story will behave usually in ways that reveal the values and role definitions of her own family group. Occasionally, children demonstrate a knowledge of other subcultural definitions of such roles, but usually they express their own cultural experiences.

Teachers tend to see children primarily in school situations. They seldom see a child responding to the dilemmas of his life outside of school. Role playing can bring outside situations into the classroom; and, as children enact their proposed solutions to problems, teachers can acquire much wider perspectives on the difficulties, perceptions, and values that shape the behavior of their students in their life outside school.

To Help Children Clarify Their Values
for Decision Making

As children participate in role-playing sessions, they have an opportunity to propose their own ways of solving human relations problems. Often such proposals are spontaneous and based on unconsciously held values. In the discussions following an enactment, the teacher-leader, *with the help of a child's reacting peers*, may guide her to consciously face her choices. In this way she is helped to become aware of her values and, in a positive group climate, she can explore the effects of various choices upon herself and others.

Thus, for example, the urge to "get even" is strong in children and usually not very discriminating. (See "Money for Marty," p. 199.) Just suspecting that another boy has stolen a favorite jackknife or top or tool may induce a boy to steal something back from his suspected despoiler. The group may point out that he has no positive evidence, only his suspicions and that what he has stolen in retaliation may be worth far more than the article he has lost. The group may ask him if there isn't a better way than retaliation to handle the problem; they may also want to know if he is sure, positively sure, that his cherished possession is really stolen and not simply misplaced. How fair is he being in judging and condemning his imagined foe? Has he really suspended judgment until all the facts are in? Has he let the fact that the other boy lives in a "bad" neighborhood, or speaks English poorly, or has a different color of skin influence his judgment? In view of these feelings, shouldn't the accusing boy actually bend over backward in trying to be completely fair? All these facets of the problem may be pointed out by the boy's own peers; and, coming from them, they have unusual weight and persuasive power.

A further complicating factor in a multicultural society is the contradictions in behavior that young people observe. To study the Bill of Rights and then discover the facts of segregation in any of its various applications, for example, creates bewilderment in logical young minds. Role playing such conflicts in values can at least make the values visible. While we do not always find immediate solutions for such conflicts, the very fact that we are aware of our dilemmas often forces us to analyze and evaluate our choices. Such experiences may make possible future resolutions of value conflicts.

The process of delineating values and value conflicts leads to further discussions and follow-up experiences in which young people can become aware of the humane considerations in problem situations. Expedient solutions can be weighed for their values: Immediate personal gain can be set against possible long-range consequences to other people and even eventual emotional reactions of the actor himself. For example, Tommy reasons that he can lie out of the fix he's in. He can say that Pete released the emergency brake when the two of them were playing in Tommy's father's car. But suppose Pete's father then has to pay for the damage incurred when the car rolled down hill and hit a tree? Pete's father works as a gardener; paying for the damages would be a heavy burden on him. He has been kind to Tommy; he has often taken Tommy and Pete fishing when Tommy's own busy father couldn't find time. Tommy knows he'll feel like a traitor and an ingrate if he plays this dirty trick on Pete. But then Tommy thinks of his own father's stern wrath when he sees the damaged car, and Tommy gets a sick ache in his stomach. "Tommy, I've warned you time and again not to play in the car when it's parked on this hill!" He could escape this wrath, Tommy knows; a lie would work. Pete is so good-natured that, when accused, he'd just mumble that he didn't know whether he had released the car brake or not. *But I'd know*, Tommy realizes; *I'd know all right!*

But even such personal experiences are not enough; children need to reevaluate their frames of reference continually. Everyone tends to generalize his or her own personal and cultural values to others. It is useful for children to learn why people in other cultures choose to behave in certain ways. (Some people will not eat meat on Friday, and others will not eat meat on any day. Some people will not call a doctor when ill. Some people will go to a baseball game on Sunday but not on Saturday. Some people take off their hats in church whereas others put them on. Some people will loyally die for their country if need be but will not fire a gun in anger against a foe. Some people let their parents choose their wives and husbands. Some people are proud of owning a big new car; some consider it a disgrace to brag or try to be better than one's friends.)

To Improve the Social Structure and Value Systems of the Peer Culture

One important use of role playing is developing a healthy group structure. Since peer groups wield so much influence on the individual in childhood and adolescence, and immature but socially powerful children can and often do set the standards, we need to work with child groups to help them (1) become sensitive to the needs and feelings of individual children, (2) become aware of how a group can either support an individual or deny him opportunities for self-realization, (3) grow critical of immature standards for selecting leaders, and (4) be appreciative and supportive of individual differences among their members.

As children become members of various groups, they need to understand the interactions, or dynamics, of group behavior. If they explore problem-story situations in which the popular boy (a good athlete) is always elected to leadership roles, even when not qualified for them, *they can discuss the problem in the safety of a situation that is not actually their own.* They can thus face the situation realistically and *with the support of their peers*, begin to define what is constructive or destructive in certain kinds of group behavior. Teachers can help children analyze what happens to their self-concepts when they are excluded or ridiculed, what happens to the quality of experience when good ideas are ignored just because they have been expressed by certain children, and so on.

Eventually, in a planned sequence of problem stories about group behavior, the time comes when children can draw up their own codes of constructive group conduct. (With adolescents who are more advanced in their abilities to generalize, it is possible to follow up their new insights with specific content on small group behavior and effective group organization.) When a group tends to exclude and deprive some children, for example, role-playing a series of problem stories on the themes of *how it feels to be left out* or *how it feels to be different* can sensitize groups to the effects of their behavior on its victims. Or, a group that is blindly following the leadership of a boy simply because he is a good athlete may be helped through the discussion following a problem story such as "The Squawk Box" (p. 310).

Gradually, as a sequel to such role-playing sessions, groups can be led to analyze their own behavior. Are the talkative, assertive members of the class, by monopolizing discussion, preventing more timid youngsters from having a full say? Are cliques fighting each other, criticizing each other, and behaving so hostilely that they disrupt class work? Are some quiet members of the class being excluded from activities because they are new, or of a different race or religion? Is some youngster, because he limps or is extremely tall and thin—or short and plump—the butt of jokes? Such analysis can help groups to compare their ways of choosing leaders, selecting organizing committees, responding to others' ideas, and so on, to what is known about healthy group behavior. We have seen classroom groups—after undergoing such self-examination—become kinder, more inclusive, and even devotedly protective of individuals' rights.

To Develop Group Cohesiveness

The *cohesive group* is one in which the individual members like one another and will support variability (differences) among themselves. Obviously, such classroom groups are a product of many factors: individual differences, past experiences, the social structure of the neighborhood subcultures, and general school and classroom policies. A teacher who is working to produce such cohesiveness in his or her classroom must work with all these factors.

Role playing can be a useful tool for this task. By carefully selecting problem stories, a teacher can cultivate respect for individual differences in the group. How it feels to be different can be explored. Ways of helping the child who is different to win acceptance and inner security can be explored; ways of *using* individual differences, too, can be discussed and enacted. The boy from another country who dresses oddly and uses unfamiliar turns of speech, for example, can be helped to learn English. His knowledge of life in other lands can be utilized by the teacher to win respect for him instead of derision.

One of the major problems of developing cohesiveness is helping young children move out of their narrow friendship cliques. They can be made aware that cliques ignore the feelings and needs of others. Exclusive factions cause nonmembers to feel rejected. Exploring, through role playing, how it feels to be left out would be one approach to counteracting cliques. Another would be to explore the conflict of loyalties to a friend (who may be unpopular) and to the wider group (which rejects that friend).

To Learn Social Behavior with the Support
of a Cohesive Group

Children will often learn through the *support* or *opposition* of their age mates in areas where they reject help from adults. This is especially true in American life in which the peer culture wields such influence over the years of middle childhood and early adolescence.

Role playing becomes an excellent tool for the exploration of antisocial attitudes and responses to situations. Thus, when Johnny role-plays his tendency to try to "get the better of another person," his classmates in the following discussion may confront him with how his actions affect other people's feelings and propose other solutions that are more socially constructive. Cheating another person, allowing him to be blamed for something he did not do, letting a lie about him go unchallenged—such behaviors may have a trail of consequences far more destructive than the perpetrator, in the sudden flush of angry impulse, foresees.

Admonition from adults is often not accepted by the hostile child, but when criticism comes in the nonjudgmental processes of role playing as *observations of their own experiences by his peers*, it can be exceedingly effective.

To Teach Problem-Solving Behavior

There is a strong tendency in both individuals and cultures to hold on to old ways, to tried-and-tested solutions. We often define new situations in terms of what is familiar in our established culture. There is great danger in continuing this behavior today. We maintain stability in groups by conserving tested and established ways of behaving. But we must learn to cope with developments that are so new that they call for the creation of new solutions.

This calls for a very different orientation than we have emphasized in schools. Instead of setting up learning tasks that mainly call for known solutions and rote learning, we must establish searching, hypothesizing, speculative attitudes. We must encourage divergent thinking, in which the individual wanders down intellectual bypaths, *inventing* new approaches to problems.

Problem solving requires the ability to face a new situation, to define the problem in specific terms, and to assess the possibilities of solution. Problem solving demands the capacity to slough off inappropriate responses and to create and test new ones. Problem solving, of necessity, involves the ability to tolerate ambiguity and to develop patience for trial-and-error searching. It requires the intellectual tenacity to follow through the possible alternatives of a hypothesis and to make choices based upon intelligent exploration of consequences. Such attitudes and skills can be learned by guided practice in meaningful problem situations.

Problem solving is a discovery process. Such a process does not flourish in a school environment that emphasizes only "right" answers and that is based on the intellectual authority of the teacher. It requires an atmosphere in which it is safe to speculate, to *guess*, to test out ideas, even at times to be *wrong*. Problem solvers need a zest for exploration; they need to learn to really listen to each other's ideas before accepting or challenging counterproposals.

Children who have experienced only preplanned learning situations with predetermined outcomes do not develop this zest for exploration, nor do they usually acquire extensive problem-solving skills. Such skills are not learned through routine lessons in problem solving but *must be learned in problem situations that have meaning and importance to the young people involved.* Only then, as they face problems they sincerely *want* to solve, can teachers help them, gradually, to acquire the specific skills of the process.

There is at present a growing concern with developing new strategies for teaching and learning. Teachers of science, mathematics, and social studies are allowing their students to gather their own data, *put it together in their own way, draw their own conclusions, and build their own generalizations.* Researchers who have concerned themselves with creativity also emphasize the need for individual exploration and programming of ideas.

In working with groups, we are confronted with the most difficult kinds of problem solving. Human situations are much more elusive than the controlled scientific experiments because they involve *people in action*, human beings interacting with each other in emotion-laden difficulties. Problem solving in social situations is always variable, dynamic, complex. It is transactional in nature.

To Teach Problem Solving at the Action Level

One reason why human relations problems are more difficult to solve than problems dealing primarily with material things is the constantly changing and unpredictable behaviors of people involved in an emotional problem. Often we *intend* to solve a human problem in a certain way, but we *act* on the basis of feelings we cannot always anticipate. Furthermore, we act not only on our own feelings but also in response to the feelings and behavior of others. The intellectual solution of a social problem situation often fails to cope with the feelings generated by the interactions of the people involved.

Because of these dynamic aspects of group behavior, we need much more practice in confronting, defining, and resolving problem situations on an *action level*. Role playing enables us spontaneously to explore the interactions of people in situations that approximate the reality; it is active exploration.

To Teach Group Problem Solving

When individuals consider a problem in solitude, they bring to it their own sensitivities and limited perceptions. Granted, creative insights are highly individual matters; nevertheless, researchers who are studying thinking processes are finding that group interaction on a problem makes available a broader range of perceptions and definitions than occurs to an individual thinking alone. One person's response stimulates further analysis by another member of the group, and a third person refines their thinking, which elicits still further additions and insights.

Furthermore, in human relations problem solving, interpersonal or group situations are involved and typically demand group action. We not only need to develop a sense of responsibility for decision making in groups, we also need to help *individuals in groups* "listen" to one another, to consider differing viewpoints, to develop ways of reconciling differences. Such skills demand both learned techniques and practice.

To Develop the Habit of Considering Consequences (Consequential, or Causal, Thinking)

In the role-playing process, one person explores, with the help of participating observers, the consequences of his or her solution to a human relations problem. In an enactment, players put that proposal into action. In the discussion that follows, the leader helps the group consider: "What happens now? How do these people feel?" In this process, impulsive and spontaneous actions can be "safely" followed to their consequences. In role playing, it should be stressed, it is safe to make mistakes; it is safe even to explore an antisocial solution to a problem because everything is on a "practice" level. Or the teacher, noting ignorance of social sanctions or insensitivity to the welfare of others, can so structure further enactments that the group is helped to a new awareness of the consequences of the actions proposed.

To Confront the Typical Ways We Tend to Solve Interpersonal and Intergroup Problem Situations

Children, even more than adults, live on an impulsive and immediate level. When confronted with a dilemma or conflict of values, they often act expediently, hoping that everything will come out all right. They need help in facing up to the dilemmas and choices in their daily lives. They need help in becoming reality-oriented, in learning from their own past experiences. Role playing gives them the opportunity to explore pertinent life situations in a nonjudgmental atmosphere. In a role-playing session it is an accepted fact that we all act hastily or impulsively at times, that sometimes we simply don't know what to do. In this atmosphere, with the emotional support of one's peers and under the skillful guidance of a leader, children can and do learn to face up to difficult problems, and do eventually develop versatile and socially acceptable solutions to many human relations difficulties. Occasionally—and this is also important—they learn to live with problems for which there are no immediate solutions.

To Teach the Feeling-Thinking-Acting Sequence

As discussed in Chapter 2, our first tendency when facing a problem is to feel, to act on our feelings, then think about the way we tried to solve the problem. The result, often, is that we wish we had acted otherwise. Children especially need to examine their impulses to action and their tendency to use expedient solutions. As they explore the kinds of choices they make—in the safe, nonjudgmental atmosphere of the role-playing session—they can be helped to see the variety of alternatives available to them in specific situations if they stop to think *before acting*; moreover, they can be helped to explore the possible consequences of the various alternatives in a particular situation, so as to choose more wisely from among them.

CONCLUSIONS

There have been many citizenship education programs in American schools. Some have been concerned with informing the student about the various levels of government and the functions of various law-making and administrative agencies. Others have sought to reorganize schools in order to give students a chance to practice good citizen behavior in school and class government. Basic to the success of these programs is the early development of strong self-concepts, a problem-solving orientation, skills in value clarification, and growth in cohesive group functioning. Young people need to be sensitized to the feelings of others so that they become concerned about the consequences *to other people* of the choices they make.

When young people are able to confront and define the dilemmas in their daily life situations and analyze their choices, they become more conscious of the values that underlie their actions. It is only as they learn to criticize and reconstruct their values that they can become responsible group members and individuals of integrity in their personal decisions.

Children need practice in facing problems on their own level and in the safe, nonjudgmental situation of the role-playing session. If we are to make headway in solving the very difficult problems of living in a multicultural urban society, we must help young people become intelligent, sensitive, responsible solvers of interpersonal and intergroup difficulties. We must help them become "open" persons who are inner directed yet able to participate responsibly with others in groups.

Our schools are a logical place to begin such training. First of all, a problem-solving orientation to learning must be established. Children should be allowed to develop a zest for solutions. Only then will they experience a sense of achievement when they solve a difficult problem. Used as a core around which a variety of communication techniques can be patterned, role playing is a procedure that seems uniquely suited to encouraging individual integrity and responsible group behavior among young people. Becoming a responsible participant in public life requires experience in being a member of caring, concerned groups who have a deep sense of responsibility not only for themselves but also for the general public. This is the essence of good citizenship.

4

Some Guidance Functions
of Role Playing

THE TEACHER AS SUPPORTIVE ADULT

Most classroom teachers have not been trained as guidance workers; and yet, inevitably, classroom teachers do much to guide and counsel their pupils both in individual instances and as a group. On the more obvious level, they administer various tests; and in many cases they identify individuals with special problems and refer them to the guidance services of the school system. On the less obvious level, if they are alert and sensitive, they not only notice tensions between factions in the classroom but catch minute reverberations of stress suffered by one or another individual; and often, either effectively or futilely, they make some effort to erase or suppress the overt animosity between cliques and to bring some measure of reassurance to the anxious, self-doubting individual. Children who are tranquil and unburdened are freer to learn; and when teachers strive to help their young charges become zestful rather than doleful, they are functioning as supportive adults—as counselors.

Role-playing procedures can serve as aids in diagnosing tensions and sources of strain in such groups; and role playing, if skillfully structured, can be of major service as a procedure for helping individual pupils to become more comfortable with themselves and more confident in standing up for what they believe. Role playing can help the classroom group to gain clearer concepts of its responsibility to support the individual. Role playing, by helping to ease tensions between individual cliques, can do much to aid the teacher in establishing an improved climate for learning.

CHILDREN'S OPINIONS OF THEMSELVES

Children see themselves, to a large extent, through the opinions of others. If an individual is warmly regarded as estimable and competent by his teachers and friends, his self-esteem is likely to be high. It is important, therefore, to maximize the opportunities for individuals to earn the respect of peers and teachers.

If an individual is underappreciated in his group, a planned sequence of role playing can do much to change his status with his peers. The teacher can give such an individual opportunities to play roles quite different from the ones assigned him by his peers, roles in which the undervalued person can demonstrate a wider range of skills and perceptions and qualities than the group ever permitted him to exhibit. And in this process, not only is the individual's status among his age mates changed, but, if he receives a supportive response from his group, his self-concept also is altered for the better. The result is often a significant improvement in his learning achievement.

The undervalued member of the group may be the butt of jokes and pranks on the part of the others, or he may be simply ignored, always left out, treated as if he didn't exist. Role playing, in which leading offenders are placed in the role of a person who is jeered at or pushed aside, often results in an awakening of sensitivity that changes scorn for the scapegoat or pariah into the beginnings of sympathy and acceptance.

The story, "George," provides an example. George was a "left-out" who was venting his anger and frustration so actively that he had become a disrupting influence. He was small for his age even in his class of first-graders. He was sullen, angry, and a problem.[1]

George

George teased, punched, kicked, scribbled on other children's papers for no apparent reason. "He hurt me, and I didn't do anything to him," was heard all day long. Talking to him didn't help, for although he seemed to understand what I was saying, his English was so limited that he was unable to express more than the simplest thoughts. Nor did other plans to help him control his aggression, to give him status in the group, to find him a friend of his own. After several weeks of trying we reached an impasse. George continued to be George, and the children were as one in their refusal to have anything to do with him.

Then one day I had an opportunity to watch him on the playground. There were the usual hopscotch and foursquare games, cowboy-and-Indian and first-grade "chase" games. George stood on one side watching but going through the motions of the games. He ran along with the cowboys but a little distance away, until they were lost in the other activities. Then he wandered to the sandbox, the sparkle replaced by his more usual serious expression. He built sand castles which were knocked down by unobservant children. The third time he built his castles he saw a trio running toward him. What was in his

[1]Reprinted by permission of the Association for Childhood Education International, 3615 Wisconsin Avenue N.W., Washington, D.C. "George Wanted In," by Marie Zimmerman Solt. From CHILDHOOD EDUCATION, April 1962, Vol. 38, No. 8.

mind I'm not sure, but as they approached he laughed and kicked over his own buildings. They charged on through as if he didn't exist. He stood quietly for a little while, then joined a group of children admiring another boy's new top. In a matter of seconds he found himself on the outside of the circle of boys. He stepped back, fury on his face, and kicked two little girls who were walking by.

"Teacher, George kicked me and I didn't do anything to him."

George wanted friends. He wanted to be a part of the fun. Being ignored was what he couldn't stand. But how to break this continuing downward spiral of rejection—aggression—rejection? The previous year his kindergarten teacher told me that he had tried to play with the other children, but they couldn't understand him nor could he communicate with them. So they went their way and he either annoyed them or played by himself. George, with his limited English, had established a pattern of behavior that was going to be difficult to change.

But what about the rest of the class? Could they be helped to understand— to feel as George felt? Perhaps the medium of role playing could help to put them in George's shoes.

The next day I told the class a story—a story without an end. I asked them to pretend that they were the children in the story and decide how it should be ended. It concerned Johnny's move to a new house, the loneliness he felt when he went out to play and saw no one he knew. They solved Johnny's dilemma very nicely by acting out the neighborhood children's inviting Johnny to play. The whole class agreed that this was good. A few days later I tried again, this time moving Johnny across the country. However, the story was complicated by the fact that the children were playing a game that Johnny didn't know. When he tried to play he made mistakes. The two solutions offered were having him go away because he ruined the game and showing him how to play. These were acted out without any comment from me. The class decided the second solution was better because it helped Johnny feel better. This indicated to me that most of the children identified with the boy in the story.

The next week we talked about Johnny again. This time the setting was across the ocean in Germany, which was not questioned in our army-centered town. The first day he went to school he felt very lonely because they were playing games he did not know and speaking a language he did not understand. He asked to play and one of the children laughed at him. Then Johnny hit him because he didn't know what else to do. Now what?

There were different ideas. "Johnny shouldn't have hit the other boy—it only made him madder."

"Well, Johnny was mad, too. The other children shouldn't have laughed."

One solution tried was ignoring Johnny, but this didn't help him. The class recognized that. They also tried having a child explain the game, but the group protested, "Johnny couldn't understand him." Then someone suggested that a child could show him what to do without talking. They tried this and decided it would work. Johnny could play and wouldn't feel like hurting anyone.

During this acting-out I weighed the children's feelings. They seemed ready to understand George, to realize their part in his problems, and to find some directions for helping him. I waited for a good day—a day when other things were favorable. It was sunny and the children could play outside. George had created a number of problems but none too serious. He left the room on a pretext arranged with the office. Then I told the class we were going to have another unfinished story—this time a true story.

The Johnny in today's story was born in Japan, a country far away. He had a big brother and sister who helped him learn many things, especially games that Japanese children like to play. They also taught him the games they learned at the schools on the army base—games that American children played. He knew London Bridge, Farmer in the Dell, and Cowboys and Indians. Then just before he was to go to school the family was transferred to America. Johnny wasn't worried. He knew all about American schools from his brother and sister. It would be fun—with lots of children to play with and wonderful things to do.

But it didn't work out that way. First there was no one to talk to, because no one spoke Japanese. When he tried to join the cowboy games, he couldn't say whether he was a "bad guy" or a "good guy." The fun went on and he could only stand and watch. He knew how to play cowboy—he even brought his gun—but they didn't give him a chance. One day he felt so angry and unhappy that he used his gun—the wrong way—and the teacher took it away. He couldn't tell her what was wrong—that he only wanted to play.

Each morning he cried because he had to go to school. His father talked to the teacher and then told Johnny that if he didn't hit the children they would play with him and he would have a good time at school. He couldn't explain to his father that he had tried and it hadn't worked.

Then came first grade: learning to read and write and do arithmetic. It was better, but there was still no one to play with at recess. The boy who sat with him at his desk always turned around to talk to the girls on the other side, and he only turned back if Johnny pinched him.

About this time the story was interrupted by a quiet question. "Is this story really about our Georgie?"

Yes, the little boy in the story is George. How did you know?"

"It sounds like him."

"George has been very unhappy since he came from Japan. He's unhappy most of the time."

"But he's a pest. He hurts us all the time and we don't do anything to him!"

"Let's see if you can tell why he hurts you." And I read the notes I had taken the day George had been in the sandbox.

"This is George's unfinished story. How do you suppose we can end it for him?"

"He can play with us. We're playing cowboys."

"We're playing kickball. He can play with us."

Out of the many responses, I suggested the group I knew George wanted to play with most. When George returned to class, for the first time he was greeted with, "C'mon, George. We're going to play tether ball and if we don't hurry the courts will be gone." The smile on his face was a beautiful and fitting end to a long, unfinished story.

It was worth noting the academic success that followed on the heels of George's social success. In September he had tested high average on the Lee-Clark—even in the vocabulary—although I seldom heard him speak. He was in the lowest reading group because he simply did not respond to reading instruction. He either bothered everyone near him or stared into space. It was January before we finally were able to help him. At this time he was just starting the preprimers. He indicated that he wanted to join the top group with his new friends. They were half way through the primer. This posed a real problem, which I thought would be solved by having him visit. Within a few days I realized he was reading with them.

By the end of the year there was no difference between his work and theirs. He is now in third grade and has retained his place among the best in the class. Many times the sight of George running with his friends on the playground revives my sinking spirits in the morass of difficulties that face us each day.

IMPROVING THE EMOTIONAL CLIMATE
OF THE CLASSROOM

Sometimes the various individuals and factions in a classroom are so hostile to one another that much disruptive clash of feeling and byplay occur, to the degree that learning is impaired. Role playing can offer significant help in bringing harmony to the stormy atmosphere. Not a single session but a well-planned series of sessions is usually necessary.

Preliminary analysis of the group structure of the class is helpful in determining the causes of dissension. Identification of the individuals who are key persons in the tangle of hostilities is also a necessity. Role playing can then be structured to show the class the results of their disruptive activity, the reasons for it, and ways of solving the issues. Such experiences can do much to bring calm and teamwork into the classroom.

Occasionally, certain members who are outside the influential cliques are given no respect by their age mates. In discussions, when these fringers make suggestions, their ideas are either ignored or mocked. An effective technique in such a situation is to play a tape recording of a discussion in which the fringers' responses, although worthwhile, win no recognition from their classmates. A role-playing session then, in which influential members of the group (perhaps the actual offenders) take the roles of the individuals whose suggestions are ignored or belittled, can do much to help the offenders discover how their behavior is affecting the victims. The class is helped, too, to realize that they have all suffered by not utilizing the worthwhile ideas presented by the unpopular members of the group.

Sometimes a committee does not function well. A role-playing session, in which other people portray the committee in action, can do much to make the individual committee members aware of why they have not worked together, of who have been disrupters and obstructionists and noncooperators.

Sometimes a fight occurs on the playground, or a group of pupils get into a brawl over taking turns in the use of play equipment. After an incident of this kind, the teacher can make the class focus on their problem behavior through discussion. Then the teacher can have the group reenact the whole incident just as it occurred. Further discussion can analyze the causes of the rumpus, the lack of consideration shown by individuals involved, the errors in tactics committed by even the well-meaning participants. Discussion can then turn to sensible ways in which the problem could have been handled, and those ways can be tested out in role playing.

Role playing can also help a group learn to appreciate individuals who are different. Often young people need to be made aware that everyone has something to contribute to the group. In fact, the odd-ball may have something very important to contribute. (See "The Squawk Box," p. 310.)

Role-playing sessions can be set up to show that the shy, soft-spoken individual in the group who never pushes himself into prominence, never interrupts when someone else is sounding off, may have special knowledge needed by the group. If given a chance, he would share it; but he needs special consideration from the others before he can speak up. (See "Bandit Cave," p. 304.) The youngster who has trouble speaking good English may be a newcomer from a foreign country who could teach the other children much about skiing or fishing with a butterfly net or gathering sea shells or what the ruins of Pompeii look like or what you can see from the Tokyo Tower. Until you really get to know another person, you may be unaware of the talents he possesses; and when a group neglects or derides or rejects an individual who is in some way "different," it is depriving itself of unsuspected riches. Role playing can demonstrate this possibility to the class.

But, even more important, children must be helped to see all individuals as of worth, just because they are people with feelings and desires, not just because they may have useful talents.

THE FEELINGS CLASS

Teachers and guidance counselors can improve the emotional climate of a classroom by means of an activity called the *feelings class*. The purpose of this activity is to "help children learn how their behaviors and feelings are related" and how children affect the behavior and feelings of others.[2] A feelings class can occur in a regularly scheduled thirty-minute period every other day or can be set up as a special occasion. These classes focus on correcting a particular behavior problem. In one class described by Gumaer, Bleck, and Loesch, the particular problems were name calling, bossiness, and verbal and physical abuse.

A guidance counselor prepared four role-playing incidents to use with a class. These incidents, all involving small children, centered around insult and rejection. For example:

1. Three girls are playing jump-rope. A fourth girl comes up and asks for a turn. The other girls scream at her, "Oh, go away! You're too fat to jump rope!"
2. A boy is inflating a basketball that is to be used by a group. A bigger boy says impatiently, "Oh, for Pete's sake, you can't do anything right! Gimme the pump and I'll do it. You go play with the kindergarten babies."
3. A girl is taking her turn at duty with the safety patrol. The boy in charge blows his whistle to stop traffic. The girl, new at the task, is slow to lean her STOP sign out into the street. The boy yells at her, "Wake up, stupid! You'll get somebody killed if you don't move faster than that!"
4. Boys are choosing up sides to play ball. A small boy is last to be chosen. Members of the team that should take him object, "Oh, gosh, we can't play with *him* on our side. He couldn't catch a ball with a bushel basket!"

The first incident was role-played. The counselor then asked the children to imagine that they were the child who had been insulted and rejected and to write down how they thought they would feel and act in such circumstances. When the children had finished writing, the counselor had them take turns reading their reactions aloud to the group. Then they discussed their feelings. In general, the children thought that they would cope with such a

[2]Jim Gumaer, Robert Bleck, and Larry C. Loesch, "Affective Education through Role Playing: The Feelings Class," *Personnel and Guidance Journal*, 53, No. 8 (April 1975): 604–8.

situation by fighting, name calling, walking away from the situation, or walking away with the intention of getting even later.

The counselor then had the children discuss the consequences of these solutions to the problem and who would bear the responsibility for the consequences. For the most part, the children agreed that they themselves were responsible for their decisions and behavior. The counselor then collected the written responses. Immediately after this, the second and third stories were role-played. Each enactment was followed by verbal discussion only. Finally, the fourth incident was role-played. This time the counselor again asked the children to write out their reactions and collected the responses.

The teacher and counselor later analyzed the written responses for types of behavior. They found that these insult and rejection experiences generated five types of responses:

1. Fighting
2. Reacting in kind—giving back insult for insult
3. Ignoring the attack
4. Seeking adult assistance
5. Talking it out.

They then compared the responses written after the first role-playing experience with those written after the fourth. They found that the children had shifted toward more acceptable responses. Instead of lashing back with name calling and fighting, the children now tended to want to seek adult assistance, to talk it out, or to ignore the behavior.

As a follow-up, another incident of the same kind was role-played a week later. The written responses confirmed the previous findings. The discussions had influenced the children's thinking and behavior for at least a week. The classroom climate had improved. Individual children also showed improved behavior in their relations with other children. The incidence of insulting and rejecting behavior had diminished.

The authors conclude: "This role-playing approach to affective education in the classroom appeared to help students understand themselves and their classmates better."[3] They also believe such understanding should be reinforced frequently by a series of feelings classes. These classes provide an excellent preparation for more extended role playing.

HELPING A TROUBLED SECOND GRADER

The following account also shows how role playing can be used to relieve disturbing situations in a classroom, help individual children, and promote tolerance and understanding.

Mrs. Nichols, who taught first and second grade in a suburban school, had nine-year-old Marilyn in her group. The girl should have been in the

[3]Ibid., p. 608.

fourth grade, but had been put here in a combined first and second grade because she couldn't do fourth-grade work—and because the principal believed that Mrs. Nichols had the patience and warmth of personality to cope with Marilyn.[4]

On the playground, Marilyn was always a focus of trouble. She was the butt of playground mischief. Inside the classroom, she was still a center of furor: a disruptive clown who would go through all kinds of antic movements with her hands and face and body, cavorting and mugging for laughs. She couldn't concentrate on work, and she kept the other children from doing so by annoying and distracting them until they lashed out at her in irritation.

Marilyn was deaf. She had never learned to talk so that she could be understood. She was not a drab, apathetic child, however, but a bright and lively youngster acrackle with energy, keenly alive to sensation and impulse. The trouble was, of course, that her energy and curiosity had no constructive outlet. Frustrated, it found expression in mischief. She acted the fool. She stole things. Inside the classroom or out on the playground, she was always embroiled in excitement, either upsetting other children or being the butt of teasing that almost drove her into screaming hysterics.

Mrs. Nichols could have asked that Marilyn be removed from the class. But she knew that if this were done, Marilyn would be permanently excluded from school, for she had a record of trouble making. In the school which she had previously attended, she had repeatedly rebelled by running away. The police had been sent to find her several times. Mrs. Nichols realized that Marilyn's last chance for an education was here, with her. Her parents, with five other children to support, were too poor to provide special schooling for Marilyn.

Mrs. Nichols decided that she would *have* to help Marilyn become a cooperative member of the class—but how? First of all, she got the P.T.A. to buy Marilyn a hearing aid. For the first time in her life, then, Marilyn could really hear. Next, she asked for help from consultants in the office of the County Superintendent. It was arranged for Marilyn to have some special tutoring in speech and reading at home.

Marilyn's problem, however, was not merely to become able to learn, but to become accepted by her contemporaries and to become a functioning and cooperating member of the class.

Mrs. Nichols decided to use role playing to help her with this problem. She then discovered that the materials she needed did not exist at first- and second-grade level.

So Mrs. Nichols created them.

She wrote a series of two-minute stories on the general theme of "How it feels to be different." She selected the kinds of happenings that intensely arouse the feelings of children, the kinds of pressures that make them behave explosively and unacceptably. Over a period of several months, she

[4]The teacher in this true account of creative work is Mrs. Hildred Nichols of the Montebello Public Schools, Montebello, California. See also H. Nichols and L. Williams, *Learning about Role-playing for Children and Teachers* (Washington, D.C.: Association for Childhood Education International, 1960).

read this series of stories aloud to the youngsters seated on the floor in a circle before her.

The first story, "Play Ball," told about a crippled boy who could not run. He did take part in the ball games, however, for his classmates ran for him. They liked him and respected him: He was very skillful at making model planes.

Another story was "A Big Boy Like You"; it was about a child who was so shy and got so fussed when grown-ups questioned him that he couldn't answer. Next came the story "There's No Room," telling how a child felt when he wasn't wanted, as Marilyn so often had felt. After that came "The Lost Ring," about a girl who sometimes stole things—though she didn't really intend to: The act was unpremeditated and disturbed her deeply afterward.

"Have you ever felt badly about not getting something you wanted very much?" Mrs. Nichols asked her youngsters before reading "What Did You Get?" The story was about a boy whose family gave no presents one Christmas because they had no money. Meeting his friends, the boy lied about what wonderful gifts he'd received. "Why do you suppose Johnny did that?" Mrs. Nichols asked the class.

After reading a story, all Mrs. Nichols usually had to do was ask a question to release a flood of reactions. Discussion would be excited and eager as the children told details from their own experiences or from those of friends. Mrs. Nichols achieved several goals simultaneously: As the weeks passed, she established and reinforced the point that people may suffer not only from physical handicaps but from shyness or not being wanted or not having money. Moreover, she was guiding the children into sharing experiences and feelings and ideas through role playing.

Often she had the youngsters dramatize one of the stories and act out roles in it spontaneously; with no structuring or rehearsing, the children would improvise as they went along. They stepped into the story characters' shoes. The "identified" with Marilyn, gradually and increasingly. They learned how much she wanted to be liked. They didn't know the words, but they became aware of the frustration and the feelings of rejection and shame that Marilyn had so often felt. Learning how Marilyn felt, they began to sympathize with her. They stopped teasing and prodding her into screaming outbursts. Instead, they began to accept her. They started including her in games. The result was, finally, that Marilyn belonged.

All the careful work Mrs. Nichols had done paid off. She had her class plan a culminating program for the end of the year, to which they invited the principal. They showed him the things they had made in a construction unit. The pupils ran the whole show themselves. And Marilyn took her turn with all the others. She didn't mumble it but gave a clear and logical presentation that the principal could easily understand. When her turn was over, she called upon the next child and sat down, just like anybody else.

Not only did Marilyn profit by this venture in teaching for better human relations, but the whole class was helped to grow in insight and sympathy. The effort Mrs. Nichols had made to mold attitudes and values *did* carry out of the classroom and onto the playground and into neighborhood and home.

ROLE PLAYING WITH MENTALLY RETARDED CHILDREN

In the course of a research project in special education (Daley and Cain, 1953) it was decided to try role playing with a group of mentally retarded ninth graders. The teachers concerned were devoted, conscientious, and eager for any help which held promise for their students. They were, however, frankly dubious about role playing. They doubted that it was practical with their slow learners. They believed that any presentation that called for more than six or eight minutes of concentration on the part of their students would not work. The consultant urged them to try it; from her experience with the problem-story procedure, she believed that even mentally retarded pupils would be able to participate for considerable periods.

The consultant came to one of the special classes, in a large, urban junior high school. The teacher was a skilled, sensitive person who had encouraged his students to develop spontaneity through use of a homemade puppet theatre. He introduced the consultant by saying that, since they had had so much fun making up stories for their puppets, he thought that they'd like to hear another kind of story that Mrs. Jones had been using with other boys and girls.

The consultant set the stage for "The Clubhouse Boat" (p. 153). This problem story had not been tailored to meet the specific needs of mentally retarded students in junior high schools but was written for average fifth- and sixth-grade students. Nevertheless, these special students gave the consultant their full attention as she read the story. It took twenty minutes to tell, with some dramatics and elaboration of detail. No pupil became overtly restless. During the presentation, many expressed their feelings in whispers and quiet comments.

When the consultant stopped and asked, "What do you think Tommy will do?," there was a long silence. Then the students began to talk. They explored the consequences Tommy would face if he kept the money. With a little encouragement, several students got up and role-played a solution to the dilemma. Even a brain-injured girl, who, the consultant had been warned beforehand, was often irrelevant in her comments, made pertinent remarks.

The class not only offered as many real solutions as "normal" classroom groups, but added considerations the consultant had never before been given. Further discussion revealed that these mentally retarded youngsters understood the story dilemma very well—*because they had held jobs and had actual experience of similar conflicts themselves.*

The adults present who were observing, and who knew these young people well, were surprised and delighted at the amount of participation in both role playing and discussion this session brought forth. Moreover, instead of showing an attention span of just six or eight minutes, the group participated in the role playing for almost fifty minutes. This tended to confirm the belief among the adults that mentally retarded youngsters have abilities that have not been tapped.

When the period ended, several students came to the consultant and told her, "That was a good story!" and they asked her to come back after lunch because they wanted to put on a puppet show for her.

At one o'clock she came back to the classroom. At the suggestion of their teacher, the group put on a puppet version of "Clubhouse Boat." They recalled every significant element of the problem story. In fact, they inserted a scene that had been merely implied in the original. Their production was complete, the dialogue natural, and they acted out a sensible solution.

When given material that touched upon the problems that were real to them, they demonstrated a level of practical judgment that was considerably above the ability which the school had been able to elicit from them before. Role playing, when structured through the problem story, enabled them to perform from their own daily life experience, and they had the exhilaration of success rather than the frustration encountered so often when dealing with academic materials.

EASING OUT-OF-SCHOOL PROBLEMS
THROUGH ROLE PLAYING

Teachers who work with role playing for some time find that they have released unexpected potentialities in their pupils that can help pupils deal with some of their out-of-school problems. For example, it was suggested to the members of two classes who had considerable experience with role playing that they might like to write their own problem stories. The results were very satisfying. Pupils produced stories that were informative about the young people themselves and therefore of help to the teachers in understanding their students. Some of the stories were used for role playing. The two classes were so pleased with the results that they planned to do more writing.[5]

Several of these stories are reproduced below, with a record of how one class role-played one of the narratives.

1. Rock Happy Judy

I was out in the backyard, playing with my friend Jack, when my sister came up and hit me with a rock. She ran around the house. Mother called Judy into the house and asked her if she hit me with a rock, and she said she didn't. There was a big argument between Judy and me. She said that somebody else must have thrown the rock from behind me. I didn't believe a word Judy said because it was all a lie. Of course just because Judy is a girl, I guess mother took her word, and told me to go outside and play and forget it. So I went outside and began to play, when up came my sister again and hit me. Then my friend and I went into the house together and told Mother. Mother called Judy in again and we had a nice little argument and Mother still wouldn't believe us. Now you try to solve this case for us.

[5]Guided and supervised by Barbara Celse Hunt, Supervisor, Orange County Schools, California.

2. Work at Home

My name is Jim and I want to tell you a story of my life.

My house has six living in it. They are my mother, father, brother, sister, and brother-in-law. The reason my brother-in-law is living with us is because they are fixing their house.

I want to write this story because I don't think it's fair. Every night after six people have dinner at the house, they go to the other part of the house. My mother says, "Do the dishes, son." I am the only living thing in the kitchen. I have to do the dishes and they go watch TV.

The class role-played this story. Jim, who wrote his problem, did not participate in the first enactment. However, he helped arrange the seating at the dinner table.

A. *Family around the Table*

(The adults did most of the talking. They tried to find someone else to do the dishes.)

MOTHER: Well, I think Jean (older brother, aged 19) should stop gadding around every night with his girl friend. He should help, too. Now, Jean, you just stay home tonight and do the dishes. It won't hurt you.

JEAN: I got a date. Why doesn't Pat (married sister) help?

(They suggested everyone in the family at one time or another help with the dishes. They also proposed that everyone take turns and also that a dishwasher be bought—but this was immediately vetoed because of cost.)

At this point, the class questioned Jim to get more information about the family. It was discovered that the sister had just had a baby; that Jean works all day, sometimes helps build a house at night, and is engaged; that the father and brother-in-law work on a house they are building at night; and that Jim gets paid for doing the dishes.

B. *Family around the Table*

(*In this second enactment Jim plays his own role.*)

FATHER: Well, I think the women should wash the dishes.

JIM (*to brother*): Why don't you help out?

JEAN: I'm too busy.

JIM: But I want to see my TV program. I think he should help.

JEAN: You need the money more than I do.

BROTHER-IN-LAW: I don't think Jim should have to do it all. Let's do them before we go to the house.

FATHER: Well, you know, you aren't going to be living with us much longer. Your house is almost finished. It will be different then.

Then the class again began to question the family members.

To Jean:

QUESTION: Why don't you bring your girl friend over and both of you help?

ANSWER: We'll be all dressed up!
QUESTION: Well, she can wear an apron. I do.
ANSWER: Gosh, I work all day. I have to have some time for fun. Besides, I help on the house some nights, too.

To Mother:

QUESTION: Why don't you help?
ANSWER: I work all day, too. Jim gets paid for this job.

To Jim:

QUESTION: How long does it take you to do the dishes?
ANSWER: Last night it took me about two hours!
REPLY: You don't know how to do them! I—

The discussion then became a sharing of experiences in dishwashing and rules for efficiency in doing the job. The final consensus of the class's thinking was that Jim should have help sometimes, that he needs to be more efficient and could arrange his time better, and that everybody has some job to do.

CONCLUSIONS

Although in most cases not trained as guidance workers, classroom teachers inevitably do much to counsel their pupils, both in individual instances and as a group. Role playing can help them diagnose tensions and sources of strain in the classroom group, enable individuals to become more self-assured, teach the group to accept and support individuals who are "different," and improve the emotional climate of the classroom.

Children build images of themselves from the reflected opinions of others around them. It is important, therefore, to maximize the chances for individuals to earn the respect of peers and teachers. Role playing can provide opportunities for underappreciated individuals to improve their status with their age mates. Such improvement often not only betters pupils' self-esteem but significantly improves their learning achievement. When cliques and factions cause a stormy emotional climate in the classroom, role playing can portray the effects of such strife, awaken consciousness of the feelings evoked, and thereby produce peace in classroom relationships.

5

Role Playing:
The Process

ESSENTIAL STEPS

Role playing is a kind of "reality practice." It enables groups to relive critical incidents, to explore what happened in them, and to consider what might have happened if different choices had been made in the effort to resolve the problems involved. Such practice provides us with an opportunity to learn from our mistakes under conditions that protect us from any actual penalty and in situations in which we have the sympathetic help of group members in exploring the consequences of various choices of behavior we might have undertaken.

Role playing can also provide a means of attacking new problems of human relations, of applying insights out of past experiences, and of trying out new methods to meet problems for which there may be no precedents in our past.

So often, when faced with a problem, we have tried to resolve it with one line of behavior, then later wished we had made a different choice! Often, in discussing a decision with friends, their comments and wider insights have provided us with a better alternative than the one we had chosen—*because the experiences and sensitivity of other people added to our own* often help us to more productive thinking.

Role playing as presented in this book employs the following steps:[1]

1. "Warming up" the group (problem confrontation)

[1] Adapted from Charles E. Hendry, Ronald Lippitt, and Alvin Zander, "Reality Practice as Educational Method," *Psychodrama Monograph* 9 (New York: Beacon House, 1947). A fine discussion of role playing.

2. Selecting the participants (role players)
3. Preparing the audience to participate as observers
4. Setting the stage
5. Role playing (enactment)
6. Discussing and evaluating
7. Further enactments (replaying revised roles, playing suggested next steps, or exploring alternative possibilities)
8. Sharing experiences and generalizing

This sequence of steps can perhaps be better grasped if the reader "experiences" a role-playing session.

FIFTH GRADERS ROLE-PLAY "THE CLUBHOUSE BOAT"

Role playing is often used in a classroom to meet an urgent need. The following role-playing session occurred in a school in which the faculty had become concerned over a sustained wave of antisocial behavior among pupils. In this particular case, the problem story, "The Clubhouse Boat" (p. 153), was selected because its basic issue, honesty, seemed to fit the troubling situation in the school. It was chosen also because it dealt with conflict between parental standards of conduct and the peer code, which was pertinent to the school situation.

The school is an attractive modern building set in a rapidly growing suburban area. The families in the school district consist of two distinct groups: former migrant workers, who have now settled down amidst the small farms into which the area was divided ten years ago and have built their own very modest homes, and a new population of middle-class families, who are building a typical big-city suburb.

The school faculty felt that the antisocial behavior of children from low economic backgrounds arose out of deprivation and a philosophy of get-what-you-can. Misbehavior among children from more privileged backgrounds was interpreted as due to their being overindulged and oversupervised. The teachers agreed that it was necessary to explore the human-relations needs of their pupils.

Sociometric studies were undertaken. Some teachers were using stories selected from such lists as *Reading Ladders for Human Relations*.[2] It was decided that the fifth- and sixth-grade teachers would explore the problem-story approach. The following is a record of one fifth-grade class's experience with role playing a problem story.

ACTION	INTERPRETATION
TEACHER: Do you remember the other day we had a discussion about Janey's lunch money? Because she	*"Warming up" the group* (Introducing the Problem): Utilizing an actual school incident to

[2]Muriel Crosby, ed., *Reading Ladders for Human Relations*, 4th ed. (Washington, D.C.: American Council on Education, 1963).

had put her money in her pocket and had not given it to me when she came into the room, it was lost. We had quite a talk about finding money: whether to keep it or turn it in.

Sometimes it's not easy to decide what to do. Do you ever have times when you just don't know what to do?

(*There are nods in the group.*)

I would like to read you a story this afternoon about a boy who found himself in just such a spot. His parents wanted him to do one thing, but his gang insisted he do something else. Trying to please everybody, he got himself into difficulty. This will be one of those problem stories which stop, but are not finished.

A Pupil: Like the one we did last week?

Teacher: Yes.

A Pupil: Oh! But can't you give us one with an ending?

Teacher: When you get into a jam, does someone always come along and tell you how your problem will end?

Pupils: Oh, no! Not very often.

Teacher: In life, we usually have to make our own endings—we have to solve our problems ourselves. That's why I'm reading you these problem stories—so that we can *practice* endings—try out many different ones to see which work the best for us.

As I read this story, you might be thinking of what you would do if you were in Tommy Haines's place.

(Teacher *reads the story,* "The Clubhouse Boat," *here summarized*):

Tommy Haines belongs to a club which the boys have organized in the neighborhood, the Mountain

---

open up a problem area, sensitizing pupils to the problems.

Creating a permissive environment: recognizing that it is not always easy to find a socially acceptable solution to a dilemma.

Children indicate how meaningful the problem is for them by bodily and facial responses.

Preparing the class to identify with the main character.

This class had already experienced several problem sessions.

This response is quite typical. Children are used to the "happy ending" pattern. The satisfaction that comes with increased ability to tackle and solve problems develops slowly, and only through opportunity to face problems.

Preparing the class to listen purposefully. This is a very important part of the process.

The story constitutes an extended warm-up, or preparation, for role playing. Characters and actions are delineated

ACTION	INTERPRETATION

Lions. An uncle of one of the boys agrees to give them a houseboat for a club if they will have it repaired and docked in the town's yacht harbor.

Tommy agrees to pay his share of the repair bill, twenty dollars. He is confident that he can manage this, because he is earning money as delivery boy for a drugstore.

To his dismay, his father refuses to let him participate, insisting that he must put his earnings in the bank.

This places Tommy in difficulty with his gang. They have had the boat repaired and owe money for it. Pete "borrows" the money for Tommy out of a purse that had been left in his Dad's taxicab by a patron.

Tommy, frantic to get together the amount he owes his gang, resorts to small subterfuges such as deliberately talking people into giving him tips and not telling his folks, or telling them that he has been given a raise in pay and even keeping several small sums given him in overpayment on orders.

Finally, the boys are in difficulty. The woman returns for her purse, and Pete's parents learn that he took money from it. They threaten to go to all the boys' fathers unless the money is returned by the next morning.

The boys manage to chip in some more money, but cannot raise enough. They insist that Tommy find the balance needed.

Tommy worries. Then, after delivering a package for the druggist, Tommy discovers that the customer had made a mistake and overpaid him $10.00. Enough to help him clear the debt to the gang!

and the problem situation is developed to its critical point.

ACTION	INTERPRETATION

Tommy is deeply tempted. He stands in front of the customer's closed door. Shall he knock and return the money—or shall he leave and keep the money he needs so badly?

TEACHER: What do you think Tommy will do? — Stimulating the class to explore possible solutions.

A PUPIL: I think he'll keep the money! — A spontaneous expression that probably reveals an impulse.

TEACHER: Yes?—

A PUPIL: Because he needs to pay the club. — Analyzing the problem.

A PUPIL: Oh, no, he won't. He'll get found out, and he knows it. — Anticipating consequences.

A PUPIL: How can he? Nobody knows he has it. — Expressing a personal philosophy.

TEACHER: (*to this last student*): Would you like to come up here, Jerry, and be Tommy?

Selecting participants
The teacher deliberately chooses the boy who expresses an antisocial solution.

(*Jerry comes to the front of the room.*) Jerry, whom will you need to help you?

JERRY: I'll need somebody to be the customer. And I'll need boys to be the gang. — Encouraging the pupil to describe the solution and situation himself.

(*Players are chosen. The teacher invites several children to participate. The setting is arranged. One corner of the classroom is the school where the gang is waiting for Tommy to come with the needed money. A chair is placed in another corner to represent the door of the house to which the package is delivered.*)

While children are never urged to play roles that they do not "feel," occasionally a child needs to be encouraged to participate.

TEACHER: Where are you going to start, Jerry?

Setting the stage
The teacher helps describe the furnishings needed and helps arrange them quickly.

JERRY: I'll deliver the package.

TEACHER: Very well. Now you people, as you watch, consider whether you think Jerry's way of ending the story could really happen. How will people feel? You may want to think of what will happen next. Perhaps you'll have different ideas about it; and when Jerry's finished, and we've talked about it, we can try your ideas.

Preparing the class to be participating observers

ACTION	INTERPRETATION

FIRST ENACTMENT

(*Tommy knocks on door. The boy playing role of old man "opens" the door.*)

TOMMY: Delivery from Central Drugstore, sir. Eleven dollars and twenty-eight cents due.

MAN: Here you are. And here's a quarter. Buy yourself a Cadillac.

(*Man closes door. Tommy counts money. Discovers he has been overpaid ten dollars. Raises hand to knock on door and call man back—then turns away. Walks across the classroom to the waiting gang.*)

TOMMY: Hey, guys, look! I got the money we need. Here!

EDDY: Swell! Now we can pay for the boat. Come on, gang!

(*End of enactment.*)

Role playing
Pretend level.
A chair is used to designate the door.

This boy chooses to "get away with it." His enactment is an expression of the (ethical) value and the anti-social behavior that have been causing concern among the school faculty.

TEACHER: Well, Jerry has given us one solution. What do you think of it?

A PUPIL: Uh-uh! It won't work!

JERRY: Why not?

A PUPIL: That man is going to remember how much money he had. He'll phone the druggist about it.

JERRY: So what? He can't prove anything on me. I'll just say he didn't overpay me.

A PUPIL: You'll lose your job.

JERRY: When they can't prove it?

ANOTHER PUPIL: Yes. Even if they can't prove it!

TEACHER: Why do you think so, John?

JOHN: Because the druggist has to be on the side of his customer. He can fire Tommy and hire another boy. But he doesn't want his customers mad at him.

A PUPIL: He's going to feel pretty sick inside, if he keeps the money.

TEACHER: What do you mean?

Discussing and evaluating
Encouraging an evaluation. The teacher is careful to be noncommittal.
A judgment.
It happens that Jerry is a boy of low mental ability; he is quite sure of himself.
An analysis of consequences.

Other consequences are foreseen, such as anxiety and guilt.
Encouraging further expression.

ACTION	INTERPRETATION

PUPIL: Well, it bothers you when you know you've done something wrong.

TEACHER: Do you have any other way to solve this problem?

Exploring for other solutions

PUPIL: Yes. Tommy should knock on the door and tell the customer about being overpaid. Maybe the man'll let Tommy keep the money.

A proposal with a wishful (fantasy) solution.

TEACHER: All right, let's try it your way, Dick.

The teacher follows through.

The consequences of fantasy solutions should be explored.

SECOND ENACTMENT

(New role players are selected, and the scene is set. Tommy delivers the parcel, is paid; the door is shut. He discovers that he has been overpaid $10.00)

TOMMY: Gosh, I better knock and call that man back!

(He knocks.)

MAN: *(opening door)* What is it, son?

TOMMY: Sir, you overpaid me ten dollars.

MAN: I did! Well—you're an honest boy. Tell you what—You *keep* the change."

(End of enactment.)

Further discussion

TEACHER: What about this solution?

SEVERAL PUPILS: It's all right! It's fine. That settles everything.

The teacher remains noncommittal.

The class accepts a fantasy solution.

TEACHER: Do you think this could really happen?

The teacher pushes for a realistic evaluation.

PUPIL: Yes. Because once I got overpaid for my paper delivery, and when I told the man, he said, "Keep it."

Generalizing from personal experience.

TEACHER: How much money did he overpay you?

Exploring the analogy for parallels.

PUPIL: A dollar and a quarter.

TEACHER: Do you think it might be different with ten dollars?

Again pushing for reality.

PUPIL: Yes. That's too much. He might give you a dollar tip.

A more realistic evaluation.

TEACHER: How do the rest of you feel about this?

Involving the rest of the class.

ACTION	INTERPRETATION

(The class agrees that few adults would tip ten dollars.)
Then, how shall Tommy solve his problem?

Guiding the class to see that they have not yet found a realistic solution to the story.

A PUPIL: I think he should talk it over with his mother.

This is probably the pupil's pattern of dealing with troubling dilemmas.

TEACHER: Why his mother, Alice?

ALICE: Well, when my Dad says no, I ask my mother.

The mechanisms that work for some.

(Grins and nods from the group.)

TEACHER: Is that the way it works for you all?

Again exploring with the class.

A PUPIL: No, it's the other way around in our house.

ANOTHER PUPIL: My folks stick together. Kids just don't have a chance.

Different families have different relationships.

TEACHER: You feel that grownups just don't understand?

Reflecting a child's thoughts so that he may explore further.

A PUPIL: Well, sometimes they jump to conclusions.

TEACHER: Do you feel that Tommy's parents were wrong?

Guiding the thinking.

A PUPIL: No. Tommy had no business promising so much money without asking his parents.

A judgment made.

A PUPIL: That was too much money for kids to spend.

A PUPIL: But once he promised it, his dad should have helped him out.

A concept of the father role.

A PUPIL: My mother would help me out of a jam!

A mother-child relationship expressed.

TEACHER: Would you like to play this, Sally, the way you think it could happen with your mother?

The teacher seizes the opportunity to explore a constructive solution, now that the class has already explored an antisocial solution and a fantasy solution.

THIRD ENACTMENT

(The setting is Tommy's home.)

Another enactment

TOMMY: Mom, I'm in an awful jam!

MOTHER: What's the trouble, Tommy?

(Tommy tells his mother the whole story.)

ACTION	INTERPRETATION
MOTHER: Why, Tommy, you should have told me sooner. Here, you pay the money (opens purse) and we'll talk this over with your Dad when he comes home. (*End of enactment.*)	Mother will help, but children do get punished, in this version.
TEACHER: What will happen now?	Probing for consequences.
A PUPIL: Tommy will get a licking!	
TEACHER: How do you feel about that?	
A PUPIL: It's all right. I'd rather have the licking and get it off my mind.	Reaching a definite attitude on the problem.
	Sharing experiences
TEACHER: Does this sound familiar, class? Do you know of an instance in which a boy or girl had to make such a decision?	Tying the situation in with known experience in a nonthreatening way. If a child wishes, he may describe someone else's experience rather than admit his own mistakes.
JIM: Yes, it happened to me once. I was borrowing money from all the milk bottles on our street. It got so I couldn't sleep nights worrying about it. Finally, my Pop caught up with me and gave me an awful licking. And was I glad.	This child chose to be direct and frank.
TEACHER: You mean it was a relief not to have to worry about getting caught?	The teacher is careful to be noncritical and casual and to generalize. Any sort of discussion, in a permissive atmosphere, may elicit such admissions of individual behavior. The teacher should safeguard a pupil from any teasing or loss of respect from his peers.
JIM: Yes.	
TEACHER: Sometimes we get into things we wish we'd never started. Was that Tommy's trouble?	
PUPILS: Yes.	
A PUPIL: But he should have told his Dad. He'd have helped him out.	
TEACHER: Why was his father so strict?	Exploring the attitude of fathers.
PUPIL: Because he wanted to teach Tommy a lesson from his own experience.	
TEACHER: Do you think that a father should help his boy decide what to do with the money he earns?	Opening up a new phase of the problem.

This class, because of previous experiences with dramatic play and sociodrama, and because the teacher observed the principles of working with youngsters in a nonjudgmental and accepting situation, was very free

and spontaneous in expression. The session lasted an hour and was continued in discussion form the next day, centering around the topic: "Who
decides how you can spend the money you earn?" The majority of the pupils
felt that children need supervision of their spending *but* that they should be
allowed to spend at least half of their earnings.

An Elaboration of the Steps

Having followed the steps in role playing through this actual classroom
session, let us look more closely at each step, its function, and the techniques
used.

1. "Warming up" the group (problem confrontation)

The warm-up serves several purposes. It acquaints the participating
group with the problem at hand. It arouses awareness of their need to learn
ways of dealing with the problem. And it involves the group emotionally in a
specific situation and thereby helps them to identify with individuals who are
coping with the tangle of human relations to which the problem gives rise.

A teacher may begin the warm-up saying, "I'm sure that all of us, at
some time or another, have been in an embarrassing situation—and felt that
a lie was the only way out of it"; or, "Sometimes our friends want us to do
something that our parents do not permit, and we get into a lot of trouble by
trying to please *both* sides." The teacher's purpose in this warm-up is to get
enough of a response from members of the group to make them realize that
each of them (and the teacher) on occasion has had to face such problems. By
his presentation, the teacher demonstrates that he is aware that children get
into difficulties and is sympathetic and wants to help—that, in fact, most
adults are on their side. The problem under discussion must, of course, be
one that is important to the young people, one with which they can immediately identify.

The next step of the warm-up is to express the problem in the vivid
details of a specific example. Doing this will involve the children emotionally.
Sometimes the group describes situations they have known that illustrate the
problem. One of these incidents may then be selected for role playing.
Sometimes an actual incident that all the children know about or have
experienced is recalled and structured for role playing. At other times the
teacher presents a problem situation that has been prepared in advance. A
scene from a film, a television show incident, or a selection from literature
can be used for this purpose.

An effective tool for the specific example is the *problem story* that is read
to the class by the teacher and that stops at the dilemma point. The problem
story provides a structured situation which, while representative of children's actual experiences, provides an often necessary "remove" that makes
exploration easier. Furthermore, such stories present dramatic spring-
boards which quickly involve the group in role playing and do not demand as
much initial skill in introductory warm-up techniques on the part of the
teacher.

The problem story must deal with human relations in terms that are both believable and interesting. The basic situation must be real and important to the group. The more convincing the story is, the more excitingly it develops, the more strongly will the listeners identify with the fictional characters. They will participate in role playing in direct proportion to the degree to which their sympathies and partisanship are aroused, or their convictions affronted.

When the story stops, a brief discussion period should be held in order to lead into role playing.

The teacher may wind up the initial warm-up comments by saying, "I'm going to read you a story about a boy who got into the sort of trouble we've been talking about. This story isn't finished. While I'm reading it, you may think of how it might end. When the story stops, some of you may want to show us some ways you think this boy may solve his problem." This last point is important. It poses a challenge to the listening group. Their attention is sharpened, and they will listen more alertly. They will identify themselves with various story characters and will try to get as much meaning as possible out of the situation. The teacher does not ask, "What do you think *should* happen now?" Such a question shuts off the impulsive, often expedient responses that need to be explored before the group is guided to think of both positive and negative consequences.

After the problem story has been read, the teacher helps the group move into discussion and then into role playing. He or she may ask, "What do you think will happen now?"; or, "What is happening in this situation?" *And then the teacher waits.*

Children are a wonderful audience. Less inhibited than adults, they vent their feelings as they listen, with sighs and groans and comments and handclaps. Even their facial expressions and body postures are eloquent. After the reading is over (if the situation is meaningful for them), they usually have much to say and are in a hurry to say it. They are boiling over with responses.

Sometimes the situation may be painful. There may be a silence when the story stops. The teacher, by waiting *serenely*, implies confidence in the children's ability to face and cope with such a problem; gradually, the responses will come.

Usually, merely by asking "What do you think will happen now?" the teacher releases pent-up debate. Suggestions follow, often with much heat and emphasis.

2. Selecting participants for role playing

In selecting participants, it is important to use individuals who have identified with the roles, who can see themselves as particular persons in the situation, who can *feel* the parts. To do this, the teacher goes "fishing." He may ask the group to describe the various characters. He may ask, "What kind of a person is Johnny?" "How does he feel?" Children who seem to identify with certain characters may be asked to play those persons. Sometimes volunteers are called for.

A caution is necessary at this point: *The teacher should avoid assigning roles to children who have been volunteered for those roles by others.* The situation may be punitive; or a particular child may not see himself in the role thrust upon him.

Usually a number of children in a group are quite vocal about what they think will happen and what specific individuals in the story will do. These responses give the teacher clues not only as to *which* children are identifying with the various roles, but also as to *how* they are identifying.

Often the teacher chooses children who indicate an antisocial solution to the problem so as to explore in action the consequences of such a solution. Or, he may select a child who will play an authoritarian or strict mother or father role, knowing that his role may typify a problem faced by a number of his young people.

Sometimes the teacher selects a child to play a part because he knows that the child needs to identify with the role as a learning experience. Such a child needs much support and help in getting into the role. (Procedures for doing this are discussed in Chapter 6.)

Primarily, the teacher chooses children who reveal by their remarks that they have identified with certain individuals in the story or have strong feelings about the behavior of specific characters. Usually the teacher should avoid choosing, for the first enactment, an individual who will give an adult-oriented, socially acceptable solution. Using this person first may result in shutting off exploration of what many children actually do think and feel in such situations. In "The Clubhouse Boat" session, recall that the teacher chose first to explore the temptation to keep the money and give in to expediency. It is by following through on such impulses and *exploring them for consequences* that children can learn from their own past experiences.

Usually, after a thorough investigation of the pupils' honest feelings and perceptions of the problem situation, in which they have revealed, by their impulsive actions and expressions, the values they hold, the teacher may come back to the child who has a mature and socially acceptable solution to propose. By that time, the children may be ready to relinquish their opportunistic solutions, since the role playing may have revealed consequences they had not foreseen.

3. Setting the stage

Before beginning the enactment, the role players *very briefly* plan what they are going to do. They do not prepare any dialogue but simply decide on a general line of action. They may decide to explore what happens if Tommy keeps the money. Or the teacher, in selecting a certain child's idea, may encourage that child to set the line of action in accordance with his own idea.

Each player is then reminded of the role he or she is to take. Role playing has most value when completely spontaneous, and each child taking part responds to the action of the other role players. There are no set speeches and no detailed plotting.

Once a simple line of action has been selected for exploration, the teacher may ask the main role player whom he needs to carry out the action. After the players are chosen, the teacher helps the actors to get "inside" the situation. He may ask, "Where is this taking place? What is it like in this place?"; or, "Where is the door?"; or "What time of day is it?"; or, "What are you doing, Mother, when Johnny comes home?" In this way he settles the players into their roles and situations.

4. Preparing the audience to be participating observers

The next step is to prepare the observing group to participate actively and intelligently. Here some listening skills must come into play. Uninstructed observers may watch passively, or become hypercritical, or be so consumed by their own ideas that they wait impatiently and inattentively for the enactment to end so that they may get turns.

We wish to help young people become good listeners to other people's feelings and ideas, to look at a problem *with* them, and see what they see. It is only by understanding another's viewpoint that young people can agree or disagree with it. Furthermore, they may also learn something from the other person's perceptions and ideas.

At the same time that we want to achieve this alert and receptive listening, we also want children to explore alternative solutions to the problem under discussion. Therefore, the teacher may begin by assigning the group various observer tasks. If she is working with a beginning group, the teacher may suggest that they judge the realistic quality of the solution that is being proposed; that is, she tells them to ask themselves "Do you think, as you watch the actors, that they are behaving in a way they would really behave in similar situations that you know about?"

The teacher may, after initial experience in reality testing, divide the group. She may ask certain children to concentrate on particular actors and decide whether those roles are being played in a way that is true to life. She may ask other children to observe how certain players feel as the action progresses. Or, she may ask some children to be thinking of the next steps (consequences) of the action.

After such instructions, the teacher keeps the way open for further solutions and enactments; she may say that she feels sure that some of the group members have other ideas about the way the situation problem should be solved, and that after this first idea has been explored, other members of the group will have a chance to try out their alternative suggestions.

It may be wise for the teacher to warn a beginning group that laughter spoils the role playing and that attentive observation *helps* the role players.

5. Role playing (the enactment)

The role players then put on their enactment. They assume the roles and "live" the situation, responding to one another's speeches and actions as they feel the people in those roles would behave. There is no set plot, only a situation—a time, a place, and, perhaps, one person's line of action (Johnny will keep the money!). Players, therefore, must think and feel on their feet, spontaneously reacting to the developing situation.

No role player is expected to present a role flawlessly. Slips or awkward moments are taken for granted; so are occasional lapses into less than formal language and gesture. When real feelings are being portrayed, language may become quite vernacular. At this point the teacher needs to use discretion; while extremes in language may not be acceptable, too much censorship will destroy the spontaneity and sense of reality.

In responding to an enactment, the group should be helped to understand, too, that the way an actor portrays a role has no reflection upon him as a person. He is simply presenting a role as he sees it. He will not be condemned for his interpretation by the teacher or anyone else. This is a very important precaution. Moreoever, no role player is evaluated for his acting. An enactment is not a play with focus on theatrical performance; it is reality exploration. Our only test is whether the group feels that the portrayal is true to life in some place or situation that they have experienced.

6. Discussion and evaluation

The discussion that follows an enactment is one of the most vital phases of role playing. While research has indicated that the actual taking of roles may have the greatest influence on attitudinal changes,[3] it is in the give-and-take of discussion that problem-solving procedures are refined and learned.

Usually, there is no need for prompting by the teacher at the close of an enactment. Discussion is fast and furious. The young people are keyed up. They bubble over with comments. They pour out their opinions of the portrayals. "I don't think a mother would say that! Mine wouldn't," is countered by, "Well, mine *would!*" Or someone else may say, "That kind of mother would behave that way." And, even more important, observations are made on the consequences of the actions taken. Thus one boy may observe that Tommy will lose his job because the druggist can hire another boy but doesn't want to lose a customer. Another youngster is concerned with how it feels to live with a bad conscience. It is in such discussions that children learn, *with the support* and often *with the opposition of their age mates*, to consider the consequences of the choices they propose.

The teacher guides the discussion with stimulating open-ended questions such as, "What is happening?"; or, "How does Jane feel?"; or, "Could this happen in real life?"; or, "What will happen now?" The questions guide the children toward thinking about the consequences of behavior.

At first, the questions direct the observers toward thinking *with* the role players. Such questions as, "How is Mary feeling?" or "What is Tom thinking?" help to focus on the action that has been presented. Later, the teacher picks up comments that lead to alternative proposals. As Mary says, "I don't think I'd do it that way!" the teacher responds with "What would you do?" If no alternatives are offered, he may ask, "Is there some other way this situation might be resolved?"

The initial role players have stimulated further thinking in the observers; and the group of observers, in their responses, broaden the perspectives of the role players. Because the observers are not as emotionally involved and committed to a line of action as the actors, the observers are in a position to see consequences to proposals more easily and to see many more alterna-

[3]Pearl P. Rosenberg, "An Experimental Analysis of Psychodrama" (Unpublished doctoral dissertation, Harvard University, 1950); Bert T. King and Irving L. Janis, "Comparison of the Effectiveness of Improvised versus Nonimprovised Role Playing in Producing Opinion Changes," *Human Relations*, 19 (1956).

tives. The entire group experiences, in a very active sense, the stress and satisfaction of problem solving.

7. The reenactment (further role playing and discussion)

Reenactment is the next step in role playing. So often in real life one wishes for a second chance to solve a dilemma. In role playing, this second chance is now forthcoming. So is a third and a fourth chance. This is the great value of role playing. *Participants can arrive at a good solution to a human difficulty through as much trial and error as is necessary.* They "discover" for themselves the complex dimensions of a problem situation and the personal and social considerations inherent in various solutions.

The role players may play their roles over and over again, changing their interpretations in the light of the suggestions they receive from their fellow group members. Or, new actors may take over the roles to demonstrate other interpretations and solutions.

Sometimes a role player precipitates a situation that leaves another role player at the end of his or her ideas. The teacher may then have to (1) guide him indirectly into further action by asking questions, such as, "How are you feeling now?" or "What kind of person are you?"; or (2) select another pupil who seems to have ideas on how to respond to the altered situation; or (3) cut the scene short and start class discussion.

New actors may take over the roles and portray them differently, or the original role players may be asked to switch roles (that is, the "son" of one enactment may play the "father" in a succeeding one). This procedure allows role players to get *inside* roles with which they were in conflict and better understand other people's feelings and views in the situation.

A surprising number of episodes may be enacted and reenacted in a short period of time. It is possible for five or six versions of a situation, with intervening discussion, to take place within an hour. Of course, the length of a discussion, or the length of an enactment, cannot be foreseen. A discussion may last two minutes, or possibly a full hour. As long as a discussion is fruitful, as long as an enactment is moving productively, it should be allowed to continue. This is an area in which teachers must use their best judgment.

This moving back and forth from acting to discussing to acting again can be a most effective learning sequence. An individual who thinks she has a rational solution to offer may find, in actual role playing, that *her feelings get in the way of her rationality.* On the action level, she may find herself so affected by her emotional response to the behavior of the other role players that she *acts* differently from the way she had intended. Such an experience gets close to reality and gives the teacher an opportunity to help the group face up to the complexity of human relations problems. Gradually, under skilled leadership, young people are stimulated to analyze their feelings and impulsive responses and thereby to bring the emotional and rational aspects of behavior into closer relationship.

There is also a kind of insight that comes to the individual as he moves back and forth from being a role player to being an observer. *This insight permits each child to come to his own conclusions on his own thinking schedule.* He programs his conclusions when ideas fall into place *for him.*

8. Sharing experience and generalizing

The last step in a role-playing session may be termed a period of general discussion, sometimes of sharing experiences, and, if the enactments and insights of the group promote it, a time of generalizing from the exploration. After a number of alternatives and their consequences have been enacted and discussed, the teacher may ask, "Do you think this problem is one that is true to life for young people like you?"; or, "Has something like this ever happened to someone you know?"

Often, individuals will volunteer examples of incidents they have known about. *Occasionally they offer personal experiences, but this should not be urged actively by the teacher since it may invite a child to expose himself to the group in ways that will harm his reputation. Therefore the teacher avoids asking, "Did anything like this ever happen to you?" unless it is in an area that is not likely to rebound on individual children.*

This sharing of experiences, this exploration of consequences of behavior, achieves several important objectives:

It helps anxious young people to discover that their problems are shared by other people—many other people. In this awareness a worried individual finds relief and reassurance. It also brings the classroom experience and the child-life outside of school into closer relationship and provides opportunity for the teacher, through his supportive leadership, to gain the confidence of the group.

Out of the enactments, out of the criticisms and suggestions and reenactments, out of the excited clash of opinions, the group hammers out some general principles of conduct. They may conclude that "Even if you get away with it, you don't feel so good inside," which may be translated to mean, "Opportunistic solutions are not worth the loss of self-respect that often results." They may see that leaders should be selected for their ability to guide the task at hand rather than on the basis of hero worship.

In this period of sharing and generalization, such principles gradually emerge. They are especially influential to the individual child because they bear the authority of his own peers.

We must be prepared to accept the fact that some role-playing sessions do not reach the level of generalization. Sometimes a session may do no more through a series of enactments than delineate in full detail the nature of the problem. It is important for young people to learn that superficial definitions of a problem situation may overlook significant facets that must be considered.

The teacher too must often content himself with a session that may only attempt repeatedly to solve the problem-story situation itself. Often it requires many role-playing sessions on a specific problem, using different stories, before a group develops insights that promote generalization. We cannot command generalization; it is a product of individual insights based on much meaningful experience.

CONCLUSIONS

Role playing, in its simplest sense, is the spontaneous practice of roles. Individuals assume them in order to practice the behavior required in various cultural situations. Role playing in psychotherapy has a special meaning that is outside the scope of this book. (Role playing intended as therapy may be termed *psychodrama* and should, of course, be attempted only by the trained clinician.[4] Role playing that is intended to provide practice in dealing with group social problems is sometimes labeled *sociodrama*.)

Here, we present role playing as an elaborate social-learning method and as a basic decision-making skill in the school program. Role playing is a group problem-solving method that involves a variety of techniques—discussion, problem analysis, and definition through (1) initial enactment of proposals (taking on of roles), (2) observer reactions to the enactments (discussion), (3) exploration of alternatives through further enactments and discussion, and often (4) the drawing of conclusions, or generalization and decision making.

Role playing provides the opportunity to explore, through spontaneous improvisation and carefully guided discussion, typical group problem situations in which individuals are helped to become sensitive to the feelings of the people involved, where the consequences of choices made are delineated by the group, and where members are helped to explore the kinds of behavior that society will sanction. In this process, young people are guided to become sensitive to feelings, to the personal consequences of the choices they make, and to the consequences of those choices for other people. The group members practice many roles, or different approaches to roles. Gradually they develop skills for solving problems of social conduct and interpersonal relations as well as for exploring many curriculum areas. Perhaps the most important aspect of the role-playing process is the fact that individuals, with the help *and* opposition of their classmates, *gradually face and make conscious their choices in the situations that are crucial to them*; through the experience of articulating, testing, and criticizing their motivations, they develop a system of consciously held values.

[4]The uses of role playing in psychotherapy, initially as psychodrama, and later in education as sociodrama, were conceptualized by Jacob Moreno, who developed and expressed his creative ideas in the now classic volumes: *Psychodrama* (New York: Beacon House, 1946), and *Who Shall Survive?* (New York: Beacon House, 1953). We are deeply indebted, as are many others, to Jacob Moreno for his theories of spontaneity and his development of the field of sociometry. He conceived the spontaneity theater and took the early theories of role and developed them into the basic work on role playing.

6

Guiding
Role Playing

Underlying the successful guidance of role playing is a set of basic assumptions about human behavior and the teaching–learning process. Most fundamental is the belief that individuals have the ability to cope with their own life situations and to grow in their capacity to deal with their problems intelligently. This is so deceptively simple that it may seem like laboring the obvious, but let us probe its significance.

If individuals have the capacity to solve their own problems, *they have to be permitted to make their own decisions and learn from their own mistakes.* Teachers often have to go along with very low-level attempts to solve problems; they should not show children the right ways, but rather, *patiently guide enactments and discussions in such ways that children make their own discoveries and gradually move to higher levels of decision making because of their increased awareness of alternatives and consequences.*

Another basic assumption in role playing is that the enacted behavior is neither good nor bad; it is simply the best idea available to the child at the time that he makes his decision. True, his first decision may not be socially acceptable; but he must come to terms with that matter *himself*, as he analyzes the consequences.

In back of this assumption is another one: We change our behavior only as we change our insights. Individuals often know intellectually what is "right" but act on feelings or past behavior patterns. The role-playing leader believes that behavior is caused and that, typically, there are multiple causes. Human problems are seldom as simple as they may seem at first glance. Furthermore, behavior occurs in a setting; the history of an incident, its emotional climate, the matrix of circumstances, all must be taken into consideration in order to understand the behavior.

When we follow through, in the discussion of motive and reason and impulse in role playing, by analyzing the *causal* aspects of behavior, the human dynamics involved, we help children cope with reality rather than merely verbalize oversimplified judgments which, too often, are little help in real situations.

Still another assumption that promotes spontaneity and sincerity in role playing is that teachers can temporarily accept negative feelings and behavior from children in order to help them accept themselves and their past experiences and to make these experiences available for further learning. Teachers therefore permit more open expression of feelings, even hostile ones, than they ordinarily accept in the classroom; this is exploration of reality. Some teachers will find this acceptance very difficult at the beginning; nevertheless, it is important that they learn it.

ESTABLISHING A CLIMATE

Given these assumptions, teachers who guide role playing are then committed to certain conditions and procedures. They must create an environment, or "climate," that encourages the frank expression of ideas and feelings, one in which:

1. It is "safe" for students to explore behaviors (both antisocial and socially acceptable).
2. It is permissible for strong feelings—even "bad" feelings—to be expressed. (We teachers are often afraid of children's feelings.)
3. The group is helped to respect the ideas and feelings of all members.

How does one create such an atmosphere? The effort poses special problems for teachers. We have been taught to punish wrong behavior and reward proper behavior. We have been charged with the character education of our students, with their learning of socially sanctioned behavior. In the classroom we set limits and do our best to promote positive behavior. Children quickly "learn the teacher," what his or her goals are, and how to respond in terms of teacher expectations. Children gradually cease to express their own feelings and ideas; instead, they respond in terms of teacher demands.

Role playing, if it is to have worth, must explore the *children's* honest feelings and ideas. We must encourage sincere, frank expression so that their feelings and perceptions may be brought to the surface for exploration in an environment where it is safe to examine both their social and antisocial efforts to meet somehow the demands that circumstances place upon them.

This position is the reverse of the traditional teaching approach that assumes that children do not know and *we* will show them how. It is based instead on the belief that individuals need opportunity and support (from their teachers and from the group) in facing and working through the life situations in which they must act, in which they must make decisions.

The teacher who uses this approach recognizes that whereas a child may begin at a low level of coping (just getting by somehow), he has the capacity to weigh alternatives and to move to more productive solutions *when he has been helped to extend his awareness of the possibilities available to him in the culture.*

In this procedure, the decision on which he or she acts (even in role playing) *is always the child's.* Not the teacher's or the group's! True, he never acts alone, inasmuch as he is confronted with situations involving other people; the procedure helps him to learn to make intelligent choices in real life; he can practice that choice making in role playing.

This commitment on the part of the teacher *not* to direct the action, but rather *to make it possible for children to choose their own behaviors,* is the critical aspect of role playing. The teacher is directive in selecting role-playing situations, in deciding whom to involve, *but is nondirective in the role-playing enactments.*

How does the teacher establish a "safe" climate for role playing? Several procedures are effective.

Since, in most classrooms, students are oriented to cues (listening for goals voiced by the teacher), one of the first steps is to demonstrate another point of view and establish at least a time in the day (or week) when students can express any and all ideas with no resulting penalties.

It will do little good to tell your class that there are new ground rules. They will have to be shown: The rules will have to be demonstrated in the teacher's behavior.

Simple ways to start are by providing literature for human understanding for the class and by using the discussion techniques developed originally by Margaret Heaton and others in *Reading Ladders for Human Relations* (Crosby, 1963). In this procedure, children are encouraged to read stories or books centering around a common theme—for example, relations between generations. Those pupils who have read a story or book on this theme (they may have read the same book or different ones focused on the same theme) are then guided by the teacher to discuss the key relationships and conflicts.

The teacher demonstrates that he or she *understands* why the characters in books behave the way they do by such comments as "It isn't always easy to do what adults expect of you," or "Sometimes you just don't know which way to turn," or "He was desperate, wasn't he?" or "She was so angry, she didn't care what happened." Such comments tell children that the teacher *feels with children* as they confront dilemmas.

After children have experienced the relatively "safe" procedure of talking about characters in books over a period of weeks, gradually the teacher can begin to use more direct, and sometimes more personal, techniques. Writing private themes about personal dilemmas may be appropriate. Using completion sentences is helpful, such as, "One time when I got very mad . . ." or "Once, I just didn't know what to do when . . ."

After such experiences, the teacher can much more easily set the stage for role playing. Again, it is wise to begin at a nonthreatening level. First role playing may center on "skills training" that does not demand much risk. The class may invite an expert to talk to them on some subject related to their studies. Role playing may be used to practice greeting the visitor and making him comfortable. Then the class may role-play the opening of discussion with the visitor, what questions they might ask, how they will share their concerns with him, and so on. Or, the class may role-play a committee going to the principal to ask permission to go on a field trip. Such skills practice encourages spontaneity and thinking-in-action. It prepares the way for deeper explorations.

When, finally, the teacher introduces real dilemma situations, the approach to the class in the warm-up is a further demonstration that it is safe to express certain feelings. He may begin by saying, "Have you ever gotten yourself into a jam in which you just didn't know what to do? I have, and it's a very frightening feeling sometimes. Once, I . . ." Or, he may say, "Sometimes we all are faced with choices that are very difficult to make. Each alternative may have advantages. How do we decide? Have you ever made a choice, then wished you had done it another way? I have!"

Children, responding to this new teacher-pupil relationship, gradually build a trust in the teacher as one who values them as persons, regardless of their behavior. This relationship, often called the *therapeutic relationship*, is summed up in the writings of Carl Rogers and his former student, Virginia Axline. Axline states: "It is the permissiveness to be themselves, the understanding, the acceptance, the recognition of feelings, the clarification of what they think and feel that helps children retain their self-respect; and the possibilities of growth and change are forthcoming as they all develop insight."[1]

The classroom teacher borrows some useful techniques from the therapist. She reflects back to role players the feelings they are expressing in their actions. As an enactment ends, the teacher may say, "You are really angry, aren't you?" (She says this only if the child reveals anger, not to lead the child to play anger.) This enables the child to say, "Yes, I am! He's been taking things from me for a long time!"

Or, the teacher may say, "It seems to me you are saying that you don't know what to do next." The child may thus be helped to state his dilemma more fully. Sometimes, after a series of enactments, the teacher says, "It seems to me that all of you are saying that adults just don't care." This summary may lead to further expression, at a verbal level, of feelings that, up to this point, have been only intuitive. By such responses, over and over, the teacher is demonstrating sympathy and understanding to the class.

When teachers wait patiently for a child to think through a proposal (rather than turning quickly to another child), when they are warm and relaxed and friendly, they demonstrate their awareness that ideas sometimes come slowly, *but will emerge* if waited for. A teacher can say, "Think it through, John. I'll come back to you in a minute."

Occasionally, as a child stumbles, hesitates, and struggles with an idea, the teacher helps by asking enabling questions, such as, "Do you mean that you think he will want to do *both* things? Do you think he can?" or "Are you wondering if this can be worked out?" In this process, the teacher must be careful not to ask leading questions, but rather to know intuitively what the child is feeling and thinking.

[1]Virginia Axline, *Play Therapy* (Boston: Houghton Mifflin, 1947), pp. 75, 77.

Perhaps the one major difference between therapist and teacher lies in the limit which must be set in a classroom. Teachers can accept negative feelings *temporarily* for the purpose of helping the child accept himself. The teacher is permissive of feelings, somewhat permissive of verbal behavior (certain limits must be set for language in the classroom), less so of physical behavior. The teacher encourages, stimulates, and sometimes directs.

The teacher retains the role of guide, of one who (1) has knowledge of subject matter and professional competence, (2) helps children anchor in reality (by accepting contributions, but raising questions), and (3) helps children to focus (order) their experiences.

In role playing, the teacher can permit much freer expression than in other classroom activities, since this is "reality practice." The teacher must be willing to follow untraveled pathways, to let one thing lead to another. By expressing *genuine empathy*, the teacher demonstrates that he can view things from the internal frame of reference of the student, that he tries to imagine how the student feels.[2]

The leader of role playing is not concerned with coercing the student into predetermined behavior. She is concerned with creating an openness to experience in which all known behavior can be examined, explored for consequences, and pondered. The teacher, therefore, remains nonjudgmental and objective; she facilitates the open exploration of life situations under the assumption that all possible alternatives are available for examination. She assumes, at this point, that there is no one right answer, although the child may eventually choose one that is right for him or may accept the fact that society defines what is "right" quite specifically in certain areas.

Just as the teacher avoids the use of coercion, so must she, at the same time, protect the child from the coercion of the class group. Children are often made to feel that they are "out of step," that they ought to fall in with the dominant beliefs (especially those voiced by popular children).

Children, however, do need to be accepted members of many kinds of groups, and the effort to maintain their position in a group may be quite healthy. Torrance points out that cliques may be needed by groups and by the individuals who compose them, as defenses. Sometimes the destruction of such cliques may rob the group of healthy modes of adapting to the demands of a situation. Unhealthy conditions develop when one clique is used, by adults, as a model for others. The group can provide the child with supporting ground to stand on, *if* the group is helped to support variability among its members.

To protect the individual child from group pressure, the teacher supports his right to do his own thinking by asking the group such questions as, "Do you think————must see this the way you do?" And, "Can we gain something from one another's ideas, if we explore our different ways of

----

[2]E. Paul Torrance writes, "The strategy of genuine *empathy* is necessary to replace the strategy of *identification*. Try to view things from the internal frame of reference of the student. Try to imagine how the student feels about things. This is then the basis for helping the student meet the requirements of the situation, as something he is doing for himself rather than as an accommodation to a powerful person." From *Guiding Creative Talent* (Englewood Cliffs, N.J.: Prentice-Hall, 1962), pp. 172–73.

seeing things rather than insisting on agreement?" or "Why do you suppose————sees this differently from most of you? Can you tell us more
about your view . . . ?"

Gradually, in such a classroom climate, children feel safe holding
different views, in being honest in their opinions. And, hopefully, the class
gradually begins to cherish and support the search for many points of view.
They learn to "listen" intently to varying opinions, ideas, proposals, to
ponder them, to engage in a real encounter with one another.

To sum up, the teacher sets the climate for role playing by his nonevaluative position and supportive attitude and by listening for underlying
meanings.

A nonevaluative position. The teacher accepts all suggestions for solving a problem in role playing (including antisocial ones) as legitimate
material to be explored. Thus a child may say, "I think Tommy should keep
the money [paid him by mistake] and pay his debt to the club." The teacher
then may say, "All right, Tom, come up here and work out your idea so that
we can see what you mean." Instead of condemning the proposal as dishonest, the teacher is trusting to the process of group examination of the
proposal, in the light of considered consequences, to reveal how antisocial
and impractical it is. By this behavior, the teacher makes it safe for children
to risk expressing their impulsive reactions.

A supportive attitude. The teacher accepts negative feelings temporarily, for the purpose of exposing "real" situations. Feelings are facts that
need to be brought to the surface, and expressing them helps the child to
recognize and release tensions. Thus, when a child, playing a role, yells "I
hate you!" or "You dirty guy!" the teacher may say, with sympathy, "You are
really angry." This is an invitation to the child to explore his feelings about
the situation.

The goal is to create an open, nonthreatening, creative relationship
rather than to coerce the child (in however kindly a fashion) into socially
acceptable behavior. The teacher is warm, relaxed, nonpunitive. He can
wait for responses and thus show his confidence that his pupils have the
ability to cope with the situation.

Listening for underlying meanings. Perhaps one of the most needed and
subtle orientations that promotes successful leading of role playing is real skill
in listening for underlying meanings. Teachers are habituated to "telling" in
most of their teaching. Modern concepts of listening demand a full giving of
oneself to *listening for the underlying meaning of what the other person is saying.*

Dwayne Huebner has given a description of the climate necessary for
real listening.

> The listener . . . establishes the climate for conversation, for it is he who deter-
> mines whether the words addressed to him are simply to be acknowledged as
> words or as signs indicating the willingness of the speaker to bridge the gap
> separating them. He may shrug off the words, listen for information, catego-
> rize the speaker, or wait to say his piece; or he may listen to the speaker,

plumbing the words for the speaker's meanings, feelings, and thoughts, which are only partially symbolized. He must be open to the speaker; the speaker senses this openness as an invitation to forsake his clichés, to expose his thoughts, to prove his own unformed notions, and to shape them so that he too gains new insights and satisfactions from the poetic form which they might take.[3]

The teacher who guides role playing is *listening* in the fullest sense of the word; she places herself at the disposal of the role players, trying, with all her senses, to feel and think *with* the children about what they are saying. The test of this listening quality in the leader rests in her ability to reflect back to the students what they are trying to say and to summarize from time to time the many perceptions that have been accumulating in the various enactments.

The teacher is constantly *demonstrating* her willingness to explore openly and sympathetically *all* the children's meanings without attaching value to some and ignoring others.

LEADING ROLE PLAYING

The teacher directing role playing must be clear about his or her functions as a guide. He is not completely nondirective. It is his responsibility to select the problems to be explored. (Exceptions occur. Occasionally a class that has experienced the role-playing approach to problem solving will suggest that they role-play a problem that has arisen.) The teacher leads the discussion, chooses the actors, decides when to cut enactments, develops the design of enactment, and probes for and selects which suggestions to follow through on. The types of questions he asks may be very decisive in pointing the direction in which the explorations of behavior will go.

Purposes Determine Procedures

Spontaneity training.   The teacher's decisions will be determined by the purposes of the role-playing session. If the purpose is simply spontaneity training—to release inhibitions and to invite active exploration—then he may be very open in his strategies and tactics. He asks only enough questions to help the children get into the role, but not enough to "set" the role in a detailed way. Thus he asks, "What is Pete like?" and accepts any useful definition. He encourages wide variety.

Skills training.   If the purpose is skills training, his questions help the children focus on acquiring skill in the task that is contemplated. He may ask children preparing to interview a resource person, "How do we make this person feel welcome?" and "How do we help him to give us the information we need? What kinds of questions do you need to ask him?" and so on.

---

[3]Dwayne Huebner, "New Modes of Man's Relationships to Man," in *New Insights and the Curriculum*, 1963 Yearbook (Washington, D.C.: National Education Association, 1963), p. 149.

Training for awareness of others' feelings.   If his focus is on sensitivity training, he necessarily spends time on questions about *feelings*, both in helping the children delineate a role and in exploring an enactment. He may ask (in working on role delineation), "How does this person feel? Why does he feel this way?" And, after an enactment, he may ask, "How is——— feeling toward————?" or "What are Nora's feelings now?" or "Who will be affected by this action? How will they feel?"

Problem solving.   If the major purpose of the session is problem solving, he may focus on both feelings and alternatives. He may spend more time on delineating the problem—through many beginning enactments— by focusing on "What is happening?" And he may probe for many alternative proposals, in an effort to get many brief enactments of alternatives; and then he will help the group choose one or two alternatives to explore in further detail. He will also spend more time in summarizing proposals for behavior and in discussing the enacted consequences.

Subject-matter exploration.   If the purpose of the session is to explore a special subject, the teacher spends time in a preliminary warm-up. For example, he might review the events that led to the Boston Tea Party. The class discusses what it must have been like to be a colonist, how it felt to be taxed without representation. Then the teacher can ask, "What do you suppose the various points of view were among different colonists? Describe one man and his possible viewpoint. Describe another." A situation is thus gradually delineated, and a role-playing presentation may result in which the events leading up to the Boston Tea Party are enacted.

The questions in this type of session focus not only on feelings and dilemmas but also on the historical realities of the time. He may ask, "How did prominent men feel about these issues?" And, "Did ordinary working people feel differently? How could we find out?" In such content uses, follow-up research is implied.

Although such varied purposes help determine the kinds of questions asked, *the questions must always be as open ended as possible.* They should suggest wide exploration and decision making by the students rather than requiring answers that are predetermined by the teacher. True, the social realities are determining factors; but the role-playing teacher must always recognize that what is accepted as fact also depends on the perceptions of individuals.

Introducing Children to Role Playing

If the children have never participated in role playing before, the teacher must be prepared to accept crude initial enactments.

Results will depend greatly on the nature of the rest of the curriculum in which the children are participating. If the school program is informal, uses group work, encourages much discussion and interaction among young people, then the class will probably move easily into role playing. But if the students are used to a highly directive, very controlled classroom environment, it will take time to establish a safe climate and to encourage spontaneity.

It is best to minimize the role-playing process at first. Simply say, after the warm-up discussion, "This story stops, but it is not finished. When it stops, you may finish it the way you think such a situation would be finished in real life." In the following discussion, invite someone up to work out his proposal for finishing the story. Be matter of fact. Just say, "Well, let's try it out and see what might happen." You will need to help beginners feel the role by asking numerous small questions such as, "How are you feeling,————(use the name of the person in the story)?" and "Where are you now?" and "What have you been doing?"

Spend some time preparing the class to be observers. Remind them that they can help explore each person's solution to a problem by cooperating with him. As leader, enter quickly to help reset the stage if a child feels uncertain about time, place, or who is involved. If a child fumbles, stop the role playing briefly and ask a helping question such as, "Who are you working for, Johnny? Do you like him?"

One real problem for beginners is that everyone wants to instruct the role players to act as he would act. You have to say to the class, over and over again, "Let's help Marvin work out *his* idea. I'll give you a chance to work out yours later."

Initial role playing is laden with self-consciousness; and children tend to get silly. When this happens, stop the role playing and ask, "Are you playing this true to life? How would people *really* behave in such a situation?" Turn to the actors and ask them questions that settle them back in their roles: "Mother, what kind of person are you? What are you doing now?" and so on. Avoid scolding or being judgmental about silly behavior. You may have to say, "You're having fun, but we're not really working on this problem, are we?" Your attitude of *positive expectance* that they will be serious and productive will help.

Do not be discouraged if first enactments are fragmentary or even irrelevant. Simply thank the role players, turn to the class, and ask for other ideas. Help the children become more spontaneous by encouraging many quick, brief enactments and *accept all ideas*.

Do not expect to move in an orderly sequence from definition to alternatives to consequences.

Perhaps the most useful advice for beginning sessions is to avoid too much preliminary discussion and move quickly to enactments. Even the follow-up discussions should be brief, at first. After many enactments, the time may be right for an extended discussion of what was proposed, how well it worked, how real it was.

Children who have not worked actively with problem solving tend to stay at a very concrete or operational level of thinking. By this we mean that they continually manipulate the specific incidents in the story rather than generalize about behavior. For example, they will insist that Tommy knock on the door and return the money (in "The Clubhouse Boat"), or they will suggest that he pay the gang, but they will seldom say, "He's caught between his knowledge of what is right and what he feels he has to do to keep his place in the club." Often, one or two children work at this more abstract level, but the rest of the class may still need to work with the specific incidents in order to think things through. Operational-level thinking is characteristic of most young children. It is our goal, as children progress into the upper grades of school, to help them move toward generalizations that can serve as guides to behavior in new situations.

Some children will hesitate to participate in beginning role playing. A little "friendly persuasion" is helpful, such as saying, "How about it, Jane? Don't you think you can be the teacher this time?" But, as a general rule, allow those children to watch the role playing. Eventually they will involve themselves. Occasionally you may have children whose experience in dramatics leads them to put on "performances." You will need to explain that we are not putting on a play, we are simply thinking things through in action.

Never evaluate the quality of performance. Instead, focus on how real the enactment was, what ideas and feelings were presented, what will follow, and so on.

The teacher of beginning role playing need not be discouraged at seeming wild behavior: hands waving madly, everyone talking at once, children issuing orders to each other and laughing hilariously at an enactment. This shows involvement. It also is the product of a first effort. Each session will bring more order and self-discipline as the teacher helps the group focus on thinking, feeling, listening to one another, doing the job. You may say, "I can't hear you all at once!" Or, laughing, you say, "Calm down, so we can hear one another."

When selecting first role players, it is wise to choose children who demonstrate by their comments that they visualize the roles. This will require much support from you. Help each child to see her role. Ask her what kind of person she is to play and what such a person characteristically does in such situations. Conjecture with her about what this person may be thinking.

Spend some time setting the stage in initial role playing. Visualize in some detail what the place is like, who is doing what, where doors are, furniture, other details.

Occasionally, the first session may be too much for a group—they may become overexcited or extremely noisy. Simply terminate such a session, saying that this will be all for this time. Then, the next time, remind them what happened and suggest that they try *really* to explore seriously the new problem story. End the session by commenting on all the useful contributions, such as "Maria helped us see how angry some people can get" or "You had so many different ways that this situation could end."

In this initial experience, you, the teacher, are walking a tightrope. You wish to help the children express their feelings honestly and spontaneously; at the same time, you must set some limits on behavior. Since first efforts release feelings in an area of low skills, you control the situation by permitting only short enactments, by asking key questions, by ending the whole session early, finishing with praise for the positive elements that emerged. You avoid scolding or criticizing. Later, after the children sense your openness to their experiences, you can set limits by helping them decide what helps and what gets in the way of good role playing.

Patterns of Role Enactments

As you lead role playing, you are confronted with a number of decisions: When shall I cut an enactment? Shall I follow through on one proposal to its consequences, or shall I call for an alternative proposal? Should I keep one actor in his role and change the others, or should I change them all?

The following guidelines may be helpful:

1. Allow an enactment to run only until the behavior that is being proposed is clear. Cut the enactment when you have enough data for discussion, or when actors and audience seem to have gained some insight, or when a skill has been practiced.

   Sometimes you cut when an impasse has been reached and the actors need help, or it is time to let another actor take over. Occasionally, you cut in order to rescue a child who is becoming emotional. Always cut when it is obvious that the action is continuing too long—that it is going nowhere, or when the group has obviously become bored and restless.

   Remember that the purpose of an initial enactment is to help the group define the situation further and identify with the characters; it does not always have to be completed to be useful.

2. You may choose to reenact the same scene if discussion of the first enactment reveals confusion about the details of events or ambivalence about the roles of the various characters. Thus, if a discussion centers on what a boy like Tommy Haines would do (in "The Clubhouse Boat"), there may be several conceptions of what Tommy is like, of what kinds of people his father and mother are. This may lead you to invite the child who sees Tommy differently to play the same incident out as he sees it.

   A first session may actually do no more than explore the dimensions of a situation through the many perceptions the children bring to the roles. This in itself is sufficient. The children have learned that the solution of a problem is highly dependent on the wide range of human responses that can be made to any given situation. Tommy may be seen as a boy who is afraid of his father, or as one who wants his father's trust, or as a boy preoccupied with his friends.

3. You may choose to keep the same subordinate actors but to change repeatedly the person playing Tommy so as to demonstrate the range of behaviors different children will bring to the role. Or, you may find that a child simply cannot manage a role—that of the mother, for example—so you change her, keeping the other players constant.

4. In other instances, an enactment may so clearly define the situation and imply next steps that it is best to let the same players follow through several enactments until consequences are fully delineated. Then the guided discussion can focus on: "What happened? Do such situations in real life sometimes work out this way?" And, "How is——feeling now?" or "Why does——behave this way?"

   In the lively discussion that follows, you, the teacher, have still further choices to make. Has this series of enactments and discussions plowed up enough ground for one session? Is your allotted time up? Or should you finally ask, "Is there some other way this situation might be resolved? Would other people act differently?" or "Is there some place earlier in this story where some other kind of action could have been taken?" Such questions take you off into a new series of enactments.

5. If you are guiding the enactments so as to reveal the consequences of a chosen line of action, it is best to help the children reveal the consequences in action rather than through discussion alone. (Their actual behavior often differs from their verbal actions—that is, from their stated purposes.) Therefore you ask, "What happens now?" And, as quickly as a next event is dimly delineated, you say, "All right, let's see what happens next. Where does this take place? Whom do you need?" and so on.

   After the enactment of consequences, which may be at an intuitional level, you help the class discuss the meanings of the presented actions. "What really is happening here? What does Mona mean? Why do you suppose she behaved this way? Will this solution work? Why?"

6. Throughout the enactments, you are careful to give the audience active roles. Pearl Rosenberg's study, mentioned earlier, has shown that role players experience more change of attitude, but that instructed observers see more alternatives, and that uninstructed observers gain the least from a role-playing session. The class can be asked (1) to observe as a whole group, in order to test the reality of the proposed behavior, (2) to divide into groups, each group watching one role in order to define the feelings or ways of thinking of the person being portrayed, or (3) to comment (in a skills-training session) on what the role player did that helped or did not help.

   Before asking for group comments after an enactment, it is useful to ask the actors to comment on their own behavior. Thus actors can express their own feelings, and this interval gives the class time to think about their own responses.

7. A key decision for you is the timing of the positive solution to the story problem. After a series of enactments that explore impulsive and expedient behaviors, probe with questions for positive solutions. Ask, "Are these the only ways out?" or "Could other ways of behaving earlier in the story have helped?" If possible, enact several of the positive suggestions for solution.

   But do not say, by your tone of voice, facial expression, or actual words, "So, you see, boys and girls, there *are* better ways to solve this problem!" By doing so, you will imply that you have been straining to reach a preordained conclusion. Instead, you review matter-of-factly what the many explorations seem to have said. You may say, "It seems to me that you have been saying that in troublesome situations like this, many different kinds of action are sometimes taken." You ask the class to restate the several proposals. Write them on the chalkboard. Ask, "Why do you suppose people behave one way rather than another?" (Remember: *behavior is caused.*)

8. This is a good time for analogies. You may ask, "In your experience, could this kind of situation happen to someone you know?" Applications can now be made, closer to home.

   If in your judgment the time is right, you may finally ask, "If you could manage this situation as you wished, what would you choose to do?" You may also ask, "Why do you suppose that———didn't choose your way?" Or if it is in a sensitive area, you may use this question for individual, private writing.

Guiding Discussions

Much has already been suggested to improve discussions. A few more guidelines may be helpful.

A good rule to observe is that lengthy discussions *follow* enactments rather than precede them. Another is that in the early phases of a role-playing session anything that can be explored by enactments rather than through lengthy discussions should be so managed. Thus, when a child says, "I think the class won't give Andy a chance to lead [in "The Squawk Box"]," you invite the child up to enact what he thinks will happen rather than having the class discuss his idea. Experience has shown that the actual role playing evokes real feelings, expresses the interactions, and further delineates the situation.

After such enactments, real discussion can be encouraged. As has been emphasized previously, the teacher's role is to guide, not direct, the discussion. To do this, you

1. *Listen with all your being to what each child is trying to say.* When a child hesitates, you may try to reflect back to him his feelings or thoughts. You may say, "You're angry at this group . . ." and wait to see if this is what the child means. If he does not respond to this suggestion, you may say, "Oh, are you wishing they would like Jimmy more. . . ." Such statements may help the child verbalize feelings he has been unable to express.

2. *Your responses are always in line with what the student is trying to say.* You respond by a nod or comment that shows that his contribution is genuinely accepted. (You do not turn away and call on some other child if his contribution is trivial; you try to find meaning in his effort.)

3. *You select some comments for immediate consideration because they hook on to the action or elaborate on a previous contribution.* As ideas rain down upon you from many children, you good-humoredly sort them out, help the children take turns, and stay in focus.

   You tell other children to hold their comments a while; new ideas will be dealt with later.

4. *You guide children to think* with *one another.* "Let's help Mary work out her idea. What did she tell us in her acting? What do you think about it?" Or you suggest, "Carmen, tell Louis your opinion," in order to stimulate class members to talk to each other.

5. *You sustain a child in his thinking.* When a child expresses an idea, you encourage him to expand on it. You may say, "Tell us more about this" or "Are you saying that . . . ?" Sometimes you deliberately distort a statement slightly so as to draw a clearer wording from the student.

6. *You point out differences in ideas.* When enough enactments have occurred to provide a number of alternatives and controversy occurs, help delineate the differences in ideas and ask children to discuss why they see the situation the way they do.

7. *You explore the complexity of situations.* For example, you say, "Let's see who is involved in this . . ." or "How many things do we have to think of before we can decide . . . ?"

8. *You raise the level of understanding by restating positions.* "You think someone will invent or develop a better way to do this?" or "You are saying it was wrong to exclude slaves from the Bill of Rights, but wasn't this attitude imbedded in the thinking of that time?"

9. *You invite other students to respond to a student's idea.* Then come back to him for a further response.

10. *You ask questions to widen the discussion.* Children often need to be lifted out of their preoccupation with their own immediate proposals to wider considera-

tions. You may ask, "Do you know someone who would have handled this situation differently?" or "Why does———behave the way he does?" or "Why are our ways of solving this situation so very different?" or "Why do you suppose problems like this arise?"

Some children respond to such questions and move up to analogies, speculation, or generalization. Others can cope only with the specifics of the story. This tells you that much more experience with confronting problem situations is needed, and much more comparison and speculation should be encouraged in other role-playing sessions.

Development in Role-Playing Sessions

As you lead role-playing sessions, you will find that children respond at different levels to the problem stories. What should you do about this? First of all, as you become more experienced, you will become increasingly able to diagnose a situation. You may have to decide on a slow, easy exploration of a problem through a number of planned story sessions, or you may conclude that a particular group of children needs only limited warm-up through one or two stories that delineate an issue before they are able to move to broad considerations and generalization. It may help you, as a role-playing leader, to think of your task in five levels.

1. *First enactments:*	Specific events are further defined—a form of beginning problem analysis.
2. *Second and third enactments:*	Roles and feelings are explored—for example, *who* is involved and *how* they feel. Data are collected.
3. *Later enactments:*	Events leading to personal and societal consequences are delineated. (Social sanctions become clear.)
4. *Final enactments* (not always achieved):	Decisions are made and values are brought to bear on the situation.
5. *Generalization* (sometimes):	Conclusions are drawn, applications made, and generalizations are verbalized.

With some groups of children and with some problems in many groups, an entire role-playing session may remain at Level One. You yourself may choose to focus a group on Levels One and Two, with certain stories, in order to develop needed sensitivities for a given class. Some stories, with some classes, will move easily through all the levels in one story session. Many classes may require much practice in problem solving through role playing before the children can consciously, deliberately, and with a maturing sense of values arrive at Level Five.

From time to time, you help the children order their thinking by asking if someone can put together what has been suggested; you may also summarize for the class saying, "It seems to me you people have been saying . . ." (in a mild, open, not final, tone). If you are *listening* to your children—their voices, actions, words—you can lift their thinking by reflecting back to them in summary form their thoughts and actions.

Promoting sensitivity. There will be moments when certain children reveal themselves as insensitive to the feelings of others. Some children may consistently reveal this trait. Several devices will help you with such children. You may ask such a child to assume the role to which he has been insensitive. Thus the boy who has been playing the classroom leader suddenly finds himself in the role of the unwanted boy. You may have to help him step into this role by asking, "What is————like? Why is he left out? What does he do that annoys other boys and girls? How is he feeling now? How does he see his situation?"

You may have to switch roles—to the roles to which he has been insensitive, placing this particular child on the receiving end of thoughtless treatment in other role-playing sessions, and planning a role-playing sequence that focuses the entire class on feelings.

Meeting individual needs. As you diagnose the needs of individual children, you may find role playing useful in specific areas. For example, you may select a problem story because it supports a child's need to be accepted *with* his differences; Hildred Nichols did this when she developed short situations to help second graders accept and understand Marilyn, the deaf child. You may use a story like "Bandit Cave" because Bobby, who is poor at sports and gets left out of games and is shy, is also a good storyteller; you can improve his status with the group by casting him (with preparation) in the key role. You may choose a role and a story that will help an insensitive child identify with others. Or, you may use a story (as did Marie Zimmerman Solt in the story of "George") to help a group understand a troubled child.[4]

Some problem areas. From time to time you will meet problems that call for special consideration. What shall you do with the child who never participates in role playing? He may have deep-seated problems that need careful diagnosis. You may, considering all that you know about him, decide this child needs special help from the school guidance services. Sometimes, however, simple devices are helpful. Perhaps he is self-conscious and shy. Selecting a role that calls for a special skill and *teaching him that skill in advance* may help. Then, when you call for someone who has this skill, he may volunteer. Sometimes structuring a role for him, asking him to play the boy who returns the money to the white-haired man (in "The Clubhouse Boat") will enable him to participate. Other times, when several roles are called for, inviting this child and someone who is his close friend gives him the support he needs.

What do you do when extreme feelings precipitate highly unacceptable language? The use of nondirective techniques can help. You can say to the child (or children) kindly and sympathetically, "I know you are furious. He's really made you furious. But," and here your voice is firm, "in this classroom we can't speak that way. Can you express your feelings in other words?"

What do you do to protect a child who portrays a highly unacceptable

----

[4]See F. Shaftel and G. Shaftel, *Role-playing the Problem Story* (New York: National Conference of Christians and Jews, 1952, pp. 61–65).

solution? You accept his enactment matter-of-factly, saying, "Henry has shown us what some people do in this situation. He is reminding us that these things do happen." In this way you remove the implication that this is the way Henry himself would behave.

What do you do when a child reveals too much of himself? For example, Therese says, "I lie, and it works for me all the time!" This is the time to accept the comment nonjudgmentally and turn the discussion to other matters, taking note of Therese's need in the meantime. *Do not confront her with her admission.* To do so would be to jeopardize the trust the class holds in you.

What do you do when you sense that a discussion has aroused guilt feelings in the group? The problem may be one of lying to get out of a deserved punishment. Such lying may be attacked vehemently by some members of the class. This is an opportunity for you to help the group acquire a healthy perspective on the matter. You may say, "We all lie at one time or another. Sometimes it is to keep from hurting someone. Sometimes it is because we are afraid or desperate." You may encourage children to talk about why people lie, how it feels to lie, what can be done to find more comfortable and more adequate ways of solving problems. By so guiding the discussion, you can replace guilt feelings with the reassurance that none of us is perfect but that we can improve with experience. Here discussion can provide a release of tensions.

CONCLUSIONS

While much can be gained from even random uses of role playing, teachers will be using a much sharper tool if it is used diagnostically. You need to know your group, its social structure, its individual needs, and the dynamics of social interaction that help or hinder children in interpersonal situations. Each child reveals his or her own needs to the skilled and observant teacher. Sociometric data are helpful. Role-playing programs can be planned for specific classes in terms of:

1. Groups that lack cohesive structure due to social competition, a power cluster, or neighborhood conflicts;
2. Individuals who need help in building their self-esteem;
3. Provincial attitudes born of suburban or small-town isolation that accentuates poor attitudes toward differences; and
4. Lack of opportunities for decision making because of a highly traditional curriculum, authoritarian subcultural components, or the presence in a class of many dependent children.

Outcomes

As you do role playing, how do you know that you are successful? How do you know when you are getting worthwhile results? How do you know when you are achieving some of the goals described earlier in this book?

How are you to judge your effectiveness in leading the kind of role playing described here?

Often, successful results in role playing are not immediately obvious; sometimes, luckily, they are. But human beings are complex. Values and attitudes are culturally imprinted outlooks and determiners of behavior; they cannot be changed by the magic of a push-button or the adding of a new chemical to a mixture. However, to the role-playing leader who has some training and experience, the effects of role playing are often quickly apparent.

What are some of the outcomes of the role-playing process?

1. Problem confrontation

An important value of role playing lies in problem confrontation and definition. If a group listens to a story, reacts earnestly, analyzes it, and shows that they have grasped the essential problem involved and perceive its richness of implications, this alone is an achievement of real value.

For example, in the story "Trick or Treat" (p. 168), two boys induce two younger lads to play a Halloween prank that unexpectedly results in serious property damage and in injury to an old man. The older boys, who are actually to blame, are safe from exposure, however; their younger dupes have been identified as at fault. By saying nothing now, the older boys can go unpunished for their actions. If a classroom group, after hearing this problem story, realistically defines the problem and expresses awareness of the issues involved—that the younger boys, who committed the mischief, were put up to it by the older boys and were, besides, too immature to foresee the possible consequences; that the really guilty pair, even if they escape exposure and punishment, will not escape their own consciences; that the younger boys, who have been misled, will probably retain feelings of resentment and mistrust—then the pupils have had an important growth-giving experience in problem definition.

2. Sensitivity to others' feelings: Awaking empathy

The *feelings* involved are, naturally, of basic importance in studying behavior. Too often, however, as we decide about how to act, we either fail to foresee the emotional concomitant of a given behavior, or we fail to estimate the full weight of doubt, self-blame, or remorse it may inflict upon us. Similarly, we may fail to foresee the impact of our behavior upon others— for example, the possible sense of belittlement and rejection it may inflict upon them.

Thus, in the "Finders Weepers" story (p. 157), three boys who have damaged a boat lack the money to pay for repairing it. They find a wallet. It contains the sum they need and a little more. They are torn between using the money to pay for repairs to the boat and returning the money to its owner, whose name is in the wallet. A group role-playing this story enacted the alternative of keeping the money. They repaired the boat, returned it to its owner, were thanked and told they could use the boat whenever they wished. They felt a great sense of relief upon extricating themselves from trouble, but, *afterward*, doubt spoiled their happiness. They had been dishonest. They *felt* guilty. One youngster said that after he had confessed such an act to his father and had been punished, he felt much better.

Such responses reveal that role-playing pupils are *relating the trial behavior to their own past experiences. They are finding answers from reality.* Clearly this is a worthwhile outcome to the role playing, perhaps even a truly important outcome.

The role-playing group may come to a generalization: Behavior often exacts a toll of feelings, and if these feelings are painful, the consequences of questionable behavior may be far too costly. When such a generalization is arrived at through an interchange of opinion among peers, it carries far more weight and is far more likely to influence future choices of behavior than if it comes as a moral or directive from an adult exhorting a group "to be good."

Sensitivity to others' feelings is, of course, the other side of this coin. In the story, "Prize" (p. 274), a student committee selects a boy as the outstanding Student Citizen of the Year who will be given an award offered by an out-of-school donor. When this donor discovers that the winner is a Chicano boy, he becomes angry. He tells the committee that he will provide another prize for the outstanding Anglo citizen of the year. The selection committee of three boys debates the matter. One says that they must refuse the second prize; another asks what's the harm in taking a second prize so that another student can win a valuable award? The harm is, of course, the fact that awarding a second prize to an Anglo boy in this situation serves to set the Chicano apart as different and is an indirect belittling of Chicanos; that such an experience sharpens the long-felt feelings of inferiority and rejection. If members of the role-playing group, through discussion and enactments, sharpen each other's insights to the point where they become aware of the ego erosion this second award will cause, they will have made significant growth in sensitivity to others' feelings.

In the story "Bandit Cave" (p. 304), a youngster is ignored by the group. He is too quiet and retiring to assert himself. He has no skills in athletics or sociability and has no close friends in the camp group. In one role-playing discussion of how it feels to be left out of activities by the group, one child said of the rejected boy, "He feels like nothing, like nothing at all." Further discussion brought suggestions on ways the lonely boy could win his way into the group; he could learn to be a good athlete, wear the kinds of clothes that are popular, be a good sport, and so on. Such discussions may be the beginnings of empathy. Such responses often have their origin, of course, in feelings of rejection that the speakers themselves have experienced. Role playing that evokes awareness of such feelings and responses of sympathy—especially in a group situation, where the opinions of peers give immense authority and sanction to values—is role playing that is achieving results.

3. Considering the probable consequences of behavior

Still another vital goal of role playing is developing a habit of taking forethought, of being alert to the probable consequences of behavior. If a role-playing group—after exploring the consequences of alternative behavior in a problem situation—realizes that they should have thought a little more before acting, they are learning a vastly important lesson.

An example may be helpful. In a story "Mr. Even-Steven" (p. 209) twelve-year-old Ken is severely scolded by his father for riding his bike through the wet concrete of a neighbor's newly poured driveway. He is told that he will have to draw out his savings to pay for repairing the driveway. But Ken is innocent. He discovers that a neighbor boy is actually to blame. The latter denies it, and Ken can't prove the other's guilt. Ken is outraged, but helpless. Then something happens that gives Ken a chance to get even with the culprit by having blame fall on him for an act of malicious mischief. The impulse to get revenge is strong; and as Ken foresees how much punishment the other boy will get, he is sorely tempted. Ken has to make a quick decision.

If, in role playing this story, your group explores the consequences of Ken's revenge, and decides that they are too drastic, that the punishment far outweighs the crime, that Ken, before getting even, should have paused to consider what the results might be, your group is acquiring the judgment to weigh probable consequences. Your group could also point out that the guilty boy might have accidentally ridden across that new driveway and that Ken's father is too harsh and the punishment too severe.

4. Ethical development: Personal integrity and group responsibility

At one time or another, every young person finds himself at odds with his group of close friends. He may wish to do one thing, but his group has decided on another. He has decided to go to a concert, but his friends have arranged for them all to hear a new rock group that night. Then again, his friends may decide upon a Halloween prank which he foresees can cause real harm. Does he go along or stand against the group at the risk of being called "chicken"? The latter sort of dilemma is particularly difficult for anyone, young or old; but the ability to say No to one's own group, when the group plans behavior that goes against one's sense of right or justice, is a very important strength. Conversely, the ability to set aside a cherished goal in order to go along with a group decision that is truly worthwhile is also, in many instances, a most difficult choice to make.

Individuals, in relation to their immediate group, must develop the skill to distinguish between conformity to group will and cooperation, between personal integrity and abject surrender. Practice in making such distinctions is important; it enables individuals gradually to acquire the judgment to guide them in their relations with any group of which they are a functioning part.

If the group, while role playing a story, begins to realize how difficult a choice is, yet sees that sometimes an individual must say No, it has grown in judgment and in integrity. On the other hand, group members recognize that personal interest may be a matter of self-indulgence, that the group's activities may be a far worthier goal, then they have also achieved a larger understanding.

In the story "Sacrifice Hit" (p. 226), Danny faces a difficult choice: His ball team votes to buy a present for a man who had helped them. But pitching in his share of money for this present will mean a real sacrifice for Danny. Certainly the group's desire to show their appreciation to their friend is worthwhile, but Danny has been saving the money to buy glasses that he badly needs, and that his parents cannot afford to get for him. If the role-playing group can see that, in this instance, Danny's need outweighs the group's purpose, they are acquiring judgment. They are learning to discriminate between human values. And if they can appreciate what a struggle this is for Danny, how difficult it is for him to stand against group pressure, to hold out for his personal need against their strongly expressed consensus, they are acquiring sensitivity to others' feelings. Moreover, the teacher can help the group realize that they should sometimes support an individual's actions instead of insisting on total conformity.

7

Dramatic Play: Groundwork for Role Playing in Social Studies

Sociodrama has been called a spontaneity technique.[1] It is a structured extension of play itself. Play is a basic means by which infants and young children begin to explore their world. It is a process of coming to terms with reality, in which the young child is beginning to manage his inner world in relation to the world outside him. He constantly revises his ideas of reality by playing them out, by testing them in action.

Erik Erikson proposed the theory that the child's play is the infantile form of the human ability to deal with experience by creating model situations and to master reality by experiment and planning.[2] Barbara Biber described this interaction:

> The free dramatic play of children during their early years serves as an extraordinarily effective mechanism by means of which they find release from emotional pressures at the same time that they clarify their understanding of their own objective experience in the world.[3]

Early childhood specialists have long understood the educational role of play. In recent years, however, as we have become more concerned with improving cognitive learning, we have retreated from using play in elementary education. We simply do not have time for "play" in our hurry to promote more efficient cognitive learning. Ironically, this attitude is a disservice to cognitive learning. Our interest in simulation and gaming is

[1] Jacob Moreno, *Psychodrama* (New York: Beacon House, 1946); and *Who Shall Survive?* (New York: Beacon House, 1953).
[2] Erik Erikson, *Childhood and Society* (New York: Norton, 1950), p. 195.
[3] Barbara Biber, *The Five to Eights and How They Grow*, undated paper (New York: Bank Street Publications), p. 4.

85

growing precisely because the utilization of spontaneity techniques enables teachers to make elaborate, complex systems more explicit to the learner.

Children need to learn by analogy, demonstration, and active exploration, *with all their senses*, if they are to become imaginative, sensitive, and creative thinkers. In our haste to develop children's intellectual capacities, we may narrow the channel of learning to symbolic forms only. Since they would then lack a solid, meaningful base in personal experience, their learning could become a mere manipulation of forms.

Jerome Bruner reminds us that "research on the intellectual development of the child highlights the fact that at each stage of development the child has a characteristic way of viewing the world and explaining it to himself . . ."[4] Reviewing the work of Piaget, Bruner emphasizes the need for children of elementary school age to go through (1) the stage of establishing relationships between experience and action and (2) the stage of concrete operations. In this latter stage the child is absorbing data about the real world and then transforming them so that they can be organized and used selectively in the solution of problems. Finally, sometime between ten and fourteen years of age, the child passes into (3) the stage of formal operations, where he is able to understand hypothetical propositions and give formal or axiomatic expression to concrete ideas.

LEARNING THE PLAY WAY

Long before children have mastered language they begin to explore the world around them through play. Children would like to actually engage in the adult work that they see about them. Unfortunately, one of the first phrases a child in our culture learns to respond to is "No! No!" In addition to our cultural prohibitions, so often derived from middle-class concerns for property, there are maturity limitations. It is not possible at age two, four, or even ten to get into the family car and drive it off to adventures unknown. Children solve this impasse by "playing it out." They dramatize life as they encounter it.

Corinne A. Seeds gave us a very fine definition of dramatic play:

> . . . When experience, firsthand, vicarious, or imaginary, stimulates children to an expression of it, through the identification of themselves with the persons or things involved in it, in order that they may get on the inside of the situation and find out how it feels to be there and control it, such activity is called *dramatic play.*[5]

Spontaneous Play of Backyard and Field

In their free play in fields, streets, and backyards, children dramatize their every feeling and impression. They explore the roles of mother,

---

[4]Jerome Bruner, *The Process of Education* (Cambridge, Mass.: Harvard University Press, 1960), pp. 33–35.

[5]Corinne A. Seeds, "Newer Practices Involving Dramatic Play," in *Newer Instructional Practices of Promise*, 12th Yearbook (Washington, D.C.: National Education Association, 1939), p. 122.

father, new baby, or big brother and often vent their frustrations in aggression toward a play mother, as they might not do in the actual home situation. The doll is spanked, the mother is defied, the father goes off gaily to work on his tricycle.

Children dramatize everything that catches their fancy, improvising equipment and organizing into groups as those are needed. Four-year-old Jimmy on a trip downtown with his mother sees a man being given a ticket for traffic violation. This dramatic episode stimulates Jimmy to organize a game of "traffic" that afternoon on the empty lot next door. Bobby, excited by the play, contributes his experience of watching fire engines go weaving and screaming through crowded intersections. Other children add their experiences—and dramatic play is on!

In such play children inevitably discover needs and meet difficulties. They are eager to understand the world into which they are growing. They have an intense curiosity about life as it unfolds for them. This drive to find out spurs them into great ingenuity in surmounting obstacles and meeting the needs of their play. Jimmy and Bobby will devise traffic signals, will hunt up whistles, and will turn tricycles into motorcycles and wagons into ambulances. Their intense desire to make the play effective will even act as a mediating influence upon individual ego expressions. Jimmy will reluctantly learn to give in and let Bobby be the traffic cop, if this is a necessary condition for the maintenance of the play. These children will continue their active pretending to the limits of their experience, and then play will end for lack of further enrichment. New experiences will set off new play patterns, momentary or extended, depending upon the maturity of the children and the depth of experience involved.

This intense drive to dramatize life activities is a powerful educational tool. Creative teachers have long recognized the contribution that dramatic play can make to growth and development and the learning process.

Dramatic Play in the Classroom

If a stimulating environment, designed to arouse the interest of children in an area of human experience, is arranged in the classroom and the children are encouraged to respond in their own characteristic ways, they often explore the area through dramatic play.

Kindergarten and primary teachers long ago recognized that play was an educative tool (Pratt, 1948). They frequently did not know the specific functions of dramatic play, but they had learned that if they created play centers in their rooms and allowed small groups to use them, the children gained satisfactions that seemed to aid the processes of socialization that so often are traumatic experiences for the child entering school. These primary teachers used the play centers as a release technique but did not attempt to manipulate the situation for intellectual development.

In the classroom today, dramatic play differs from casual play in that the teacher feeds it with developmental experiences until it assumes a sequencing that leads children to ever-expanding understandings and skills. Not only is it used to help young children explore and experiment with the social relations of their own immediate environment under teacher guidance, but it is also used as a social studies technique to help children acquire concepts in and identify themselves with cultures and events that may be at a remove in time and space. For example, a group of children respond with enthusiasm to an arrangement of pictures and books about pioneer life in the time of Daniel Boone and to an exhibit of a replica of a long rifle, a candle mold, a hunting knife, a powder horn, and a suit of pioneer clothing. The group's immediate response is to take the gun and hunt game. Their concept of a pioneer is a man with a rifle.

In the sharing period after playing, the teacher asks how the gun was used and if this method of use was the way the real pioneer gun was actually employed. Pursuit of these questions leads to seeking authentic answers and then reading for further information about pioneer weapons. The children learn that not only was the pioneer gun used for defense but that it also provided a means of procuring meat. This understanding leads to a study of pioneer hunting, care and preparation of the meat, pioneer cooking, and to a study of the vast variety of foods other than meat which the Indians introduced to the white settlers. With each addition of information, dramatic play proceeds to progressively higher levels in terms of activities portrayed and accompanying satisfaction for the players.

In the course of playing the conflict with Indians the teacher has the opportunity to help the children explore how it felt to be in strange country and to be attacked, why the Indians attacked the white men, how it felt to be an Indian when your land was being overrun by another culture. As the experiences are played and further questions are raised under teacher guidance, the entire culture of pioneer days is explored. Moreover, as the children seek "props" with which to make their play increasingly lifelike, they manufacture rifles, powder horns, costumes, and other real objects as needed. They undergo the life processes of cooking over open fires, building cabins with logs, and spinning wool thread. These enterprises, of course, involve them in learning to plan, to do research, to use tools and materials appropriately, to measure and estimate, to learn to work and live together cooperatively.

This interweaving of many learnings is the great merit of dramatic play. Such play satisfies children's needs for play and for manipulating materials and for activity and communication goals. At the same time, the children are acquiring concepts that lead to extended knowledge, skills, and attitudes that are important for individuals growing up in our American culture but that children in their immaturity may not see as important.

The success of dramatic play in the classroom depends on the teacher's clearly defining its goals. The purpose of dramatic play is to provide an environment that will stimulate children to explore, *in their own way*, to the limits of their experience, the activities of a selected social studies area. It is designed to help children identify themselves emotionally with the people whose lives they are adopting, their life activities, and the time and place involved. Children thereby develop a *real interest* in the activities being experienced and *real felt needs* that will impel them forward to vital learnings. Another major concern is to involve children in a common enterprise in which they can learn to work and live together democratically and meet their own basic personality needs.

To achieve these goals teachers work for spontaneity of expression on the part of the children. They get this spontaneity by

1. Providing some vivid contacts with the selected social studies area through an arranged environment of things that children can handle and use, and, sometimes, by introducing a dramatic story about the selected area;
2. Allowing the children to explore the environment, and begin to play in their own way, *with no instructions from the teacher*; by permitting them to *discover* their own difficulties and *feel* the need for better organization and further knowledge;
3. Avoiding an audience situation. (This is not a stage play or the presenting of a story to an audience; it is the reliving of an experience, each child trying to be a person or animal and *think* his way through the developing situation.)
4. Avoiding criticism of the children's activities. It is important that *the children shall not try to do what they think the teacher wants them to do, but rather that they reveal in their own way* what they know or think they know about the area. By a technique of sharing experiences and by discussion, the teacher will get them to question their own procedures and to want to find out more in order to improve the hunting, cooking, or building activities. Then the enriching experiences the teacher provides as a follow-up of the discussions will not be teacher-imposed, but rather a means of meeting the children's own felt and expressed needs.

In summary, dramatic play in the classroom is an education technique in which children explore an area of human experience (1) by reliving the roles, activities, and relationships involved in that experience in their own way; (2) by acquiring, under teacher guidance, needed information and skills; and (3), by increasing the satisfactions inherent in play that is meaningful and extensive. Dramatic play encompasses the following procedures:

1. The introductory situation is an arranged environment planned by the teacher.
2. Children explore the arranged environment and are permitted to respond in their own way, to manipulate tools and materials and discuss them.
3. A story may be read by the teacher to further the interest of the children in the selected area and to provide initial data for use.
4. Children are invited to play any part of the story or set their own situation.
5. First play is spontaneous and unguided, but is carefully observed by the teacher.
6. Play is followed by a sharing period in which satisfactions are expressed and dissatisfactions are clarified, under teacher guidance, into statements of questions and expressed needs.
7. Planning for meeting the expressed needs includes the processes of problem solving, making rules, assigning work to be done.
8. Play proceeds on higher levels (involving more accurate activities and more interrelationships and interpretations) as a result of enriched experience.

ORGANIZATION AND PROCEDURES

What are the techniques and procedures involved in dramatic play?

There are no absolute rules or methods for dramatic play. It is essentially a dynamic process. As children interact with ideas and experiences, they shape them into play patterns. The play is always new, spontaneous, evolving. It has a quality of its own because children feel free to *be* the people and the animals as they see and feel them, in their own way.

While there are no absolute procedures in the guidance of dramatic play, some techniques have been found successful. We present them here with the hope that they may be of help.

The Arranged Environment

The arranged environment, previously described, serves to arouse the immediate interest of the children in the area of experience presented. Usually, if there are realia such as a gun, a metate, chop sticks, or a loom in the exhibit, the children respond by wanting to handle them and to demonstrate their use to each other.

If the children bring to these articles a sufficient background of experience and information, they are ready immediately to launch into play. For instance, the long rifle usually evokes immediate action—Daniel Boone is off to explore new country. Or, if a little boat is in the exhibit, it is at once put into action by being pushed along the floor with accompanying "toot-toot" sound effects.

However, if the meanings of the articles are less clear to the children, they may begin by handling the articles curiously and asking questions. Then the teacher's next step is to enrich the children's knowledge by means of a vivid story, one that will quickly involve the children in the activities of the period concerned. Thus, in a Hopi unit, reading the beginning of Grace Moon's *Chi-Wee* may be advisable.[6] Enough of the story is read to develop a full incident. Then the teacher invites any who wish to play out the incident.

Beginning Play

Usually, after the reading of a story in an area in which the children have a meager background, the play becomes an actual reproduction of the story itself. The teacher helps to organize the first play by asking who the people and animals are that the children will play and by guiding the choice of players. The other children are then permitted to go on to other activities—drawing or painting, looking at books and pictures, and so on. An audience situation is avoided.

If *Chi-Wee* is used, for example, the first play might be the incident of Chi-Wee's finding the red clay for the making of the fine pottery the trader wanted. The children would probably attempt to play the finding of the clay, the sharing of the meal, and the mother's procedures in making the pottery. The children would soon find that they did not know enough about the ways of serving and eating a meal in a Hopi home and the process of pottery making to make the play interesting. The children may become self-conscious as a result, and even silly. This is the teacher's signal that they

---

[6]Grace Moon, *Chi-Wee* (New York: Doubleday, 1925).

have reached the end of their knowledge and play must stop for further enrichment.

The play may thus be stopped the first time after five or six minutes. It has lasted long enough to make the children aware of their difficulties but has ended before it has deteriorated into confusion and disorder.

In beginning play, children often use the few real objects at hand and even improvise equipment to help establish the reality of the play.

During this play time the teacher has taken notes on what the different children did and on evidence of further needs. For example, she notes how Jack threw the rabbit stick while hunting and that the women remaining in the pueblo "set a table" for dinner.

Sharing the First Play

When the teacher calls the group together after the first play, she may begin a sharing period by a casual comment such as, "That looked like fun." The children may respond by telling some especially good incidents they acted out in the play. Then the teacher may say, "Mary, I noticed you serving the meal. Just what did you do?" Mary is encouraged to show how she served the meal. This enables the teacher to guide the group into a discussion of how the Hopis prepared and served meals.

Actually, the teacher is helping the group realize that they need to know exactly how Hopis served meals. This leads to a *"We Need to Find Out"* list with an Item 1 of: "How Do the Hopis Serve Meals?" Item 2 on the list may be "What Utensils Do the Hopis Use?"

Gradually, the teacher guides the discussion: (1) to give satisfaction and recognition for the fun and good thinking that went into this first play; (2) to build an attitude of dissatisfaction with sketchy information and a desire to obtain accurate information and items for use in the play; (3) to make definite plans for obtaining that information and for making the items needed; and (4) to help the group formulate rules for better social interaction as they play.

For several days, during dramatic play time, the children may continue to use the plot of the story read to them as the basis of their dramatizing, enriching it with the details they are learning through reading, looking at pictures and films, undergoing industrial arts experiences, taking excursions, and through other activities the teacher provides to meet their growing needs. Gradually, as they acquire a wider knowledge of Hopi life, they may suggest other episodes to play, or the teacher herself may suggest that they might enjoy making up new incidents about life in a Hopi pueblo. While the story is used to initiate play, the children are encouraged to deviate from it and to develop new play patterns continually. The purpose always is not the perfection of the story, but the wide exploration of the life of the people being portrayed.

Dramatic play on the primary level operates on the same principles as with older children. The starting point with young children, however, is usually their own immediate environment. They are ready to build and play immediately since they work with manipulative materials such as blocks, toys, and wood for construction. A group of primary children react to an arranged environment of a dairy farm, for example, with a response similar to that of the Hopi situation, except that they may begin at once to run the trucks, use the blocks to build corrals for the animals, and use apple boxes for barns and houses. *They build and play simultaneously.*

It is only as the unit plans develop that the activity that becomes construction work with wood is assigned to a work period separate from the dramatic play period. Even then, the primary child who is making a truck for the farm will stop work when he has nailed the engine to the truck body and will take time to run his truck (and deliver some milk) before he has the wheels on the vehicle. Older children, on the other hand, can wait and plan. They often postpone dramatic play for several weeks while making the things with which to play. Thus an upper-grade group will work for a long time, hollowing out boats for harbor play, and will wait for the unfinished vessels before playing. In contrast, again, primary children will use blocks for tugs and liners until their constructed craft were ready for service.

Follow-Up

After the first play time, as we have seen, the teacher works for the emergence of felt needs in the sharing time. It is in this sharing time that the teacher guides the group. This is the opportunity for *the asking of provocative questions*, for the pointing up of attitudes of inquiry, for skillfully assuming that of course "we want to do this the way it is really done," and for helping the children learn more about the actual processes and relationships. This sharing period is a golden time for developing techniques of problem solving and critical thinking.

The quality of the dramatic play and its growth to ever-higher levels depends on how the teacher follows up the play needs expressed in the sharing time, and on what plans the group makes. Let us consider the Hopi play a little further. After the two items were listed on the board, the teacher did several things. She helped the children list sources from which they could find the answers to their questions. She had a reading lesson in which the children read about making pottery and rabbit hunting and then discussed their findings. She shared with the children books and pictures of the women's work in the pueblo. She provided a pottery lesson for the class so that they could experience a major activity of the women in the village and make dishes for use in play. She planned a corn-grinding experience for the same reason.

Now the types of experiences that the teacher can provide are almost endless and depend upon her knowledge of the field and her judgment of what should be fed into the growing unit as a "next" experience. They are a series of teaching strategies. There are times when she provides a carefully planned excursion to a direct center of experience, such as the harbor, the freight yards, the farm, or a newspaper plant. Sometimes the excursion may be to a museum. Or an expert may be brought in to share his knowledge with the group. At other times, or even in conjunction with these activities, the teacher may use instructional aids. Always she seeks to weave in the use of significant reading material so that the children may become more and more aware of the importance of reading. At the primary level she frequently guides the development of an experience chart or presents an informational chart to the group.

Another procedure that pays high learning dividends is putting children directly in touch with the life processes of the area, such as grinding corn, weaving, making paper, or making boats that float. Then the children learn to do things as they were really done by people striving to meet their basic needs. Properly guided, these activities help children to relate historic and geographic conditions to anthropological concepts.

As children plan, work, and develop the dramatic play, the teacher guides them to see the necessity of improving their skills in order better to achieve their goals. She provides specific learning periods for this purpose. These specific learning periods are kept separate from the dramatic play time to safeguard the spontaneity of the play period and to promote serious study habits.

If the procedure of (1) responding to a stimulating environment, (2) playing dramatically, and (3) sharing experiences is followed up by the teacher with enriching and specific learning experiences, children will play on increasingly higher levels. Though the first play period can end after five minutes for lack of sufficient knowledge, the second period can go on for fifteen minutes because the children will know more and can actually do more. Increasingly, the tendency is to extend the length of play time until, toward the end of the curriculum unit, there are occasional play periods for summarization purposes that last an hour. Moreover, the play grows qualitatively. This gain is the fruitful result of deepened and extended understandings.

Some Practical Considerations

1. How many children should participate?   Ideally, all the children in the class should play at one time. At the start, only a few may desire to participate. But as the play goes on, others enter in as their interest is caught and grows. Also, as they make tools or ships or trucks, children will put them into use and are thus naturally swept into the group activity. When all the children play at one time, a common sharing period enables the teacher to guide the development of the same felt needs for the entire group.

Sometimes it is not possible to have the entire class in one play group. Space limitations or the nature of the play may limit the number of participants. With young children it is not advisable to divide the class into more than two groups. If every day one group has a dramatic play period, each group is able to play every other day. An interval of more than one day between the periods is not advisable, since young children forget quickly and continuity of expression is lost. With intermediate grades, however, it has been found practical to use three groups, each one participating in play every third day. It is best to keep the group membership as constant as possible, so that the same children work out the play sequences together long enough to get a continuity of experience.

When classes are divided into groups, needs that emerge from one play group may not necessarily be felt by the rest of the class. It then becomes necessary to arrange class sharing periods, from time to time, in which all groups discuss together the important needs that have emerged in any one group or in all groups. This procedure will help knit the class needs together into a common set of purposes.

2. When should dramatic play occur?   The play period is a matter of scheduling convenience. Some teachers prefer to have it during the latter part of the morning, following a reading or research period, when enriching ideas have been explored. This also enables her to plan follow-up activities, when advisable, that afternoon while questions are clear and immediate.

With primary children, dramatic play ideally occurs daily unless other needs interfere. In the intermediate grades dramatic play may be stimulated by the arranged environment and then postponed for several weeks, while the children concentrate on construction and industrial arts activities in order to make the things with which to play. Then play may proceed intensively for many days, with construction and industrial arts at a minimum or standstill.

3. How long should the dramatic play period be?   In its early stages, dramatic play should last from five to fifteen minutes at the primary level. Gradually it may grow to thirty minutes. Fifteen minutes or more should be provided for sharing time, varying with the need and the ability of the children to concentrate and sit still. As interest rises and the children develop driving purposes, their interest span lengthens; even young children will often sit, absorbed in thinking and sharing together, beyond the usual time span for their age.

In the intermediate grades, play may grow to forty-minute periods with at least twenty minutes for sharing time. There will come climaxes in play patterns, especially toward the end of a study, when these older children will have so much to share that occasional long periods of an hour or more should be provided to enable them to use their knowledge and materials to full satisfaction.

4. Where should dramatic play be done?   Most teachers have to operate almost entirely within the confines of their classrooms. This necessity does not rule out dramatic play. As some types of social studies units develop, a space may be cleared on the floor so that the growing farm or harbor or community or log cabin can be arranged for use. Dramatic play can be done in that space.

In some areas of the United States it is often possible to go outdoors. Some teachers have been quite successful in building and using out-of-door harbors or in carrying much of the play paraphernalia for pioneer life studies outside. Going outside enables the entire class to play and helps relieve much of the tension that arises when teachers must continually restrict expression because the noise may disturb the class next door. If a small classroom must be used, much ingenuity is possible in turning desks into trees in a forest, aisles into roads, and so on.

5. *How much should the teacher enter into the play? What is her role?*   The teacher's role is that of *facilitating*, not directing, dramatic play. She assists with the minimum organizing needed to get a group started. She may *help* decide who will play which roles. (She does not order the choices!) She may ask leading questions to limit the area of play. For example, if it is a pioneer play period, she may ask who the people are in the hunting expedition, what time of day and year it is, and where they plan to hunt. She guards against making too many suggestions, however, because then the play pattern becomes hers rather than the children's. The teacher's real guidance occurs in follow-up experiences. The test of the meaningfulness of those follow-up experiences is whether they emerge spontaneously in later play. *If the learning was meaningful, it will be used by the children*; if it is never used, we may question the significance of the experience or how well done the teaching was.

In the primary grades, the teacher may sometimes casually enter the play and participate, in order to indicate some things that are fun to do. For example, the six-year-olds are building houses and stores with blocks. No play between children has emerged. Miss Brown takes a miniature man and walks him into a store and asks Gordon, the boy builder, if he has some tomatoes for sale. This starts interplay in a situation in which the children have been playing in isolation before.

The teacher's main role is that of quiet observer. She jots down items that will help her guide the sharing period. She may note interesting and significant play incidents, evidences of partial understandings that need elaboration or evidences of need for new information, the need for further play materials or facilities, difficulties in social behavior, and evidence of individual personality needs. Then, at sharing time, by casually glancing at her notes (but not reading them as a judgment) she can weave into the discussion the points she has noted.

In order to be alert to the emerging needs, the teacher must be observing and noting actively while a play period is on. She cannot assign a group to play and then go off to help a reading group. This would nullify the educative value of the play, for she will not know what has occurred and therefore cannot give appropriate guidance.

6. *On what basis should we group children for play?*   When dramatic play is in its formative stage, it is wise to let grouping occur spontaneously and naturally and to allow those who wish to participate to come together and help the children divide into regular play groups, if grouping is necessary.

There are many considerations that determine the grouping of a class. It is well to divide the highly creative individuals among all groups. Often it is wise to separate conflicting personalities. Sometimes if an aggressive new leader is removed from a group, qualities may develop in children who have been shy or reserved.

7. What should we do with the child who does not wish to participate? Occasionally there are children who do not wish to play. Since wholehearted participation is basic to the concept of dramatic play, forcing this child to take part would violate our goals. Let him observe. Try to involve him in making things that serve the play. The time will come, for most children, when they enter the play of their own accord. If it does not come, it is best to let such children do other things.

8. What should we do with disrupters? This is a difficult problem to solve. Since one of our purposes is to promote individual growth, eliminating a disrupter from the play may be a way of denying him opportunity to solve his problem. Why does he disrupt? Does he crave attention? Perhaps a good role may aid him. Is he insecure? Helping him to acquire some special skill or information that improves the play may be a solution. All possible factors should be explored.

Sometimes, however, an individual child's needs are too complex to be met by simple solutions and he persistently spoils the experience for the other children. It may become necessary to remove him temporarily or permanently from the dramatic play group. Of course the teacher continues to work on his needs. She must consider the welfare of the group as well as that of individuals.

SOCIODRAMA: AN EXTENSION
OF DRAMATIC PLAY

Dramatic play offers teachers a method of guiding children into social studies experiences through dramatic exploration of human activities. It is focused on exploring roles and acquiring content.

Sociodrama is an extension of dramatic play. It is primarily a group problem-solving tool focused on human relations. Children who have explored their world through dramatic play develop the capacity to enter freely and imaginatively into the more structured explorations of sociodrama or role playing. Teachers who are interested in the educational usefulness of role playing would do well to consider dramatic play as a preliminary experience to role playing.

8

Extended Role Playing

THEMATIC SEQUENCE IN ROLE PLAYING

Although even a single session of role playing can often help a group confront a problem in human relations, far more growth in insight and empathy is achieved by role playing that extends over a series of sessions and is focused upon various aspects of a single theme.[1] Role playing can be most effective when a group deals with a general problem through a *cumulative sequence* of sessions. Each successive role-playing experience reinforces and enriches both the emotional impact and the understanding of previous sessions. Each new session should build on the preceding experience; this is another way of saying that the goal of role playing is growth in maturation. An effective impetus for changed behavior is awareness of probable consequences, and extended role playing upon a crucial theme offers optimum potential for growth toward behavior that can change in the light of foreseeable results.

An example may be helpful. Occasionally the members of a class are an uncongenial, quarrelsome group, and the classroom climate is charged with tension. Personality clashes between key individuals are frequent. Conflict between factions causes many daily eruptions and costly delays in the learning process.

---

[1]In support of this hypothesis, see Jerome S. Bruner, Jacqueline J. Goodnow, and George A. Austin, *A Study of Thinking* (New York: Science Editions, Inc., 1962), p. 242. "First of all, to understand the intelligent or adaptive nature of behavior, one must work with units larger than a single response, no matter how 'molar' that response may be. One must, moreover, work with *sequences* of response if one is to appreciate the unfolding interplay between successive responses in reaction to prior consequences."

The establishment of effective working relationships in the classroom has traditionally held high priority for teachers concerned with promoting educational achievement among their pupils. Although much of learning is ultimately an individual task, in the modern school it takes place in a social environment. Pupils learn through interaction with the teacher, by working in committees, by discussing with classmates, by checking homework assignments over the telephone. Their motivation to learn is influenced by their position in the classroom social structure, by the peer group standards toward classroom activities, and by the supporting or conflicting pressures from a great variety of forces which are a part of their life space.[2]

A sixth-grade class in a laboratory school was causing their teacher a great deal of anxiety. So much strife was flaring up between rival groups and individuals in her classroom, so much spiteful bickering was occurring that the orderly learning process was disrupted and the basically able group was failing to make normal progress. As members of one group attempted to recite when called upon, others would make jeering comments; naturally, the first group would retaliate in kind.

Especially distressing to the teacher was the fact that a number of vulnerable youngsters were having a severely damaging experience. One girl, who had had difficulty in previous grades, was becoming increasingly frightened, unhappy, and hostile; her present experience, the teacher suspected, might set so bitter an edge of failure upon her aspirations that she might never regain confidence in learning. One particularly withdrawn boy, similarly, had stopped making any effort to participate. And others, the teacher realized, whose problems she had not yet fully learned, were receiving an experience that might become an irreversible setback.

The teacher was spending far too much time and effort in maintaining discipline. Repeatedly she had tried to make the class see how destructive their behavior had become, but without success. She could have enforced discipline by a stern use of authority; but this she was reluctant to do, for she foresaw that it would leave her, metaphorically, holding down the lid on a cauldron of seething, barely suppressed feeling. Rather than force an outward compliance, she preferred, if possible, to change the troubled classroom climate.

She discussed her problem with a consultant. She explained that her pupils were children of professional and academic people and were highly competitive. They had had a teacher, the previous year, who pitted them against each other for achievement, and as a result, they were set in a critical attitude toward everything said and done in the classroom.

"In some way, I have to calm this group down," she told the consultant. "But I want to do it in a way that leaves them comfortable with me and with one another."

"It may help if you can get the individual members of the group to realize what feelings they are arousing in each other."

"How can I do that?"

---

[2]Robert S. Fox and Ronald Lippitt, "The Innovation of Classroom Mental Health Practices," in Matthew B. Miles, ed., *Innovation in Education* (New York: Teachers College, Columbia University, 1964), p. 271.

It was decided to try role playing. They planned a sequence of role-playing stories, all of which dealt with the same theme: how a person feels when he is rejected by his group. Five such stories were used in the sequence.

The consultant directed the sessions while the classroom teacher observed from the back of the room. In the first session, the story entitled "The Squawk Box" was used.[3] In this story a very able youngster (Andy) is denied a chance to use his knowledge in a classroom project. He is rejected by the children because he is different: He has formal manners, uses adult language, and dresses very neatly. Moreover, instead of trying to overcome the group's hostility by being ingratiating, he fights back by being sarcastic, for which he has more than a little talent.

The consultant read the story to the group and stopped at the dilemma point. Discussion, then role playing followed. The session proved surprisingly diagnostic: The teacher learned important facts about the group. The pupils who volunteered to play roles were those who were suffering most from rejection; and in the role playing they reflected their own experiences in the classroom. On the other hand, the influential members of the class—leaders of cliques and their close friends—refrained from taking roles. Instead, they made critical comments to one another about the individuals who did play roles.

"Isn't he something?"

"Thinks he's smart."

After the enactment, the role playing was discussed and the central issue raised: How could Andy be helped to win acceptance from the classroom group? The children suggested that he dress like the others, learn to play games, and learn to take a joke.

The role-playing leader then asked the children if they thought that these suggestions would solve Andy's problem. One boy said, very emphatically, that this would *not* solve his problem, that for example Andy would not be permitted to be the equipment engineer unless Jerry (the power clique leader in the class) would let him. Another boy supported this statement, saying, "Jerry is the power in that bunch, and everyone knows it!" Another child added that Jerry would never let Andy in and no one else would if Jerry wouldn't.

These comments were most significant. There was a cynical acceptance in this class of the role of influential persons and the need to get along with them. It is important for the teacher to know who are the most influential individuals in the classroom group. Research provides some support for the hunch that individuals who play active roles in role playing undergo more change of attitude through the experience than do individuals who sit in the audience and observe.[4] If key students were given roles as the sessions proceeded, their attitudes would be more likely to change. Not only would the influential individuals be given a chance to learn how it feels to be rejected, but their consequent changes of attitude would influence the attitudes of their followers.

[3]The stories used are included in Part III of this volume.

[4]Pearl Rosenberg, *An Experimental Analysis of Psychodrama* (Unpublished doctoral dissertation, Harvard University, 1950).

In the next role-playing session, the second problem story of the thematic sequence, "Bandit Cave," was used. In this story, the boy who is rejected by the group is a quiet youngster who reads a great deal and who would have much knowledge to contribute to the group if he were given a chance. He does not fight against the treatment he is receiving, either constructively or by being sarcastic and hostile; instead, he withdraws, participating less and less in the activities of the group.

Again the consultant read the story to the group and invited discussion and role playing. Surprisingly, the role playing aroused very strong feelings in the listening group. For them, the lot of the rejected boy was deeply poignant; to them, he seemed so alone and deeply hurt. The leader of one clique summed up the feeling of the class by saying, "He feels like he is nobody. Just nobody at all."

The fact that this classroom leader voiced his own feelings in public this way set a seal of approval on openly expressing sympathy for the rejected boy in the story; in effect this authoritative reaction freed this influential boy's followers to avow their own feelings publicly. The result was that this role-playing session aroused a high pitch of open empathy.

Feelings of rejection were explored still further in the succeeding sessions, in which a group of three stories dealing with children's expectations of rejection were used. In the first story, "Judy Miller" (p. 294), a girl returns with her family to a community from which they had moved two years previously. She had had many close friends there before the family moved away, and while absent she had missed her friends intensely. Her unhappiness was so deep, in fact, that it had been one of the chief reasons why the family had returned to the town. But now, back again, she suffers acute disappointment. Her old friends have acquired new cronies. Increasingly, during the first days of her return, she feels left out of things. And, when the members of her group are invited to a party and she is not, she feels bereft and heartsick. She no longer has any friends, she realizes; her former friends, on whom she had counted so heavily, no longer care much about her.

She is mistaken. The night of the party, to which she has not been invited, finally comes. Her mother sends her out on an errand. When she returns home, she finds the house full of young people—all her old friends. They are waiting for her, and when she enters, noisy greetings welcome her. The party to which she had not been invited along with all her former friends is her own party—a surprise party given to welcome her back home.

In the discussion that followed the reading of this story, almost every pupil in the classroom stated that he or she had had just such an experience of feeling left out. And they were delighted by the happy ending to the story: it obviously soothed a common hurt.

More important, of course, this discussion alerted the group to another aspect of common behavior: Sometimes we *expect* to be mistreated; sometimes *we are too quick to jump to conclusions about other people's behavior.*

In the next session, a second story, "Johnny Kotowski" (p. 296), was used. In this story a boy who is the star pitcher for his sixth-grade baseball team is a candidate for captain of the team. When the election is being held, Johnny Kotowski overhears the teacher-coach of the team listing his (Johnny's) defects to his teammates: Johnny is hot-tempered, he stutters, he cannot run as fast between bases as the bigger boys, he tends to slow up in a tight spot, and so on. Johnny is crushed. To him, this is a betrayal. The fact that everything the coach has said is true only makes the hurt keener. Johnny slinks away, feeling humiliated and rejected. Later, however, Johnny learns that the coach was listing his handicaps only to show the group how much Johnny had learned to overcome; the teacher had been making the point that Johnny had had the strength of character to overcome a great many defects. The result is that Johnny is chosen team captain.

The final story was "Jimmy Garrett" (p. 297). In this story a young black boy comes to believe that he has been rejected for a job as delivery boy and blamed through prejudice for stealing a bike which he had actually retrieved for its owner. But the policeman who he thinks is coming to arrest him has come, instead, to thank him for saving the bike and to help him get the job he wanted.

What were the results of this sequence of role-playing experiences? This sequence of role playing played a part in changing the climate of the classroom. The teacher expressed it in this way: "Before, they were beastly to each other, but now they are decent human beings." The isolated youngsters had been given a chance to take part in an absorbing group activity; their status with the group improved, and their self-concept and morale had consequently become healthier as the other children extended friendship to them. The girl who had hated coming to school because she had been so bitterly unhappy now was bringing classmates home to play. The withdrawn boy, still quiet, was participating more and more in classroom activity. Toward the end of the term the class was functioning productively at a very satisfactory level.

The basic strategy was to induce the influential leaders of cliques to *play roles that helped them gain insight into how it feels to be rejected.* The experience had sensitized them, had given them heightened empathy for their isolated classmates. Of course, this experience was not the only factor that operated to transform these warring cliques into a more "cohesive" group; the fact that they all participated in an exciting project that involved them emotionally, that they shared a common experience in problem solving, was of real importance. Also, as the weeks passed, they grew to know each other better under "action" circumstances that provided reasons for them to appreciate individual abilities. The personality and ethical feeling of the teacher, too, was a potent influence for change.

To sum up: It is unreal to hope that a problem in social relationships can be solved in a single role-playing session. A change of attitudes and values requires time, emphasis, and reinforcement.

Themes for Extended Role Playing

Some of the themes into which the stories presented in this volume can fit are listed below. In general, these themes touch upon aspects of ethical behavior; their focus is to help young people grow in individual integrity and group responsibility.

Just how attitudes and values are acquired is not obvious; perhaps they are absorbed—or better yet, *achieved*—by an extended process of heightening awareness and empathy that come from a sensitively understood poignant experience. Such experiences can be provided in the classroom by role-playing situations that are structured upon the generalizations implicit in these listed themes. These experiences are immediate yet removed enough so that they exact no penalties for mistakes and provide a second— even a third or fourth—opportunity for a decision.

The stories in Part III were written to illustrate a number of ethical themes. The stories are listed in groups or patterns to support these ethical considerations. The themes are listed below. However, the stories are sufficiently varied and numerous to fit a much wider range of themes than those we have listed. When a problem of human relations arises in the classroom, the concerned teacher can select specific stories from these groups that may fit the problem troubling her class. The stories can be rearranged in a wide variety of patterns to fit themes applicable to many classroom situations.

Themes for Extended Role Playing

1. Honesty
2. Fair-mindedness
3. Unfair revenge
4. Rules are for everyone
5. Self-acceptance
6. Prejudice
7. Feelings of rejection
8. Anticipation of rejection
9. Integrity in friendship
10. Responsibilities of the group toward individuals
11. Responsibilities of individuals toward others
12. Cooperation within the group

Selecting a Thematic Sequence of Stories for Extended Role Playing

To illustrate how stories are selected for extended role playing, suppose, for example, you wish to work on problems of honesty. The theme for the sequence of role-playing experiences could be as follows:

I. Theme: Honesty

A dozen stories in this group deal with problems of honesty. From among these stories, the teacher can select three to five (or more) that seem particularly applicable to the needs of the group. The aspects of honesty touched upon are lying, cheating, hiding someone else's possessions, letting another person take the blame, social lying, and not returning a found article.

Lying:

1. "Boy Out on a Limb"
2. "Lost Ball"
3. "Little Echo"
4. "The Un-Invitation" (social lying)

Cheating:

5. "Paper Drive"
6. "A Long Nose Has a Short Life"

Letting Another Person Take Blame for Your Wrongdoing:

7. "Rocket Shoot"
8. "Heavy, Heavy Hangs Over Your Head"
9. "Trick or Treat"

Not Returning a Found Article:

10. "Money for Marty"
11. "The Clubhouse Boat"
12. "Finders Weepers"

II. Theme: Responsibility to others

These stories overlap in the ethical considerations with which they deal. For example, stories dealing with aspects of honesty are also concerned with the responsibility to others that an ethical individual must feel. Sometimes, merely pointing out that it is dishonest to let another person take blame for a wrong one has committed keeps the matter on a vague, abstract level; whereas pointing out just how that other individual is injured by a damaging act for which one is responsible puts the matter on a plane of individual feeling that is far more real and meaningful.

Letting other people take the blame for your wrongdoing.   Such behavior is, of course, dishonest; but involved, also, is failure to face up to one's responsibility to others. Stories dealing with this problem include:

1. "Trick or Treat"
2. "Heavy, Heavy Hangs Over Your Head"
3. "Rocket Shoot"

In these stories, the person who has committed a wrong can, *by keeping silent*, evade punishment for that wrong, but, by keeping silent, he is failing to establish the innocence of the person who is wrongly blamed for the misbehavior.

Setting a bad example.   Sometimes young people can break rules (like going swimming, fishing, or hunting in places marked *Keep Out*), have fun, and safely evade detection. But, other young people will often take note and decide to imitate. Usually there are good reasons for prohibitory rules: beaches, for example, marked *No Swimming* may be subject to dangerous undertows, and young people imitating older individuals' behavior in ignoring signs may get into serious trouble. Setting an example is an important facet of the individual's responsibility and concern for the welfare of others.

   4. "Blind Fish"
   5. "Frogman"

In these two stories, the central character commits an act that breaks the rules and safely gets away with it. But other youngsters then want to imitate his behavior. The central character can foresee the possible harm that might come to them, but if he does not permit them to do what he has done, he is a spoil-sport, a hypocrite who is bitterly resented by his friends.

CONCLUSIONS

Even a single session of role playing, in some instances, can help a group solve a problem of human relations. In general, however, far more growth of insight and empathy is achieved by role playing that extends through a series of sessions focused on a single theme. Such sessions should be planned as a cumulative sequence in which each successive role-playing experience with various aspects of the general theme reinforces and enriches the understandings of previous sessions.

The problem stories in this book are listed in patterns to implement a number of ethical themes; moreover, the stories are varied and numerous enough so that many teachers, dealing with a problem not listed here, may be able to select stories to make a pattern that will better apply to the specific problem causing concern.

PART TWO

Preparing Teachers
to Lead Role Playing

9

Training Teachers
to Lead Role Playing

Good ideas or techniques often fail in the classroom because teachers have an incomplete grasp of what is required to make the procedures work. So often teachers say, "I tried role playing and it doesn't work." They would be more accurate if they said, "I tried role playing, but I didn't know how to make it work."

A common assumption held by teachers is that learning to lead role playing consists of simply following a set of directions. More than that is involved. To recap some general principles, skill in role playing requires

1. Understanding that the process is a group problem-solving procedure based upon spontaneity, exploration of alternative solutions to problems, and consideration of the likely consequences
2. Skill in using nondirective responses and questioning techniques—learning how to ask open-ended questions that sustain students' thinking and are nonjudgmental
3. Establishing a climate of trust—demonstrating by one's own behavior that you, the teacher, are listening, protecting students' ideas, giving opportunity for all viewpoints to be aired, and shutting down invasions of privacy
4. Practice—there is no substitute for *learning in action* in order to discover your own hidden agendas, to learn how long to run an enactment, to learn how to facilitate the thinking of your students
5. Willingness to learn by making mistakes—most teachers' insights into the role-playing process will come from analyzing their own behavior during role-playing sessions.

TRAINING

There are a number of ways to organize training sessions. A role-playing course can run a quarter or a semester, typically involving two- or three-hour sessions twice a week. Summer workshops can be one or two weeks long, and weekend workshops for school districts usually involve a Friday evening session and an all day Saturday session.

All these sessions are based on *learning through doing*. The most effective strategy is to give a brief introduction to the process and its characteristic steps, have the group try some simple situations, and then go into further theory and analysis. While it helps to have a skilled leader guide these learning sessions, it is possible for a small group of teachers to get together and make considerable progress on their own.

Following are some strategies appropriate to several approaches to learning to lead role playing for informal groups, the week-end or one-day workshop, the longer workshop, and a formal course.

Informal Groups

After familiarizing yourself with the basic process and steps, invite a few colleagues or friends for an evening of "fun with role playing." As few as six people can provide a basis for such exploration—enough to provide both actors and observer-participants. Briefly explain the idea of spontaneous exploration of a dilemma situation, the taking on of roles, and enacting possible solutions to the situation.

Use simple, nonthreatening, even humorous dilemmas for this initial experience. (A number of such stories are included in this section.) Present the situation and invite enough discussion to get people involved. Select role players and act out several possible solutions, changing role players as individuals express different ideas of what might happen. Do several situations with minimum discussions of techniques until everyone has a "feel" for taking a role and a sense of the steps involved. If this is a professional group, the leader can plan a follow-up session with more detailed analysis of the process, moving from humorous situations to more crucial and serious dilemmas. After some experience with participation in role-playing sessions, the group can be introduced to the skills involved in leading role playing.

A careful reading of descriptions of role playing (see Chapters 5 and 6) can provide a basic background for understanding the role-playing process.

Each member of the group should undertake to lead a session and have the help of the group in critiquing that session. Then each member can begin to use simple situations in his or her own classes, gradually building skill through successes and failures. Always remind the hesitant trainee that "No one will know how well or poorly it went—and you can learn from your mistakes."

The following guide can be helpful. It is a shortened version of the elements presented in Chapters 5 and 6.

**Suggestions for the Teacher
(as Leader of Role Playing)**

1. *Setting a climate for role playing.* The climate is the key to realistic role playing. The leader must demonstrate through his (or her) own behavior that he knows that many problems are not easy to solve, that we often behave impulsively and get into difficulties, that there is no necessarily one "right" solution. He guides the group to think of "what *will* happen" rather than "what *should* happen." The *should* aspect will emerge from the group's growing insights as they role-play the situation. The teacher works for open-ended exploration.

2. *Selecting role players.* After a "warm-up" and the presentation of a situation or problem, role players must be chosen. The teacher may ask such questions as "What is———like?" "What is our situation (or problem)?" "How does———feel?" or "What will happen now?"

   Such questions call for responses from different individuals. This enables the leader to select the people who seem to be identifying with roles in the situation or with aspects of the problem. Such people are ready to role-play.

   When possible, select first for role playing people who evidence impulsive or socially poor solutions so that these may be opened up and explored for their consequences. Save the positive and socially acceptable solutions for later enactments so that the entire gamut of behaviors may be laid before the group for evaluation.

3. *Preparing the audience to be participant observers.* Prepare the audience to observe purposefully. Suggest to the observers that
   a. Some identify with particular roles and think through whether that would be the way they would play them
   b. Observers check the performance for realism
   c. Observers try to gauge the feelings of the actors confronting the problem in action
   d. Observers think through the solution that is being developed by the actors and consider other solutions that might be offered.

4. *The enactment.* The leader helps the role players get into action by asking such setting-the-stage questions as
   "Where will this take place?" (and helps set the stage by indicating tables and chairs that might be used and other available real or imaginary props)
   "What time of day is this happening?" or
   "Where in the story are we starting?"
   "What are the various people doing?"

   An enactment does not have to go to completion. The leader may stop it when the role players have clearly demonstrated their ideas of what will happen. Sometimes the teacher may want to allow a situation to be played out to the bitter end so that the consequences become dramatically clear to the group.

5. *Discussing and evaluating.* After the enactment, the leader must be careful not to be judgmental. He (or she) may end the enactment, thank the performers, and ask the audience: "What is happening here?"—an open-ended question.

   The leader may further the discussion through such questions as
   "How does———feel?"
   "Could this *really* happen?"
   "What will happen now?"

"Why does————behave the way he does?"

"Are there other ways this situation could end?"

Finally, after a number of enactments, the leader may ask, "Could this happen to you or people you know?" in order to relate the problem to the students' own lives.

6. *The reenactment.* Further enactments may represent other persons' ideas of how the roles could be handled or how other people might have behaved in the situation. Further enactments may involve exploration of alternative solutions. Often the group may take the situation that was presented by the first role players and carry it forward in terms of further consequences.

7. *Sharing experiences and generalizing.* The leader's question "Where are we now?" may precipitate some generalizing or review of the various solutions that have been explored.

   The leader may also ask, "Is this a true to life situation?" in order to elicit from the students examples of similar problems in their own experience.

   Quite often a role-playing session may have achieved only a further definition of the problem or dilemma. The participant-observers may not yet be ready to generalize. This should not disturb the teacher. It may take a number of sessions before children accumulate the knowledge and develop the insights that lead to generalization.

Some Hard Spots

1. Quite often teachers find much difficulty in overcoming the directive role. A teacher may believe that he or she is being truly nondirective as he or she leads a role-playing session. The truth may be that the teacher is responding, in discussion, only to those students whose ideas fit the teacher's own preconceived notions of how the session should go. This results in the leader selecting a line of action that fits his or her own preference. This is usually an unconsciously held position (the teacher's own hidden agenda). To overcome this fault requires practice in asking open-ended questions, making open-ended statements and nonjudgmental responses, not focusing on just the one proposal but covering a range of ideas. Beginning leaders of role playing can be helped to overcome this fault by having an observer critique their functioning, or by tape-recording the session so that the leaders can listen to their own performance and spot faulty techniques.

2. It has been suggested here that training in leading role playing can begin on an informal, humorous basis. Because people are self-conscious when they first do role playing, there may be clowning and laughter from the group. Gradually, by focusing on the situation and asking role-centered questions, the instructor can help the group to discard farce and to become serious in its enactments.

3. Another difficulty in doing role playing is to help the people who are observing the role playing to move from an audience role to a participant one. Assigning observation tasks and calling on the observers for their reactions will help.

4. Timing is important. The beginner usually lets an enactment go on too long. An enactment should be cut as soon as a clear line of action has been delineated and discussion started.

The Short Workshop

The short workshop—usually a Friday-night-to-Saturday-afternoon session—has necessarily limited goals. The leader can only hope to introduce teachers to role playing and give them some *initial* experience with the process and the skills involved. The following is a practical format:

Friday evening: 7:30 to 9:30 P.M.

1. Introduction: What is role-playing?
2. Use a short "fun" situation and involve the group in a role-playing session. The story entitled "The Weight Watcher" (p. 119), for example, provides an easy, relaxed way to introduce people to role playing.
3. Analyze the session, briefly, in terms of process.
4. Use another short, humorous dilemma story from the group in Chapter 10 (or any other source) and after enacting it, have the group do further analysis.
5. Summarize, then present the agenda for the all-day Saturday session.

Saturday morning: 9:00 A.M. to noon.

1. Introduce the group to more serious role playing by using either a story such as "Paper Drive" or a filmstrip, such as "The Big Eye," or a film. The film *Paper Drive*, because it involves a teacher, is a good take-off vehicle.[1]
2. Involve the group in active role playing, using as many alternative solutions as the group can suggest and as many role players as possible.
3. Allow time for extensive discussion of all the ideas presented.
4. End this session with a detailed analysis of the elements of role playing demonstrated in this session. For example:
   Taking on roles
   Expressing feelings
   Discovering the transactional process
   Listening to another's ideas
   Doing antecedent/consequential thinking
   Drawing conclusions
5. At about 10:30 A.M. take a break.
6. After the break, present in greater detail the role-playing process and the strategies involved in leading role playing. At this time it is helpful to distribute a mimeographed sheet of *Suggestions for the Teacher (as the leader of role playing)*.
7. Organize the workshop members into groups of eight or ten people to practice role playing in the afternoon sessions.

Saturday afternoon: 1:15 to 4:00 P.M.

1. The small groups are given a large picture, a filmstrip,[2] or a short problem story (for example, "Money for Marty" (p. 199) and sent to different rooms with

---

[1]George Shaftel and Fannie Shaftel, *Paper Drive*, A Values Film, Dimension Films (Los Angeles: Churchill Films, 1972). Other films in this series include *The Clubhouse Boat* and *Trick or Treat*.

[2]George Shaftel and Fannie Shaftel, *Values in Action* (ten filmstrips) (Minneapolis: Winston House, 1976); idem, *People in Action: Problem Pictures for Role Playing and Discussion* (New York: Holt, Rinehart & Winston, 1970).

instructions to select a member of the group to lead the session, then to enter into role playing. In this short initial experience, they are instructed to use the *Suggestions For the Teacher* as a checklist after the session with which to evaluate their experience. Groups may change leaders at any time in order to give as many people as possible a chance to try leading a session.

2. At approximately 2:30 P.M. the entire workshop reassembles to share experiences and raise questions.
3. The rest of the time is devoted to a discussion of role playing in the curriculum. Where does it fit? What purposes can it support? What is its range of possibilities?
4. The members of the workshop are finally given a working bibliography that includes books on theory, practical applications, and teacher experience in using role playing in the classroom.

The Longer Workshop

In a workshop of two- or three-weeks duration there is, of course, time to (1) give the participants more experience in partaking of role playing themselves and (2) have the small groups move into practice in leading role playing more systematically.

1. Start with short humorous situations.
2. Do simple skills role playing—for example, how to apply for a job, how to introduce a foreign visitor or a new student to the class, and so on.
3. Do short dilemma situations.
4. Do the more elaborate dilemma problem stories.
5. Finally, do controversial situations. And, always, rotate the leadership so that everyone has experience in leading sessions.

The problems and questions that emerge in these group practice sessions can then form the basis for workshop seminars and open the way to related theory and curriculum.

The Formal Course

A formal university course in role playing is "formal" in the sense that it is an organized class and has some built-in requirements. In many respects it is a laboratory course that has an action arena.

Perhaps its most unique quality is that the participants learn by doing and in the process confront the need to learn more by reading, discussion, and analytic thinking. The number of students enrolled should be limited so as to maintain a manageable situation.

The first session involves a brief explanation of the course structure and introduction to the processes involved in role playing. The instructor may then introduce role playing with an informal, nonthreatening situation, such as "The Weight Watcher" story, one that everyone can identify with immediately. If many young people are in the class the instructor might begin with a dating situation. The result is often the establishment of an immediate sense of community with everyone talking, sharing ideas, and getting to know each other.

This session can end with a reading assignment in such materials as this book, the Chesler and Fox book,[3] or other materials, and a description of the requirements for the course. This may include

1. Participation by everyone in role-playing sessions and eventual leading a session in class
2. Systematic reading assignments
3. Writing role-playing incidents
4. Responsibility on the part of each class member for finding a group (children or adults) to lead in a role-playing session, tape-recording or videotaping that session, and writing an analysis of it with the help of a guide sheet provided by the instructor
5. Presentations by the instructor on theory, strategies, and curriculum applications as well as the use of film, filmstrips, and other materials.

Each week the class has some role-playing experience, starting with story situations provided by the instructor. These problems range from humorous incidents to skills training to serious problem dilemmas.

Theory presentations may involve such topics as Jacob Moreno's spontaneity theatre and his rationale for psychodrama and sociodrama, the role of empathy in the development of the humane person, open processes of teaching, how to work with controversial issues, and, eventually, the curriculum possibilities of role playing.

Early in the course students begin taking responsibility: preparing a role-playing situation in advance, then leading sessions with the class. This is always critiqued by the group and the instructor. It is emphasized that we learn by making mistakes—that such mistakes are golden opportunities to look at the pitfalls, to diagnose needed skills, to advance understanding of theory.

A NEW DIMENSION

Each week the instructor leads a role-playing session designed to introduce various dimensions of the use of role playing. Early in the course the problem situations used are simple, involving low complexity, and of a nonthreatening nature. Gradually more serious topics can be introduced, such as community-school controversies, intergroup and interracial problems, and so on.

The following session, involving an incident that actually occurred early in the civil rights struggles, is an example of the deeper probing into controversial issues that can occur in a class that has developed some elements of trust and a sense of community through a series of role-playing experiences.

[3]Mark Chesler and Robert Fox, *Role Playing Methods in the Classroom* (Chicago, Ill.: Science Research Associates, 1966).

The Empty Seat

In a student body of about four thousand in a college in Southern California, forty of the students were black. They usually grouped together for mutual support. One night, about 11:00 P.M. five black students entered the single eatery on the campus that was open at that hour. All tables were occupied, and the only seats available were six at the counter. At the hostess's suggestion, the five black students seated themselves there. A white man entered, and the hostess offered him the remaining empty seat.

He protested, "I won't sit next to those niggers! You'll have to find me another seat."

The hostess turned on the five black students, saying: "Why don't you get out! You're nothing but trouble!"

Everyone in the restaurant heard this.

When the black students tried to assert their rights, not one of their white classmates or the faculty members present came to their defense.

The next day some of the whites tried to apologize for not having the courage to speak up.[4]

This incident was used in a role-playing class which included teacher internes, their supervisors, and some experienced teachers. The objective was to help them explore their own interracial attitudes.

After describing the incident, the instructor set up a role-playing situation. The hostess was chosen and white students were selected to play the five black students. A group of people seated around a table were assigned the roles of faculty members, while the rest of the class was assigned to play the other students in the eatery. The white man who objected to sitting next to the blacks was finally chosen.

The enactment started. When the white man began shouting, the hostess turned venomously on the five "blacks," ordering them out. The five blacks protested and refused to leave. In the midst of this controversy the "faculty members" got up and left.

A black interne, G., role-playing a white student, suddenly shouted "Call the police!" Two men (from the "faculty" group that left) returned as policemen.

"What's happening here?"

"Those fellows," G. said, pointing to the students playing the blacks, "started a fight here."

The class began to protest, saying, "That's not what happened!"

"Yes, it is," said G., quietly, now speaking as a black. "That's the way it is. The blacks get blamed, even when they're innocent."

There was a moment of silence. Then someone said, "I never realized that before." And the talk started! The class stayed an hour past dismissal time, deeply absorbed in the experience of exploring why the whites had not responded, what each thought he or she might do in such a situation, and how it felt to whites to be blacks in these circumstances.

The two black internes and a Mexican-American interne became

---

[4]Fannie Shaftel, "Role-Playing: An Approach to Meaningful Social Learning," *Social Education*, 34, No. 5 (May 1970): 556.

unusually articulate, and everyone listened. If time had permitted, there could have been further enactments in which whites could have explored other ways of responding in this situation.

What had happened? The polite barrier of words used as defenses against unpleasant realities had been broken; instead, ideas were being dealt with at a feeling level. The acting out of the situation encouraged spontaneous responses rather than guarded maneuvers. In this moment of truth, members of the class recognized that they had been so socialized in the process of growing up in American culture that they accepted forms of discrimination as realities of life, seldom aware that they themselves were participating in that discrimination.

In reenacting the episode, some members had their awareness heightened by a confrontation with the real-life experience of the black and Mexican-American members of the group.

Writing Problem Stories

A new dimension of learning occurs as students write and present their own problem stories. Structuring a real dilemma is not easy, as they quickly realize. But using a good dilemma story—that presents real alternatives and, often, no complete victories—is the key to productive role playing.

As practicing teachers (student internes and sophisticated classroom teachers) bring in and share their role-playing experiences from their own classrooms, many critical issues in teaching emerge for discussion. These discussions often lead to a gamut of considerations that are not only educational and developmental but social.

An important phase of their training is an out-of-class role-playing practice assignment.

Assignment

1. Select a role-playing dilemma situation. (Either originate one or use one that is already in print). Lead a role-playing session with your own class of children (or other group). Tape-record or videotape the session.
2. Listen to your tape, and analyze the session in terms of
   a. Whether you think the warm-up really involved your listeners. What is the basis for your conclusion?
   b. Whether you selected role players appropriately. Did key players have ideas they were ready to express?
   c. How well did you set the stage for the action. Did you place your participants into roles and settings clearly and quickly?
   d. How you decided which lines of action to follow. Did you have difficult decisions to make? What was the basis of your choice?
   e. How well you used the following:
      (1) Open-ended questions
      (2) Reflecting back individual feelings and ideas for clarification
      (3) Summarizing a discussion (by reflecting back what you think the students are saying)
3. Summarize what you had as your goals in this role-playing session. How well do

you think you achieved your goals? Specify on what criteria you base your conclusions.

4. Discuss your strengths and weaknesses as revealed by your leadership of this session. What elements do you especially need to work on?

The following account is one student's response to this assignment.

A Role-Playing Session

I gave a role-playing session to my Freehand Drawing Class. I wanted to introduce role playing as a technique to develop skills on how to act in certain social problem situations. I wanted to make the first session as simple as possible. I used a situation in which a boy takes a girl to a restaurant only to find when once he is seated and looking at the menu that he is unable to pay the prices.

Warming up students to the situation so they could identify and respond to the problem seemed to be successful. Instantly students reacted to the situation and recalled similar instances in their past experience. This specific problem seemed to be one that encouraged involvement on the part of the student. Nobody was really on the spot to expose sensitive and "touchy" feelings. I think I should have let my students talk it out just a bit longer in order to let them develop their ideas more concretely. I think I rushed them into role playing a little too soon. I believe I chose the role players appropriately. Those students who seemed to have an idea how the situation should be played were asked to play it out.

The stage for action seemed adequate. I wish I had talked to the observers sooner about their role in the process. While I think the observers were reacting and identifying with the players, I feel if they had been more attentive to the role players they might have tried to solve the problem in more depth.

My job as role-playing leader was greatly simplified by the lack of complexity of feelings that the problem-solving situation called for. The search for as many alternatives as possible was my main line of action. My most difficult decision was: When should I cut off the line of action? In most cases, I feel I cut off at the appropriate time; but in other instances, I feel that if I had let it play out longer, we might have come to stronger and clearer conclusions.

I tried to use as many open-ended questions as possible. I probably should have used more variety in my questioning to bring out more viewpoints. I believe I let the students do most of the talking. I don't think they ever felt that they were looking for the right answer for the teacher.

I found that reflecting back individual feelings and ideas for clarification brought strength to the problem-solving. For example, after one particular enactment, I clarified how the girl felt, and she elaborated upon the problem even further. I wish I had done this more often. I felt I rushed through the summary of a discussion. I should have slowed down and reviewed the other solutions we had used earlier in the session so the students could either agree or disagree or add or modify the problem-solving. I think they would have gotten a better idea of the goals and purposes of role playing rather than considering it simply as an opportunity to act and have fun.

My main goal was to introduce the technique of role playing as a way for developing social skills in delicate situations. I wanted my students to feel positive about the technique. I also wanted my students to experience a different method of problem solving, of developing skills in a very active way rather than in the more passive method of discussion alone. As far as the success of these general main goals is concerned, on the whole I feel positive. The students were actively participating throughout the session. In fact, I wish there had been less talk on the part of the observers during the role playing. Many students stayed after class to hear parts of the tape. Several asked questions on role playing and asked if we were going to do it again.

As far as the success of the problem solving and skill development, I am much more in doubt. Much of the weakness of the problem solving can be attributed to weak timing on the part of the leader and the self-consciousness of the students in a first role-playing session. There was a natural tendency for both the role players and the observers to see the process as a form of impromptu entertainment. I refer to the several occasions of applause that were given for clever retorts on the part of the role players. I believe this whole attitude is a characteristic of any group in their first role-playing experience.

I was weak all through the session in clarifying points and in summations. For example, after the last role-playing enactment, I should have summarized all the different solutions that were brought up in class and then asked if there were any more alternatives for solving the problem. I feel I have a general feeling for the technique, especially after this session. I need smoothing out at the rough corners—for example, How much talking should be done by the instructor? What are the correct questions? When should they be asked? I feel I need more confidence and ease with the process; yet, each time I have the opportunity to be the leader, I gain more security.

I feel my strengths came when I asked the role players what was happening. Open-ended questions are invaluable for bringing out student responses. I think the students understood that I wasn't looking for any right answers or passing value judgments. I think I communicated clearly to the group. There never seemed to be any doubt as to what was the problem to be solved. I think my weaknesses are those that only experience can correct. I find role playing to be an exciting and meaningful way to developing sensitivity and insight to social situations.

CONCLUSIONS

Learning to conduct role playing involves the teacher in the most basic considerations inherent in the teaching-learning process. It helps teachers to develop an understanding of how to establish communication with and between students and how to facilitate genuine intellectual interaction with nondirective techniques. It demonstrates the potency involved in joining the affective-cognitive domains. Teachers discover qualities in their students that were not apparent in conventional classroom relationships.

Leading role playing, obviously, is a skill that requires training and practice. While a skilled leader can greatly enhance the training process, groups of teachers can help each other to acquire such skill with the use of carefully selected materials. Many teachers, of course, already use some of the procedures of role playing in their classroom teaching. For them, growth in leadership skills will be rapid.

10

Materials for Learning
by Doing

This chapter presents ten dilemma stories that have proven effective for learning role-playing techniques. The first, "The Weight Watcher," is something of a classic. The author has used it for almost thirty years all over the United States with groups varying in size from twenty to two thousand; and always the story has proved a success. Its dilemma point arrives with the sudden impact of an O. Henry ending, and its portrayal of human frailty is so universal and so contagiously funny and forgivable that it never fails to both appall and delight. Moreover, the story is true; it happened to a family friend.

After practicing with the first few light-hearted stories, the training group can go on to those involving more serious issues. Growing familiarity with the role-playing procedure permits the group to work its way into deeper areas with increasing confidence.

MATERIALS FOR ROLE PLAYING

Humorous Dilemmas

1. "The Weight Watcher." This story involves two people and a minor act of unintended burglary and self-indulgence.
2. "The Dinner Date." What do you do when you take a girl you want to impress out to dinner, and you find you don't have enough money?
3. "The Helpful Wife." With all the good will in the world, one can try to help another person in the worst possible way.
4. "A Good Impression." Being invited to the boss's house for dinner can be a pleasant experience—or an unqualified ordeal.

5. "Welcome to Our City." Finding your way around a strange city at night can lead to surprising complications.
6. "The Windfall Syndrome." An embarrassment of riches—when is honesty dishonesty? When are good intentions suspect?

Dilemmas of Tact

7. "The Mess." The issue is tact.
8. "Listen, Doctor." Can you, must you, dare you correct the boss?
9. "Advice and Dissent." Giving advice is a thankless and sometimes risky effort.

A Serious Dilemma

10. "Paper Drive." Dealing with a classroom problem, this story is very effective in teacher education classes. It is also a powerful story to use with children.

Dilemma Exercises for Teacher

11. "The Mimic"
12. "The Trick"
13. "Language, Language!"
14. "Outside Authority"
15. "Whose Word Can You Take?"

HUMOROUS DILEMMAS

The Weight Watcher

The Problem: How do you learn to resist temptation?

Introducing the Problem: Say to your group, "Have you had occasion to watch a friend or relative trying to break the habit of smoking? It's so difficult! There is probably only one other addiction that's even harder to break: the habit of eating. This is the story of a person—a fine, honest, caring person—who was addicted to eating, and the consequences thereof."

So many of us have to watch our weight. So long as we say No to that second helping of steak or that luscious dessert, we manage to look nice in our clothes. But somehow, if we eat just a stingy couple of ounces of cheesecake or that extra-high mound of spaghetti, our thrifty calorie banks make a showy brag of extra deposits, and the straining seams of our clothes shout to the world of our gluttony.

Well, anyway, my friend Nora decided that her willpower needed the extra prop of group sanction. She joined the Weight Watchers Club. It's something like Alcoholics Anonymous. If you slip from grace, in your despair and remorse you can call upon a fellow member to come hold your hand and help you make new resolutions. Weight Watchers does even more: It gives you specific directions. It lists menus for you with kind and quantity specified in exact detail. Furthermore, the group has arranged with several restaurants to provide menus shrewdly tailored to keep your personality within bounds.

Wonderlings Cafeteria was one of those cooperating restaurants. Nora had gone into Wonderlings for lunch. She felt depressed and knew therefore that she was vulnerable. (If she had gone into Blum's, she'd have probably backslid in spectacular fashion.) Resolutely, then, as she walked along the serving counter in Wonderlings, she selected only those few dishes that were approved: a leaf or two of skinny lettuce, a thimbleful of cottage cheese (low calorie), a dab of carrot, a dab of spinach, and meager samples of other foods guaranteed to make eating a trial by boredom.

Bearing her trayful of these Spartan goodies, she sought a table. The place was crowded, and the only empty chair was at a table for two by the wall at which a young man was already seated, busily eating. Nora approached him and asked, "Would you mind?" as the young man looked up. Since his mouth was full, he just nodded. She unloaded her tray and sat down.

As she picked up her fork to start, she glanced at the young man's plate and saw what he was eating. A hot wave of nostalgia and appetite hit her like a flush of fever. Cake doughnuts! He was eating big, thick, sugar-coated delights laden with luscious jam. Food to make the blood thrill with youth and vigor! Not in years had she indulged herself with such ambrosia.

Resolutely she forced her gaze down at her own sparse victuals. But she couldn't close her ears and the young man opposite her was a noisy—well, hearty—eater. But did he *have* to chomp his food with such gusto? Did he *have* to guzzle his coffee like a snoring rhinoceros? A decent respect for the opinions of humankind—Whoa! she told herself. Let's not make a federal case of it. Straining, she swallowed a mouthful of soybean steak.

Opposite her, a fork clattered, a chair scraped. When she looked up, the young man had risen and was leaving, stalking off with the sturdy power of the well-fed.

She turned back to her food, then stopped, fork in mid-air, breath caught in her throat. The young man had departed leaving a cake doughnut on his plate. A whole, untouched, beautiful, wonderful doughnut lying there neglected and unwanted.

For a long moment she just stared.

To this day, Nora doesn't know how it happened. But somehow, that cake doughnut found its way off that young man's plate onto her own. Somehow, that doughnut levitated itself into her fingers, up to her mouth. And she took a great big, enormously delightful mouthful. And another, and another. She didn't gobble, mind you; she didn't really gulp it down. But it was half gone—just as the young man returned to the table with his second cup of coffee. . . .

Dinner Date

The Problem: How do you impress a person you want to admire you?

Introducing the Problem: Say to your group, "Have you ever tried to do something very well, but tried so hard that you ruined your effort? Sometimes the best-laid plan can backfire. This is a story about a young man who tried very hard to make a good impression on a young woman, a young man who planned carefully but ran into the unexpected."

Mike Patton and his roommate, Tony Bender, were in their room in the men's dorm at State College. Mike, who had been talking on the telephone, hung up and turned excitedly to Tony.

"Hey, I just got a date with that great girl I was telling you about!"

"Good. When?"

"Tonight, for dinner. Say, how about letting me wear your dark suit?"

"Not a chance."

"Look, Tony, I really want to make an impression on this girl. It's— important to me."

"So important you'll lend me five bucks until the first?"

"It's a deal! Here."

"Where you going to take her to dinner?"

"You know the city better than I do. Where do you suggest?"

"The Regency Room is tops. Expensive, though. And if this chick of yours is real hungry. . ."

"The Regency Room it is. This is no everyday event."

"You'll impress her, all right. She'll think you're filthy rich and act according."

"Okay! This'll be a night to be remembered!"

"You just may be right."

Susan Daniels was as excited as Mike when she dressed for their date, that evening. "But what bothers me, Alice," Susan told her roommate, "is that I don't know how to order a nice dinner from a big fancy menu."

"Just blink your eyes and say, real sweet, 'You order. I know it'll be wonderful.' That'll flatter him."

"And make me look like a ninny!"

"You really like this boy."

"I do."

"But aren't you a bit out of your class? I mean, you're just a new freshman and he's a senior?"

"Junior. But he was out of school last year, traveling in Europe. I don't want him to think that I'm so green I should still be wearing braces on my teeth."

"Well, if he takes you to a really nice place. . ."

"That you can count on."

"Show him that you have a mind of your own."

"And discriminating taste."

"Right."

"*Good* taste."

"So, when he makes suggestions for dinner, listen. And agree."

"In principle."

"But order something a little better, on the one hand—"

"And something a little more modest on the other."

"You catch on fast, Susan."

"I hope he doesn't take me to some awfully *expensive* place!"

"Oh, Susan, that's just what I was afraid you'd say. Look, the fact that he wants to take you to dinner in the city instead of some beanery near the campus shows that he wants to look good to you. He wants to make a big impression. Let him."

"I sure will. Hey! What'll I do if the menu is in French?"

"Just point with your finger."

"And get fried tripe? No, thanks. Besides, he'd think I had an I.Q. of minus seventy."

"There's the doorbell. He's here."

"Wish me luck!"

Mike and Susan drove up to the city. In the Regency Room, they were shown a table by a window with a wonderful view of the city lights. The waiter brought menus and handed one to Susan and one to Mike. They studied the long line of gourmet dishes.

"Susan," Mike said, "this place is famous for its seafood. But the prime rib is awfully good too, and so's the London Broil."

"Prime rib is just what I'd like," she said, "very pink, and a tossed salad with roquefort dressing."

"Good. And, I think, a dry white wine would be just right. For dessert, the French pastry here is . . . ."

"I think I'd like Cherries Jubilee."

"Swell!"

Then Mike gulped as his eye ran down the list of prices on the right side of his menu. Prime rib, $9.95. And, since everything was à la carte, salad was $2.50. And Cherries Jubilee was $2.45. He did some quick mental arithmetic. He had started out with thirty-two dollars. He had figured that would be ample; in fact, he'd thought he'd have enough for an after-dinner drink. Then there was the tip. And the parking fee.

But he didn't have the full thirty-two dollars. He'd loaned five dollars to Tony. And he'd decided to play it safe and fill his gas tank before driving to the city. He'd been too bemused to keep a sharp count. The fact was that he just didn't have enough money to pay for a dinner for two at the Regency Room.

Then the waiter bent over and asked, "Cocktails?"

Susan said, "Some sherry, please."

Mike said . . .

The Helpful Wife

The Problem: How do you get along with people who are impatient with rules and regulations?

Introducing the Problem: Say to your group, "Does it make you uncomfortable to break a rule, even in a very minor way? Are any of you the kind of people who develop intense anxiety over disregarding regulations? If you drop a candy wrapper on the sidewalk, do you look over your shoulder for a cop? This is a story about a woman like that, whose worst fears came true."

Parking downtown was always difficult. Too many people tried to park their cars in too few spaces.

Tom Williams was an impatient and busy man. He didn't drive a car himself; he was so nearsighted that even thick lenses did not make driving any easier for him. His wife drove him on necessary errands.

Whenever they had to go downtown to make a deposit in the bank or cash a check, Tom insisted that his wife park at the curb in front of the bank. She hated to do this. The curb was painted red and had the words *No Parking* painted in emphatic yellow letters on it. She was a timid, middle-aged woman and did not want to have a hassle with a traffic cop and get a ticket. But Tom insisted and she usually complied.

He insisted again today, as they went to the bank, that she park at the curb out in front.

"But, Tom. . ."

"All I have to do is cash this one check. I'll rush in and rush right out. You'll be all right!"

He hurried in. But evidently he had to stand in line in front of the teller's window. Moments passed. Mrs. Williams's nerves grew screamier with every breath. Today she'd get it, she just knew. Today would be just once too often. Sure enough.

"Lady, can't you read?" demanded a stern, official voice, "This is a No Parking zone."

The enormous policeman reached into a pocket for his little book.

She almost choked with panic. Tom would not forgive her if she got a ticket.

"But officer," she blurted, "I'm just waiting here for my husband to come running out of that bank!"

For an instant the officer froze. Then he whirled around, his eyes narrowing, his hand reaching inside his coat, as Tom Williams, indeed, came running out of the bank. . . .

A Good Impression

The Problem: How do you make a favorable impression upon a new boss?

Introducing the Problem: Say to your group, "We all like to impress our employers with our sterling qualities. We all want our boss to know how hard we are trying to do a good job, how talented and industrious and punctual and reliable and conscientious we are. But sometimes such efforts can backfire. This is a story about a person who was too reliable."

As Tony finished breakfast, and grabbed his hat and coat to rush off to work, he suddenly stopped.

"Gosh, I almost forgot!" he blurted. "Linda, you sent my new suit to the cleaners, didn't you?"

"I did. Just as you *insisted*."

"And your white dress?"

"Yes, dear. Why the sudden concern?"

"You haven't forgotten, have you?"

"Forgotten what?"

"Good Lord!—*tonight's the night*."

"For what?"

"Dinner with my boss! At his house. He wants to meet you and he wants us to meet his wife."

"Oh dear. I. . . I guess I did forget. But I'll pick up the clothes and everything'll be ready."

"And get your hair done."

"But that's next week. . ."

"Dent the budget. It's for a good cause. Got to rush!"

That evening, all dressed up, Tony and Linda left their apartment early in order to weave through heavy evening traffic and still get to their destination on time. Tony drove anxiously and murmured with relief as they reached East Glenwood Avenue on schedule.

"Not too early," he said as he parked at the curb, "and not too late."

It wasn't a huge house, but it wasn't small, either. They noted that the driveway was lined with tall, carefully groomed trees. The garage had room for three cars, although only two were parked in it, one being an old Beetle.

"What's he like, your boss?" Linda whispered.

"He's nice. Austere, pipe-smoking type."

"Born rich?"

"Don't know."

"His wife—does she spend the evening giving young wives advice?"

"Here I am a stranger, remember? Let's just be awfully nice."

"And eager and worshipful. . ."

"Look, this guy's my boss and I like my job!"

"Don't worry, dear." She patted his arm reassuringly. "They'll love us."

They reached the front door, and Tony pressed the doorbell button. They waited. Nothing happened. Tony pressed the bell again.

Linda said, "I hear a vacuum sweeper. No, it's just stopped."

They heard footsteps. Then the door opened. A slim woman looked inquiringly at them. She was wearing faded jeans, a man's shirt with the tail hanging out, and a towel wrapped around her hair.

"Good evening," Tony said. "We're Mr. and Mrs. Scott."

A puzzled crease came between the woman's brows.

"Yes?"

"Would you please," Tony said very politely, "tell Mrs. Hamilton that we're here?"

Her puzzled frown deepened.

"I'm Mrs. Hamilton."

"Oh!" Tony gulped, then plunged ahead. "Mr. Hamilton expects us, I believe?"

"I see. He got home just a little while ago." She turned and called into the house, "John! Can you come to the door?"

Linda and Tony looked at each other, the same consternation beginning to build in each of them. And then Mr. Hamilton came striding into the entrance hall. He was in his shirtsleeves, a pipe in his mouth, a newspaper in his hand. He stared in surprise at Tony.

"Oh, hello, Tony! What brings . . ."

And then a look of consternation also came to his face, a look that took on an edge of panic as he turned to his wife.

He and Tony started to speak together.

Tony said . . .

Mr. Hamilton said . . .

Welcome to Our City

The Problem: How do you prevent a slight mistake from becoming a big mistake?

Introducing the Problem: Say to your group, "Have any of you ever, quite innocently, blundered into an awful predicament? This is a story about two people who did just that."

Alice sighed with relief when they turned into the lobby of the big apartment house. Tom had refused to take a cab from the theatre, insisting that it was a lovely night and they should walk. Alice, still humming tunes from *My Fair Lady*, was in such a euphoric mood that she agreed.

"Here we are," he said, "and I found the way back on the first try."

"Don't brag. You were here just five years ago."

"I told you, it's safe to walk the streets. Although," he added, as they crossed the lobby, "it *is* past midnight and we might still be mugged in the elevator. Maybe we better walk up?"

"Ten flights? Oh, no!"

"Then let me look first," he said, making a big show of peering into the cage as the elevator door opened. "Ah! Empty. In we go before any assorted thugs, creeps, finks, and acidheads can pop in after us."

He pressed a button, the door ached shut, and the elevator crept rheumatically upward.

"This 'lift'," Tom said, "lacks ambition. It hates to go up in the world."

"If you were as old. . ."

"And decrepit."

Alice yawned. "Gosh, I'm sleepy. It'll be good to crawl into bed." She started singing softly, "The rain in Spain, falls mainly. . . Say, that was a good revival. Mark Easter's grand as Professor Higgins. Better than Rex Harrison."

"At singing. Not *acting*," Tom objected.

"And so much handsomer."

"Just younger. Us mature types, we like *mature* actors."

The elevator shuddered to a stop. In this elevator, Tom broke his habit of gallantry toward women by striding out the door ahead of Alice and glancing down the hall in both directions.

"No muggers, no ghetto juven-eye-uls, no Mafia hit men. You got Nancy's note on you?"

"Yes, but I memorized it anyway, just in case." She drew a piece of paper from her purse and read, " 'When you come out of the elevator, turn left, go down the corridor to the sixth door. It'll be unlocked. . .' "

"Okay." He took her arm and counted as they walked. "One door. . . two doors. . ."

At the sixth door, he grasped the knob, tried it, turned it, pushed—and the door opened.

"Right on!"

"Shh! It's late. They're probably asleep." She lifted the note and read on: " 'Go straight down the hallway, past the study and bedroom, to the living room. . .' "

"Listen to Matt snore!"

"Shh!"

He hunched his shoulders and exaggerated walking on tiptoe, stage-whispering dolefully: "Professor Thomas James McCrary and his lovely wife Alice were apprehended by municipal police on charges of unlawfully entering the domicile of Mr. and Mrs. Matt Landiss. . ."

"Hush, Tom! Matt works hard and needs his rest."

"Okay, here's the living room. What next?"

Alice read: " 'The sofa in the living room is a comfortable folding bed. It'll be open and made up. Go to bed, sleep tight, and wake up when you smell coffee gurgling and bacon sizzling and popovers popping. Love, Nancy.' "

"Smell *gurgling?*" Tom echoed, shocked. "Smell *popping?*"

"Oh, stop grading papers!—and get undressed."

Tom shucked off his topcoat and jacket. He glanced appreciatively around the large living room.

"The Chez Carlson. As a pad, not bad."

"Awf'ly nice of them to invite us to stay overnight."

"Even if we did twist their arm a little."

"I'm sure we're not the only tourists who call up their friends when they get to New York."

"Besides, the local hotels are veddy greedy."

Tom always undressed so fast, he seemed to shake off his clothes. Used to sleeping bare, he slid under the sheet without pausing to don pajamas. Alice, who was tired, took a little longer. After undressing, she reached into their big tote bag and drew out a nylon shortie.

It was then that the little dog came pattering into the room. It wriggled joyously up to them, its hind quarters wagging a blur of welcome.

Alice saw the dog and froze.

"Tom. I didn't know the Carlsons had a dog?"

"They don't. Matt's allergic."

"They do. Take a look. Here, Poochie!"

The little dog gave a miniature yelp of pleasure. Tom, in the middle of a yawn, choked and sat up.

"What in the. . ."

"Tom!" Alice's low voice suddenly had an edge of hysteria. "I heard a door creak. The *front* door, I think."

Listening rigidly, they heard voices and footsteps—voices and footsteps that grew louder as they neared, coming down the long hallway toward this living room.

It was Alice, as the awful truth came home to her, who gasped, "Oh, no! No!"

"What's wrong?"

"Oh, how awful!"

"Calm down. Maybe the Carlsons have more guests. . ."

"No! Tom—Oh, I can't face them. . ."

"I said what's wrong?"

"Tom, *what floor do the Carlsons live on?*"

"I thought you knew?"

"But I thought you knew!"

Tom gasped, "My God!" as the sheer horror of it all hit him. "Quick, jump into bed!" he hissed. "Pretend you're asleep. Maybe they'll think *they're* in the wrong apartment!"

Still talking, the newcomers opened the door, entered the living room; and then, in harsh abruptness, their footsteps ceased and their voices quit in mid-breath. For one long moment, silence held the room in shock. And then. . .

The Windfall Syndrome

The Problem: How can a fine, conscientious person become an opportunist and still retain her self-respect?

Introducing the Problem: Say to your group, "All of us at times, to some small degree, have been opportunistic and felt pangs of guilt about it. Have you ever had a newspaper thrown by mistake to your front door—and kept it? Have you ever started to use a pay phone and discovered change in the slot? You kept the change because there was no easy way to return it to its owner. Have you ever found a purse with money in it? If you have, you turned it in to the Lost and Found, of course, but didn't you—for just a moment—want to keep it? Here is a story about a very nice, very admirable lady who—through an error—received a windfall, and what she did and didn't do about it."

Abigail Addams had a startling nightmare. It recurred nightly for a week. It did not fade with waking but persisted, and left her racked between euphoria and despair. In substance, the dream went like this: The doorbell rang, and she answered it—to find officers of the law seeking her and serving a warrant for her arrest. The arrest was then reported shockingly in the newspapers. She envisioned the news stories very clearly.

> *Abigail Addams, 45, wife of Thomas L. Addams, principal of Madrona High School, was taken into custody last night. Asked by reporters if she were guilty as charged, she said, "I have done exactly what I'm accused of doing."*
>
> And the social society columnists wrote, *"Prominent civic leader crowns her record of good works by going to prison for theft. Nothing petty, mind you: Grand Larceny."* And: *"The Addams caper is no mere local brouhaha. Washington is involved. The FBI is investigating."*

At this point Abigail would wake up, heart pounding. Her vigorous mind would fight panic with logic and reason, but to little avail.

It should be noted that Abigail Addams is a gentle, loving, sympathetic, honest person. Very honest. And thrifty. And strong-minded. But she has the defect of her virtues.

It had all begun a week before. That previous Wednesday had started out badly. After breakfast, Abigail had had to write a difficult letter to her younger sister who had requested a loan with which to start orthodontia for her daughter. Abigail had been unable to help. She had had to explain that they had two youngsters in college to support, and that her husband had been helping pay to keep his mother in a rest home for the past two years.

The old saw says that troubles all come at once. That same morning Abigail's daughter Lucy had phoned to say that she'd been invited to the junior prom by a fellow she adored and that she simply *had* to have a ravishing new dress! Abigail understood and sympathized, but No. In her mind, too, Abigail was composing a letter to her son Andy. This one also hurt her to write. He had made good enough grades to become eligible for a year overseas at his university's Tokyo campus. But the added expense, Abigail would have to tell him, was beyond their resources.

That same morning, before she started writing her letters, the mail arrived. Among bills and ads was one important communication: a letter from the U.S. Treasury Department. Abigail immediately phoned her husband, not even waiting to open the envelope.

"Tom, the tax refund from the IRS has come."

"High time," he snorted. "You better deposit it right away, just to make sure I don't overdraw the account. It's for the full five hundred and sixty-six dollars, isn't it? Look."

She opened the envelope, took out the stiff check, and said, "Yes, five six six—and. . ."

"Okay. Got a faculty meeting. See you later!"

"Tom, wait. . ."

But he had hung up. She studied the thin cardboard check with its various slots.

"Five hundred sixty—well, it looks like. . ."

She put the check down on the table and stared at it, biting her lip. "Oh, no! It can't be. Well, it looks like. . . Am I going out of my mind?" She stood up, took a turn about the room, came back, and peered at the check again. "Well!" She slapped her hand down on the table, hard. "Now we've got another hang-up. Another long wait and miles of tangled red tape. . ." She laughed, but there was little mirth in her laughter. "Maybe I should be crying. Or *swearing*."

She frowned in intense thought for a minute. She picked up a pencil and doodled figures on a slip of paper. "*I've got to be calm, unemotional, and logical,*" she told herself. "*For the thinking person there's always a solution.*"

She snatched up the telephone and called her husband.

"Tom, I think you'd better come home for lunch."

"Can't. I told you—faculty meeting."

"This is an—emergency."

"Okay. But just give me some idea. . ."

"I don't dare!" she said and hung up to prevent futher debate.

She started to do housework but gave up. She was too excited, too aware of dazzling vistas suddenly opened to her startled view. Impulse ran away with her. She pulled note paper from a slot in her desk and began writing. She wrote her daughter Lucy to go ahead, buy that ravishing dress, and wear it with success! She wrote her son Andy to plan for that year in Tokyo. She wrote her sister that she would send a check shortly for the orthodontia. Finally, she addressed an envelope: *Internal Revenue Service, Washington, D.C.* She wrote a brief note, stuck it inside the envelope, and put a stamp on it. She placed the unsealed envelope inside her purse.

She looked at the clock. Almost noon. Tom would be home soon. She quickly prepared soup and a sandwich for him.

He came storming in just as she finished. A big man, he made the floor quake with the force of his stride.

"Abby, where's that refund check? It was for the full five hundred and sixty-six, wasn't it? They didn't reduce it?"

"No, darling. You have no grounds for complaint."

He peered at her. "You know, Abby, you look—pleasantly stunned."

"You," she said, "are a discerning man."

"Deposit that refund check right after lunch. I've written checks for pressing bills."

"Don't worry. There'll be enough money in the bank."

"Abigail, why did you make me rush home for lunch? What's the emergency?"

"I've always wondered," she said dreamily, "how it would feel to be struck by lightning. Now I know."

"What are you talking about?"

"You know how everything marvelous and miraculous always happens to somebody else? Well, it finally happened to us."

"A tax refund—miraculous? Really!"

"Tom, dear, we are through the tunnel. Over the hump."

"Abby, dear, when you start digging up dead metaphors, you just plain scare the hell out of me. What's wrong?"

"You haven't asked to see your tax refund."

"Okay, I ask. Where's that refund check?"

"Since you ask so nicely, dear, here it is. Look upon it."

"And weep?" He looked at the check. He blinked, he frowned, he held it closer to his eyes. "Something's wrong," he whispered.

"Not necessarily."

"Something's very—very. . . Oh, my God!" He collapsed upon the sofa.

Abigail said, "It's like being hit on the head with a gold mine, isn't it?"

"Somebody's made a mistake—a helluva mistake!"

"Oh, just a misplaced decimal point."

"What'll we do, Abby? My God, we can't just. . ."

"How much is it for, if you can read that lofty language?"

"I can't believe it!"

"My own first reaction," Abigail said.

"There has to be some simple explanation."

"Why fight it? We're rich. We're wealthy. We're. . . You know, I never in my whole life expected to be this close to. . . to Beverley Hills and Biarritz and Eden Roc and Princess Grace, and. . . well, rich enough to buy anything, without asking the price. Go on. Read it. Read it out loud. Maybe it'll sound different from what it looks."

Tom slowly read aloud from the check, "Five million, six hundred sixty-six thousand, six hundred and sixty-six dollars. . ."

"And sixty-six cents," Abigail added. "Out loud, it sounds twice as rich."

"It's a mistake. It's a crazy mistake."

"Don't carry on so. It's only money. Scads and scads of money."

"It's an error, that's all. It's a computer error!"

"Of course. But such a lovely error."

"Damn!"

"The question is, Tom. . . Are you listening?"

"I feel sick at the stomach. . ."

"I know. But help me. What do we *do* with this—windfall?"

Discussion: At this point, the reading can stop. The role-playing leader can direct the group to go into a discussion of the situation.

Role Playing: If the discussion reveals varying points of view on the problem, the leader can ask for volunteers to play the various roles and start them role-playing a solution to the problem and the possible consequences of that solution. If the discussion does not lead to role playing, or if the group is curious as to what happens next, the leader can continue to read the story.

Tom caught a long, shaky breath. He shrugged helplessly. "Abby, you've got to send that check back."

"Yes."

"I mean it!"

"Of course, dear. Don't shout."

"*Today.*"

"Right away," Abigail agreed. "This very afternoon."

Tom rubbed his sweating face. "When you told me over the phone that the tax refund had come, I wrote a check for the insurance and a check for the installment on the new roof. . ."

"Yesterday I wrote a check for the Fuller Brush man."

"Lord, we'll have so many checks bouncing they'll register 7.5 on the Richter scale!"

"Eat your lunch now."

"I'm numb. Right now, Cherries Jubilee would taste like potatoes."

Tom ate and sleep-walked back to his job. Abigail dressed herself impeccably in her best suit, then went to the bank.

At the counter, she carefully made out a deposit slip for $5,666,666.66. Then she endorsed the government check. For a long, breath-choked moment, she looked at the check. She had never seen such a big check in her life before; she would never see another. She sighed and then walked briskly to a teller's window.

The teller smiled hello as Abigail presented her passbook and the deposit slip and the check. The teller opened the passbook and picked up a pen to write the sum inside. He looked at the deposit slip, he blinked, then he looked at the check. His eyes widened and his jaw dropped and color faded from his fleshy cheeks.

"B-but Mrs. Addams. . ."

"Yes?"

The man swallowed hard.

"This . . . is a big check."

"Standard size, I think."

"I m-mean, the amount. . ."

"Oh, that."

He turned the check over, studied the back, then reexamined the front, stalling for time and words.

Abigail said tartly, "Would you prefer that I deposit my money elsewhere?"

"Oh, no, no! But. . . Please, let me take you to our Mr. Barclay."

He came from behind his cage and led her to the office of one of the bank officials, laid the papers before him, and quickly briefed him in agitated whispers.

Abigail said, "Please, Mr. Barclay, is there a problem?"

Mr. Barclay—a small, pepper-and-saltish man—tried to assume a judicious mien. He made a steeple out of his fingers that shook slightly. He spoke very carefully, "Mrs. Addams, h-how did you get this check?"

"Exactly the way we've always gotten tax refunds from the Internal Revenue Service: delivered by the United States mail."

Mr. Barclay turned a little green about the gills.

"This is just a *tax refund?*"

"Right."

"Good Lord! How large were your taxes?"

"That's a private matter, I believe, but I don't mind telling you. We paid $6,457 in federal income taxes."

"*And you got over five million in a refund?*"

"Mr. Barclay, you are shouting at me."

"Oh, s-sorry, sorry! But. . ."

"Mr. Barclay, this is a perfectly genuine check from the Treasury Department. Don't you recognize it as such?"

"Oh, yes, yes indeed, it's just that. . ."

"And it *is* a tax refund."

"But possibly. . ."

"An overpayment, yes."

Mr. Barclay's relief was vivid. He nodded very soberly. "Perhaps," he suggested, "a. . . a *large* overpayment?"

"Right."

"Even a. . . preposterously large overpayment?"

"Mr. Barclay, come right out and say it. The amount on this check is a computer error."

"Exactly!" Mr. Barclay's relief was now ecstatic.

"But it's not all error!"

"Oh?"

"What I mean is, part of this money is rightfully and legitimately ours. We've been waiting months and months for this refund, and I don't intend to wait another crawling eternity!"

"Mrs. Addams, please. I urge you to send this money back."

"That's exactly my intention."

"Good!" He slapped palm to desk with satisfaction.

"All except the five hundred sixty-six dollars and sixty-six cents that belongs to me."

He frowned. "I don't follow."

"This is a perfectly good government check, isn't it?"

"Yes."

"You really *don't* think I counterfeited it?"

"Of course you didn't!"

"Then there is absolutely no reason why I can't deposit it in any bank that I wish, is there?"

"No, I suppose not. But you said. . ."

"Here. Watch."

She leaned over his desk, opened her own check book, and carefully wrote out a check—payable to the Internal Revenue Service—for five million, six hundred and sixty-six thousand, one hundred dollars.

"But that's not the whole amount," Mr. Barclay objected.

"It's the whole amount less my tax refund, which is rightly and legitimately mine!"

She drew the stamped, addressed envelope from her purse and showed Mr. Barclay that it was addressed to the Internal Revenue Service. She showed him the explanatory note she had written. She placed both her note and her personal check inside the envelope and sealed it.

"And you can drop this into the mail box yourself, if you wish," she said. "Okay?"

Mr. Barclay nodded in reluctant acceptance.

"Even so, I'd prefer that you'd just send the government check back," he said.

"But I told you. I need my tax refund. Now do I go to another bank with this deposit?"

He stood up decisively, handed the check and deposit slip to the teller, nodded, and said, "Business as usual, Walter. Mrs. Addams. . ."

"Yes?"

"This won't happen again, I trust?"

"Never!"

That night she told Tom what she had done. He just grunted unhappily. Later, in bed, she lay sleepless with euphoria. "This was Thursday," she told herself. "By Monday. . ."

On Monday, she wrote a note to her son Andy: "I'm enclosing a check for $1,500. This will pay those extra costs for your year on the Tokyo campus. Just don't buy any geisha girls!" Tuesday, she sent a check to her sister to start the orthodontia. Wednesday, she sent a check to her own daughter, Lucy, to buy the prom dress. Thursday, she went to a travel agency, and paid—by check—for a two weeks' vacation in Hawaii for herself and Tom. That would be a birthday surprise for her husband.

Friday, she reined in her grandiose impulses. But on Monday again, she soared on the wings of euphoria: Wilson's posh department store was having a sale on their twenty-four-dollar-a-yard carpeting. She contracted to have the living room, dining room, hallway, and master bedroom recarpeted. And she paid in advance—by check—and thereby pried loose an additional discount.

That evening, Lucy came home from school across town for dinner. And that night, during dinner, the doorbell rang in two sharp, peremptory bursts.

"I'll go," Abigail said. But as she pushed back her chair, she felt suddenly giddy and faint, as if she were having a premonition.

She opened the front door. Two men and a woman stood there, all very official of demeanor, all grim-faced.

"Mrs. Abigail Addams?" one asked.

"Yes?"

"I'm Special Agent Monahan, Federal Bureau of Investigation." He held out an open leather folder, revealing a badge. "This is United States Marshall Gohegan, and Mrs. Loran of the Internal Revenue Service. May we. . ."

Somehow, in spite of her tight throat, Abigail managed to say, "Come in, please. I g-guess I've sort of been expecting you."

They followed her into the living room. Lucy and Tom left the table and came in, looking puzzled. She made introductions.

Tom asked, "What can we do for you?"

Agent Monahan, Marshall Gohegan, and Mrs. Loran all faced Abigail. Abby fought back a hysterical giggle as she had the sudden wild urge to ask them to omit the blindfold and to give her a last cigarette. She would die gamely. Instead, she said, "All right, what can *I* do for you?"

Discussion:

Role Playing:

Special Agent Monahan said, "Last week, Mrs. Addams, you received a check from the Treasury Department."

Abigail nodded, "We did. A tax refund."

"Mrs. Addams!" The IRS representative was obviously making a great effort to be calm and reasonable. "You do have a refund coming to you. For five hundred and sixty-six dollars and sixty-six cents. But that Treasury check was for almost six million dollars!"

"Not quite," said Abby.

"Mrs. Addams, that check was a mistake."

"*What else?*" Abigail thought; and some imp of perversity made her say: "One of the most important lessons my father taught me was to take responsibility for my mistakes."

This playing with fire was more than Tom could take. In his most reasonable manner, he said, "Mrs. Loran, we understood at once that the sum of that check was a computer error."

"Then why didn't you return the check?"

"Oh, but I did return the money," Abigail said.

"We haven't received it."

Tom turned to Abigail, his face suddenly troubled. "Abby?"

"I did return the government's money."

"But I tell you," Mrs. Loran insisted, "that the check has not been returned!"

"I didn't send that check back. I sent my own personal check," Abigail said quietly.

"Your *what?*" Mrs. Loran gasped.

Tom, equally stricken, blurted, "You wrote your own check for over *five million. . .*"

"I deposited the government check in our bank. I wrote a new check, which I mailed to Washington."

All three officials chorused, "Why?"

"Because I retained the amount of money due us as a tax refund: five hundred and sixty-six dollars and sixty-six cents. That's why."

"And the rest?"

"I'll repeat: I sent back my check for five million, six-hundred sixty-six thousand, one hundred dollars."

Special Agent Monahan said, "Madam, we have only your word."

"I can show you my check stub."

Tom groaned. The IRS person sighed in defeat over the firmness of Abigail's innocence, then asked, "When did you mail your check?"

"Last Thursday, a week."

The IRS person caught a shaky breath. "Mrs. Addams, it is my duty to inform you that if your check does not reach our home office on schedule. . ."

"*What* schedule? We're talking about the United States mail!"

"I will come back with a warrant for your arrest on charges of grand

theft. The penalty, Mrs. Addams, can be a long term in a federal penitentiary. You understand?"

Tom blurted in outrage, "Mrs. Loran, idle threats are unnecessary!
You have my wife's word."

"Mr. Addams," Mrs. Loran snapped, drawing a paper from her purse,
"I make no idle threats. Here is a list of your wife's recent . . . activities."

"Activities!"

"Mr. Addams, we have learned in our investigations that you are hard
up for money. And yet, last week, your wife contracted to have this house
recarpeted, wall to wall, and paid in advance. By check. Also, she went to a
travel agency and paid for a two weeks' Hawaii vacation—*for two*—paid in
advance, by check."

"But she couldn't have!" Tom gasped. "We haven't got the money!"

"And further investigation," Mrs. Loran continued sternly, "I'm sure
will reveal still other expenditures of money you haven't got. Mrs. Addams,"
she looked sternly at Abigail, "conviction will mean a long, long term."

Without further ado, Mrs. Loran and the two federal men turned and
left. When the door closed behind them, Tom turned on Abigail.

"For Heaven's sake, Abby, *what is this all about?*"

And Lucy demanded, "Mother, you sent me a check, too. Have you
been spending the government's money?"

"Certainly not," Abigail said.

"Abby, you did send that money back to Washington?" Tom demanded. *"Didn't* you?"

"I certainly did. Just as I told you I would."

"Then how could you write checks for so much money?"

"It's very simple," Abigail said serenely.

"Then *tell* us!"

"Remember, I sent a check back to the Treasury Department for every
dollar above the five hundred and sixty-six they owed us?"

"So?"

"I mailed that check on a Thursday. First-class mail. When it got to
Washington, I don't know. But bear in mind that last weekend was a three-
day holiday, so no mail was delivered until Tuesday. When my check
arrived, I don't know. But I'm sure it went into the proper channels. It was a
personal check, remember. For a large sum, sure. But the government deals
routinely with lots of large checks. So it went along to the Treasury Department, was shuffled off to be recorded somewhere, went to a clearing house,
and will eventually get back to our own bank here to be paid."

"But Mrs. Loran said her office had no record of it?"

"Maybe it wasn't recorded until today. I suspect when she calls back
tomorrow, she'll learn it has been received. But meanwhile. . ."

"Meanwhile what?"

"That check is in banking channels, being stamped and photostated
and what not, being shuffled along with a dozen million other checks.
Eventually it'll be in the United States mails again. Maybe it's there now. But
it will finally get back to our own bank. But until it does, we're. . ."

"We're what?"

"Until that check's finally cashed—oh, don't you see?"

"We're *what*?" Tom repeated, through gritted teeth.

"We're rich."

They stared at her. Lucy gasped, "Mother, are you out of your mind?" And Tom groaned, "Oh, Abby!"

Abigail smiled, "Relatively speaking, of course. Let's say, we're *slightly* rich. You see, every day until that check is cashed, our balance in the bank increases by about eight hundred dollars."

"How?" Lucy demanded.

Tom said despairingly, "She's talking about the interest."

"Of course, dear. Five percent interest compounded daily on five million, six hundred sixty-six thousand. . ."

"But it's a checking account, Mother, and banks don't pay interest. . ."

"Lucy, you remember how mad I was when your father insisted that we move our account from the old bank near here to the one downtown? Because the new bank pays interest on checking accounts."

"Oh!" Lucy said, her face lighting up. "So you're getting interest."

"Five percent, compounded daily," Abigail said. "Tom, don't you *see*? I put the money where it's earning big daily interest for us—and it's that interest that I've been spending!"

Lucy blurted, "So the principal isn't touched at all!"

"Exactly."

Lucy laughed in utter delight and relief. "Mother, you're a genius!"

But Tom was shaking his head in utter despair. "Abby, Abby, what shall I *do* about you?"

"But, Dad, Mother hasn't. . ."

"Genius, you call her. What she's done is. . . Oh, hell, let's call it what it is: just plain larceny."

"But, Tom, I've returned the government's money."

"You've *used* the government's money. It's the government's five million that's earned all the interest you're spending. Not our money. Abigail, you're a crook."

Abigail's face whitened. She looked from her daughter to her husband. "Genius, Lucy says. Crook, you say. So what *am* I? And what," Abigail begged, "do I do now?"

Discussion: What is Abigail? Resourceful?—in a small way. A crook?—in spite of herself?

Role Playing: Selected or volunteer actors role-play a solution to the problem. . . and extrapolate the consequences.

DILEMMAS OF TACT

Humorous dilemmas can serve as a pleasant introduction to the role-playing process. It is important, however, after experience with less critical issues, to turn to more serious concerns. The purpose of these exercises in decision making is, after all, problem solving. The next group of stories could be called "Dilemmas of Tact." Following them is the story "Paper Drive" which has often been used in teacher education classes because it has proved to be very effective. Following "Paper Drive" are a number of very short capsule situations that involve both teaching and social problems.

The Mess

The Problem: The issue is tact—that is, sensitivity to other people's feelings, particularly their needs for a sense of personal dignity and self-esteem.

Due to a minor accident in a classroom, a potted plant has fallen on the floor, and the mess has to be cleaned up immediately. The teacher and two aides are preparing the room for a tour of visiting parents. The visitors are due any moment. The teacher's impulse is to delegate the clean-up task to one of her helpers while she greets the principal and visitors. But one of her helpers is a black woman who works very hard at a menial job and is now trying to improve her life situation by training to become a teacher. The other aide is a stately white-haired woman, the wife of a prominent doctor, who is a volunteer. Whom should the teacher ask to clean up the mess? If she delegates the job to the black woman, will she be reminding the woman of her past menial status? If she asks the white woman to do it, will she be offending a prominent member of the parents' group?

Introducing the Problem: Ask your group, "Have you ever, while shopping in a store, been mistaken for a clerk and been asked to show some merchandise? Have you ever, while gardening in your backyard, stopped to answer the doorbell and been asked by a stranger (as if you were a servant) if the lady of the house was in? How did that make you feel? If you were at a party, how would you feel if someone asked you to get a towel and wipe up the mess from a fallen dish? The following story involves people's sense of dignity."

You are a classroom teacher. With the help of a teacher aide, Mrs. Ady Gorman, and a parent, Mrs. Whitney, you are busy preparing your classroom for a parents' night event. You expect fifty-odd parents to troop through the room and look at exhibits of their children's work that you three women are now placing on stands and hanging on the walls. You are all working frantically to finish arrangements, because it is almost 7 P.M. and people are already starting to arrive at the school. You are especially tense because you're new here and have prepared a little speech of welcome that you haven't yet had time to memorize as well as you wanted.

Your two helpers are very willing, but you have to direct them where to hang drawings, on which cupboards and stands to place the last exhibits. Ady Gorman, your teacher aide, is a black woman of thirty-six, an earnest, very independent mother of twins. She is a widow; she works hard as a cook to support herself and her children. But she's ambitious to become a teacher. After attending a workshop, she has been assigned to you as an aide. Your other helper, Mrs. Whitney, is a woman of fifty who lives in the neighborhood. She was a teacher until she married a doctor. Now she plans to run for the school board and is helping you as an aide in order to refresh her knowledge of classrooms. It is obvious, from her smart clothes, that her husband is prominent and successful.

From down the hall, you hear your principal's voice. He's taking the first arrivals for a tour of the building. They'll be at your doorway in a moment.

It is, of course, at just such times that the unexpected little crises occur—and balloon into big ones. You have been planning to replace the fraying rope that holds a potted plant near the window by the desk, but just haven't gotten around to it. Now, when the wind blows a door shut down the hall, the tremor is enough to break the last filaments of rope holding the plant, and the pot crashes to the floor, creating a moist, muddy mess of clay shards and spilled dirt and leaving the plant a pitiful huddle of green in the wreckage.

Ady Gorman utters a startled gasp. Mrs. Whitney murmurs an "Oh dear!" of despair. You swallow hard; and you think, "Somebody's got to get a broom and dust pan and paper towels and clean up that mess! People coming in will step in it. . ."

You're wearing your best shirtmaker dress. You can ask Mrs. Gorman to clean it up, or you can ask Mrs. Whitney, only she's dressed so smartly. . . . But already people are at the door.

"Mrs. Phillips!"

Your principal, in the doorway, is beckoning to you. He has several of your pupils' parents in tow. You turn to your two helpers. You say:

Listen, Doctor

The Problem: Most people become defensive and angry when blamed for making a mistake. They feel threatened and belittled. For an employee to correct a self-important boss requires an especially acute sense of tact and propriety. To correct someone in a way he or she can accept demands empathy and skill.

Introducing the Problem: You might say to your group, "Have you ever been caught making a mistake and been corrected in public? Like saying, 'Between you and I,' and someone pipes up, 'Me, *me, me!*' Does your face turn a burning red? Do you feel resentful? Furious?

"Suppose you're at the other end of the transaction. You hear someone making a honey of a mistake. One that can have serious consequences. And the mistake is being made right in front of the people who'll suffer the consequences. Suppose it's your employer who's making the mistake. You can correct him. You should correct him. But, if you do, you'll be in trouble, later. This is a story about such a problem."

You are an office nurse. You have just recently started working for Dr. Morrow. You respect him, although you don't like him, yet. You think that he is a very able family doctor, but you find him a bit aloof and demanding. With patients, however, he is warm and understanding. You wonder if he hasn't deliberately cultivated that very good bedside manner; if so, he's been successful. He charms patients, he instills deep confidence, and that's basic to good therapy. In all, you like your job—and that's fortunate because you need your job.

But this morning you face a crisis.

Dr. Morrow always walks to the door with his patients. He is coming from his office now, and you hear him saying heartily to Mr. and Mrs. Coughlin, "I won't keep you longer. Don't want you to miss that plane. Getting reservations is tough this summer."

"Especially to Honolulu," Mrs. Coughlin says. "I wrote four letters while I waited on the telephone to get through to the airline."

You like the young Coughlins. She's a kindergarten teacher, and he's an artist just beginning to make a name for himself. He has severe allergies and asthma.

Dr. Morrow says, "I'm so glad you're leaving this Los Angeles smog for the summer. Hawaii is a happy choice. I've never been there, but I hear that the trade winds blow so strong all the time that smog can't build up. It gets pushed out to sea so fast that the air remains pure. Your asthma will clear up. You'll be comfortable, and you'll get a lot of work done."

You almost gasp in shock as you hear this. Mr. Coughlin will *not* be able to breathe better in Hawaii. You know. You've been there. What Dr. Morrow says is true: The constant trade winds do blow the auto exhaust smog away from the island. But the air is not pure and clear: For the same trade winds blow so much pollen from the mountain slopes overgrown with flowering shrubs that Honolulu is one of the worst places in the world for asthmatics—at least, for those asthmatics affected by pollens. For Mr. Coughlin to go there now, when he's been so sick with asthma, may be a very serious mistake. . . unless, of course, he's not affected by pollens. But if he is. . .

Your impulse is to blurt all this out to the Coughlins and Dr. Morrow. But you hesitate. *Should* you? Should you, an office nurse, correct a doctor? In front of his patients? You like your job. You need your job. But if Mr. Coughlin reacts to pollens. . .

You say:

Advice and Dissent

The Problem: Giving people advice is a thankless—and sometimes risky—thing to do. All too often individuals don't want advice but approval for what they already plan to do. If you do give advice, and it's followed but proves incorrect, you get blamed. If you give advice and it proves correct but *wasn't* followed, then the other person is chagrined and resents you. He blames you for not convincing him that he should have followed your advice. Knowing all this, there are times when you are asked for advice and you don't want to give it. You know you can't win. But what do you do?

Introducing the Problem: You might say to your group, "Sometimes you find yourself in a spot like this: Your best friend introduces you to his new girlfriend (or, if you're both girls, to her new boyfriend). Your friend is obviously smitten with his (or her) date. Later, he asks you what you think of his new girlfriend (or she asks what you think of her new boyfriend). Suppose you think that the person is a walking disaster? Can you speak honestly to your friend? You hate to hurt his (or her) feelings. But you hate to lie, too. What can you say?

"Suppose you have a job you like and want to keep. Then your boss asks you for advice on something you have lots of doubts about but which he is sold on. He wants your opinion. Maybe you think what he wants to do is crazy. But maybe you're wrong. This is a story about such a situation."

You are Jim Martin, vice-principal of Hartson Elementary School in a suburb of Los Angeles, a job to which you've just been promoted. It is a week before school is to open in September, and you've come to the office for a planning session with your principal, Mrs. Williams. She's in her middle thirties, just back from getting a doctorate at a midwest university. She's new to the school. From previous meetings with her, you realize she's determined to make the central administration discover how able she is.

"Jim," Mrs. Williams says to you, "I've been thinking we might make a try at team teaching this semester. On a strictly experimental basis, of course. We'll put just two class groups together and see how it works. What do you think?"

You ponder a moment. "Team teaching has been strongly criticized. . ."

"In some quarters. Some bad mistakes have been made. It's not necessarily wrong. It can have real advantages. I'd like to select a pair of teachers who can work together in harmony and can complement each other's strengths. Such an arrangement could enrich classroom experiences for the children, don't you think?"

"Yes, but—I mean, there are other aspects. . ."

"You've taught here for years. I'm new here. I don't know my teachers. You know them well. Which two—or even three—of them do you think would make an ideal team?"

"I'm. . . Well, I'm not really convinced that team teaching works."

"That's a common opinion, and it's one reason I want to try it. I want to demonstrate that, if the team is properly selected, and properly guided by those responsible, team teaching *can* work! Which teachers in this school do you think would make a successful team?"

"But they might—prefer to keep their individual classrooms."

"Naturally, we don't want anyone on the team who feels strongly about keeping her own classroom. But I'm sure that if we ask for cooperation in the proper spirit, it would not be refused. So who would you recommend that we ask to take on this project? Miss Harris, for one?"

You tense up. You're on the spot. Your principal is asking you for your advice. You've already intimated that you question the wisdom of team teaching in this school. She hasn't listened. So you realize that her mind's made up. She's going to make a big thing of this project for the superintendent's office. You realize that if you suggest two teachers for the team, and she takes your advice and the project *fails*, she'll blame you. On the other hand, if she does not take your advice, but chooses other teachers and the project fails, she'll feel that you were right and she was wrong. And she'll be constrained with you and resent you. She'll try to hide her feelings, but either way you will be a source of chagrin to her. Of course, the project might succeed. But you've intimated you doubt it. And if it succeeds, she'll figure you just don't have a big enough vision to be her right-hand person in this school.

"Jim, what do you think? Miss Harris? And who'd make a good teammate for her?"

You say:

A SERIOUS DILEMMA

Paper Drive

The Problem: This story deals with problems of honesty—specifically, with the rationalization that if your opponent is dishonest, you are justified in being dishonest too. (This story is best used in fifth, sixth, and seventh grades.)

Introducing the Problem: Say to the group, "Have you ever been in a game or a contest which you wanted to win very much and discovered that the other side was cheating? Were you tempted to cheat too, then? This is a story about such a situation."

Miss Hendry's sixth-grade students were eager to win the annual Paper Drive. The classroom bringing in the most paper during the week of the contest was to be given a picnic at the Pink Horse Ranch. Hot dogs and ice cream would be free. Swimming and movies, and rides on the roller coaster and boats and ponies, too, would be free. At the start of the contest, Miss Hendry did not believe that her group had a chance to win. But each day, after school, her students busily gathered paper and tied it into compact bundles and delivered it to the big trailer waiting at the rear of the school yard. As the end of the week drew near, excitement in the classroom rose to fever pitch.

Friday morning, she had to remind the group, "You're still in school, children. Please pay attention."

"We're going to win, Miss Hendry!"

"That's fine, but meanwhile, let's get some classwork done."

"We're too excited!"

"Just calm down."

They did—a little. But this was the last day of the contest, so she was patient. At 3:30, the children rushed out, and she remained behind to work late.

She was at the back of the classroom, an hour later, when through the slats of the venetian blinds she saw three of her students bringing a heavy bale of paper to the school yard. The awkward bale was resting on a small coaster wagon they were pulling up the alley behind the school. As she watched, the wagon overturned, and the bale fell off. The cord tying it broke, and the paper came loose in a mess on the pavement. Hastily the youngsters gathered up the paper into a clumsy package again and retied it. But not before Miss Hendry, to her amazement and dismay, discovered the awful truth.

Wrapped in folds of the newspapers—which had momentarily opened to reveal their contents—were pieces of rusty iron junk. Her students were hiding heavy pieces of old iron, probably gathered from junk heaps, within the bales of paper. *To increase their weight!* So that they would deliver the heaviest amount of paper and win the contest.

She opened the window and called to them, "Andy! Sue! You and Pete come in here at once."

They came in. They flushed uneasily as they stood before her.

"You have pieces of heavy junk hidden in those bundles of paper, haven't you?"

Andy nodded. He stared at the floor, not meeting her stern glance.

"To make your bundles heavy?"

Andy nodded again.

"Have you been doing this all week?"

"Just since Wednesday."

"You three only, or has the whole class been doing it?"

"The whole class," Sue said.

Miss Hendry sighed in despair. "Don't deliver that bundle to the truck," she ordered. "Take it—some place and hide it!"

They scuttled out as if released from jail.

Miss Hendry sat down at her desk and took thought. What should she do? She hated to expose her students. Her own face began to burn with shame and regret. What would the parents think of her as a teacher when word got out that her group had been cheating in an effort to win the paper drive? If her class had not profited by this cheating, she decided that she would not expose them; instead, she would preach them a very hot sermon Monday morning on honesty. . . .

After dinner that evening, she heard local news on the radio—and learned the outcome of the paper drive. It was good news, but it left her miserable with worry.

"The sixth-grade class of Glenwood Elementary School, taught by Miss Belle Hendry," said the announcer, "has won the annual paper drive sponsored by the Junior Chamber of Commerce. The class will be given a rousing big picnic at Pink Horse Ranch as a reward. In addition, a surprise dividend for the group will be a big turkey dinner, a ball glove for each boy, and a school ring for each girl.

"Runner-up in the contest was the sixth-grade class at Wilson Elementary School, which was a close sixty-seven pounds behind in the weight of paper gathered. . . ."

Miss Hendry felt sick at heart. Her group had won—by cheating. They did not deserve this victory.

What she felt must have been plain on her face when she met her class on Monday morning. The group became very quiet and tense.

"Well," she said slowly, "you won the paper drive. But you won it in a way that makes me deeply ashamed. Some of you packed pieces of iron junk in the bales of paper you brought to the truck." She paused. Nobody in the group gasped in surprise; evidently *all* knew and *all* were involved in the cheating. "You are going to write a letter, as a class, to the Junior Chamber of Commerce. You will apologize for having won the drive unfairly. You will say that the real winner is the sixth-grade class at Wilson School. Do you understand me?"

"But Miss Hendry," Sam Martin protested, "we cheated because the Wilson sixth grade was cheating."

"Oh, no!"

"Yes! Those Wilson boys were spraying garden hoses on their bales of paper. Making them wet so they'd weigh heavy. Then letting them stand in the sun so the outside would dry, and then wrapping dry paper around them. That's why we packed junk in our bales!"

"Is this *true*?"

"Yes, it is!"

"Did any of you actually see this being done?"

No one answered immediately.

"We *heard*—"

"My brother heard them talking about it," Sue Nolan said.

"But even if they *were* cheating," Miss Hendry went on, "do you think that made it right for *you* to cheat?"

"But, gosh, Miss Hendry, we didn't want them to win!" Sue blurted.

"If you make us withdraw from the paper drive, the Wilson sixth grade ought to withdraw, too!"

"But I can't go to their teacher and tell her that her class was cheating," Miss Hendry said firmly. "I have no proof. I'd just be repeating gossip and rumor. That other teacher would be justified in telling me that I'm a bad loser, and to mind my own business."

"But if you make us confess that we've cheated," Andy said, "you'll be helping that other class to win by cheating!"

"But I can't overlook your dishonesty and let *you* win by cheating," she said.

"You mean," Andy protested, "that you'll let *them* win by cheating?"

She started to answer—and could not; indecision held her silent. If she said nothing, she would be helping her students to profit from dishonest conduct. But if she made them confess their cheating, she would be helping the other group to win by dishonesty. What should she do?

DILEMMA EXERCISES FOR TEACHERS

These capsule dilemmas can provide role-playing material for teachers in training. They can also serve as models and examples of dilemma situations that the group can contribute to the class.

"The Mimic."   A substitute teacher has come to take over a class. As she speaks to the group, a boy in the back of the room mimics her. The children

around him are paying attention to him instead of the teacher and are convulsed with suppressed laughter.

She can ignore him; she can reprimand him; she can send him from the room; she can use other methods to discipline him and gain the full attention of the class.

"The Trick."   A substitute teacher has been told that a certain boy is a troublemaker. He is not to be allowed to leave the room. She has been warned that he is very tricky and always uses sly devices. Now he insists he must go to the lavatory. Should she let him, knowing that it may be a trick?

"Language, Language!"   A substitute teacher is new to a class of well-to-do suburban children. She announces an assignment. One boy utters an "Oy vey!" and another boy exclaims "Oh, shit!" What should she do? Ignore them? Call them to task?

"Outside Authority."   Two boys in a ghetto school are very disturbed when they come to class. The teacher asks them to settle down. They say they don't have to. She asks what's troubling them. They tell her that a policeman stopped them, questioned them, made them move on. And they weren't doing anything!

Should she ignore the incident? Should she try to argue the boys into a more reasonable attitude toward policemen, despite the fact that she is dealing with children who look upon policemen as enemies and always speak bitterly of them?

"Whose Word Can You Take?"   On the playground, a small child is crying. You ask the child why. He tells you that two boys have hijacked him and taken his lunch money and bus fare. He points to the two boys. They deny it hotly, claiming they have just arrived on the school grounds. The teacher doesn't know them and doesn't know whether they are telling the truth or lying.

11

Role Playing
in the Preservice
and Inservice Training
of Teachers

Role playing is uniquely suited for use both in the preservice preparation of teachers and in the continuing professional education of experienced teachers. It provides a way of simulating classroom situations, teacher-parent encounters, and other school relationships. Educators know that there is no substitute for actual experience, and for this reason include student teaching and internships in preservice programs. Most teacher education programs, however, have not been able to provide trainees with enough direct classroom experience. They are usually too brief and often occur under less than optimal conditions.

Numerous reports recount the effectiveness of role playing in helping prepare future teachers for their various roles and responsibilities. By using role playing to simulate many classroom situations, problems, and encounters, instructors of future teachers can help their students translate theory into action. Such role playing enables students to test both their understanding of theories and methods and the complexities of applying them to real situations.

In a manual for training teachers in the biological sciences, David L. Lehman describes in some detail how he used role playing to develop certain skills and personality traits in teachers.[1] After discussing the basic techniques, he presents many sample situations that show how role playing can be used in the biology teaching laboratory. He includes typical situations

[1]David L. Lehman, *Role Playing and Teacher Education: A Manual for Developing Innovative Teachers* (Washington, D.C.: Commission on Undergraduate Education in the Biological Sciences, 1971). Published by The American Institute of Biological Sciences, 3900 Wisconsin Ave., N.W., Washington, D.C. Supported by a grant from the National Science Foundations. Library of Congress Catalogue no. 76–145578.

such as student-teacher interviews, teacher-parent phone calls, and student-teacher-parent conferences. He discusses how to handle bored and unmotivated students and describes inservice workshops and school board meetings.

Leonard S. Kenworthy describes his experiences in using role playing in the preservice and inservice preparation of social studies teachers.[2] He emphasizes the many values of role playing as a training technique. He points out that while students are often very adept at verbalizing what they have read about role playing, they assimilate such material best after repeated experience with role playing. Role playing gives them insight into the many behavior patterns they will find in a typical classroom. Many prospective teachers and inservice teachers also gain a better understanding of themselves through role playing and the analyses that follow in class or private conferences. Kenworthy notes how students become more secure regardless of whether their first role playing succeeds or fails—that is, whether the first attempt hits the mark or has to be reenacted and discussed by peers. Role playing is also an excellent method for helping experienced but overly directive teachers become facilitators of learning and observers of behavior. Kenworthy presents many other valuable suggestions for using role playing as a general teacher-education procedure.

In their own experiences with preparing elementary teachers and in field work with experienced teachers, the authors have found that role playing provides reality practice in many dimensions of teaching. First is the problem of classroom management and discipline, a subject of special concern to teachers, particularly novices. Role-playing techniques can help teachers explore such fundamental problems as organizing group work and then dealing afterward with other problems such as disruptive students, classroom fights, and aimless behavior in activity periods. Second, role playing is very useful in simulating methods of teaching various subjects. Such role-playing sessions help teachers appreciate the value of planning, clarifying their goals, and perfecting their class presentations.

As we have mentioned, organizing group work is a major problem for both experienced teachers and novices. Role-playing procedures can be used to explore certain problem behaviors that frequently occur in small groups. Teachers can learn to cope with the class clown, the domineering student, the procrastinator, and the passive student by assuming these roles themselves. In the teacher education laboratory, the author found that group work among teachers themselves often tends to break down after the third week. By means of brief role-playing sessions, the author explored some possible underlying reasons for difficulties in group work. They then presented ways in which the student-teachers could make positive contributions to the group. This effort not only helped the future teachers become productive members of groups, but also taught them some basic techniques to use in their own classrooms.

Student teachers—and even experienced teachers—often need guidance in handling relationships with parents, administrators, and other

---

[2]Leonard S. Kenworthy, "Role Playing in Teacher Education," *The Social Studies*, 64, no. 6 (November 1973), 243–46.

teachers. Role-playing techniques can realistically simulate situations such as employment interviews, faculty conferences, and parent conferences in order to expose blind spots of which some teachers are unaware.

Finally, a frequent and basic problem occurs for student teachers when their philosophy of teaching is in conflict with the philosophy and methods of their resident teachers. When such problems are explored in role playing, students can be helped to find positive ways to reconcile the conflicts. They can be helped to clarify their roles in someone else's classroom as different from what they might choose to do in their own future classrooms.

SITUATIONS FOR USE
IN TEACHER EDUCATION

The literature in teacher education includes a number of publications on critical incidents in teaching in which experienced teachers and supervisors volunteer classroom crises from their own classroom work. These incidents provide reality practice for prospective teachers. The following examples indicate some possibilities.

Never on Thursday

Instructor's goal.   To open up the subject of classroom discipline.

You are a substitute teacher in a fourth-grade class. This is the second day of a three-day assignment. After recess, you suggest to the children that this is a fine time to take out their diaries and write in them. Johnny, who has been disruptive the entire morning, says, "We don't do that on Thursday." Whereupon all the children start beating on their desks and chanting, "We don't do that on Thursday!"

You wait until everyone but Johnny has quieted down. He is still banging on his desk. You say, "Johnny, please leave the room and go to the office."

Johnny says, "I won't!"

What will you do?

Have half your class role-play this situation and select two people to play the teacher and Johnny. The other half will be observers.

Princeton Bound

Instructor's goal.   To help teachers deal with parent goals in ways that will help both child and parents.

You are an interne in a fifth-grade class, holding your first parent-teacher conference with Christopher's mother. Although he is a child of normal ability, he is tense, daydreams a lot, and seldom finishes his work.

You welcome his mother, Mrs. Galt, who immediately begins to describe the family plans for Christopher. He has already been enrolled by his father for entrance to Princeton University, his father's alma mater. She says, "We want you to really put pressure on Christopher. He must achieve!"

What do you do?

The Interview

Instructor's goal.   To open up some ethical dilemmas that confront the beginning teacher.

You are applying for a beginning teaching position in the Alpha district. You need this job to help your husband finish his graduate work at the university, and it is the only position open in the area. The interviewing committee consists of Mr. Ames, the principal of the school with the vacancy; Miss Sims, a consultant; and Mr. Motts, a teacher.

After introductions, Mr. Motts says, "Mrs. Jones, I firmly believe that every teacher must begin the school year by laying down the law. You have to show students who is boss. Where do you stand on this?"

You are a teacher who believes that an atmosphere of cooperation in a classroom is important. You believe in first demonstrating to a class that they and you together can build a good class community. You know that it takes time and patient guidance to create such an atmosphere.

How do you respond to the question?

Dress Code

Instructor's goal.   To help teachers deal with colleagues with whom they may differ on issues.

You, a first-year secondary teacher, have been appointed to the joint faculty-student policy committee. The chairman of the committee is also chairman of your department. He opens the meeting with this statement, "It's time we take a stand and require a strict dress and grooming code. Sloppy and casual dress in this school can't be tolerated any longer."

Mike Penn, a student, quickly says, "Students feel very strongly that the way they dress is a personal right."

You fought for this same right in your college days. What do you do now?

Abdul Speaks No English

Instructor's goal.   To help a class accept a newcomer and to make a new child feel welcome.

You, a third-grade teacher, have just settled your class into their activities for the morning when your door is opened by your principal, who leads a frightened-looking child into the room. Your principal says, "Mr. Lang, this is Abdul. He speaks no English. I'm leaving him in your care." And he leaves before you can object.

You have a small, confused, scared little boy on your hands. You can almost see him cringing under the onslaught of stares of the other children.

What do you do?

Mrs. Johnson

Instructor's goal.   To open up the issue of racial discrimination in the classroom. Some prospective teachers are unaware of their own prejudices.

You teach seventh grade. The mother of one of your students, Tom Johnson, has phoned to make an appointment to see you. It's after school now, and Mrs. Johnson enters your classroom. You see from her manner that she is angry. You invite her to be seated, and you ask, "Is something wrong?"

"Yes," she says. "You've been preparing your students for the science competition at the county fair. But you've entered only white students. Why? Tom developed a good project. You gave him a good grade on it. Why didn't you enter it? Maybe you're a racist!"

What do you say?

The following situations were written by experienced teachers in a graduate class in sociodrama and related classroom techniques. While the preceding situations were planned for use in skills training, the following situations involve more pointed dilemmas and will provide practice in handling such difficulties in the classroom.

Noise Pollution

The last period of the school day, a tardy student plays his portable radio very loudly while walking into class. An English teacher, Mr. Smith, acting upon the principal's instructions to confiscate all radios played during class time, stops the student and demands his radio. The student refuses to give it up.

Mr. Smith is a dedicated, extremely responsible white teacher. He believes that rules must be maintained at all cost. The black student, a known militant, believes that his white teachers are out to get him. He also feels that his music gives him a kind of inner strength that enables him to cope with the school setting; he is rarely without his radio.

What do you, as Mr. Smith, do?

No Help Wanted

You're a teacher in a middle-class junior high school. One of the boys in your home room is from a Christian Science family. He carries a card signed by you that exempts him from all medical care or discussions of anatomy or health. You have complied with this request all year. One day on your way out of school, you notice a lot of commotion on the playground. You learn that this boy has been in a fight; he is bleeding from the mouth and appears to be in much pain. There are no other adults around; the boys around you are frightened and waiting for you to help him. You ask one of the boys to go to his home and find his mother while you try to think what to do, recalling your agreement not to administer any medical care.

What do you do now? What if the mother isn't home?

Don't Hold My Hand

At a day-care center, preschool children are engaged in some group activities. The center is designed as an outlet for children to play and do as they like in a supervised situation. The children are now all holding hands in a circle, except for a little boy who refuses to take another child's hand, thus blocking the activity. The teacher walks over to this child, Chuck, a five-year-old white boy, and asks him to please hold Shirley's hand. Shirley, four years old, is black

"I won't," Chuck says. "*Her* hand is black."

What should the teacher do?

The Fight

You are a new sixth-grade teacher in an inner-city school. The children in the class range in age from ten to fourteen. It is a nice spring day; you are returning to your class about 1:05 P.M. after the lunch break and after the children have filed in from the playground. As you enter the classroom, you see two big boys fighting furiously in the back of the class while the other pupils watch.

You could stop the fight by physically separating the combatants. But you feel that you must do something immediately to show the class that this kind of behavior is unacceptable. You think that if the two fighters are made to feel ashamed, then they and the class would see the error of this kind of activity. With this thought in mind, you say, "Well, you two boys are really something. This is terrible. If you want to fight, fight up here in front of the room where everybody can see you. Give us a big show and a big laugh." You expect that this will stop the fighting and result in some self-examination.

The two boys look at each other, and then to your utter amazement, they start to fight again with even more animosity. One boy yells, "I'm gonna kill you, you bastard."

The door opens. The principal, Mr. Thompson, walks in and says to you, "What's going on here?"

What do you say or do?

The following incident is included, even though it is dated, because such difficult ethical dilemmas do occur, and teachers need to explore, with the help of their peers, how to deal with these issues.

The Medal

Friday afternoon, after lunch, is sharing time in Miss Allan's fifth-grade class. This afternoon the children have brought in a wide variety of things: pictures, a real mess kit for camping, articles from newspapers and magazines, and stories of unique experiences to share with their classmates.

Joanie shows the postcard her sister has sent her all the way from Alaska. This nudges Mike to volunteer his contribution: a medal won by his father in Vietnam. Several children get excited about it and ask Mike questions. He tells about his father's tour of duty in Southeast Asia.

Joey says shyly that his father says we shouldn't ever have gone to war in Vietnam and that it's wrong to kill people for any reason, wrong even to have guns.

Tina agrees. She says that's what she learned in church. "Thou shalt not kill."

Joey goes on to ask Mike, "You mean it was okay to kill the Viet Cong?"

"Sure," Mike says. "They were the enemy!"

Joey says, "Why? What did they do? Miss Allan, is it okay to kill people if they're your enemy?"

If you were Miss Allan, what would you say?

PART THREE

Curriculum Materials
for Role Playing

12

Moral Development

HONESTY

The Clubhouse Boat

The Problem: The issue is conflict between peer group and parental stand-ards. To a ten- or eleven-year-old, keeping faith with his group is an all-important goal. Too often parents, in their concern for certain standards they wish to maintain for their families, ignore this need of the child to be like the rest of his age mates. In this story, the boy's needs to be like his peer group are so hindered by his father's restrictions that the boy is forced into possible antisocial behavior in order to meet his obligations to his age mates.

Introducing the Problem: You may ask the group, "Most of you, at one time or another, have found yourself in a spot in which you had to decide whether to obey rules your parents set down for you or to do what your friends are urging you to do. It's a difficult spot to be in, isn't it? This story deals with such a problem. The story stops but is not finished. As I read, think of ways in which the story could end."

Tommy Haynes listened big-eyed as his chum Eddie Blake excitedly ex-plained, "We *are* getting the houseboat! Listen, here's what's happened. Dave Allen's uncle has this houseboat down near the yacht harbor in Port Redwood City. He's going to give it to us, to the Pedal Pushers Club. For a clubhouse!"

"Oh, boy!" Tommy blurted.

"Only, we got to get it repaired. It leaks. It's not a big job, he says. If we'll get the hull repaired, we can have the Sea Lion! And Ed Mays says he'll bring his movie projector and keep it aboard, and my Dad says I can have our old T.V. to use in the club."

"Swell!"

"But we need money. There's six of us, and if we each chip in twenty dollars, we can swing it. Can you raise twenty dollars, Tommy?"

"Sure! I started delivering for the First Street Drug Store, and I make eight dollars a week. I already got eight dollars, and payday is tonight. I'll have sixteen dollars. I'll get the rest next week."

"That's fine. My mom says I can cash the savings bond my uncle gave me on my eighth birthday. I got to go and tell Andy Simons now."

"I'll bring the money over to Dave's house tomorrow," Tommy promised.

He rode on to the drugstore and was busy delivering until six o'clock. Mr. Ekblaw paid him his weekly wage of eight dollars, and Tommy rode on home to supper.

After the meal, his dad asked, "Tommy, did you get paid tonight?"

"Yes, I did, Dad. Mr. Ekblaw's sure a nice man to work for."

"Got the money on you?"

"Yes."

"Better give it to me. I'll put it in the bank for you."

"Oh, I need it, Dad. And my eight dollars I gave you last week, I'll need that too."

Mr. Haynes frowned. "Look, Tommy, I let you take this job, though you certainly don't need it. But I figured that it would do you good to earn money and learn to save."

"Oh, sure, Dad. Only right now—"

"There's only one way ever to start to save, son. That's always right now."

"But, Dad, I got to have it."

"What for?"

"The Pedal Pushers Club is buying a houseboat, and we each . . ."

"What!" Mr. Haynes exploded.

"The club is getting a houseboat from Dave Allen's uncle."

"Giving it to you?"

"Yes!"

"It can't be too good."

"We've got to get the hull repaired, so it won't leak."

"Good heavens!" Mrs. Haynes said.

"Oh, it'll be all right once we get the hull fixed. Then we're going to keep it tied up near the yacht harbor. That's why I need the money right now. I got to put in my share."

Mr. Haynes was shaking his head. "Listen, son. *Right now* is the best time for you to start learning that the best place to put your money is into the bank!"

"But, Dad, the club's depending on me to put in my share!"

"Son, when you get your pay, you're going to bring the eight dollars to me. I'll give you two dollars spending money. But the rest I'm putting into the savings bank for you. And to that, as long as you keep your job, every week I'll add a dollar. By the end of the year, Tommy, you'll have a respectable sum in the bank. You'll be proud of it."

"Dad, please . . ."

"No! And that's final. If there's anything I hate, it's whining. You know that!"

Tommy left the dining room, went to his own room, and flung himself down on his bed.

There was dismay at the next meeting of the Sea Lions.

"Oh, gosh," Dave Allen said disgustedly, "this wrecks the whole deal! If Tommy can't put his money in, then we're shy of the full amount. We've had the leak fixed, and those people want their money right now. What're we going to do?"

Eddie said, "That Mr. Bidwell, who fixed the hull—he won't put the Sea Lion back in the water until we pay him all we owe."

Pete Myers said, "Tommy, I think maybe I can raise some money to lend you. But you got to pay me back, or I'll be in trouble."

Tommy looked at their dismayed, accusing faces. Suppose he said yes? But where would he get the money if his dad took most of his pay?

"Gee, Pete, that's great," Eddie said. "Of course you'll pay him back, won't you, Tommy?"

Tommy couldn't speak. He only nodded.

Pete Myers said, "Some lady lost her purse in Dad's taxi the other night, and Mom's got it put away in the dresser drawer, until somebody claims it. There's over twenty dollars in it. I'll borrow the money for you, Tommy. But you sure got to pay me back, so I can put the money back in the purse."

"I'll try."

Tommy was in a constant agony of fright that week. Suppose he couldn't pay back the money, and the owner came and found the money missing? They'd accuse Pete's dad of stealing . . .

Tommy made a discovery Monday afternoon. He had to deliver a package of aspirin and vitamins to a house on the Lake Street hill. He was puffing and sweating from effort as he rang the doorbell, and when the kindly woman who answered looked at him, he said impulsively, "Golly, that's some hill!" She said, yes it was, and when she paid him for the drugs she gave him a half dollar extra. It was his first tip and he stood there confused, staring at it. She smiled at him and said goodbye.

It gave him an idea.

On his next delivery he had to go out to the edge of town. After handing over the package to a flashily-dressed man at the given address, he stood there, sort of waiting, and said meaningfully, "You sure live 'way out."

It worked. He got only a quarter, but that was a help. At home he said nothing of these tips, just hoarded them carefully in his bureau drawer. He worked hard. Tips were something he had never thought of. Tips might help him solve that awful problem so heavy over his head. He did not dally on his deliveries; the more customers he brought drugs to, during his brief working hours, the more chances for that extra piece of change.

Wednesday night he got another surprise.

The druggist, Mr. Ekblaw, grinned at him when he said good night, and remarked, "You're a hard worker, Tommy. I'm afraid maybe I'm gypping you a little on the pay. You'll get two dollars more, Friday night. Ten bucks."

Tommy's eyes shone.

"Thanks, Mr. Ekblaw!"

That night, in his room he counted up his tips. He had $2.60.

It was next evening that a Mrs. Black on Page Drive overpaid him fifty cents. He didn't know until he reached the drugstore and handed over the money to Mr. Ekblaw. Mr. Ekblaw returned the fifty cents to him.

"Tommy, you got some of your money in this," he said. "Better keep it in separate pockets."

Tommy flushed, and leaving work, he knew he should head back to Page Drive . . . but he pedaled straight home, and there was such a sick churning in his stomach that he left his food on his dinner plate. His mother's forehead knitted as she looked at him.

"You feeling sick, Tommy?"

"I'm all right!" he said vehemently and went to his room.

His mother shook her head and wondered aloud, "Now what's wrong? Boys sure are a worry!"

Mr. Haynes looked up from his paper, frowning. "Tommy's working pretty hard and for just eight bucks a week. You know, I think I'll stop by the drugstore and tell Mr. Ekblaw that Tommy has had his tryout now, and deserves a little raise in pay."

"Maybe that'll make Tommy cheer up," Mrs. Haynes said . . .

It was the next afternoon at the drugstore that Tommy got an unexpected phone call. Mr. Ekblaw called him.

"Somebody wants to talk to you, Tommy. Sounds kind of urgent."

As he took the phone, Tommy wondered who it was. His friends knew better than to call him at work.

It was Eddie Blake, and he sounded as if he were scared sick.

"Tommy, we got to talk to you. Right away!"

"Gosh, Eddie, I'm working."

"We're waiting at the schoolyard corner. Next delivery you make, you go by there. Hurry!"

In Tommy's stomach was a gone, hollow feeling as he hung up.

Mr. Ekblaw looked at him as he came out of the phone booth, and the kindly druggist said, "Tommy, something wrong?"

"N-no, sir."

"Well, take this stuff out to 1218 Vistillas Drive. You ask for eleven dollars and twenty-eight cents."

The boys were waiting at the school corner as Tommy rode near. Eddie beckoned him, and they moved into a huddle on the empty playground.

"The awfullest thing's happened," Dave burst out. Tommy saw that Dave looked disgusted, that Eddie was sore, and Pete Myers looked white and scared.

Eddie Blake came right out with it. "Tommy, the woman who left that purse in Pete's dad's taxi came hunting for it. Pete's ma gave it to her, and she opened it and found twenty dollars gone. She was going to call the police, but

Pete's ma promised that it would be returned. Then she asked Pete, and he had to tell her all about it."

Dave broke in, "And his ma says Pete's got to quit the Pedal Pushers. He can't hang around with us any more at all!"

Eddie went on, "Pete's ma told his dad, and his dad says the club'll either get him that twenty dollars by tomorrow, or he's going to see all our dads and tell them what happened!"

And Dave added, "Tommy, you get that money for us!"

Tommy choked up; tears blurred his eyes. "I c-can't," he said.

"Look, Tommy," Eddie went on. We've raised some of it. We got about twelve dollars. Haven't you got any money at all?"

"Maybe—four dollars—"

"Good, good! But, Tommy, you just naturally got to raise the rest by tomorrow."

"I got to deliver this medicine," Tommy said.

Eddie said: "Tommy, if Pete's dad goes to all our fathers and tells them—well, there'll just be no more Pedal Pushers Club. You got to have that money for us by tomorrow."

"I'll try," Tommy whispered. . . .

He passed 1218 Vistillas Drive, realized with a start that he had gone too far, and turned back. A white-haired man answered the doorbell and grinned at him. Maybe it was Tommy's woebegone expression, but anyway, he gave Tommy a little lift of heart after paying for the medicine, by tipping him a whole half dollar, saying, "Buy yourself a Cadillac, sonny," and smiling as he shut the door.

Tommy put the change in his pocket, and straightened out the bills carefully to put them in his wallet. He got a shock. The old man had overpaid him. Given him, instead of a ten-dollar bill, two bills—two new ten-dollar bills stuck together. Overpaid him ten dollars.

Tommy raised his hand to knock on the door.

And hesitated—that ten dollars—why, it would more than make up the money he needed. With his tips it would make up the sum Pete needed to give to his dad.

Tommy stood there, arm lifted, frozen . . .

Finders Weepers[1]

The Problem: This story concerns the dilemma of being honest when it would be easy and convenient to be dishonest in order to solve a burdensome problem.

Introducing the Problem: Say, "Have any of you ever found a pocketbook on the street? If you have, I'm sure you wondered whether to keep it or turn it in to some

[1]John E. Warriner, John H. Treanor, and Normal H. Naas, *Teacher's Manual: English Grammar and Composition, VII* (New York: Harcourt Brace Jovanovich, 1960). Pp. 128–30. Reprinted by permission of the publisher.

lost-and-found department. Here's a story about some boys who found a wallet with money in it just when they needed money very badly. This story stops but is not finished. As I read, try to think of ways in which the story should end."

They had been told not to use the boat. Eddie's Uncle Ross had been very definite about it. "I have a good reason," he told them. "Storms come up real sudden on this big lake. You might get caught out in one and drown. So fish and swim and hike all you want. Just leave the boat alone." But the boys had not obeyed.

They had had a lot of fun—swimming, fishing, hiking, and just loafing on the beach in the warm sun. But all the time the rowboat had rested there in plain sight, both an invitation and a challenge. Finally Pete had lost to temptation. While Eddie and Tom were in swimming, Pete had pried loose a staple that held the locked chain and freed the boat. Then he had rowed out into the lake. Eddie had yelled angrily at him; his uncle had been very kind to invite them to stay with him for the week, and they should have respected his wishes. But, in the end, Eddie had enjoyed using the boat too.

This morning, the last day of their stay, the boat was missing. Eddie's uncle had said goodbye to the boys and gone off to work. They had cleaned up breakfast dishes and gone out on to the beach to swim. Eddie then noticed that the boat wasn't in its usual place.

"Pete, you used the boat last night. Where did you leave it?"

"I pulled the bow up onto the sand."

"Didn't you *tie* it to anything?"

"I was in a hurry. But I had it almost halfway up onto the beach."

"So when the wind came up during the night," Eddie said disgustedly, "the waves washed the boat free. No telling how far it's drifted by now. Come on, we have to find it!"

They found the rowboat a mile away, resting drunkenly on sharp rocks that jutted out from shore. The boat was half full of water—the rocks had punched a hole in the bottom.

"That's just fine," Tom said angrily. "Pete, you have to pay for the boat!"

But Eddie said, "No. We're all in this. Anyway, I think it can be repaired."

They hauled the boat out. They got a boat-builder from nearby Lakeport to come and look at the boat. It could be repaired, he said. The repairs would cost $30. The boys added up their cash. They had, in all, $11 more than the cost of bus tickets home.

"Can we send you the rest of the money?" Eddie asked.

"Yes, but I'll have to keep the boat until you do."

After the man hauled the boat to his shop, the boys worried.

"Where'll we get the $19.00 we'll owe him?" Tom asked.

Eddie said, "Gosh, I'd sure hate to have Uncle Bob pay it himself, but he'll have to if we don't."

"We'll have to ask our folks for the money," Tom said.

"If my Dad hears how we broke our word, after Uncle Bob had been so good to us," Eddie said, "I'll *really* be in trouble!"

Pete said, "Now your uncle won't ever ask us here again."

"All your fault!" Tom told him angrily . . .

It was Tom who found the wallet, on the bus station floor.

He picked it up and said, "Look!" drawing the other boys aside. "Maybe this'll get us out of trouble."

But Eddie said, "Look inside. The owner's name must be in it."

Inside the wallet were two ten- and two one-dollar bills and a check—it looked like a paycheck—for $292.00.

Eddie said, "There must be a Lost and Found desk here. We'll turn the wallet in."

"You crazy?" Pete said. "This money'll pay for fixing the boat!"

"Look at the identification card," Eddie said. "This wallet belongs to a Mr. Martin Sands. The bus company will return it."

"Listen," Pete said insistently. "We'll just take the cash out, and say there was no money in the wallet when we found it. Don't you see, Eddie? Pickpockets hang around bus stations like this. The owner will figure that somebody picked his pocket, took the money out of the wallet, and then threw it away, so's it wouldn't be found on him if he got searched by a cop."

"But that paycheck . . ."

"We'll leave the paycheck in the wallet. Pickpockets don't mess around with checks, they just take cash that can't be traced. The owner will be so glad to get this big check back that he won't mind losing the cash. He'll figure it's just the reward he had to pay to get his paycheck back!"

"No," Eddie said.

"We'll vote on it," Pete insisted. "I say keep the cash!"

"And I say return everything," Eddie said.

"Tommy, how do you vote?" Pete demanded.

And Eddie urged, "Say it, Tommy. Keep the money? Or give it back?"

Tommy swallowed hard. Tommy said:

Boy Out on a Limb

The Problem: The issue is honesty—specifically, telling the truth about misbehavior and being punished or keeping quiet and allowing the wrong person to be blamed.

Introducing the Problem: Children are often in one kind of trouble or another over care of property. This might be a good story to use in one of those frequent occasions when adults complain of some act of vandalism committed by school children. If there is not an immediate incident to serve as a springboard into this situation, you may simply ask the children, "What was the last occasion you damaged some property while playing, when you didn't really mean to do any damage?" After some discussion, you can say, "I'm going to read you a story about such an incident. The story stops but is not finished. As I read, try to think of ways the story might end."

Bobby Allen's father had promised to take him fishing that Saturday afternoon. Out of excitement Bobby had risen earlier than usual for Saturday; and after breakfast, he faced a long, long wait until afternoon.

"Run outside and amuse yourself, dear," his mother urged. "But be quiet. Edie's got a bad cold and I'm keeping her in her crib so she can get a lot of sleep today."

Outside, he walked out the front gate to the street. He saw none of his friends; most of them, he knew, had already gone downtown to see the Saturday morning movie.

Abruptly the quiet street was made noisy by the racket of a motor coming from the Mapes's yard, two houses down. Oh, oh, he thought; his baby sister wasn't going to get much sleep while all that noise was going on.

He hurried down the sidewalk and saw that the roar was coming from a small cement-mixer. Two men were putting finishing touches to a new driveway for Mr. Mapes. He stayed on while they finished pouring fresh mix between the wooden forms and watched while the men smoothed the surface of the last square of concrete. Done, they finally hitched their mixer to a small pickup truck and drove away.

Bobby sat down on the curb and yawned. It was such a *long* wait until one o'clock. And then he cheered up. Al Brady was coming down the street. With a dog, by golly. Al was new on the block, and Bobby had not played with him much as yet, but now he greeted Al as if they were best friends.

"Hi, Al. Can you play?"

"I guess so."

"What kind of dog is that?"

"Red setter."

"Does he know any tricks?"

"No. He's just eight months old."

"Don't you know how to train him?"

"No."

"I'll show you. I used to have a fox terrier. Let's go into your yard."

They walked into the Brady yard, next door to the Mapes's place.

Bobby asked, "What's his name?"

"Champ."

"Here, Champ," Bobby called. "Here, Champ!"

The young setter wagged his tail furiously and came up to him, eager to play but wary of a stranger.

Bobby patted him, then said, "Sit down, Champ. Sit down!"

And with the command, Bobby pressed on the dog's flanks, forcing him to sit on his hind legs.

"See? Just practice that with him. Will he fetch?"

"Yeah, he'll go after a stick or a ball."

"But will he bring it back?"

"Yeah, sure!—sometimes."

Bobby threw a stick, saying, "Get it, Champ. Get it!"

Champ lunged after the stick, picked it up in his big mouth, and lay down and worried it.

"Bring it, Boy! Bring it here," Bobby called.

Champ's ears went up and he studied Bobby—but just sat where he was.

"Bring it, Boy!"

The urgency in his tone had results. Champ came to him, carrying the stick in his mouth; but when Bobby reached for it, Champ ran across the yard and sat down and proceeded to chew the piece of wood.

"Champ!" Bobby said disgustedly. "You ought to call him Chump!"

The dog trotted over to his master, leaving the stick behind.

Bobby said, "That's because he's never been given a reward for bringing something. When he does a thing right, you should give him something. Then he'll learn. Watch." He ordered, "Sit down, Champ," and pushed down on the setter's back. Champ sat down. Bobby took from his pocket a piece of last week's licorice whip and held it out. Champ sniffed it suspiciously, then ate it ravenously.

Again Bobby threw a stick, ordering, "Fetch it, Boy!"

Champ lunged after the piece of wood.

But Bobby had thrown the stick a little too hard. It sailed over a low picket fence, into the Mapes's yard. Champ sailed right after it—down upon that new concrete driveway. Champ landed running in that last, still half-wet square of concrete, and every lunge he took at a slant along the drive left four big imprints that looked like bear tracks.

Al breathed a gasping "Wow!" and added quickly, "*You* threw the stick, Bobby!"

Bobby stared, fright in his eyes.

"My pop will be mad," he said.

Champ found the stick and lay down and gnawed it.

"Here, Champ!" Al called urgently.

The setter cantered back toward the fence—right across the wet concrete again.

"Get him out of there!" Bobby yelled at Al.

"*You* threw that stick over there," Al repeated angrily. "Come on, Champ. Come back here!"

The setter paused and sprang, clearing the fence but leaving final imprints like tiny bomb craters in the soft cement.

Bobby said breathlessly, "I've got to go home, Al!"

Bobby leafed through his new encyclopedia until lunch time. He didn't enjoy it much; he had a stomachache and he felt too hot.

At noon, his father arrived. Hurrying indoors, he smiled at Bobby and said, "Soon's we have lunch, we'll climb into the car and head for the lake."

Bobby didn't feel hungry, but he forced himself to eat.

And then the telephone rang.

Bobby knew at once what it was about. He felt sick.

"Yes, this is Allan," his father said into the phone. "How are you? . . . What's that? Your new driveway? . . . Oh, but look here, we don't have a dog. . . . Your wife saw it? You mean actually with her own eyes? . . . Oh, I see. . . . Is that so? . . . I'll ask him. I'll get the straight of it. I'll call you back."

And the way Mr. Allan hung up was grim.

"Bobby, I want to talk to you."

"Yes, Dad?"

"Were you playing with some dog in the Brady yard this morning?"

Bobby gulped. He looked at the tablecloth and his stomach knotted and he felt as if he were going to upchuck his lunch.

"Dad, I—was trying to train Al's dog to fetch. I threw a stick, only it went over the fence into Mr. Mapes's yard, and the dog jumped over the fence, right onto the soft concrete, chasing the stick."

"So that's how it happened."

"Y-yes, Dad."

"All right. I'll phone Mr. Mapes to get his driveway smoothed up and send the bill to me. And—you'll have to take your punishment, Bobby. You didn't intend any harm, so I'll be—easy."

Bobby licked his lips and didn't say anything.

"You will be confined to your own yard for a week. Maybe—next Saturday—we'll go fishing. If you haven't busted any windows or burned down any houses meanwhile!"

The afternoon began in very dull fashion. Bobby, confined to his yard, had to amuse himself alone, for neither Mike nor Arthur would come into his yard to play. They were busy on bicycles in the street.

Then Bobby got a break: His cousin Phil arrived to see him.

"Hey, my brother Ned's joined the Air Force," Phil announced. "He's going to be a jet pilot."

"Dad," Bobby said, "was a helicopter pilot in Vietnam."

"What'd he do? Pick up wounded?"

"Yeah, and once he got shot down! His engine busted, and he crashed. They had to send another chopper in to get him."

Phil darted around the grassy plot of yard making noises like a jet engine, roaring and swooping. Bobby opened up on him with a pair of make-believe machine guns. "Hrah-hrah-hrah-hrah!"

Phil stared around the place. His gaze focused on the big apple tree in the Rea yard that thrust a thick limb over Bobby's yard. His gaze moved to the stepladder that stood against the garage.

"Hey, Bobby, can you get a rope?"

"Yeah, we got one in the garage."

"Quick, get it!"

Quick, Bobby got it.

"But what for?" he demanded.

Phil threw the rope over the big limb of the neighbor's apple tree. He tied the stepladder to one end of the rope and hauled the ladder up until it swung free, a foot off the lawn.

"You see, Bobby? This is a ladder hanging from the rescue chopper. Now we got to climb up into it. While they're shooting at us!"

"Hey, Dad won't let me hang a swing from that limb. He says it might break!"

But Phil was already climbing up the ladder. It swung, and swayed, and tilted, and turned, and Phil had to hang on tightly. But his dark eyes shone with delight.

"Climb, Bobby! They're shooting at us. Climb for your life!"

Bobby gingerly caught hold of the ladder and put one foot on it, then the other. The ladder swung 'way back, so that the boys were leaning far over on their backs. The ladder swung and rocked, and Bobby's face lit up with scared enjoyment.

Cra-a-ck . . . and the tree limb broke under the combined weight of boys, ladder, and high excitement. The branch broke near the trunk. Ladder, boys, and high excitement plunged earthward. The ladder hit first, the boys were jarred loose, and they hit the grass separately. The limb landed inches away and broke into four different pieces from the impact.

"Wow!" Phil gasped. "What a crash!"

He laughed shakily, and Bobby laughed too.

They stood up and dusted themselves off, still laughing.

But the laugh stuck in Bobby's throat as he saw the damage. That falling limb had broken a big notch in the fence, crushing a fine climbing rose. Over in the Rea yard, the thick limb had crashed down upon a big orange-colored garden umbrella, breaking down the table below it and crushing a lounge chair; and over on this side of the fence, in Bobby's own yard, the limb had smashed flat his baby sister's playpen.

"Golly," Phil breathed, all the fun gone from his voice. "I got to go home!" And he hurried off, almost running.

Bobby glanced at his mother's kitchen windows. She didn't seem to be there. Turning, with shaking fingers, he untied the rope and ladder from the broken limb and carried them into the garage and set them in their proper places.

He wandered into the house. His mother was in the dining room, at the telephone, ordering groceries.

Bobby picked up a book and tried to read, but the type was a blur to his eyes. . . . What was his father going to say when he saw all the damage? What was he going to *do*? . . .

What Bobby's father did say, when he returned late in the afternoon, was, "Bobby, what in the world happened out here?"

Bobby had difficulty forming words.

"D-dad, that big limb—it fell off the tree . . ."

"I told Rea he ought to have that old tree pruned!" Mr. Allen exploded. "I told him over a month ago. Now, when the first breath of strong wind comes along . . . look at Edie's playpen! If that baby had been in it, she'd have been killed!"

Mr. Allan bent over the playpen wreckage.

"Dad . . ."

"I'm going over after dinner and tell Rea what I think of him. It's criminal negligence to let an old tree like that be a hazard to your neighbors. I'd *told* him to get it pruned! I'll make him pay for the playpen and for rebuilding the fence, too."

"Oh, no," Bobby gasped.

"What?" Mr. Allan said, turning to Bobby. "What did you say?"

Bobby said . . .

Little Echo

The Problem: The issue is that of honesty—specifically, the "white lie." Parents often set standards of ideal behavior for their children which the parents themselves do not observe. Children, on their part, are apt to justify their own misconduct by citing the misconduct of others. In this story a child deliberately deceives her mother after a disillusioning experience with white lies on the parent's part. This misbehavior is a consequence of a double standard set up by adults: One code of behavior for themselves, another for the child.

Introducing the Problem: You may ask the class, "Have any of you ever told a lie, a little 'white lie' in order to get out of doing something you didn't want to do? This is a story about a girl who lied, and what happened as a result. The story stops but is not finished. Try to think of ways in which the story might end."

When the telephone rang in the late afternoon, Nora was busy drying her wavy dark hair, in preparation for a party that night.

"Nora," her mother said, "it's for you. Mrs. Kyne."

Nora gasped in dismay. "Oh, my gosh, *no!*"

"Hurry, dear!"

Running to the phone, Nora asked, "Mother, is today the tenth? It is!"

"Indeed it is!"

"What'll I do?" Nora begged.

"About what?"

"I told Mrs. Kyne I'd sit with their baby tonight . . ."

"Oh, *no*, Nora!"

Nora's mother held her head.

"Mrs. Kyne?" Nora said.

"Yes, Nora. I called to ask if you could possibly come fifteen minutes earlier? We have to start out earlier so we can pick up some friends."

Nora hesitated and licked her lips, her mind racing.

"Oh, Mrs. Kyne, I'm awfully sorry!" she wailed. "But I won't be able to come over tonight at all . . ."

"You won't!" Mrs. Kyne sounded aghast, dismayed, and politely infuriated. "But, Nora, my dear, I absolutely have to have you! We have to visit my husband's employer, and it's so late I couldn't possibly get anyone else."

"Can't you call Beulah Allen? She usually sits for you."

"Beulah is playing at a piano recital tonight. Nora, you must come!"

"But, Mrs. Kyne, I . . ." Nora thought desperately. "I have a rash on my chest and back. Mom thought it was poison oak, but the school nurse says it isn't, and said it looks more like measles, and we're waiting for the doctor and . . ."

Mrs. Kyne blurted a "Good heavens!" of despair. "Well, stay in bed, child. Mr. Kyne will simply have to go without me." And she hung up, too upset even for a polite goodbye.

Nora hung up, with a "Whew!" of relief. But the relief curled up in smoke when she turned and met her mother's eyes.

"Nora Belle Bayliss!" Every word was underlined in an increasing surprise, shock, horror. "What did you tell Mrs. Kyne?"

"But, Mom, I do have this rash on my back . . ."

"You have a few miserable little hives, which you get every single time that you eat too many sweet pickles."

Nora turned red and looked at the floor, unable to meet her mother's eyes. "But, Mom, what could I do? I'm going to Ellen Ames's party tonight, and I just couldn't think of anything else to tell Mrs. Kyne."

"Nora, what you told Mrs. Kyne was an out-and-out falsehood!"

Nora felt hot tears push into her eyes. "Oh, Mom!" she cried.

"When did you make this date with Mrs. Kyne to watch her baby?"

"Two weeks ago."

"And she has been counting on you all this time. Now you let her down. I just can't tell you how *surprised* I am, Nora. I'm shocked."

"Mom, I'll—I'll call Mrs. Kyne back and tell her I'm coming."

"No, I don't want her to know that you had not told her the truth. I don't want people to know that my daughter. . . . In fact, I think, Nora, the best punishment I can give you is to *make* your story the truth." Her voice became firm. "You're not going out tonight, Nora. You're going upstairs to your own room, you're going to undress, and you're going to bed! I think that that is the best lesson I can give you."

It was the following Saturday, in mid-morning, when Mr. Bayliss called home to say he thought he had a buyer for the house. He'd bring the people over in an hour. Could Mrs. Bayliss have the house ready to show?

"I couldn't possibly," she gasped. "But I will!"

She hung up and grabbed the vacuum cleaner.

"Nora, darling, help me. We've got to get the house all straightened up before Dad arrives!"

"I'll vacuum, Mom. You dust."

Mrs. Bayliss was very anxious to sell their home. Here in Altadena, just under the high rampart of Mount Wilson, and some twenty-odd miles from the ocean, summer weather was very hot and dry. Besides, their house was a two-story Cape Cod type of structure and had no insulation in the roof. As a result, in summer time the upstairs bedrooms were just bake ovens. Also, there was no breakfast nook in the kitchen. And the yard was small. Mrs. Bayliss had lived with these disadvantages for ten years without serious injury to her self-respect. But, just now, she had discovered a lovely new house for sale near the beach.

Mr. Bayliss was *not* eager to sell their present home, but he had finally agreed that if they could make a good sale, he would buy the modern house that Mrs. Bayliss wanted.

"Nora, we've got to have everything just shining for these customers! So they just can't resist buying!"

"We will, Mother."

Mother dusted like fury. Nora vacuumed the living room and dining room rugs, the hallway runner, then started upstairs to do the bedroom rugs.

Through a window she saw a car stop at the curb and a woman start up the walk to the house.

"Mom! There's that Mrs. O'Manion coming to see us."

"Good heavens!" Mrs. Bayliss blurted. "She'll expect me to sit and talk over P.T.A. for a solid hour. Nora, darling, don't answer the bell. Don't make a peep!"

Nora froze, her heart pounding, as the doorbell jangled. Nora held her breath. Again the doorbell ding-aling-alinged for a long, impatient moment. Then Mrs. O'Manion rapped on the door with her knuckles, as if she suspected the bell wasn't working. Again she rang the bell, holding it down so that it rang endlessly.

Finally Mrs. O'Manion gave up, turning and hurrying down the walk to her car, her heels tapping wrathfully and her shoulders moving with an angry, insulted twitch.

Mrs. Bayliss waited until Mrs. O'Manion's car turned the corner before she said, even then in a whisper, "All right, Nora!"

Nora had finished vacuuming the upstairs bedrooms when all of a sudden she remembered. "Oh, my gosh!" she cried out. "Mother! *Mother!* I'm supposed to go to Dr. Amos at eleven this morning to have these braces on my teeth fixed."

Mrs. Bayliss plumped down on a chair, as if hopelessness had drained her knees of strength.

"Nora, darling!" As if it were Nora's fault. "We just *can't* go."

"He charges if you miss an appointment and don't cancel it."

Mrs. Bayliss went to the phone, sat there a moment, frowning in thought, then dialed the dentist's number.

"Dr. Amos? This is Mrs. Bayliss. Doctor, I'm awfully sorry, but I won't be able to bring Nora in this morning. We just went out to the garage to drive downtown, and I discovered I'd left my ignition on all night, and the battery is dead, and I can't start the car. I called our garage, and they tell me they can't send a man up for another hour, so. . . . Thanks, Dr. Amos. We'll come in Monday, then. 'Bye." And she hung up, and sat limply with a "Whew!"

She got a glimpse of Nora's face, then, and Mrs. Bayliss reddened. Getting up quickly, she hurried to the kitchen, saying, "Nora, change into your blue dress. Hurry, dear!"

Dad was well trained; he arrived not precisely on the dot, in an hour, as he'd said, but a good five minutes *past*, giving them a little leeway. So they were dressed and ready, and the house shone like a dime that had been rubbed with quicksilver.

"Dear, this is Mr. and Mrs. McHenry. My wife, Mrs. McHenry and Mr. McHenry. And my daughter, Nora."

Mrs. McHenry was a plump, big woman, and Mr. McHenry was a plump big man. Both were graying, both had rather severe, expressionless faces.

Nora followed behind as her mother led the McHenrys from room to room. Mother was being awfully friendly and talkative; she talked almost too much and too fast, Nora thought. Mrs. McHenry just looked; and if she felt anything about what she saw, she didn't let it stampede her into wasting a word. Mr. McHenry, though, began to thaw out.

"My, my," he said appreciatively, as Nora's mother opened the French doors at the end of the living room and let the sun flood in.

"My, my," he said, when Mother showed them the kitchen, which had cupboards on three sides, from floor to ceiling.

"My, my," he said when Mother opened the door to the basement and showed them the two hot-air furnaces and a full concrete foundation that would baffle termites.

And he said, "My, my," again when Mother led them upstairs and showed them the bedrooms with windows on *three* sides.

Mrs. McHenry's careful armor of indifference cracked then. "These are lovely, lovely rooms," she said, so positively that Nora almost wanted to hug her. "Tell me, Mrs. Bayliss. Upstairs rooms like these are bright and airy, yes, but in summer don't these rooms get stifling hot?"

Mother said, right off, "We've lived here for ten years, Mrs. McHenry, and we have been entirely comfortable. There is simply nothing about this house that I personally would want to change. It just breaks my heart to think of moving, but I have to consider my husband's and my child's needs, and living across town will be better for them."

Mrs. McHenry nodded. She looked at her husband. She didn't say anything, but her husband smiled as if she had whispered in his ear.

"We like the place," he said. "We'd like to buy it. Your broker told us the price and all. We'll just go see him now and leave a deposit. I think we'll be quite happy here."

Mother said, "I'm sure you will!"

And when the McHenrys left, Mother hugged Dad, overjoyed.

Nora walked thoughtfully to her own room.

Thursday night, during dinner, the telephone rang. Mother got up from the table and answered.

"It's for you, Nora. Marylee."

Nora put the receiver to her ear and said, "Hi."

"Nora, are you coming over to study with me, tonight?"

Marylee sounded all excited. Nora said, "I was going to ask Mother if I could. Why?"

"Let's go to the State tonight! There's a swell picture showing."

"But, golly, Marylee, tonight's Thursday . . ."

"Aw, gee, Nora, can't you go?"

"I want to." Nora thought hard. She wasn't permitted to go to movies on a week night when there was school next day.

"Mother!" she called. "Marylee wants me to come over and—study our history. Can I go?"

"Why, yes, dear. Be back by bed time."

"Okay, Marylee!" Nora said into the phone. "I'll be right over. Oh, say, I owe you seventy-five cents for school milk money, don't I? I'll bring it along."

Mother gave her the money she asked for, and she quickly slipped into her coat, grabbed her history book, and started out. At the door, however, she hesitated. Somehow she didn't feel excited and happy about going to the movie. She felt depressed. She felt worried.

"Oh, Mother?"

"Yes, dear?" Her mother smiled. "I suppose you really could study better if you stopped at the drugstore on the way over to Marylee's and bought a sack of salted almonds. All right, here's a dollar."

Nora took the money but still looked uncertain.

Mother asked, "That's what you wanted, isn't it?"

"Oh, Mother," Nora said, "I . . ."

RESPONSIBILITY FOR OTHERS

Trick or Treat[2]

The Problem: The issue is honesty—specifically, responsibility for others in a situation in which two boys, guilty of leading smaller boys into trouble, can escape all blame by saying nothing and allowing the younger boys to be punished for the misdeed.

Introducing the Problem: Say to the group, "Have you ever been tricked into doing something mean and hurtful to somebody else? Or have you ever been on the other side? Have you ever, without really intending to, induced other children to do something that got them into trouble? This story deals with such a problem. The story stops but is not finished. As I read, think of ways in which the story could end."

Pete's father was very firm in his stand. "I want this clearly understood, Pete. No serious damage this Halloween. Ordinary trick or treat, okay. Have fun. But keep it just fun. No malicious mischief. I want your word on this."

"Okay, Dad. I promise."

But Pete's friend Sandy groaned when Pete told him.

"What'll we do? Wear the same old cowboy costumes that everybody else has got and just knock on doors and collect a bag full of jellybeans?"

"That or nothing."

As Pete got dressed in the old cowboy rig Halloween night, he discovered it was much smaller than it had been last year. He was outgrowing it. Maybe, he thought, he was outgrowing Halloween entirely? Oh, well, one more time.

He met Sandy outside. Carrying bags for loot, they marched from door to door in their neighborhood, saying "Trick or treat!" and collecting handfuls of jellybeans, molasses kisses, homebaked cookies and squares of fudge, wrapped hard candy, and apples. It was a pretty dull business, Sandy grumbled over and over.

Nothing unusual happened until they ventured into the big trailer camp several blocks away. A couple of younger boys had started tagging after them. They also were wearing cowboy suits, and that enraged Sandy

[2]Adapted from John E. Warriner, John H. Treanor, and Norman H. Naas, *Teacher's Manual: English Grammar and Composition, VIII* (New York: Harcourt Brace Jovanovich, 1960). Pp. 136–40. Reprinted by permission of the publisher.

even more. Their masks, however, were just narrow eye-covers, and Pete recognized one of them as eight-year-old Ronnie Hites who lived on his block.

"Quit following us!" Sandy snapped at them, and they hung back for a few moments, but came on again.

Pete and Sandy started knocking on trailer doors and were given treats. But at the fifth trailer, a sour-faced old man opened the door, and at sight of their masked faces and costumes he flew into a rage.

"Go on, beat it! Get out of here or I'll throw dishwater on you!" he shouted; and as they backed away, he slammed his door shut.

"What an old crab!" Pete said, surprised.

"No treat," Sandy said, "so he gets a trick."

"Let's soap his windows."

"Sissy stuff. No, we've got to think up a real good one for him."

Sandy noticed that a car stood in front of the next trailer, lights on and motor running. Somebody had evidently stopped, had gone into the trailer, and was planning to leave in a moment or two. Sandy also noticed that, between the trailers, lines were stretched between T-posts on which to hang drying clothes. His quick wits leaped to a possible use of these resources.

He drew a Scout knife from a pocket. Reaching up to one of the clotheslines, he cut it at his end and then ran to the other end and cut it there. He hurried back and started tying one end of the rope to the front hitch of the house trailer.

"Sandy," Pete whispered angrily, "no rough stuff. I promised my Dad."

"That's right," Sandy said, but he finished tying the knot. Straightening up, he looked around the dark camp. "You promised *you* wouldn't play any rough tricks. So okay. *You* won't."

"You're included! I said *we* wouldn't!"

"Okay. Hey, you!" Sandy called, low-voiced. The two younger boys, Ronnie Hites and his pal, were hovering nearby, watching. Ronnie came forward. Sandy handed the end of the rope to the eight-year-old. "Can you tie a good knot?"

"I can tie a square knot," Ronnie said proudly.

"Fine! Just tie this rope around the bumper of that car."

"What for?"

"To play a trick, that's all. You chicken?"

"I ain't chicken," Ronnie said sturdily.

He took the rope, went to the rear of the waiting car, and carefully started tying a knot.

"That car'll tow the trailer away," Pete started to object.

"No, it won't," Sandy said. "It's just clothesline—it'll break. It'll just give the trailer a jerk."

"Oh," said Pete, and laughed. "The old guy'll think it's an earthquake!"

Ronnie finished his knot—then ran, for the door of the nearby trailer opened and a man came out. Pete and Sandy also crouched back in the darkness as the man got into his car. His door slammed. The engine revved up as he stepped on the gas—and then the car started forward.

The car moved ahead—and the rope lifted taut, and broke with a violent twang; but it held just long enough to give a jerk to the house trailer, a strong, unexpected forward jerk. Pete discovered something, then, that he had not noticed before; he had thought that the trailer would roll forward a few feet. But the trailer's wheels had been removed, and it could not roll. The trailer had been set up on permanent supports, on wooden blocks. And now it was jerked off those blocks: it lunged forward and crashed to the ground.

"Pete, come on!" Sandy whispered and started running. Pete followed after him.

Behind them, the car had stopped. The trailer door had opened. Somebody was shouting angrily, "*Grab those kids!*" . . .

There happened to be no school next day, so Pete slept late. When he finally rose and went to the kitchen for some breakfast, his mother was in the backyard, talking to the next-door neighbor, Mrs. Long, over the back fence.

"It was the Hites kid," Mrs. Long was saying. "Just eight years old! The trailer was badly damaged. The poor old man'll have to pay a couple hundred dollars, maybe, to get it fixed up."

"I'm sure glad Pete stayed out of trouble," his mother said. "His father had really laid down the law to him."

Pete's appetite for breakfast vanished. He waited in dread for his mother to come inside.

"What did Ronnie Hites do?" he asked.

"Crazy little tike tied a man's house trailer to a car," she said. "When the car started off, it yanked the trailer off its blocks, and when the weight of the trailer came down on those blocks, they ripped up through the floor. The old man inside was pouring himself some hot tea, and when he was flung off his feet by the jerk he got a bad burn. That Ronnie is in real trouble. You sit down, son, and I'll get you some oatmeal."

Pete forced the oatmeal down his throat. . . .

As soon as he could leave, he went to Sandy's house.

"Sandy, what we going to do about Ronnie Hites?"

"Nothing."

"He may tell the cops that a couple of older boys told him to tie that rope to the car!"

"So what? Ronnie doesn't know who we are. We were wearing costumes and masks. He can't give us away."

"He can tell the cops we were wearing cowboy costumes . . ."

"So were at least a dozen other boys in this neighborhood."

"But he's being blamed for it all!"

"Sure. He tied that rope to the car."

"But it wasn't really his fault. He didn't know what might happen. A little kid like that— he just did what we told him to do."

"Now he knows better."

"We can't let him take all the blame!"

"So what do you want to do?" Sandy demanded. "Tell your father that it was all *your* fault? After you promised him? And you want him to pay for all that damage?"

Pete gulped. He wanted to do the right thing, but . . .

Blind Fish

The Problem: The issue is honesty—specifically, obeying rules and responsibility for others. One of the important growth needs of middle childhood is learning to abide by rules. The child who does not learn this is in constant conflict with age mates and adults in school and community.

Introducing the Problem: You may say to the group, "Most of us, at one time or another, have broken a rule set by parents or school or other authorities. Sometimes nothing happens; sometimes nothing happens to us, but does happen to other people. This is a story about such an incident. The story stops but is not finished. As I read, think of ways in which the story could end."

From the edge of the pool, Mr. Brady, the camp counselor, yelled, "Oh, Mike! Come here!"

Mike thought, "*Oh-oh, I'll get it.*" Reluctantly he swam toward the bank where Mr. Brady stood.

The counselor's face was stern.

"Look, Mike. You know the rules. This is the second time that you've gone in swimming here during hours when it's not permitted. Why?"

Mike pulled himself onto the rim of the pool. "Mr. Brady, I just don't like fire-making and building lean-tos and learning the names of birds and plants. Swimming's the only thing in this camp I like."

"But do you know *why* you're not permitted to go in swimming between ten and twelve in the morning?"

"I guess you don't want anybody going in swimming all by himself."

"Why?"

"Well, if he got into trouble, there'd be nobody around to pull him out of the water and he'd drown."

"Mike, even the best swimmers sometimes get cramps. If that happened to you, and you were here alone, there'd be nobody around to help you. Come on, now, climb out. We're hiking to Crystal Cave, and if you want to come, get ready."

"Yes, Mr. Brady."

By the time Mike got dressed and came out, the dozen boys going on the hike were already in the back of the big truck parked out in front of the Camp Waterman office. Mr. Brady was giving them a short talk.

"We'll hike through the cave. I want you all to stick to the trail. There's a reason for that, and I want you to understand it right now. Underground exploring is actually underground mountain climbing, for caves are rugged, and our path will wind along cliffs and shoot down into deep pits. You could easily have a bad fall. So I'm laying down this rule: Everybody sticks with the party. We'll move in single file, and no boy is to step out of his place in the line. All right, let's go."

The truck took them halfway up the side of Mount Sherman. On a grassy flat circled by live oak and sycamores, they parked the truck. Mr. Brady led them up the bed of a tiny creek, to the back of a box canyon, where the little stream emerged from a dark hole in the mountain wall.

Each boy had a Scout flashlight. In addition, Mr. Brady had brought along four gas lanterns. He pumped them up, now, lit them, and assigned one to every fourth boy in the file.

Then, carrying one of the lamps, Mr. Brady led the file through the cave entrance into a dark, narrow tunnel. The path underfoot was soft and moist. It followed along the tiny creek, and the boys moved carefully so as not to slip and take a header into the shallow water. They bunched close at first, and were silent, awed, and a little frightened by the dark walls crowding close around them. Here underground, their flashlights seemed dim, but the Coleman gas lamps gave off a warm, reassuring flood of light.

Abruptly, the narrow tunnel ended. The boys found themselves in a cave chamber so great that they could not see the ceiling, nor the far walls.

"Turn your flashlights straight up," Mr. Brady said.

They obeyed, the slender cones of light whipping up like antiaircraft searchlights. And, far overhead, they saw the myriad sparkles that marked the ceiling—the glistening tips of long icicles of stone that hung from the arched roof.

"Stalactites," Mr. Brady said. "That's a drop of water at the tip of each one of them."

He turned his flashlight level to the ground. Far across the lofty room they saw the opposite wall, at least a hundred yards away. It was a big cave, all right.

"Let's move on," Mr. Brady ordered.

He led the file across the chamber. At the far wall, a dozen corridors opened off this big central room. Mr. Brady stopped.

"Those tunnels run into other big rooms. This cave system honeycombs the mountain, and parts of it have never been explored. A man lost in here could likely wander around for days and starve to death. That's why," he said firmly, "we're sticking to this main path."

He led them into a broad hallway that widened and became higher until it was like the still, echoing interior of a cathedral.

Mr. Brady said, "Gather around."

The boys crowded about him. There in the wall before them was a niche, hollowed like a bowl, which held a little pool of crystal clear water. On the bottom of the bowl were round white objects, smooth and shining, like birds' eggs, white and lovely.

"Cave pearls," Mr. Brady said. "Not really pearls, but a lime formation. Come on."

Presently he halted the column once more. In a low spot at the base of the wall were shallow dish-shaped holes that held a white liquid. They looked like bowls of milk set out for kittens.

"Moon milk," Mr. Brady said. "Not really, just water full of a sort of lime mixture that hasn't hardened solid."

He led on. Mike, at the end of the file trudging after the counselor, noticed the huge shadows everybody cast on the walls. The swinging Coleman lamps made those shadows seem to lunge and leap like giants in a crazy war dance. Their path, following the little stream, twisted through a forest of columns and on into another high-roofed chamber. Here the creek widened into a broad, shallow lake so still that the water seemed not to be moving at all.

Mr. Brady stopped, bent down, held his lantern out over the water. The boys moved close to him. In the pool they saw a small sleek fish.

"Blind fish," Mr. Brady said. "They have never, in all their lives, seen light. Let's go on."

The boys stared at the fish, then turned reluctantly to follow Mr. Brady around the lake and on into another corridor.

Mike, at the end of the line, slowed his footsteps. Tony Pringle, next ahead of him, looked back. Mike beckoned to him, and Tony stopped and came back.

Mike said, "Tony, let's get us some of these blind fish!"

"What for?"

"Don't you see? Bill Toland's got some guppies, and Steve Akers has some fighting betas, and Nick Barton's got some of those long-tailed, big-eyed Japanese fish. But nobody's got any *blind* fish. Bill brought his aquarium to school, for the science class, and Miss Mason made a big fuss over 'em. We'll bring in some blind fish, and that'll really be something!"

"How'll we catch 'em?"

"Scoop 'em up in a mess kit. You hold my lamp. I'll do the catching."

Mike waded out into the shallow pool. Bending, he lowered the mess kit into the water, moved slowly toward a little school of the tiny fish, and scooped them up.

"Got three of them, Tony! Here, I'll put 'em into your kit."

He caught a dozen of the blind fish.

Tony, tired of being a mere onlooker, put the fish into his drinking cup. Then, lantern in one hand and mess kit in the other, he waded into the water.

"Tony, let me carry that lantern."

"Okay. That'll make it easier . . ."

Tony didn't finish. It was odd. One moment he was standing in knee-deep water, turning to talk to Mike—and the next moment he was sliding, falling, vanishing down under the water. And the brilliance of the Coleman light just as abruptly died and was followed by a surprising and shocking darkness. Mike knew what had happened: Tony had stepped into a deep hole.

Mike plunged ahead and dove—and his groping hands caught Tony. Mike headed for the surface, kicking strongly. Their heads came up into the air. Tony gasped and screamed. His arms caught around Mike's neck and he clung with panicky strength. They went under again.

Mike wasn't frightened. "They do it every time," he thought. He got an arm inside of Tony's elbows, and as they broke surface again, he pushed back against Tony's chin, pushed his head back until Tony's hold on him broke. Dragging Tony with one arm, Mike started swimming.

His feet touched bottom. He stood erect, gasping for breath, holding Tony up. Mike got scared, then. Not of drowning, but of the darkness. It was so utterly unbroken, so solid, so heavy, so suffocating. Fumbling at his belt, Mike unhooked his flashlight, lifted it, and pressed the button. It was supposed to be waterproof, but if water had gotten into it . . .

The light came on; Mike grinned in relief. Tony was shivering now, his teeth chattering, and he began to cry.

"We're all right," Mike told him. "Here, you hold this flashlight. I've got to dive down and get back that Coleman lamp."

"I s-swallowed water," Tony sobbed.

Mike dove back into the deep hole and groped along the bottom for the gas lantern. He had been in a sweat from hiking hard, and the water was icy cold. Something happened to Mike that had never happened before. He found himself doubling up, his stomach knotting in the awfullest pain he'd ever felt. "I'm getting cramps!" he realized. He had to get into shallow water. He had to reach shore before his muscles locked on him and he sank like a rock.

He struck out with arms, trying his level best, but was so doubled up that he couldn't use his legs at all. He got scared, panicky. He had never felt so utterly helpless in his life. He let out a yell—and strangled, his mouth full of water. *"I'm going to die,"* he thought. *"I'm drowning."*

Then he felt rock under him. A hand grabbed his elbow and hauled him out; he was able to gulp air into his stinging lungs.

The pain eased. He was shivering, lying on the bank and shivering.

"What happened to you?" Tony was demanding. "You sure scared me!"

"I'm all right. Just leave me alone."

Lights neared, and they heard voices.

"Hey, Mike! Tony! Where are you?"

"Here!" Tony answered, and waved the flashlight.

Charley Ames and Jeff Hollis and Georgie Parker and Fatso Landiss came hurrying down the trail.

"Say, you guys! What's the idea of dropping out of line?"

"Mr. Brady sent us to find you."

"What you doing, anyhow? Going in swimming with your clothes on?"

Tony said, "Wise guys. Look!" Triumphantly he showed them the drinking cup with the dozen blind fish, so small and graceful, swimming in it.

"Blind fish!" Charley Ames blurted.

"Uh-huh," Tony said. "They're scarce. They're worth a lot of money."

"Where'd you get them?" Georgie demanded.

Tony jerked his chin toward the pool.

"Caught 'em."

"With what?"

"Mess kit."

"Boy, I'm going to get me some!" Charley Ames said.

"Me, too," Jeff Hollis said.

Mike scrambled unsteadily to his feet. "Hey! Don't you go into that water," he said.

They looked at him.

Charley retorted, "You ain't gonna tell *me* what to do."

"If you can get some blind fish, I can," Jeff said.

"You guys ain't going into that water!" Mike shouted at them.

"Who's going to stop me?" Charley snapped.

"I'll call Mr. Brady!"

"You got some blind fish," Jeff said. "The rest of us are going to get some, too."

"Keep out of that water," Mike repeated. "It's icy cold, and . . ."

"You got some blind fish but you don't want us to have any!"

"I'm telling you, I'll call Mr. Brady!"

"If it's all right for you and Tony to catch 'em, why isn't it all right for us?"

Frogman

The Problem: The issue is honesty—specifically, responsibility for others. Two boys have broken regulations to spearfish for big trout in a forbidden pool. Other boys now intend to imitate them. And if the other boys go ahead with their plan, it is very likely that they will get into serious trouble. The two boys who have already broken the rules will, if they permit their friends to imitate their behavior, probably be causing them to commit a serious breach of regulations and to get severely punished. (The story "Blind Fish" deals with the same issue but is appropriate for a younger group.)

Introducing the Problem: Ask the group, "Have you ever done something that was risky or forbidden, because it might be dangerous, and felt scared but excited about it afterward—and then had your kid brother or sister or other young people say that if you did it, they could too? This is a story about such a happening. The story stops but is not finished. As I read it, think of ways in which it could end."

Mike turned the pickup truck off the highway and into the darkness under the trees, stopped, and switched off the engine and headlights.

Danny, on the seat beside him, whispered: "You sure nobody saw us turn in here?"

Mike just laughed. Slipping from behind the wheel, he jumped to the ground, then climbed into the back of the truck. Hastily he pulled off his clothes, then drew on a rubber frogman's suit. He pulled his flippers onto his feet and hefted a "scuba"—aqualung—onto his back. Finally he picked up a waterproof flashlight and a long fish spear with its powerful elastic "gun."

"Mike," Danny whispered, "if anybody passes over the bridge, they'll see your light in the water!"

"No traffic this late at night. But if a car does come, slap the water twice with your hand. I'll turn off my light."

"Be careful, will you? Guys've drowned wearing gear like that."

"Relax, Danny."

Mike lowered himself to the ground and walked with flapping flippers to the river edge. Danny followed. They were parked on the bank of the Truckee River, between the Tahoe City bridge and the Lake Tahoe dam.

Mike waded into the water, the flashlight beam guiding him. Danny watched as Mike sank lower and lower until the water covered his head and the flashlight beam was a weird, greenish glow under the surface. Nervously, then, Danny watched the highway. *"If we're caught, we'll be in real trouble,"* he was realizing.

The river, at this point, was blocked by a dam. In the pool below the dam lived many large trout. In California, fishing is not permitted close below a dam. As a result, these trout had lived long lives and grown to enormous size—up to fifteen pounds in weight.

Mike Albee and Danny Ames were junior counselors at Pine Knob Boys Camp. Mike was seventeen and Danny was sixteen. Mike had an older brother who had been a frogman in the Navy. Two weeks ago Mike had a bright idea: "Let's borrow my brother's diving gear and spearfish some of those big trout in Truckee River!" he had suggested to Danny. To Danny, at the time, it had seemed like a good idea. But now that they were actually doing it, Danny was scared. If a game warden or highway patrolman came along . . .

In the wide pool, Mike was kicking his flippered feet, slowly propelling himself along close to the bottom. The lamp strapped to his head sent a narrow cone of light ahead of him. He held his spear gun ready, nerves tensed to aim and pull the trigger when he sighted a fat trout.

Moments passed. The mountain water was icy cold, and the chill knifed through his rubber suit.

There! Into the tapering funnel of light ahead of him a long, deep-bellied trout swam lazily. Mike reacted with swift precision. He aimed the spear gun, pressed the trigger, felt the rebound of the heavy elastic. The big trout seemed to leap convulsively in the water, and Mike felt a heavy pull on the line. Wishing he could yell in triumph, he hauled in delightedly on the line attached to the spear.

Danny, shaking with nervousness as he watched from the bank, saw Mike rise up out of the river and trudge toward the bank. And Mike was holding aloft a huge trout!

"Look at the size of him, Danny! Big enough almost to feed the camp."

"Yeah. Come on!"

"Hey, wait. Here. Get into the rig. It's your turn."

"I don't want a turn," Danny said. "Let's get . . ."

"You chicken?"

The question was blunt and cold. Danny felt his heart turn over, felt a hot flush of shame.

"All right. Give me the rig," he said angrily. But even as he started putting on the frogman's outfit he raged at himself: Falling for that chicken stuff! Sure, you're scared. Why be afraid to admit it? More guys've got into trouble from being afraid to admit they were chicken than anything else. If you're right, let them call you chicken!

"Pull the straps snug," Mike was saying. "Get a big one. It's easy."

"Watch for cars."

"Relax. You're jumpy as a cat in a dog pound."

Danny waded into the stream. The icy water lifted around him, its chilliness burning through the suit and rising up his legs and stomach and chest. He shivered and his teeth chattered. Steadying himself, he started swimming underneath, kicking his flippered feet. Lifting the spear gun, he peered ahead into the narrow beam of light from his lamp.

Then he saw it. A fish. Caught full in the light. A trout bigger than Mike's!

Afterward, he never remembered taking aim or pulling the trigger, but suddenly the fish shot out of sight and the line from the spear was tugging him through the water. He set his feet on the bottom and pulled and hauled the dying fish to him. Then he swam back and staggered up out of the water, shouting to Mike, "Look! This one's bigger'n a cow!"

Mike grabbed his arm and yanked him up onto the bank. He whispered angrily, "Shut up, for Pete's sake! A car passed and stopped and is turning around. The driver must've seen your light in the water. Drop the fish. We got to run!"

Danny obeyed. They reached the trees and clambered into the pickup truck. Mike started the motor. As he gunned the engine and swung the little truck out onto the highway, Danny looked back. He saw a man standing on the riverbank, bent as if peering down at something. The man turned, looked their way, but did not follow.

He had found the big fish, Danny realized. The spear was still sticking through the trout. The man must've understood at once what had happened. If he was a law officer, he would follow them; if not, he would probably report the incident to the sheriff's office. . . .

"Jeepers, what a fish!"

"What did you use for a worm? A boa constrictor?"

"Bet you had to haul 'im out with a tractor."

Mike and Danny had brought their catch into the older boys' dormitory; now a crowd of them was staring at the big trout.

"Going to have it mounted, Mike?"

"No. We'll eat it tomorrow. Let's give it to Mrs. Dade."

"She's probably sleeping."

"No, there's a light in the cook shack."

Mrs. Dade was elderly and skinny but vigorous, and a wonderful cook who liked and understood boys. She didn't sleep well, so she often read late;

and if anybody was absolutely dying of starvation, he could sneak to the cook shack and bum a cup of hot chocolate and a doughnut from her.

Mike and Danny tiptoed to the cook shack, taking care not to wake Mr. Allen, the camp director, who slept in the main office.

Mrs. Dade, in a robe, was reading in her rocking chair.

"What's this?" she demanded. "A delegation to protest the hogwash I've been feeding you?"

Mike held out the trout for her to see.

"Ain't he something?"

"Looks like the one that swallowed Noah," she admitted. "You going to stuff and mount it?"

"Let's eat it tomorrow!" Danny blurted.

"Come on," she said, rising. "I'll make room for it in the refrigerator. That trout's big enough to give everybody in camp a taste. Mr. Allen will be going into town tomorrow. We'll eat Moby Dick here for lunch. But, boys, don't go back for his cousins, you hear me?"

Danny nodded, reddening. Mike just laughed. . . .

The game warden arrived next morning while everyone was at breakfast. He was a stocky man with a pockmarked face and a worried expression. Mr. Allen rose from his chair at the head table to greet him.

"I'm Johnson, from the Department of Fish and Game," the warden said, loudly enough for everyone to hear. "Mr. Allen, we suspect that several of your boys went spearfishing in the river below the dam last night." He turned and faced the suddenly quiet roomful of boys. "Any of you boys involved?"

Some boys shook their heads; others looked blank; nobody answered.

"We found a fish on the bank, right beside the pool, with a fish spear still sticking in him. Any of you own a spear gun?"

Again he got no answer; the faces looking at him were all still and tense.

"Whoever speared that fish will face charges of fishing with illegal equipment, fishing at night, and fishing in closed waters. He will probably pay a fine of over a hundred dollars and have to spend time in Juvenile Hall."

"Wow," somebody murmured; someone else uttered a low whistle; another boy groaned, "What a way to spend a vacation!"

Mr. Allen, who did not get mad very often, looked very upset now.

"If any of you boys were involved in this—raid," he said sternly, "I want you to stand up. Now."

Mike didn't stand; Danny didn't stand. But Danny felt that the hot flush of misery on his face must betray him as clearly as a shouted confession.

Mr. Johnson said, "I don't have a search warrant, and I wouldn't insult Mr. Allen by asking him to open every locker on the place. But I will ask you boys: Which one of you bought a fish spear at the Lake Sports Shop in Tahoe City last week? The owners tell me that such a spear was sold to a tall, dark-haired boy from this camp. I want that boy to stand up."

Danny's heart sank. Mike was tall and dark-haired; and, in fact, it *was* Mike who had bought the spear.

Then a boy stood up. Not Mike, but Lee Monahan, who was also tall and dark-haired.

Lee said: "I bought a fish spear at the Lake shop, Mr. Johnson, but I sent it home as a birthday gift to my brother, who's going down to Catalina to do some skin diving in the ocean."

Danny almost gasped aloud. Lee was lying. Lee was a quick-witted guy, and he was covering up for Mike.

But the game warden was not easily fooled.

"Mr. Allen, mind if I look in the camp refrigerator?"

Danny felt a sickening wave of alarm come over him again. The big trout was in Mrs. Dade's refrigerator; it would furnish the final and positive proof of guilt.

"Not at all, under the circumstances," Mr. Allen answered the warden. "This way."

He started out of the dining room. Mr. Johnson followed, and a group of boys tagged after. Mike grabbed Danny's arm and drew him along with the others. Danny felt so ill he was afraid he would lose his breakfast.

They filed into the big camp kitchen. Mrs. Dade, drinking her second cup of coffee, looked inquiringly at them.

Mr. Allen said, "Mrs. Dade, please excuse us. Do you have a big fish in your refrigerator?"

"I do. Why?"

"Mind if we take a look?"

"Help yourself. Bottom door."

Mr. Allen opened the refrigerator door, and there on a big platter was the fish. Using both hands, Mr. Allen drew out the platter and held it up for Mr. Johnson to look at. Spread out over the platter were clean, appetizing slabs of a fish that had been gutted and cleaned and cut into cooking-ready fillets. They might have been trout or halibut or cod or barracuda as far as any ordinary glance could tell.

Mr. Johnson's eyes were snapping with suspicion and frustration. "What did that fish look like?" he demanded.

"Wet, scaly, and dead," Mrs. Dade said. "What does any fish look like?"

"I mean, what kind of fish was it?"

She shrugged. "Just fish. The butcher may have mentioned, but I've got too many other things to remember."

Mr. Johnson glared at her, then turned and stalked angrily out.

Danny heard Mike, beside him, choke back a laugh; but Danny didn't laugh, didn't even feel like laughing. He was thinking that first Lee Monahan had lied to protect them; now Mrs. Dade had saved them by covering up for them. The mess was spreading like some kind of runaway infection. . . .

Then, several nights later, when Danny was undressing for bed in the tent he shared with Mike, two boys came in. They were Lee Monahan and Eddie Ames.

Lee said, "Danny, we want to borrow that frogman outfit that you and Mike used. Okay?"

Danny stared. "What f-for?" he stammered.

"What d'you think for?"

Eddie said, "We were up at the dam today. There's bigger trout than the one you guys got!"

"Where's the gear?" Lee demanded.

"It's Mike's. You'll have to ask him."

"So we'll ask him," Lee said.

"I don't think you guys ought to go spearfishing there."

"Why not? It was all right for you, wasn't it?"

"But . . . Anyway, we lost the spear."

"I got a new spear gun from home today. Come on, Eddie," Lee said. "Let's go find Mike."

"You know," Eddie remarked as he turned to follow Lee, "I bet we could shoot a deer with that spear gun. We could rig up a jacklight, and that would draw a deer close enough so we could hit it easy with the spear . . ."

Danny sat there, after they left, in acute misery, thinking . . .

Mike came in.

"Mike, did Lee and Eddie find you?"

"No. What do they want?"

"To borrow the frogman outfit, so they can go spearfishing."

"Let 'em have it."

"But suppose they get caught?"

"That's their problem."

"You heard what the game warden said!"

"So did they."

"We're older. We're counselors."

"They're not babies."

"But we set the example!"

"So now we can just mind our own business."

"But, Mike, we can't let them get into trouble!"

"Don't see what else we can do."

"We can refuse to let them have the diving gear."

"Then everybody in camp would figure us for a couple of heels."

"Or we can tell Mr. Allen that Lee and Eddie are going spearfishing. . ."

"I'm no lousy stool pigeon!" Mike said furiously. "You squeal on them and you know what the whole camp'll think about you, don't you?"

"Yeah." Danny caught an unsteady breath, then insisted, "Mike, we just can't let them have the diving gear."

"Then somebody will squeal on *us*! I don't put it past Lee Monahan to tell Mr. Allen that the frogman gear is in our locker and that we speared that big fish. Mr. Allen would turn us over to the game warden!"

Vividly, Danny foresaw the results of that eventuality. Being arrested. His name in the paper. Trial before a judge. Writing his mother that he had to pay a hundred-dollar fine. That he must spend thirty to ninety days in jail. . . .

Outside the tent, then, they heard voices and footsteps approaching.

Mike said, "That must be Lee and Eddie now, coming for the diving gear."

"Don't give it to them—that game warden is going to be watching that pool awful close. Lee and Eddie may get caught!"

"We can't help that."

Yes, Danny thought, we can. He could go to Mr. Allen. He could confess that he and Mike had speared that big fish in the refrigerator. Mr. Allen would seize their diving gear. Then Lee and Eddie couldn't get into trouble.

"Mike, let's tell Mr. Allen the whole thing!"

"And have him hand us over to the game warden? You crazy?"

Then Lee and Eddie were entering the tent. *"Now,"* Danny realized. *"You can stop it now—if you go tell Mr. Allen what you did. If you've got the guts. . . ."*

Rocket Shoot

The Problem: The issue is honesty: accepting blame for a wrong committed even though someone else thinks he is guilty and has already accepted the blame. Two boys have started a fire in wheat fields by accident. A logger, who drove across the area and lost a bottle of gasoline, thinks he must be to blame and has accepted the guilt. The boys, if they keep still, will not even be suspect; but they know that the fault may well be theirs. Should they keep still?

Introducing the Problem: Ask, "Have any of you ever been in a spot where you suspect that something you did may have caused serious damage to somebody's property, but you are not absolutely sure that you are to blame? This is the problem in this story. The story stops but is not finished. As I read, think of ways in which the story could end."

Chris carefully assembled the rocket while Ronnie looked on. To the twenty-inch steel tube of the combustion chamber, Chris fastened the wooden nose cone. Then he filled the combustion chamber with the propellent—a mixture of three parts zinc dust to one part powdered sulphur. He tamped the charge in, working with patient thoroughness. Next, to hold the powder in, he inserted the burst-diaphragm, to which he had already attached the igniter wires. These wires he ran through the opening of the nozzle and screwed the nozzle into place at the base of the rocket. Finally, then, he clamped the six-inch fins into place. Now the rocket was ready to blast off.

"Ronnie, you carry the launcher. Let's go!"

They rode out of town on their bikes, down a country road out into wheat fields. The rocket, Chris figured, had a range of a quarter-mile. When they were at least half a mile from the nearest house, he stopped.

"Let's set 'er up!"

Leaving their bikes in the road, they walked out into a field. They set up the launcher—a V- shaped trough of metal with slanting braces. Chris placed the rocket on the launcher and unrolled the wires of the igniter a distance of sixty feet to a little ditch. He attached one wire to the pole of a dry battery.

"All right, Ronnie. You count-down!"

They crouched down in the safety of the ditch. Ronnie, his voice shaking with excitement, began counting: "Ten. . .nine. . ." on down to "three. . .two. . .one. . .*Blast!*"

Chris touched the second wire to the other pole of the battery. A long moment seemed to pass. Then the building pressure of exploding gas within the combustion chamber of the rocket burst the diaphragm; smoke and flame shot out of the nozzle, and the rocket inched up the launcher, lifted into the air twenty—fifty—a hundred feet—hesitated, wobbling as its comet's tail of fire dwindled; dropped half-way to earth – and then, as flame suddenly blasted strongly again, shot ahead once more. But it was off-course. It had veered and twisted. "She's burning uneven!" Chris shouted in dismay, for the rocket was flying parallel to the ground, about a hundred feet up. It whipped over the tops of a grove of trees and vanished from sight.

"Guess I just didn't tamp the powder down right," Chris said gloomily. "So she burned unevenly."

"It was a good shoot," Ronnie said loyally.

"Yeah, sure. We aim at the moon and hit the house next door. Fine shoot. Let's go pick it up."

But they couldn't find the spent rocket in the wheat field. Finally they gave up and pedaled home.

Chris first heard the fire trucks roar down the road as his family sat down to supper that evening.

"Oh, oh," Mr. Carter said, "a fire." He hurried to the door and looked out. "Look at that red sky. Must be a big one!"

Chris looked. To the west, the cloudy night sky burned with a sullen, crimson glow.

Mr. Carter telephoned to the local paper. When he hung up, he said, "The fire's burned out over fifty acres of ripe wheat and is spreading fast. Burned a barn, too. That fire will cause thousands of dollars of damage before it's put out."

"Wheat fields?" Chris echoed. "Where, Dad?"

"The Bronkmyer Ranch, to the west."

That, Chris realized, was where he had fired off his rocket that afternoon. He went to his room, feeling sick and scared. . . .

At breakfast next morning, the local newspaper had a surprising story about the wheat field fire. The article said:

> Blame for the fire that burned over the field of wheat on the Bronkmyer Ranch has been definitely placed on William Hawes, who owns a small ranch adjoining the big Bronkmyer holdings. Firemen found the remains of a shattered glass jug in the area where the fire is believed to have started. Chemical tests on charred vegetation show that the jug had contained gasoline. Firemen believe that the jug, lying in the wheat, acted like a magnifying glass to focus rays of the hot sun on dry fuel to start the fire. Heat made the jug shatter and then the spilled gasoline further fed the flames.
>
> Mr. Hawes had been cutting timber with a gasoline chain saw in a grove near the fire site last Saturday. When questioned he freely admitted that he

carried gasoline for the saw in such a jug. The jug, he says, must have fallen from his jeep as he took a shortcut across the Bronkmyer fields on his way home.

Chris paused in his reading. He felt a happy surge of relief. He wasn't, after all, to blame for the fire! But his relief did not last. That jug, he thought; it had been lying out in the wheat since Saturday. Why hadn't it caused a fire the first day it was out there?

Maybe it hadn't caused the fire at all! Maybe something else started the blaze. Maybe that something else was a rocket that went crazy and landed in the field still hot enough to set dry grain to slowly smoldering until a spark fanned into flame? A spark could smolder in the vegetation for hours.

Chris read on: "Mr. Bronkmyer has *No Trespassing* signs posted on his property. He has announced that he intends to sue Mr. Hawes for full damages. While the loss is less than first estimated, it is thought that it may amount to four or five thousand dollars."

Five thousand dollars!

And Mr. Hawes wasn't a rich man at all.

That sick, lost feeling came back to Chris's stomach.

"Ronnie," he said, when they met in the schoolyard later, "I'm wondering if my rocket started that wheat field fire!"

"Don't tell anybody!" Ronnie gasped.

"Maybe, if they find my rocket, chemical tests will show it started the wheat to burning."

"But, gosh, Chris, you'd be in awful trouble!"

"I g-guess so." His name would be in the paper. His mother would cry. He'd have to quit tinkering with rockets. Maybe Mr. Bronkmyer would even sue his father for damages.

"But nobody's found the rocket," Ronnie said. "You just keep still."

"Then Mr. Hawes will have to pay for all that burned wheat."

"You want your Dad to pay for it?"

"No."

"So what're you going to do?"

Chris said, "I think that we . . ."

Heavy, Heavy Hangs Over Your Head

The Problem: The issue is that of honesty—of confessing to one's guilt when someone else is blamed for a fault of one's own. Linda, baby-sitting for Mrs. Mallory, tries on a string of pearl beads from Mrs. Mallory's bureau. The string breaks and some of the pearl beads are lost. Later, Mrs. Mallory accuses Linda's friend Nora of losing the pearls. Linda can clear Nora of blame only by confessing her own guilt in the matter. Involved, in addition to honesty, is integrity in friendship.

Introducing the Problem: Say, "Sometimes you get into trouble by sheer accident, when you had no intention of doing anything wrong. Have any of you ever unintentionally broken something that belonged to somebody else and felt just sick about it? It happens to all of us. It happened to Linda in this story. But Linda's problem is more complicated because her friend Nora is blamed for the damage. Maybe some of you have been in such a spot. This story stops but is not finished. As I read, think of ways in which this story might end."

This was Linda's first job of baby sitting for the Mallory family. The baby went right off to sleep, soon after the Mallorys left.

Linda watched television in the living room for a long while. Bored finally, she got up and wandered through the house. She had got this job with the Mallorys tonight because her friend Nora Baker had given her name to them. Nora was their regular sitter. Tonight, Nora had a bad cold, and her mother had kept her at home.

Looking into the bedroom closet, Linda gazed with a hungrily appreciative eye at Mrs. Mallory's wardrobe. Such lovely dresses and such smart suits! Linda felt an impulse to try some of them on but checked it. She did baby sitting for half a dozen different families; she never touched their belongings or opened their refrigerators or sampled cookie jars.

But the jewel box on Mrs. Mallory's dressing table was more temptation than Linda could resist. The box lay open, revealing pieces of costume jewelry that were magically lovely to Linda's eye. She picked up a string of pink pearl beads that shone with a lustrous glow. She put the string about her throat and peered into the mirror, studying the effect; and she sighed, for the beads were so shiny and beautiful.

"Oh, darn!"

The string had broken. Pearls cascaded down her dress to the floor. She bent to pick them up, and gasped in alarm. Some of the pearls had fallen through an open register in the floor—the cold air return of the heating system. She could hear the lost pearls rolling down the long, insulated pipe toward the furnace in the basement.

And then, out front, she heard a car turn into the driveway, heard the engine race momentarily as the driver shifted gears, then die into silence as he stopped the car. The Mallorys were back!

Working swiftly, she scooped up the pearls still on the floor, thrust the partial string and loose beads into a vase on a stand in the hallway as she hurried back into the living room. Sitting down, she grabbed up a magazine and pretended to be reading. Her heart was beating so violently it seemed that the Mallorys must hear it as they entered.

But they sensed nothing wrong. They paid her, thanked her, and Mr. Mallory took her home.

As she lay in bed afterward, worry was a torment that would not let her sleep. She scolded herself bitterly; she should never have touched Mrs. Mallory's belongings.

She did try to reassure herself: a string of pearls left out in the open on the bureau like that—they were just costume jewelry. They had to be! She would go with Nora, next time Nora sat for the Mallorys, get the string from the vase, take it out and have the pearl beads restrung and pay for the job herself. . . .

But she received a shocking surprise when Nora called her, several evenings later. Nora was baby-sitting at the Mallorys.

"Linda, Mrs. Mallory fired her cleaning woman today. For *stealing!*"

Linda gasped, "Wh-what?"

"Uh-huh! Mrs. Mallory went to put on her pearl necklace and it was gone! The pearls weren't real—that is, they were cultured pearls—but Mr. Mallory paid over a hundred dollars for them in Tokyo."

Linda plumped down on a chair, the strength suddenly gone from her legs.

"Have—have they looked everywhere in the house for the pearls?"

"They sure have. Mr. Mallory kept saying that they would turn up, and anyway he wouldn't fire a poor cleaning woman without *real* proof. But Mrs. Mallory was so mad she wanted to go down to the police station tomorrow and swear out a warrant for the cleaning woman's arrest!"

"Oh, no," Linda choked. "Nora, I'm coming over."

"Sure, come on."

For a while Linda had to listen to Nora talk. In an agony of impatience, Linda sat with Nora in the living room in front of the TV set. Then, saying, "I'm going to the kitchen for a drink," Linda walked through the house.

In the hallway, she upended the vase on the stand—and the torn string of pearls and loose gems fell into her palm.

Quickly she poured them into a covered casserole on the sideboard. There the necklace would soon be discovered.

The next afternoon, Mrs. Mallory telephoned her. In a strained voice, she asked Linda to come over that evening after dinner.

When Linda arrived, she found Nora—angry and white-faced—sitting in the living room with Mrs. Mallory.

"Linda," Mrs. Mallory began, "I've already told Nora what's happened. Today I found this string of pearls in a casserole on the sideboard. The string is broken and a dozen of the pearls are missing. I missed the necklace several days ago and thought it was stolen. Obviously, it wasn't. It's my guess that somebody took them from my bureau top and tried them on—that the string broke and some of the pearls were lost. And that this person then hid the remaining pearls in the casserole."

"I didn't do it!" Nora blurted. "I've told you!"

Mrs. Mallory continued right on: "Now, this casserole was empty yesterday. I know, because I used it. The only people who have been alone in the house since yesterday are you, Linda, and Nora. You were both here last night. Nora tells me that she has never seen the pearls before. Linda—now tell me the truth! —did you hide the pearls after breaking the string?"

"Oh, no!" Linda said. "I've never seen them before either!"

"Then, Nora," Mrs. Mallory said firmly, "you are the guilty one."

"But I'm not, I'm not!" Nora insisted. "Please believe me. I've never seen those pearls before. Not even once!" And, unable to check herself, Nora began to cry.

Mrs. Mallory's angry glance moved from Nora to Linda, then back to Nora again.

"Nora," she said sternly, "a few weeks ago, I asked you to sit for me and you told me you couldn't because you had a bad cold. But that same evening I saw you in a movie with some friends, having a gay time. Nora, I just can't take your word.

"My pearl necklace, with so many of the pearls gone, isn't worth much now. I'll discuss replacing it with your father. He may or may not feel any responsibility. As for you, I don't want you to baby-sit for me any more. And don't give my name to anybody as a person who will recommend you for a sitting job. Please go home now."

Nora got up to go, and Mrs. Mallory turned to Linda.

"Linda, will you stay tonight and baby-sit for me?"

For a moment Linda could not answer, she was so choked up. Nora, going to the door, was crying into her hands. Linda felt that she must jump up, stop Nora, turn and blurt out to Mrs. Mallory that Nora was a fine person, that Nora *was not to blame* for losing the pearls, that Nora would never lie about such a thing . . .

"*But I can't,*" Linda told herself. "Nora doesn't need sitting jobs. I do. Her father makes good money. He can afford to replace that necklace. My folks don't have any money. I just *can't* admit I did it!"

"Well, Linda?" Mrs. Mallory asked.

The Apple Orchard

The Problem: The issue is a conflict between self-preservation and responsibility for others. A group of boys creep at night into an orchard to steal apples. One boy falls out of a tree and is hurt. They realize that he needs immediate medical care. But if they try to carry him away, they may cause him to suffer serious internal injury. The alternative is to go to the nearest house—the home of the orchard owner—and ask that an ambulance be called. But if they do this, the owner will also call police to arrest them for stealing his apples.

Introducing the Problem: Say, "Sometimes you do something that's wrong but you figure that you can run fast enough, or think fast enough, to keep out of trouble. Then something you never expected happens, and you find yourself in a spot you can see no way out of. This is a story about some boys who got themselves into this kind of a fix."

A group of boys are on their way to an orchard to steal some big, ripe Delicious apples. They feel a little thrill of guilt as they pass a gas station and see a police car parked there. A block away, they hide their bikes in bushes; and moving stealthily, they pass the house of the orchard owner, Mr. Kelly. Through a window that flickers with the blue light of a television set, they see him inside watching it. Back of the house, they reach the orchard. In the dark, they climb the trees and feel along the limbs for the big apples.

Eddy calls out in fright. The others hear a heavy thud.

"Eddy, you all right?" Andy hisses. "Mike, I think Eddy fell out of the tree. Let's take a look . . ."

The boys gather around the groaning boy on the ground.

Mike says, "Gosh, I think he's hurt bad. We got to carry him out . . ."

Andy says; "No! That's the worst thing you can do, if he's broken something . . ."

Pete says: "Yeah. A rib can puncture his lung."

"What'll we do then? We just can't leave him here!"

Danny says: "We've got to leave 'im. We can go to the gas station and telephone his father to come get him. That way, nobody'll know we've been here."

"You know where they live? It'll take his Dad half an hour to get here. At least!"

Mike says; "Look, we've got to get help *right now*! We can go to the house and tell Mr. Kelly and he'll phone for an ambulance."

"And for a police car," Danny objects, "to grab us for stealing his fruit! No, we don't do that! But anyway, how do we know Eddy's broken any ribs? Maybe he's not hurt all that bad. Let's just carry him to my house. My Mom'll take care of . . ."

But Mike broke in furiously, "I've told you! Carry him, and if he *has* broken something inside, he's a goner! We've got to get an ambulance."

"Then it'll get to the cops. They'll ask who was with him, and he'll tell our names."

"No, he won't. We'll warn him."

"He's not a squealer."

Pete says, "Look. Let's make a stretcher with jackets and sticks and roll him onto it real gentle and just carry him out to the street. That's just a little ways. Then we can call an ambulance, and we say he was knocked off his bike by a hit-run driver."

"Beautiful," Jim blurts.

And Pete goes on, "That way, nobody'll blame us. In fact, they'll give us credit for helping him!"

But Mike still insists: "No! We don't roll him onto a stretcher. We don't move him!"

Jim says, "But we can't just run off and leave him!"

INTEGRITY IN FRIENDSHIP RELATIONS

Birthday Present

The Problem: The issue is individual integrity—specifically, integrity in personal relations, such as keeping a promise to a friend.

Introducing the Problem: Say to the group, "Sometimes we promise to do things with friends and get ourselves into a conflict of promises. Haven't you ever agreed to go one place with one friend—and then unexpectedly had a chance to go to a better place with a friend you like more? Then you wish you hadn't made the first promise. This story I'm going to read deals with such a conflict. The story stops but is not finished. As I read, try to think of ways in which the story could end."

Susan Burns got a late start on her 4-H project that Saturday morning. She had had to stay home and help her mother take down the living-room curtains so that they could be sent to the cleaners. Done, finally, Susan rode her bike down Mulberry Street toward the Morton place, where she kept the steer she was fattening for the county fair in June.

As she pedaled along, a station wagon passed and several girls called hello to her. She waved back, recognizing Dotty Burton, Ellen Hewes, and Edie Jones, riding with Dotty's father. The station wagon was pulling a boat on a trailer; and as Susan noticed the boat, she felt a pang of envy. Dotty's father was evidently taking Dotty and her friends out to Frenchman's Lake. He was going to teach them water-skiing. Dotty was already good at it.

Susan wished that she knew Dotty and her friends better; Dotty might ask her along some time. Susan's family had moved to Hamilton just a month before, and she was a new girl in school. Luckily she made friends easily, or she would have been out of things entirely, like Wendy Norris.

She thought of Wendy just because she saw her coming out of the Pritchard house with little Timmy Pritchard. Wendy earned money baby sitting. It wasn't just that Wendy was small for her age; she was a city girl who didn't know the first thing about ranch country. She was new here, too, although her family had been living in Hamilton for over six months.

Reaching the Morton place, at the turn of the street, Susan dismounted from her bike and walked back to the barn where she kept her steer. There she got busy throwing feed to the sleek Hereford and cleaning up the stall. When she saw Wendy and little Timmy walk past the barn door, headed out to the corrals, she saw no reason to warn them away.

The first clue she had of trouble was when she heard Wendy calling, "Hi, Sookie!" and little four-year old Timmy echoing her in a shrill, "Hi, Sookie!"

Susan had picked up a brush, intending to smooth down the steer's coat. She stopped, arm uplifted, frowning.

Sookie? Sookie was the gentle old Jersey cow the Mortons owned. But Sookie had been put on a trailer and hauled out to pasture yesterday. That wasn't Sookie out in the corral now, that was . . .

"Good gosh!" Susan blurted. "They'll get killed!" She dropped the brush and looked around frantically for a pitchfork but saw none. Then she heard little Timmy cry out in fright. Susan grabbed up a horse blanket and whirled and ran out of the open door of the barn. And as she looked at the corral, she gasped in alarm. That fool kid, Wendy. She had taken Timmy right into the corral.

"Come back!" Susan yelled. "Come out of there!"

Wendy and Timmy had crawled under the bottom board of the fence and walked into the corral—had walked toward "Sookie," probably intending to pet her. But that wasn't Sookie in the corral; that was Comanche. And Comanche, now, was lowering his head, pawing the ground, and snorting his anger.

"Run!" Susan screeched. "*Run!*"

But neither Wendy nor Timmy moved; they stood frozen in their tracks, paralyzed with fright. "*If only I can get there in time,*" Susan gasped to herself. Already Comanche was beginning to move; Comanche was working himself into the rage that would launch him into a rush.

Susan flung herself to the ground, rolled under the fence, bounced to her feet, and ran her level best. Again she screamed, "Run!" as she passed Wendy and Timmy. She darted straight at Comanche. Her intention was to whip the blanket across the big bull's face, and this she tried to do. But the blanket caught on Comanche's horns and was torn from Susan's grasp. Susan did not waste an instant trying to clear it but kept on running. If only she could draw the bull after her . . .

She glanced back over her shoulder fearfully—and stopped. The bull wasn't chasing her. That blanket, snagged on Comanche's horns, was hanging over his eyes, blinding him. Comanche, head lowered, was trying to shake the old blanket off his horns.

Wendy had finally come to her senses. Pulling Timmy by the hand, she was running toward the fence as hard as she could make the little boy go. Susan breathed a heartfelt "Thank goodness!" of relief and followed them. She walked at first, but then she darted into a run as she saw the blanket go flying from Comanche's horns. The bull glanced around, snorting, saw the children, lowered his head, and again started into a rush.

Wendy and Timmy were at the fence. They flopped down and rolled under the bottom rail—and Susan came right after them, into safety.

As they scrambled to their feet, Comanche reached the fence and bellowed at them. They jumped back in fright.

"What's the matter with Sookie?" Wendy asked Susan, stammering.

"For Pete's sake," Susan demanded furiously, "don't you know a bull from a cow?"

"You m-mean that ain't Sookie?"

"No, that ain't Sookie," Susan snapped, "that's Comanche."

"Ain't he a pet?"

"Sure, like a rattlesnake's a fishingworm, he's a pet."

"Gosh!"

"Yeah, gosh. Now take Timmy home before something else happens."

Timmy's mother had heard him crying and had left the house and was hurrying toward them now.

"Timmy, dear, you all right?" she called. "What happened, Wendy?"

Wendy swallowed hard, still too scared and confused to give a clear answer. Timmy pointed to the bull in the corral and, as his mother reached them, buried his face in her skirt and began to yell. Susan turned away, headed back to the barn, disgusted with the whole hullabaloo.

"Shush, Timmy," his mother said soothingly. "You're all right, dear. Wendy, what happened?"

"He—went in there," Wendy said, pointing toward the corral.

Mrs. Pritchard gasped. "Oh, he's *always* getting into things. That awful bull! He might've trampled Timmy. But you got him out."

Wendy pointed to Susan.

"Susan came—she ran in . . ."

"You brave girls. You saved Timmy's life!"

"Oh, what gush," Susan thought. If she heard any more of it, she would be sick to her stomach. She hurried into the barn to finish tending her steer.

But she did hear more of that gush. At dinner, that evening, her mother said, "Susan, did you see the story about you and Wendy in the paper?"

"*What?*" Susan gasped.

"Listen." Her mother read from the local evening paper: "Girls save tot from bull. Susan Burns and Wendy Norris, both eleven years of age, saved four-year-old Timmy Pritchard from possibly being goared and trampled by a bull in a corral on the Morton place this morning. Timmy had climbed into the corral, thinking that the bull was a cow that the children often pet. Luckily, the older girls noticed him in time. The bull, enraged, had started toward Timmy. The two girls ran into the corral. While Wendy grabbed the tot and hurried him back to the fence, Susan distracted the bull by striking him across the face with an old saddle blanket she had snatched up. Mrs. Pritchard, who reported the incident, says that undoubtedly her little son's life was saved by the prompt action of the courageous girls . . ."

Susan made an inelegant sound with her lips.

Her mother said, "Susan!"

"But that's hogwash."

"You didn't haul Timmy out of the corral?"

"Yes, sure, but—Wendy didn't do anything."

"You're going to be less generous than Wendy?"

"What do you mean?"

"According to the paper here, Wendy insisted to Mrs. Pritchard that all the credit for saving Timmy should go to Susan Burns."

"Oh."

"That's pretty nice of Wendy."

"But, doggonit, it was her fault that Timmy got into the corral in the first place."

"You sure? You saw it happen?"

"Oh, what difference does it make?" Susan said disgustedly, and gave up on the whole thing.

But it did make a difference—at school, next morning. Both Susan and Wendy were teased about being heroes by the other children. Susan shrugged it off; Wendy turned red with discomfort.

"Susan did it all," she tried to explain, but nobody listened.

Susan could have exposed Wendy; she could have told everybody that Wendy was a dope who deliberately walked into a corral to pet a prize bull; but Susan kept still. She knew how much scornful teasing this would bring down on Wendy.

Something else that was different happened: Wendy was usually left out when the girls played games. But today she was included. Another difference was that Wendy attached herself to Susan and began to follow her around.

Formerly, Wendy's mother had taken her to school every morning in the family car. Now Wendy came to the corner where Susan waited each morning for the school bus and climbed aboard after Susan and sat beside her. Susan didn't mind; Wendy wasn't a pest who kept talking if you wanted to sit in silence and think lazily. If you wanted to talk, Wendy talked; and sometimes she was interesting, because she was a bookworm who knew a little about a lot. Girls who liked Susan began to treat Wendy in a more friendly fashion. Wendy began to share Susan's growing popularity.

As Wendy became happier, her class work began to improve. She would speak up now, instead of sitting silently until the teacher called on her.

Late one afternoon when Susan got home from school, she found a strange woman sitting in the living room with her mother.

"Susan, dear, this is Mrs. Norris, Wendy's mother."

Susan said hello and started to her room.

"Wait, Susan," Mrs. Norris said; "I want to thank you for what you've done for Wendy."

"But I haven't done anything."

"You've let her be your friend. Wendy hated school here and was doing badly, although she's bright. Now she's happy with school, thanks to you."

"Actually, I'm kind of new here myself," Susan said.

"But you make dozens of friends without even trying."

"Well, I—guess so," Susan admitted.

Among her new friends were Dotty Burton, Ellen Hewes, and Edie Jones. Dotty was the most popular girl in the class.

One afternoon after school, as Susan and Wendy waited for the bus that would take them home, they saw Dotty, Ellen, and Edie get into a station wagon driven by Mrs. Burton. The car moved up to where Susan and Wendy were standing.

Dotty called, "Susan! You want a lift home?"

"Why, sure. Thanks!"

Not until she got in, and the car started off, did Susan realize that Dotty had not invited Wendy, too. Looking back, Susan got a glimpse of Wendy's face, looking hurt and crushed, before the car turned a corner.

Susan said, "I usually ride home with Wendy."

"Wendy?" Mrs. Burton said. "The girl who was standing near you?"

"Yes."

"I'm sorry, dear, but I'm in such a hurry now I really can't turn back to get her."

"No loss," Dotty Burton said, and Ellen and Edie laughed.

They stopped at Susan's house to let her out.

Dotty said, "Sue, Dad's going to take us to Tomales Bay some Saturday soon, to go clamming. Like to come along?"

"Sure, that would be swell," Susan said.

Wendy wasn't at school next day. She did come the following day, however. When Susan asked why she'd been absent, she said, "Oh, I had a cold." She did look kind of sick.

"A cold? And you got over it in one day?"

"Maybe it was just an allergy," Wendy said.

But Susan's mother, when she asked her what an allergy was, wanted to know more; and when Susan told how she had left Wendy standing at the bus stop and gone off with Dotty Burton's crowd, she nodded her head and said, "Yes, that would make Wendy sick, Susan. Sick at heart."

"Wasn't my fault, Mom."

"She does count on you a lot."

"Doggonit, am I going to be saddled with that drip the rest of my life!"

"She's a nice girl, dear."

"Sure, but . . . Hey, I'm going clamming with Dotty and her crowd!"

"Wonderful. When?"

"Don't know yet. Dotty'll tell me."

Several days later, Susan received a letter in the mail—an invitation to a birthday party. It was Wendy's birthday party, on Saturday, the 14th.

"Do I have to give Wendy a present, Mom?"

"No have to about it. But don't you want to?"

"Well, sure. I'll get her a book."

"That would be fine."

On the bus next morning, Susan said to Wendy, "Thanks for inviting me to your party, Wendy."

"You'll come?"

"Sure, I'll be there. Who else did you invite?"

"All the girls in our room."

"That's nice."

So it came as a surprise to Susan—a disastrous surprise—when on Friday night she got a phone call from Dotty Burton.

"Hey, Susan, you be up and dressed at 5 A.M. tomorrow morning!"

"What for?"

"We're going to the beach to hunt clams. Remember?"

"Tomorrow?"

"Sure. Dad says it'll be the right kind of low tide. I told you it would be some Saturday soon."

"B-But—aren't you going to Wendy's birthday party?"

"When we could go clamming instead? Don't make me laugh. Wouldn't go anyway. She gives me a pain."

"Look, I—I think I got to go to her party," Susan said.

"Say, I invited you first, didn't I? I asked you over a week ago, and you promised you'd go."

"I did," Susan admitted. "But you said we'd go clamming *some* Saturday, not exactly . . ."

"So you owe it to me to go clamming with us."

"But Wendy's feelings will be hurt."

"So who cares? See you tomorrow. Be waiting for us at 5 A.M.!" Dotty said, and hung up.

Susan was so silent at supper that her mother asked, "What's the matter, dear?"

"Mother, what do you mean when you say that you have a 'prior engagement'?"

"Oh, that means . . . Well, somebody calls you up, for example, and asks you to come to dinner. But you've already promised somebody else you'd come to *their* dinner. That's your *prior engagement.*"

"I guess I can't go to Wendy's birthday party. I got a prior engagement to go clamming with Dotty Burton."

"Susan, dear, Wendy will be hurt!"

"But I do have a prior engagement."

"Was it definite? Seems to me you said it was *some* Saturday."

"Whatever Saturday, I promised to go."

"You mean you *want* to go?"

"I've got to go!" Susan said wildly.

"Would you really do that to Wendy?"

"I've got nothing against Wendy."

"She'll really be hurt, Susan. She'll think you don't like her. She'll think you prefer to go with Dotty and her crowd."

"Maybe I do!"

"But you accepted Wendy's invitation. You're willing to go back on your word?"

"Oh, darn it! What *should* I do, anyway?"

"It's your decision, dear."

"I wish I'd never heard of Wendy Norris!"

"Don't get upset. Go ahead and phone. Whichever way you decide, you settle it now. You phone Wendy—or Dotty—and say you're awfully sorry, but you can't go."

Miserably Susan sat down at the telephone.

Whose number, she asked herself, should she dial? Wendy's . . . or Dotty Burton's?

Lost Ball

The Problem: The issues are honesty and personal integrity. Sometimes young people are so frightened of their elders that they lie to escape punishment for infraction of rules.

Introducing the Problem: Say, "Sometimes you get into trouble without ever intending to, by accident. Then, trying to get out of it, you get yourself into even worse trouble. In this story I'm going to read to you, a boy breaks the rules when he was really trying hard to mind them. This story is unfinished; when it stops, I will ask you to finish it. While I'm reading, think of ways in which the problem of the story might be solved."

Johnny Lucas was idling out in front of his house. A streetcleaning truck went past, and behind it the gutter filled with a rapid current of water. Johnny considered making a sternwheel paddleboat out of a cigar box, with paddles that would be slung on rubber bands that could be wound up to turn them. Trouble was, his Dad didn't allow him to play in the street. Traffic came zooming downhill here. It would be an hour, probably, before either his father or mother returned from shopping. Should he risk playing in the street?

He forgot the matter then, as he saw another eleven-year-old boy coming down the sidewalk. It was Lon McCassland, and he had a softball in his hands.

"Hi, Lon."

Lon looked at him. "Hi."

"I got a Superman comic . . ."

"Seen it."

"Let's swing on the rings."

"I can't play in your yard."

Johnny followed with his eyes as Lon threw the softball up and caught it, and tossed it again and caught it behind his back.

"Hey, Lon. Let's play Andy-Over!"

"Your Pop doesn't want me to play in your yard. *My* Pop doesn't want me to play in your yard. *I* don't want to play in your yard. That makes it unanimous."

"I mean, you stay out here *in front* of the house, and I'll go around in back."

Lon considered. He'd come down the street because he had no one to play with. He nodded. "Okay."

Johnny ran around to the rear of the Lucas home and waited.

From out in front came Lon McCassland's high-pitched yell "Andy-y-y-Over-r-r-r!"

Presently, high over the house, Johny saw the ball rising, saw it slow, and arch, and come slanting down toward him. He ran back, and almost caught the ball. It tore through his fingers and bounced against the garage. He snatched it up.

Then it was his turn.

"Andy-Over-r-r-r!" he shouted, and threw the ball high as he could over the roof of the house, and watched it rise and curve and start down on the far side, and drop out of sight.

He waited. He'd thrown pretty hard. Presently he began to have worries. If the ball had gone over Lon's head, out into the street, it might start rolling downhill, to the boulevard below, where traffic was heavy and constant. They might never get the ball if it rolled down there.

He grew tense. No yell of "Andy-Over!" came from Lon.

And then, around the edge of the house, at the driveway, he saw Lon. Lon beckoned. Lon looked scared.

Johnny hurried to him.

"Didn't you catch the ball? What's wrong?"

"Come see," Lon whispered.

Johnny followed Lon out in front. Lon pointed to the car at the curb. It was Johnny's folks' car, an old convertible.

"What happened?" Johnny demanded.

"Look!" Lon said hoarsely.

Johnny looked. In the fabric top of the car was a hole.

Lon said, "The ball landed on the car and tore through the roof. The ball's in front, on the floor, and the car's locked!"

"Oh, my gosh," Johnny breathed. "My Dad'll just . . ."

"Get my ball."

"You better run on home, Lon. I'm going out in back."

"First you get my ball!"

Johnny tried the car door.

"But it's locked."

"Get a key! I ain't going home without my new ball. My Pop'll strap me good."

"I haven't got any key."

"Go in and get one from your mother."

"*And tell her what happened? Oh, no!*" Johnny thought to himself.

"Can't. She's downtown, shopping."

"Johnny, your folks've got an extra key to the car. Everybody has. It's in your mother's bureau, or your dad's desk somewhere. You go get it."

"That's right."

In the tall file in his father's study . . . Johnny ran indoors. In a couple minutes he was out, with a key.

He unlocked the car door. The ball was down on the floor, under the clutch pedal. He climbed in and groped around on his hands and knees on the floor for the ball.

Johnny's mother always left the car in gear on this hill, because of the steep grade, and because the hand brake didn't hold well. Dad had trained her always to cramp the wheels into the curb. Now, as Johnny crouched on the floor, fumbling under the clutch pedal for the ball, his shoulder nudged the gear shift lever and pushed it out of gear.

The front tire slid along the curb, and the front wheels straightened as the car started rolling.

Lon yelled wildly, "Johnny, look out!"

But Johnny was down on the floor, groping for the ball. In a moment, Lon realized, the car would be at the steep part of the sloping street. The car would gain momentum, would roll down onto the boulevard at the bottom of the hill, out into that stream of traffic.

Lon ran to the moving car. He tried to get the hand brake—Johnny was on the floor, in the way—so Lon grabbed the steering wheel and jerked it savagely, twisting the front wheels back toward the curb.

But the front wheels jumped the curb. The car careened up onto the parking strip—and crashed into a tree, coming to an abrupt, jolting halt.

Lon jumped from the car. He murmured, "Oh—oh!" as he looked at the front of the car.

Johnny backed dazedly out of the door and stood up, rubbing his head, where he'd bumped against the steering column as the car hit the tree.

He walked around in front, stopped short, and just stood there, staring, aghast. The grill was smashed in; the front of the convertible was wrecked.

Lon grabbed his ball and ran up the street toward home.

Johnny didn't notice at all. He was thinking, "Oh, gosh, will I catch it now . . ."

"All right, start over, and tell it slow," Johnny's father said sternly that evening. "You and Lon were playing ball?"

"Yes-s, Dad."

"I thought I made it plain to you that I didn't want that McCassland boy on this property?"

"But we were playing out in the street, Dad."

"Oh, so that's different, huh?"

"And Lon was batting . . ."

"How often have I told you not to play in the street? You want to get run over by a truck? Why do you think I've bought you all the play equipment in the back yard?"

Johnny stared at the rug and did not answer.

"Well, go on," his dad said.

"Lon hit the ball, and it went up high, and it came down right on the car, and broke through the top."

"As if that isn't enough," Mr. Lucas remarked. "Then what?"

"Lon wanted his ball back, so—so I got the extra key, and—gave it to him. He opened the car door, and got in and was feeling around for the ball, and the car started rolling . . ."

"He must've pushed it out of gear."

"It looked like the car would roll downhill, so he turned the steering wheel, to bring it against the curb . . ."

"And the car jumped the curb."

"That's right."

"And smashed into the tree!"

"Well, I won't stand for it!" Mrs. Lucas said angrily. "If that harum-scarum boy were grown up, I could put him in jail. It's illegal to meddle around with somebody else's car! Ed, you go right over to see this McCassland kid's father. He's going to have my car repaired, or find himself with a lawsuit on his hands."

Mr. Lucas nodded.

"Come on, Johnny."

"Oh, Dad, I—got to do my arithmetic!"

"That can wait. This is important. It's a civic duty, Johnny. When you see somebody damage property belonging to somebody else, you're duty bound as a witness to testify and help the owner get pay for the damage done. Come along."

"But, D-Dad, I don't feel so good."

"For Pete's sake, what's *wrong* with you?"

"My stomach hurts," Johnny said, and he wasn't pretending.

"You'll live."

They walked down the block to the McCassland house. Mr. Lucas rang the bell, and the door was opened by Mr. McCassland.

"Why, hello there, Lucas. Come in, come in. Nice to see you."

Johnny followed his dad into the living room.

Young Lon was there, squatting on a hassock, watching television. He saw Johnny, and started to speak, but noticed how worried and miserable Johnny looked. Lon gulped and said nothing.

Mr. Lucas came right out with it: "McCassland, I don't know whether your boy's told you yet, or not . . ."

"Told me what? Sit down, Lucas. Johnny, there's a chair for you, over by Lon."

"McCassland, the boys were playing ball out on the street today . . ."

"That's not so good."

"And your son batted a high ball that came down onto my car and tore through the top."

"Oh?" Mr. McCassland was a big, hearty man who smiled easily and a lot. He frowned now, and it made him look sad and older. "Lon didn't mention it."

"Then, trying to . . ." Mr. Lucas went on; but at the same time Lon started saying, "Dad, I didn't . . ."

"Lon, Mr. Lucas is talking," Mr. McCassland said firmly.

"But . . ."

"You wait."

"Then my boy got the key to the car," Johnny's father continued, "and Lon got in and groped along the floorboards to find his ball . . ."

"No, that's not it! I was just . . ."

"Don't interrupt!" Mr. McCassland said sharply.

"And Lon must've touched the gear shift. Anyway, the car started rolling downhill."

"Good Lord!" Mr. McCassland paled. "He might've got killed! And wrecked your car, too."

"Yes, if he hadn't twisted the steering wheel and sent the car against the curb."

"But, Dad, I was just. . ."

"You'll let Mr. Lucas finish!"

"And the car jumped the curb and smashed into a tree. Wrecked the front end. There may be other damage."

"Did you see this happen, Lucas?"

"No, I didn't. But Johnny was right there."

"I didn't do it!" Lon burst out.

"Lon, I'll talk to you later!" Mr. McCassland was furious. "Mr. Lucas, you get your car repaired and send me the bill."

"You don't have to pay . . ."

"When my own son damages property belonging to somebody else, I do have to pay for it and I *will* pay for it," Mr. McCassland said. "I'm going to make sure that you remember that, Lon. You're going to be punished. You've been saving up to go to boys' camp this summer. You'll keep on saving your show money and what you earn cutting grass, but you'll use it to pay me back for repairing Mr. Lucas's car. You understand?"

Lon's lips quivered. He turned to Johnny.

And he said wildly, "Tell your Dad the truth! Go on, tell him what really happened!"

Johnny couldn't look at Lon.

Low-voiced, Johnny said, "I've already told him."

Johnny's dad shifted uncomfortably on his chair.

"I'm afraid," he said then, "that one or the other of you boys is lying. Let's get the truth of this right now."

THE "GETTING EVEN" SERIES: BEING FAIR

One of the strongest of all emotional experiences is the sense of outrage felt when one has suffered injustice. In the first wild heat of such a mood, one wants to pay back in kind for the wrong that has been inflicted. Young people and children are especially prone to experience burning desires to "get even." But behavior motivated by the urge for revenge is often unwise and far out of proportion. The wronged individual too often inflicts a wrong greater than the one he has suffered. Moreover, when a so-called wrong is studied dispassionately, it often proves to have been something far different from the vicious act it seemed at first.

This group of stories is based upon the desire to get even. Role-playing this material will provide practice in *exploring the feelings and the consequences* of behavior based upon the need to strike out at someone who has wronged you.

In using these stories, the role-playing leader should help the group analyze:

1. How an individual feels who has suffered a wrong.
2. Why the individual who committed the wrong behaved as he did.
3. Why people try to get even.
4. Whether the way of getting even is a punishment that fits the crime.
5. What will be the consequences of the act of revenge upon people other than the original wrongdoer.
6. How the person who is getting even will feel later about his revenge.

To bring the problem close to home, you may ask: Have you ever had experiences in which someone

1. Humiliated you?
2. Played a trick on you?
3. Stole from you?
4. Tattled on you?
5. Lied about you?
6. Took credit belonging to you?
7. Blamed you for an act you did not commit.
8. Destroyed something you cherished?
9. Excluded you?
10. Could have cleared you of undeserved blame but did not bother to do so?

Younger children are especially prone to have violent desires to get even for real or fancied wrongs. It is, perhaps, a sure sign of maturity that one, when wronged, can be detached enough to study the unjust behavior before trying to get even. It is an even surer sign of maturity when one can recognize the reasons why an individual wronged one and sympathize with him. It is a still higher level of maturity when one can see a way of getting revenge for an act of wrongdoing, but can recognize that the consequences are likely to be far more evil than the injustice suffered, and can forego the satisfaction of revenge.

Money for Marty

The Problem: The issue is honesty. If someone has cheated you, is it fair to cheat him in return? Bryan owes Marty money he has borrowed but not paid back in spite of Marty's repeated requests. Marty has a chance to get his money back; he can steal it in a way that will cause Bryan much trouble.

Introducing the Problem: Say to the group, "Have you ever lent something to a friend who just never gets around to giving it back? If you have, you can remember how provoked you felt. This story is about such a happening. The story stops but is not finished. As I read, think of ways in which you might end it."

Marty had put his foot on a shiny dollar. Nearby, on hands and knees, Bryan was searching through the grass, carefully parting the blades to peer between them for a silvery telltale glint.

"Marty, help me," he pleaded. "I lost my dollar!"

"Too bad," Marty said. "Too bad you didn't pay me what you owe me before you lost that money."

"Oh, I couldn't pay you out of *that* dollar!"

"Oh, no? Well, you are, chum, you are," Marty said to himself. He was really disgusted with Bryan. He had lent Bryan money for a movie just a week before, when Bryan already owed him for a hot dog and a Coke. But Bryan who was good at mooching always managed to forget any debts he owed.

"I couldn't pay you from that dollar," Bryan explained, "because it isn't mine. Besides, it's special. It's a coin from my Dad's collection. I brought it to school to show to Mr. Dolan. He collects coins. I didn't tell my Dad I was taking it. He doesn't like me to mess with his collection. Besides, this coin isn't worth just a dollar. It's scarce, so it's worth a lot more. Dad'll really be sore!"

"So you're in trouble," Marty thought. "Well, go ahead and squirm. You got it coming to you." Then Marty thought of Bryan's father. He'd really be rough on Bryan.

Marty almost lifted his foot, almost said, "Hey, look. . ." but checked the impulse. Bryan needed a lesson.

But this would be so tough a lesson. . . .

Tell-Tale

The Problem: Getting even can sometimes be extremely unfair: The revenge can be a far greater wrong than the original hurt done to the person trying to get even. In this story, two boys are exposed as authors of a prank. To get even with the person who exposed them, they arrange for her to seem guilty of stealing from a lunch box.

Introducing the Problem: You may say to the group, "When you've done something wrong, and someone tattles on you, you feel very angry toward that person, especially if you were punished severely. You really want to get even. But getting even can sometimes lead you into serious trouble. This is a story about such a case. The story stops but is not finished. As I read, try to think of ways in which the story should end."

Ken had worked out a clever plan to create some excitement. He and his pal were bored and just aching for something to happen. Ken's big idea promised to be a lot of fun. But Ken needed Jimmy to help because Jimmy wasn't afraid of snakes.

During the morning recess, they carefully stole back into their classroom. Their teacher, Miss Moffatt, was busy doing playground duty. At the rear of the classroom, on a long work table, was a natural history exhibit the class had been preparing. Jimmy opened a cage, reached in, grasped a young gopher snake just back of the head, and took it out of the cage. He wasn't afraid of it; in fact, he had caught the snake in his own backyard and brought it to school just a week ago.

Ken leading the way, they hurried into the cloakroom. Ken glanced along the rows of lunchboxes set on shelves.

"Here. Put it in Lenore's."

Ken opened the lunchbox, and Jimmy carefully stowed the snake inside.

"I'll bet she screams like she was bit by a rattler," Ken whispered.

"She'll probably think it *is* a rattler," Jimmy said scornfully. "Okay, close the box."

"Come on, let's get out of here."

They met Dora in the doorway to the hall. She looked at them suspiciously but said nothing.

"Think she saw us?" Jimmy whispered.

"No," Ken said, making his voice confident because he wasn't, but wanted to be.

At lunchtime, Lenore performed as well as the two boys could have hoped. In fact, she even surpassed their expectations.

Rain had started to fall outside, so Miss Moffatt had asked the children to eat at their seats. "No commotion, *please*," she had requested. Everyone got his or her lunchbox; everyone had gone back to his or her seat; everyone had started opening his or her lunchbox with eager appetite. Only Jimmy and Ken had delayed; taut and aquiver with expectancy, they waited for the excitement. It came.

Lenore opened her box—and as the little snake reared its head up, tongue forking redly from its mouth, Lenore screamed. Lenore had a strong pair of lungs and sturdy vocal chords, and she really put her heart into the effort, for she was scared. She screamed as if a lion had leaped at her. She shrieked and jumped from her seat and flattened herself back against the wall.

Several other girls screamed too; but some of the boys laughed.

"Children! Children!" Miss Moffatt's stern voice finally clamped control on the hullabaloo.

Some of the boys spoke up then.

"Miss Moffatt, there's no reason for Lenore to bawl like that. It's just a gopher snake."

"A little one. Like the one in our cage."

"It *is* the one from our cage," Dora said shrilly. "Miss Moffatt, Jimmy and Ken put it in Lenore's lunchbox. I saw them in the cloakroom during recess."

Miss Moffatt looked at the two boys.

"Aw, we didn't mean to scare her silly," Jimmy said.

And Ken added, "It was just a joke, Miss Moffatt."

"I think," the teacher said soberly, "that you two boys should give some serious thought to the possible consequences of such mischief. You'll stay after school each day for the rest of the week."

"Oh, no," Jimmy gasped.

And Ken said, "We got a Little League game to play! Jimmy's pitching, and I'm catcher."

"Shouldn't you have thought of that before you played your trick on Lenore?"

"But Jimmy's our best pitcher," Ken protested unhappily. "Besides, I got a birthday party tomorrow after school!"

"I suspect that the best birthday present anyone could give you, Ken, is an awareness of how important it is to look ahead to the possible consequences of your behavior," Miss Moffatt said. "All right, it's one o'clock. Everybody to work."

Jimmy and Ken smoldered as they served their time after school.

"That Dora! I'm going to fix her good," Jimmy said.

"We ought to put her in a barrel of cement and dump her into a river," Ken suggested.

The big idea came to Jimmy as he and Ken were walking home.

"Say, I know how to fix Dora!"

"How?"

Excitedly, Jimmy told him. . . .

Next day, at recess again, Jimmy and Ken stole back into their classroom, to the shelves on which the lunchboxes were kept.

"There's Brenda Norton's lunchbox."

"What's she got in it?"

"Look—two hardboiled eggs, a liverwurst sandwich, and a jam sandwich and a thermos of milk and a big, thick slab of cheese cake and a red apple."

"No wonder she's so fat."

"Take the eggs?"

"No. Anybody might have eggs. We'll use the liverwurst sandwich and the cheese cake. She'll miss them. She'll really scream if those are stolen."

"Yeah. Now where's Dora's lunchbox?"

"Here."

"Open it."

Ken obeyed. Inside were just two thin peanut butter sandwiches, nothing else.

"Plenty of room," Ken said.

Jimmy leaned over to place Brenda's liverwurst sandwich and thick cheese cake inside.

"You really think," Ken demanded, "that Miss Moffatt will believe that Dora stole this stuff?"

"Sure she will!" Jimmy insisted. "Dora has stolen stuff out of lunchboxes before. Miss Moffatt knows it. In the fourth grade. You weren't here then."

"Maybe Dora was hungry?" Ken said. "Maybe that's just a story and she never really did it?"

"Look, she tattled on us, didn't she?"

"Yeah."

"She needs a good lesson, doesn't she?"

"Yeah," Ken admitted. "Hey, hurry, will you! Somebody's coming down the hall. Put that stuff in and let's go!"

Jimmy reached to lower the liverwurst sandwich and slab of cheese cake into Dora's lunchbox. He hesitated.

Frantically Ken whispered, "Quick, we got to leave. Put that stuff in and shut the box. Well? . . . you doing it or not?"

Jimmy said:

Eyewitness

The Problem: The issue is personal integrity. The problem is how to control the violent urge to get even for a wrong done.

Introducing the Problem: Ask the group, "Has someone ever played a joke on you that hurt your feelings so badly that you wanted to get revenge on him (or her) very much? This is a story about such a case. The story stops but is not finished. As I read, think of ways in which the story might end."

It happened during the afternoon recess. John was wearing his gray slacks and blue jacket—the new clothes Mrs. Latham had bought him just a week ago. It was the first time he had worn them. Mrs. Latham had urged him to wait until after school to dress up, but he was so impatient to be ready when his Uncle Walter came for him that he had insisted on putting on his good clothes. The evening would go fast enough as it was—too fast, in fact. But dressing up before school was a mistake, and John realized it when he reached the school yard.

"Hey, look at John. All dressed up."

"Where you going, John? To a funeral?"

He just grinned and did not try to answer. The reason he was dressed so nicely was too important, too wonderful, to share just yet; later, perhaps, he'd feel like talking about it.

The remarks had continued during the noon hour, and started again at the afternoon recess. Now something worse happened.

"Hey, John. Come over here," Andy Byers called to him.

John walked over.

Andy was the biggest boy in the sixth grade and very popular. John had started school here just a month ago, and so far Andy hadn't paid much attention to him.

"John," Andy began, in a serious, confidential way, leaning close and speaking in a low tone, "do you know what the man said to the shovel? *Hit the dirt!*" And Andy pushed John, pushed him hard.

John went over backwards. In fact, he flipped over Tony Barnes, who had kneeled down behind him. John landed flat on his back on the ground. Andy and Tony and the other boys stood around and howled their laughter.

For a moment John did not move. He wasn't hurt, just numb with surprise. The laughing made him flush with humiliation, and he started to get up. He put his hands down to raise himself. His hands sank wrist-deep into mud. Then he felt dampness at his back.

He scrambled to his feet. He twisted his neck to look around and felt his back and his pants. He had fallen into a muddy spot left by the sprinklers on the school lawn.

The stricken look on his face made the boys laugh all the harder. Blindly, John turned and swung his fist at Andy. But Andy, a head taller, merely caught his arm and pushed him again. Then the bell rang; recess was over, and everybody ran to enter the building.

Fighting back tears, John went to the boys' room, took off his jacket, and tried to wipe the mud off with paper towels. Presently he gave up; the coat was a mess; his slacks were a mess; he was a mess.

He went to the school office and asked permission to use the phone. Calling home, he said, "Mrs. Latham, I won't be home right after school. Tell Uncle Walter I can't go with him."

"Why not, John?" Mrs. Latham wanted to know; she sounded a bit shocked.

"I—got into a fight."

"I hate to write your father that you couldn't come to see him because you were kept after school for bad behavior," she said disapprovingly. "He's going to be terribly disappointed."

He said goodbye and hung up, biting his lip. Mrs. Latham provided a foster home for John. His mother was dead, and his father was a seaman on an oil tanker that got into San Francisco only two or three times a year. John's younger sisters, twins, were in a foster home in Redwood City. When their father made port, young Uncle Walter, who was unmarried, gathered them all up and rushed them to the city for dinner and a show or a ball game with their father. Tonight, they had planned to see the Giants play. The whole family would have been together. Now, John realized, he'd probably have to wait six months to see his father. . . .

The rest of that afternoon was wasted, he could not focus on studying. His thoughts seethed. That was such a dirty trick they had played on him! Any other day, it wouldn't have been so bad. But to dump him into the mud *today*!

Usually, John went straight home after school. But this afternoon John delayed, to make good his story that he had been kept after school.

Andy and Tony and Pete—the biggest boys in the sixth grade—horsed around on the play equipment in the schoolyard, until finally a teacher shooed them homeward. John, having nothing else to do, followed them.

A new road was being constructed across the side of a hill near the school. Earth-moving equipment was parked there now; the workers had just quit for the day.

To the big boys, this equipment was a challenge. They climbed aboard the big dirt carry-all, the enormous roller, the big tamping machine that seemed studded with railroad spikes. John watched, frowning. They had been warned at school to stay off the big machines.

Andy, on the seat of the big tractor, twisted the steering wheel and shifted the gears, making a roaring sound with his mouth as he pretended he was taking an enormous Sherman tank across a battlefield, ramming enemy tanks, capsizing them, crushing them, as his main cannon blasted enemy pillboxes and his turret gunner knocked down enemy planes trying to strafe him.

"He'd better not go off and leave the emergency brake loose," John thought. And when, finally, Andy jumped down and followed Tony and Pete on home, John climbed aboard the tractor. "Huh," he snorted, "what a dope!" For Andy *had* left the brake loose. . . .

Reaching home, John mowed the lawn before entering the house for dinner. Mrs. Latham looked sharply at him but did not scold.

"Maybe your father'll put into San Francisco again soon, John," she said reassuringly.

He just nodded. But he could not sleep well that night. Disappointment made him jittery and restless. When he did finally doze off, the heavy drumming of rain on the roof woke him. He felt headachy when he left for school.

In mid-morning, his teacher, Miss Allen, was called out of the room and was gone for a long ten minutes. When she returned, several people were with her—a policeman, a burly man carrying a construction worker's hard hat, and a fourth-grader named Mamie Anderson.

Miss Allen said to the class, "Boys and girls, as you know, you have been asked not to play on the road construction machinery making the new street south of the school. Yesterday, several of you disobeyed that rule. The result is that an accident has occurred. Luckily, nobody was hurt. I say luckily, because somebody might easily have been killed. What happened was that a boy released the brake on the tractor parked on the hill. The tractor rolled during the night and left the road. Now tell me—did any of you boys release the brake on that tractor?"

She studied the group. The policeman and the construction worker eyed the pupils. Then Mamie Anderson turned to the policeman and whispered something to him.

Miss Allen continued, "The tractor started rolling down the roadway, went over the edge, slid down the bank, turned over, and slammed into a garage. The garage wall was caved in, and the side of a car parked inside was also caved in. If the tractor had rolled a little farther, it might have crashed into a bedroom of the house, in which people were sleeping. I'll ask you again. Which one of you boys played on that tractor after school yesterday?"

No one spoke up; each boy sat rigid. John finally glanced at Andy, thinking, "Serves him right. He's got it coming to him. I'm glad of it." Andy was biting his lip and staring fixedly at his hands knotted together on the desk before him.

"Miss Allen," the policeman said "we know who the boy is. Mamie has recognized him. She doesn't know his name but she can point him out. I'm sorry to interrupt your classwork, but I have to take this boy down to Juvenile Hall."

The construction man added, "His parents are going to have to pay for the damage done. We've chased kids off those machines until we're tired of it. We've got to make an example now."

Miss Allen said, "Please don't blame the whole group for one boy's misbehavior." She looked at the class. "Whoever it is, I'd like him to come forward of his own free will."

Slowly Andy stood up. He looked sick, he was so scared.

John, unable to keep still, blurted out: "I know what really happened!"

Andy turned and looked at John. Everybody stared at John. Miss Allen asked, "What do you mean, John?"

John swallowed hard, trying to sort out his racing thoughts. Be quiet! Andy's got this coming to him. Why should you do anything to help a guy like him? . . .But Andy wasn't really to blame for the tractor accident.

Swiftly, John thought how he could explain the accident to the policeman: Sure, Andy *had* played on that tractor. And Andy had let loose the tractor brake, and had shifted the gears, pretending he was driving the darn thing. And when he had jumped off the tractor, he had left the brake loose. But I climbed onto the tractor after Andy left, and I set the brake. That's not all. I put the gearshift into reverse. That tractor never could have rolled by itself. The rain was at fault. It had come down hard last night. The tractor was standing on the soft shoulder of the new road, right at the edge of a drop-off. The road had just been graded and the dirt was soft. The rain had loosened the dirt. No other way to figure it! The edge of the road shoulder caved in, just washed away, and the tractor tipped off balance and then dropped down the slope. *I'll bet it never rolled forward at all,* John reasoned, *and there's a way to prove it!* Look at the brake. See if it's still tight. Better yet, look at the gearshift. If it's still in reverse, that'll be positive proof that the tractor never rolled forward. It just couldn't have! *I'll bet anything that gear's still in reverse.*

But after what Andy had done to him, why should he bother to help Andy? Why in the world should he even say a word to clear Andy of blame?

"John," Miss Allen repeated, "do you know anything about the accident?"

"Well, I—I did see Andy playing on that tractor," John said slowly, and hesitated.

"So? Is that all you've got to say?" Miss Allen pressed.

Just nod your head, John told himself. *That's all you've got to do. . . .*

You're Not Invited

The Problem: The issue is the problem of controlling the urge to get even for being slighted; specifically, the problem is acquiring the judgment to weigh how vastly disproportionate taking revenge on someone for hurt feelings may become and recognizing that getting even can hurt both victim and perpetrator.

Introducing the Problem: Say, "Sometimes somebody says or does something to you that hurts your feelings very deeply. It happens to all of us, and when it does, it is only human to want to get even. This is a story about such a happening. The story stops but is not finished. As I read, think of ways in which this story could end."

Alice was the only girl in the classroom not invited to Millie's party. Alice kept hoping as days passed that Millie meant to include her, that the lack of an invitation was just an oversight. Actually, Alice was not a close friend of Millie, but then, neither were half of the girls who were invited. Alice felt worse about being left out when Luella, her closest chum, suggested that they go to the party together, and Alice had to say, "I'm not going."

"But everybody's going!"

"I'm not."

"You mean," Luella gasped, "that you're not invited?"

Alice nodded and turned away, too choked up to answer. But why, she kept asking herself. Why was she, of all the girls in the class, the only one not included?

She could not hide her feelings from her mother. At dinner, the day before the party, her mother asked her, "What's wrong, dear?"

"Oh, nothing really important, Mom. Millie Bailey's having a party and didn't invite me."

Her mother's pretty face saddened.

"We're still new in this town, dear. Be patient."

Later, after Alice had gone to bed, she heard her father and mother talking, low-voiced, in the dining room. The house was very quiet; her parents did not realize that even their careful, soft-toned speech could be heard by Alice.

"Maybe I'm wrong," her father was saying, "but Alice sure looked down-in-the-mouth tonight."

"Yes, she's really low."

"Why?"

Her mother told him about Millie's party and ended, "The only reason I can think of why Millie didn't invite Alice is me. I work as a waitress at a drive-in, and I make slangy talk with the truck drivers. In this town, that means you're dirt."

"So that's it," Alice's father said.

But my mother's a fine, decent person! Alice told herself, in outrage. They've got no right to think she isn't as good as they are!

Her father was saying, "Maybe you'd better quit your job."

But her mother said, "I can't just yet. We couldn't carry the payments on the house and the hospital bills."

"Change to another kind of job."

"Nothing else I can do would pay as well, counting the tips. Besides, it makes me mad! I'm doing a decent job."

"A waitress in a highway cafe ranks pretty low on the social scale."

"But the Baileys, of all people. Putting on airs. Telling everybody that their boy is in the army overseas when he's in prison for drunk hit-and-run driving!"

"Ssh."

"Oh, nobody can hear us."

"We don't spread gossip."

"It's not gossip; it's a fact."

"We're not supposed to know it. You found out only because I'm in the sheriff's office. If it got around, the sheriff would guess that there had been a leak in his office."

"Just the same, I resent the whole thing! The Baileys have really got something to be ashamed of. We haven't."

"And they really are ashamed," Alice's father said thoughtfully. "They wouldn't have spread a lie around if they weren't terribly upset about their boy."

"That's right. It's a heartache."

Alice lay awake for a solid hour, thinking hard; and gradually, she saw a way she could get even.

They were such *nice* people, Millie Bailey's family! Her father was the manager of a big new chain store in the little town, and her uncle was running for mayor. Really nice people. But their older son got drunk, caused a car accident, and ran away. Didn't stay to see if he could help anybody he might have hurt. Just drove away—and so stupid that the cops caught him, anyway, and now he was in prison somewhere. And the family was so ashamed they lied about it. Spread a story that he was in the army overseas. *That* was what would make people really disgusted with them. Now people would sneer at them.

Alice saw just how to handle the news. She would tell the story to Joanie Lucas. Everybody called Joanie a blabbermouth. She'd whisper the worst kind of gossip in your ear and beg you not to tell anybody ever—and then go and tell it herself to everybody she met. Telling her a confidence was really broadcasting.

Finally Alice fell asleep. For the first night in almost a week, she slept well.

After eating a good breakfast, next morning, she called Joanie Lucas. She asked Joanie if she'd go to the movie with her that night; it was Friday night.

"Movie?" Joanie said. "But aren't you going to Millie's party?"

"I should say I'm not," Alice answered. "Don't tell me that *you're* going."

"Sure I am. But why aren't you?" Joanie demanded.

"You mean you don't *know?*" Alice gasped.

"Don't know *what?*"

"It's the *awfulest* thing. . ." Alice said, lowering her voice to almost a whisper. "But, gosh, I don't *dare* tell you over the phone. Wait till I get to school."

"Gosh, *hurry!*" Joanie whispered back.

As she walked to school, Alice began to have some misgivings. If she knew Joanie, the broadcasting had already begun. Spreading this story about Millie Bailey's brother—wasn't it spreading gossip of the worst kind? But it's not just gossip; it's true! Yes, but wouldn't a lot of people be hurt? Millie, her parents, her brother. . . But haven't I been hurt by the way they're treating me? And they haven't any reason to treat me like this! And wasn't she broadcasting something she had *overheard?* She was being left out of a party, true; but she'd get over it, all right. But how about Millie's folks? They'd be so terribly ashamed. . . .

Joanie had already been talking. Alice realized that as soon as she reached the schoolyard, for Joanie and Millie and a knot of angry girls turned toward her as she approached.

"There!" Joanie said triumphantly. "Alice'll tell you! Alice, tell them why you're not going to Millie's party."

But Millie Bailey broke in furiously, "She's not coming to my party because I haven't invited her, that's why!"

"Even if you had, she wouldn't have come," Joanie retorted. "Tell them why, Alice!"

But then an interruption occurred. Their teacher, Miss Carter, joined the group, looking very stern.

"I overheard some of this talk," she said. "You girls know how I feel about spreading malicious gossip."

Joanie said, "But it's not just gossip. Is it, Alice? You said it was *awfully* important."

But Miss Carter said very firmly, "Alice, you have evidently told Joanie something that is mean, spiteful, and probably untrue. I shall ask you first, to apologize to Millie. Then you are to stay after school to explain your behavior to me and to give me a good reason why I should not report this whole incident to your mother."

"Tell her, Alice," Joanie urged. "Tell her!"

"Sure," Millie said scornfully, "go ahead, give your imagination a workout. Tell us, tell everybody."

But Alice stood taut, silent. Speak up? Here? Before everyone?

Miss Carter said, "I'm waiting, Alice, for your explanation or your apology."

Alice said:

Mr. Even Steven

The Problem: The issue is that of getting even. So often, all of us have a wild but very human impulse to get even with someone who has wronged us. This impulse can lead us into very destructive and unjust behavior.

Introducing the Problem: Say, "Have you ever had somebody do something to you that was so inconsiderate, so mean, that you wanted to do something really awful to him by way of getting even? This story deals with such a problem. This story stops but is not finished. As I read, I'd like you to try to think of ways in which you might end the story."

Bob's father was very angry with him.

"I thought you were a responsible kid. When I gave you that bike, I was sure that you had the good sense to handle it properly."

"What did I do?" Bob demanded, surprised.

"You know what you did!"

Mr. Ames wasn't exactly shouting, but he was really upset and angry. Bob thought frantically. I haven't set fire to anything. I haven't broken any windows playing ball.

"I haven't done anything," he insisted again.

"Mr. Scanlon's new driveway?"

"What about old Scanlon's new driveway?"

"You rode right across it. Right after he got through smoothing fresh concrete."

"Oh, no!"

"You left tracks in that concrete two inches deep. He didn't discover it until the concrete had set. Now he has to rip out a big section and pour new concrete. He's so mad he's threatening to sue me."

"Dad, I didn't do that!"

"A neighbor saw you."

"*Nobody* saw me. Because I didn't do it."

"Mrs. Holzer saw you from her front porch."

Bob gasped. "She's a liar!"

"Bob!" His father never used that tone unless he was deeply aroused.

"But, Dad—"

"I've told Mr. Scanlon to have the driveway fixed. You'll pay for it. I get off work at two today. We'll go down to the bank and draw out your savings. If you haven't enough money to pay for the repair, you'll sell your bike to make up the difference."

And that was that. . . .

A little later, Bob looked at Scanlon's driveway; and as he looked, he wondered how in the world Mrs. Holzer had got the notion that she saw him riding across the fresh concrete. He had not done it. But someone had certainly left two deep ruts across the width of the driveway. Mrs. Holzer had evidently seen it happen. But she was nearsighted. She wore glasses with lenses that looked half an inch thick.

"It wasn't me. She saw someone else do it," he realized.

But who? Then Bob remembered. Russ Adams had just got a brand-new bike. Russ lived on the other side of this block. Maybe Russ, Bob reasoned, had been circling the block; he had come racing down the sidewalk and without even slowing up had crossed old man Scanlon's new driveway. Scanlon was a chintzy guy. He probably had a box standing in the middle of the walk with a penciled sign saying *Keep Off.* He was a bossy old coot who was used to giving orders without bothering to explain. So, naturally, if Russ had noticed the sign at all, he had merely glanced around to see if Scanlon was watching—and not seeing him, had rolled right on across the driveway. Then, discovering that the concrete was soft and he had rutted it, Russ had probably raced away as fast as he could pedal.

" 'Course, maybe it wasn't Russ at all," Bob reflected. "But then, who else *could* it have been?"

Worrying, he walked around the block to Russ's house and turned down the driveway.

Sure enough, Russ was in the garage, tinkering with a new bike. Oh, oh, Bob thought—maybe his wheels'll show fresh concrete on them.

Russ's dog, Trigger, came up to him and nuzzled his hand with a big wet nose. Trigger was a large Boxer, thick of chest and powerful, but very good-natured with people.

"Hi, Russ," Bob said. "Hey, that's a swell-looking bike."

"Uh-huh." Russ did not seem especially pleased to see him.

"Russ, did you ride across old man Scanlon's fresh-laid driveway?"

"His what?"

"He just had concrete poured for his driveway. Did you ride across it?

"Heck, no!"

He said it loudly, nervously, and did not look Bob in the face as he spoke.

Bob examined the bike for specks of clinging concrete. The wheels and tires, however, were spotless; so shiningly spotless, so free even of dust, that they glistened.

"You just *washed* this thing?"

"So I washed it! What's it to you?"

"Look. Old Lady Holzer saw a kid ride across Scanlon's driveway. She thought it was me and told Scanlon. He told my father. But I didn't do it. Did you?"

"No!"

"You're a liar."

"I tell you I didn't!"

Russ was almost crying and was scared; Bob was positive that he was lying.

"Look," Bob said, "I'll have to pay for it if you don't own up that you did it."

"Get out of here. Go on, get off this property!"

Bob looked at him, realized argument was useless, and turned and left. Trigger followed him.

"Go on back," Bob angrily told him, but the big Boxer just licked his hand and trotted comfortably on ahead, settling into a steady zigzagging walk down the street. The husky dog was so sociable that he went for a walk with almost anybody who passed the place.

Moodily, as Bob started home he wondered what to do.

Russ was afraid to tell the truth. Probably his old man had not really wanted to give Russ a bike and had agreed only after Russ had begged and begged; but he had probably warned Russ—you get into trouble with that thing *just once*, and I'll sell it! So Russ was scared.

He stopped. He was passing the big Dorfmyer place. Mr. Dorfmyer raised chickens. Often, after mowing his huge lawn, he would open the chicken runs and let the white Plymouth Rocks out to wander over the grass to feed on the freshly mowed greens. The trim white chickens were now scattered all over the wide yard, clucking contentedly, their heads nodding down in a stitching motion as they pecked at the ground.

Bob looked across the street at Trigger, who was looking through a fence bemusedly at a small but frisky terrier who felt safe enough, with the fence between them, to growl threats at him. Trigger, though so nice to people, was a chicken-killer. In fact, Russ's father had brought him in from their little ranch because Trigger had made enemies for him among his neighbors. Here in town few people still raised chickens; but Mr. Dorfmyer was one of them, and he and Russ's father had already had a run-in over Trigger. The Boxer had already had a taste of Dorfmyer pullets. Mr. Dorfmyer had made threats, and Russ's father had made threats right back. But Russs's father *had* warned Russ to keep Trigger out of trouble, or Trigger would be sent to the pound.

Bob saw his chance. Russ liked Trigger. Liked him a lot. And Russ was so afraid of his old man that getting into trouble with him would be a real punishment.

Bob called, "Here, Trigger!"

Obediently the big Boxer trotted across the street and came to him. Then Trigger sighted the chickens through the fence and stuck his blunt muzzle between the upright pickets and whined with eagerness, drooling.

Bob looked around warily. He saw no one close by on the quiet street. All he had to do was open the gate and say, "Go get 'em, Trigger!" And then the feathers would really fly! The chickens would squawk like crazy; neighbors would pop out of houses all around; Old Man Dorfmyer would run outside, and shake his fists and screech at Trigger, and maybe rush back inside and come out with a shotgun, or go to the telephone and yell for the police, and then he'd phone Russ's father and swear and say he'd get his lawyer busy and sue for thousands of dollars, and Russ's father would say he could sue his head off; but when Russ's father got home, then Russ would really be in hot water.

That's what Russ is doing to *me*! Making my father raise Cain with me. Letting me pay for the damage he's done. So okay! Now he'll get a taste of his own medicine. He's got it coming to him!"

Bob took a step to the gate. Trigger followed, pawed at the gate, whining with eagerness. All Bob had to do was open it, and say, "Get 'em, Trigger!"

Bob heard a long-drawn distant whistle: wheet, wheet, whe-ooo!

It was the clear long note that his mother whistled when she wanted him or his brother to come home. It meant, Bob realized, that his father was home, waiting to take him to the bank to draw out his money to pay for having Mr. Scanlon's driveway fixed. He had to hurry home.

But it would take just a second to open the gate, to give Trigger a push, and run—

13

Social Studies

TEACHING CITIZENSHIP

Often a young person faces a most difficult choice: whether to cooperate in a decision made by his group or to resist it. It is very hard to say No to one's friends. Yet it is vitally important for an individual to have the courage to say No to his cronies when, in his best judgment, No should be his answer. On this base rest responsibility and self-respect; without this integrity, it is impossible to function as a conscientious citizen. But saying No *does* take courage. For anyone to stand against the desires of his close friends, especially when the group expresses its desires in concert, requires an unusual degree of conviction and hardihood. Among children, such dissent is all too often rewarded with abuse and rejection.

When *should* an individual cooperate with a group? When is cooperation just abject surrender? When is refusal to cooperate an act of unworthy self-indulgence, and when is it an act of courage and wisdom? The answer varies according to the special circumstances of each case; such a decision requires a serious and insightful evaluation of the issues involved.

It is all too human for the individual to stifle his qualms and go along with the crowd. A group of boys may be planning a prank that, in the judgment of one member, may do someone serious injury. This member may even voice an objection, but the group is enthusiastic, and his objection is raucously pooh-poohed. He foresees that if he persists in saying No, he will be jeered at and told to go home to his mother. Similarly, a group of young girls may be mistreating a newcomer by ignoring or ridiculing her; one member of the group, out of sympathy for the newcomer, may want to charge her friends with callous bad manners. Again, this inwardly dissenting individual will, too often, stifle her good impulse for fear that she, in turn, may be made to suffer by the group.

Of course, on occasion just the opposite kind of dilemma occurs. An individual may have an overwhelmingly selfish desire for something, but his group asks that he participate in some idealistic and worthwhile venture that makes it impossible for him to realize his own goal. Too often, the individual may give lip service to the group project but actually sabotage it out of sheer inability to relinquish his own cherished purpose.

Young people need help in acquiring the good judgment to decide which course is the more ethical and humane. They need help in acquiring the courage to make a choice and stand by it in spite of abuse or disappointment. They need help in maintaining the inner stability and security to weather such emotional storms without crippling their self-esteem.

The group, too, needs guidance in learning to accept and support the dissenting individual. Perhaps, in the last analysis, individual integrity cannot exist without group responsibility for understanding and respecting the member who says No to its Yes. To reach such levels of social maturity, groups need many opportunities to face up to and cope with crucial issues.

Some individual-versus-group choices can be roughly described as dilemmas in which:

1. The individual has a worthwhile personal goal, but the group has a frivolous purpose. If the individual cooperates with the group, he will lose his own serious goal ("Sacrifice Hit").

2. The group has a serious and worthy purpose, but the individual has a self-indulgent goal. If he cooperates with the group, he will fail to gain his selfish goal ("Shutter-Bug").

3. Both the individual and the group have serious, worthwhile goals, but they are in conflict; if the individual persists in resisting the group decision in order to gain his own purpose, the group goal will not be achieved, and vice versa.

4. The group may be planning some action which may possibly cause serious hurt to someone. The individual wishes to prevent this happening, but if he objects or interferes, he may be rejected by the group ("The Menace in the Tree" and "The Junior Cavemen").

Can a general rule be laid down to guide the individual and the group in making choices between such conflicting personal and group issues? Perhaps it is valid to say this: that the more worthwhile purpose should be honored. It is not always easy, however, to decide which is the more worthwhile purpose. Sensitive judgment is required; this is not easily come by and requires practice.

Young people can learn how to deal with crises of decision making by living through them at a remove. They need practice in confronting choice-demanding situations, in defining the issues and alternatives involved, in foreseeing the consequences of their choices, in recognizing their own emotions, and in making decisions that they can live with afterward with self-respect. Practice in making decisions with-or-against the group can help young people build the confidence and inner security that will enable them to be more ethical and humane in their choices.

The responsibility of the group to understand, respect, and support the dissenter is, of course, a vital necessity. How can it be achieved? The group that *makes an active effort* to understand the emotional crisis of the dissenter in its midst, even in an imaginary situation, acquires some degree of empathy for the dissenter. As each individual in a group experiences a dissenter's role, he is sensitized to it and made sympathetic. The group that practices solving such dilemmas will increasingly acquire the empathy and wisdom to respect and support differences of perception and purpose.

The Menace in the Tree

The Problem: The issue is conflict between a group and an individual. Should the individual surrender to group will against his own inclinations and sense of right? In this story, a group of three boys are playing a prank. Jimmy wants to call a halt when it seems to him that their victim is someone who may be hurt by their mischief; the other boys insist on going through with their prank.

Introducing the Problem: Ask, "Have you ever been with a bunch of friends who wanted to do something reckless that you did not really want to have a part in, and you were too afraid of being called "chicken" to make objections? Perhaps your friends' plan wasn't reckless but just wasn't sensible, and they all seemed to want to go ahead with it—and you didn't want to be the only person who wasn't cooperating. This story deals with such a problem. The story stops but isn't finished. As I read the story, try to think of ways in which the story could end."

The three boys crouched in the dark shrubbery at the back of the garden. They had been waiting, tense and eager, for long minutes.

Jimmy, keenest of hearing, heard footsteps on the sidewalk. Jabbing Pete, he whispered, "Somebody's coming!"

"Sounds like two or three people!"

"Okay, okay. I'm ready."

The tree-lined street was dimly lit by a street lamp, blue in the distance. Few cars passed on the quiet residential avenue. An occasional couple or group of boys and girls, returning from an early movie, had sauntered past at intervals. It was for such a group that the three boys waited.

Here, hidden in the bushes a hundred feet from the sidewalk, they felt safe from discovery and pursuit. Pete held a ball of kite string. Tom crouched beside him, and Jimmy kneeled behind them.

The kite string, invisible in the darkness, stretched at a long slant to the middle of an elm tree that loomed over the sidewalk, bent over a bough, and hung straight down, suspending a bag of waxed paper containing water.

When somebody passed beneath the tree, Pete would let go of slack in the string, and the bag of water would drop. It would startle the passerby. He would think something was up in the tree and making an attack on him, and he would jump and blurt out in surprise. If the passerby were a woman, she would utter a shriek; if a bunch of giggly girls, they would scream and chatter like crazy. If the bag hit somebody on the head and split, that somebody would think a miniature cloudburst had used him for a target. If the victim happened to be a big, husky man—well, no telling what might happen.

"He's getting close," Tom whispered.

"They. Two men."

"Oh, boy! We'll have to run."

The two men, talking earnestly, were walking at a brisk pace and drawing quickly nearer.

Jimmy felt a dart of fear. Two men. If they got mad, they'd be good and mad.

"They'll chase us."

"For gosh sake, stop shivering!"

"Don't be so chicken."

Closer the men came, almost to the tree . . .

"Now!" Tom whispered.

Pete let go the coils of slack in the string.

The bag of water dropped until the string was tight.

"Hey!"

"What's that?"

The two men had jumped back and stood tense now, peering up into the darkness of the foliage above their heads.

"Just a bird, prob'bly."

"Maybe a cat."

They moved closer, straining to see among the branches.

Pete carefully pulled the kite string, drawing the bag up into the darkness of the leaves.

One of the men—the younger one—strode decisively to the tree trunk and started climbing up.

"Careful, Jack. If it's a cat, it might claw you," the other man warned.

"Might be a racoon. I'd like to catch it."

Hearing this, Pete chuckled. Tom choked back a laugh, but Jimmy was too nervous to think it funny.

He whispered, "Maybe they'll see the string."

"Too dark," Pete said confidently.

And he was right.

"Come on down, Jack," the older man said. "I want to get home."

The young man delayed a bit, straining to see among the leaves, then gave up. He climbed down, rubbed his hands together, and brushed off his clothes.

"Whatever it was, it isn't moving now."

"Maybe just a branch fell. Let's go."

The two men left, walking on down the street.

Jimmy finally let out a long breath of relief, but Tom and Pete were somewhat disappointed.

"Pete, we're not letting the bag fall down far enough."

"I'll let out more slack."

"But it'll hit somebody smack on the head," Jimmy pointed out.

"Sure. That's the idea. Hey, here comes somebody."

"Sounds like two people again."

"No—just one."

It sounded like more than one, Jimmy realized, because this person was using a cane and tapping along at a slow shuffle.

"Somebody old," he whispered.

"Maybe it's Old Lady Corbin," Pete said.

"Good!" Tom added.

But Jimmy stirred uncomfortably. Old Lady Corbin was a mean old witch, sure. If you passed her house on roller skates, she came out and screamed that you were making too much noise. If you batted a ball into her fenced yard, it was goodbye ball; if you climbed over her fence to get it, she'd yell murder and phone your parents to complain that you had trampled her flower beds; then she'd come hunting for the ball and if she found it, she'd keep it.

But she was real old. She was using a cane because she had had a fall and broken a hip that had never mended right. She had a weak heart; Jimmy's mother had said she'd pop off one day in one of her rages.

Suppose, now, when the bag dropped down over her head from the tree, she got such a fright that she jumped back and fell down and broke her hip again. Or suppose she got so mad she screamed and tore around more than was good for her!

"You ready, Pete?" Tom whispered. "She's almost . . ."

"But maybe that's Old Lady Corbin," Jimmy blurted.

"Nobody ever saw her out at night," Tom said, "except on her broom, maybe . . ."

"But maybe it is," Jimmy insisted.

"You chicken or something?" Pete snorted. "If you don't like what we're doing, beat it on home."

Jimmy gulped. What should he do? He could warn her. He could yell to the old lady to watch out. Or he could grab hold of the kite string and prevent the bag from falling. But it he did, Tom and Pete would despise him. They'd tell him to stay away from them, to go on home and play with dolls. But if they *did* drop the bag and the crippled woman *was* Old Lady Corbin . . .

"Pete . . ."

"Shh! She's almost there!" Tom said.

And Pete said, "Right . . . on . . . target!"

He could grab the string, Jimmy realized. He could stop the prank. But if he did . . .

The Junior Cavemen

The Problem: The issue is again whether to cooperate with the group or oppose it. A bunch of boys are out on a hike and are playing pranks on an unpopular member. The pranks are becoming progressively crueler and one boy is outraged. But if he protests and resists, the group may reject him. He is a newcomer who wants very much to have a secure place with these boys.

Introducing the Problem: Ask the class, "Have any of you ever been with a bunch of boys or girls who kept picking on you, making you the fall guy for a lot of jokes that were funny to them, perhaps, but very unpleasant to you? Or have you ever been with a bunch who were picking on one person and making him miserable? Maybe you wished, at the time, that you could stop it, but you didn't know how. This story deals with such a problem. The story stops before it is finished. While I am reading, try to think of ways in which you would end the story."

When Ben walked into the house, his mother looked at him and realized at once that he was feeling happy.

"Who gave you a million dollars?" she asked.

He stared at her.

"What million dollars?"

"You're feeling good, aren't you?"

"Uh-huh."

"Why?"

"Oh, nothing much. Going on a hike."

"Okay, give. When, where, who with?"

"Giant City Game Refuge—all day Saturday."

"And who with?"

"Ted Dolan and his friends."

"Ted's the boy who's such a good softball pitcher?"

"Yeah. How'd you know, Mom?"

"You've been talking about him and his friends for weeks. They're big-shots at school, huh?"

"I guess so."

His mother smiled at him.

"Okay, you can go. You'll need chow for—two meals?"

"Yeah. Lunch and probably we'll cook up something before coming home. By rights, we should stay overnight, but those kids' folks won't let them." Ben's voice held a note of superiority. His father was a state ranger, now in charge of the Giant City state park. In the few months since the family had moved to this area, Ben had become familiar with the rugged park. He wouldn't have minded sleeping out in it overnight, even alone. "Their folks probably think there're grizzly bears and timber wolves hiding in the caves."

"You can walk off a cliff in the dark, Ben. Well, I'll fix up a pack for you."

"Thanks, Mom."

He went to his room, and Mrs. Cagle breathed a little sigh of relief. Her husband had been transferred to this job at the beginning of summer. In the short time that they had been here, Ben had had little chance to make friends and had been very lonely. But now, finally, Ben was making friends—for that she was grateful.

Giant City, far down in southern Illinois, is a wilderness of limestone cliffs and caves and stony corridors and rock slides, much of it overgrown with brush and dense timber. Saturday morning, Ben guided the group of boys into the park.

"Boy, what a mess of scrambled geography!" Ted Dolan said, as they eyed the cliffs reaching up from the roadway.

"Ben," Syd Gold asked, a little anxiously, "you got a compass and map with you?"

"Don't need 'em."

"We could get lost awful easy."

"Not if you knew the place like I know it."

"You must have built-in radar."

"My Dad taught me how to get along in the hills."

The five boys, respecting his knowledge and woodsman's skill, followed him into the stony maze of Giant City. He led them along new trails that his father's crew had opened up, and into areas of craggy beauty none of them had ever seen before.

"Say, this is really something," Ted said.

"Hey, wait," Syd begged. "I got to get a picture here."

Ben liked the group. Ted was a fine athlete and the natural leader of the group. Syd was the brainy, talkative one. Andy was quiet (like me, Ben thought); but he always pitched in when work had to be done. Tom, the biggest boy, was strong but so awkward that he was poor at athletics; but he was good humored, always making jokes at his own expense. The only boy in the group Ben did not immediately cotton to was Joey Bayne. Like himself, Joey was a new member of the group. Joey talked a lot, mostly about himself; Joey had a loud, rough voice and used a lot of gutter language. He took offense easily and was quick to use his fists. Ben wondered why the boys had ever included him in their group. Probably the boys' church youth group leader had urged them to befriend him. They didn't, however, seem to like him. What happened at lunch time showed that.

"Here, Joey, try one of my sandwiches. I got some extra," Ted said.

Joey had eaten the one slim sandwich he'd brought, so he took Ted's thick sandwich and bit into it ravenously.

Something odd happened.

Joey's eyes suddenly grew huge and round with horror. He gasped. He choked. He spluttered food in a shower over his shirt front.

"It b-burns!" he gasped.

"Here. Drink this."

Syd handed him a camp cup full of water. Joey took a huge mouthful—and then he really was sick. His face turned greenish white. He jumped up and ran into the woods and was sick.

"What's wrong with *him*?" Tom asked, amazed.

Ted and Syd couldn't answer; they were guffawing, laughing their heads off.

Andy, grinning a little worriedly, said, "Red peppers. Mexican peppers in his sandwich."

"And drinking water full of s-salt," Ted gasped, trying to choke back his laughter, "didn't help at all!"

So the whole thing had been planned and prepared in advance, Ben realized.

"Think you're so funny, don't you!" Joey quavered. "For two cents . . ."

He had to turn and heave once more, and the boys again doubled up in laughter. He did look funny, Ben thought, but not to himself. Another minute, and he'd clout somebody.

Ben took his canteen to him.

"Here, drink this, Joey. It's good water." And, turning to the group, Ben said, "Let's get going. Lot to see."

He led the group into a newly opened part of the refuge.

Here, in this region of limestone cliffs near the Mississippi River, it was as though a cluster of huge skyscrapers had fallen flat to earth and shattered over many square miles of ground. The result was a crazy jumble of cliffs and chasms and gloom-filled, echoing caverns and passages.

Ben showed Syd the best vantage points from which to take pictures. Ben also showed Tom and Andy where to dig to find old arrowheads. Ben led the way through tunnels and over rockfalls and along paths slanting up the face of cliffs.

"This trail is like poison," Joey Bayne said. "One drop'll kill you!" And he laughed at his joke.

At least, Ben thought, he's getting over being mad.

It was then that Syd saw a long, slender object moving across the path before them.

"Hey, look!" he whispered, catching Ted's arm. "A coral snake!"

"No," Ben said, "just a king snake. Nonpoisonous."

"Let's catch it," Ted said. "We'll put it in Joey's lunch box and when he opens it . . ."

"No," Ben said.

Ted and Syd looked at him, their faces suddenly angry.

"You telling me what I can't do?" Ted demanded.

Ben wanted to say: Lay off Joey; he's having a bad time. But instead he said, "This is a game refuge, remember? My Dad's in charge."

"That's right," Syd said.

Ben led on and Ted said nothing more.

Nobody paid much heed to the passing of time, they were all so interested in exploring. Hunger finally made Syd look at his watch.

"Hey, it's past five o'clock. It'll be dark before we find our way out to civilization!"

Ben said, "Doesn't matter. I know the way. Let's eat."

He built a campfire in the mouth of a huge cave. Its light cast their shadows in huge distortion upon the back wall—as if they were giants, of long ago, sitting in council. Outside, sunset dimmed into gloomy dusk; and the wind fretted through the twisted passageways of Giant City, moaning like a lost ghost.

It was night by the time they finished eating; and it seemed abruptly, and menacingly, dark when Ben poured water onto the campfire to quench all embers.

"I sure hope you know the way home," Syd said to Ben.

"Look, if I had to, I could lead you out blindfolded, and I'm not bragging."

"But let's not try it," Ted said.

The accident happened soon after they started hiking. Ben led, the rest strung out in single file on the trail. As they walked along, he was thinking that he liked these boys. They were a good bunch. It was then, at the rear of the file, he heard Joey yell, "Hey, wait—Help! Help!"

The boys stopped, hurried back along the trail.

Andy was crouched at the cliff edge, shining his flashlight down. "That Joey," Andy said disgustedly. "Draw a line on the floor and he'd trip over it."

"What happened?" Ben demanded.

"He slid off the trail. Listen to 'im holler."

"Help me up!" Joey was screaming.

Ben examined the slope below. It was almost straight down, for its upper half, then sloped out; the slope, covered with thick shrubs, had cushioned Joey's fall. From the strength of his yells, he hadn't suffered anything but fright and scratches.

"You all right, Joey?"

"Yeah, but help me up!"

"Can't. Got no rope. Anyway, you can just walk along the bottom of the cliff there. You'll come to a break, where you can climb back up to the trail. We'll move along right above you. Use your flashlight."

Ben's calm soothed Joey.

"All right, I'm starting."

And then Ted got another of his wild ideas.

"Hey, Ben! Syd! You guys," he whispered. "This'll be good! Keep real quiet. Let's move fast, now—and leave Joey behind."

"He'll get lost," Ben said sharply.

"That's right!"

"You mean, leave him out here alone all night?"

"Sure, he won't freeze or anything. Ain't no bears or wolves around to hurt him. Weather ain't even chilly!"

Andy chuckled. "Serve him right for lagging behind. Next time he'll keep up."

"He'll be scared," Ben said.

"And how," Ted said. "He'll sure remember this night!"

"I mean, he'll be *really* scared," Ben insisted.

"You chicken or something?" Ted demanded.

"I'm just saying that . . ."

"Gosh, Ben, you don't like anything we want to do! Well, you can just stay out of it."

"Come on," Andy urged. "Let's get off a way and make noises like howling wolves."

"Joey'll be shaking like a leaf!" Syd said.

"Come on, then!" Ted commanded. "You coming, Ben, or aren't you?"

Ben hesitated. I could teach the bunch of them a good lesson, he thought angrily. I could easily, in the darkness, slip away from the group—and join Joey. I could lead Joey out of Giant City to the highway to town, while the rest of them wandered around in the dark passageways, lost. They'd be lost the minute I left them. They'd discover what it was like to be lost at night in the woods! But if I play this trick on them, Ben realized, they'll be through with me. I won't have any friends but that no-account Joey . . .

"You coming, Ben, or not?" Ted demanded.

Ben said . . .

Shutter-Bug

The Problem: The issue is whether to cooperate or to oppose one's close friends. Sometimes a member of a group finds himself in strong opposition to the emphatic, united wishes of the rest of the group. Such opposition is especially difficult for the disagreeing individual when the group consensus is focused on a worthy goal and his own conflicting purposes relate only to himself and might, in some instances, be considered mere self-indulgence.

Introducing the Problem: Ask the class, "Have you ever wanted something very badly, then discovered that somebody else needed that thing just as badly as you did? This story deals with such a problem. Listen carefully as I read. The story stops before it is finished. Think of ways in which you might end the story."

It was a treasure to Jimmy Norton: a twenty-year-old press camera. It belonged to his Uncle Tod, who was a veteran news cameraman. With that camera he had taken historic pictures of flood damage, of forest fires, of gunmen being tear-gassed into submission, of oil tanks blazing in a lightning-caused fire, of troops landing on D-day, of earthquake ruins, of visiting statesmen at the United Nations.

Jimmy, at twelve, was quite a good photographer himself. He hoped some day to be a crack photojournalist who traveled around the world taking pictures of events that caused headlines in the press. By that time, of course, he figured that he would have a whole battery of fine cameras; but now he wanted nothing so much as that bedraggled old press box of his uncle's.

Right now, Jimmy and two of his friends, all members of his Scout troop, were on a sort of scavenger hunt. They were combing their neighborhood for "white elephants." Their church was going to hold a rummage sale to raise funds to buy an organ for a mission church overseas. The plan was to ask people to donate articles for this sale, articles that, while no longer of real use to their owners, were still useful enough to find a buyer at prices that were irresistibly low. People were glad to donate, for a really worthy cause, such items as old radios and broken-down sewing machines and vacuum cleaners and coffee grinders and abandoned toys—all broken but mendable.

So far, Jimmy and his friends had had good luck in their hunt. They had gathered in an old TV set, five old radios, a power lawnmower that needed a new motor, two pairs of scuffed cowboy boots, a Civil War rifle, a portable phonograph that needed a new arm, a tired cavalry saddle, and a grandfather clock.

"Hey, Jimmy," Pete asked, "isn't this your aunt's house?"

"Yeah. She'll give us something sure. She's real nice."

His Aunt Mary answered the bell and beamed at the three boys.

"Hi! Come in—come in. I've been baking. You fellows don't think that some fresh cookies and lemonade would be out of order just now, do you?"

Their ear-to-ear grins were sufficient answer to that.

As they munched and guzzled in the kitchen, Jimmy explained that they had come for white elephants for the church rummage sale.

"I've got just the thing for you!" she said, rising from her chair. She hurried into another room and came back. "Here. Look at this!"

"Boy!" Ed gasped.

And Pete said, "Hey, that's something! It'll really sell."

Jimmy said nothing; he couldn't. He just stared, his heart a sick, heavy lump in his chest.

His aunt had brought out his uncle's old press camera.

She said, "This isn't all. More junk goes with it. I'll get the rest."

Junk! Jimmy's face grew hot with outrage as his aunt brought in the accessories that went with the camera—a flash gun, tripod, separate backs for roll and sheet film, wide angle and telephoto lenses. Junk worth its weight in money!

"Gee," Ed breathed in delight, "what a haul!"

And Pete said, "I'll bet that'll sell for real money."

"B-but, Aunt Mary," Jimmy protested, "this stuff is old, maybe, but it's still too good to j-just give away!"

"Oh, no. Your uncle finally got the fine new camera he has been daydreaming about for months. He doesn't need this stuff any more."

"This outfit's good enough to put up for auction at the sale," Ed said soberly.

And Pete added, "I'll bet it'll bring in over fifty dollars. Maybe a hundred. That'll sure help a lot toward buying the organ for the mission."

"Aunt Mary," Jimmy insisted in desperation, "you've got to check with Uncle Tod first . . ."

"No," she said comfortably, "I heard him say he was going to give all this stuff away."

"To me!" Jimmy blurted. "He promised it to me."

Aunt Mary looked suddenly stricken.

"Oh, Jimmy! I didn't *know*. Boys, I—I'm sorry. I hate to disappoint you, but . . ."

"Aw, heck, Jimmy," Ed protested, "you already *got* a good camera. Nobody in the gang gets as good pictures as you do!"

Pete added, "Look what a big awkward thing that old box is, anyway. I can just see you packing it up Mt. Baldy. It'd break your back."

"Besides, think of the money it'll bring at the sale," Ed went on.

"Fifty bucks, at least," Pete said. "You know how much the mission needs that organ. You heard what Reverend Michaels said: The gift that counts most is the one that the giver wants most."

Aunt Mary broke in, "But if Jimmy really wants this camera, it's his, of course."

"Aw, Jimmy, how crummy can you get!"

"I'd hate to live with that on my mind," Pete snorted.

"Now, boys," Aunt Mary said.

"Aw, come on, Ed," Pete said, "Leave 'im here with his loot."

But Ed pressed, "Jimmy, think how much that fifty dollars would help. What d'you say?"

Jimmy caught a shaky breath and said:

The Un-Invitation

The Problem: The issue is integrity in human relations. Should pleasure for a group be bought at the price of pain for an individual? Mary has invited six girls to go to the Fair with her on her birthday. But, for the seven of them, she has, she discovers, only six books of tickets. Someone has to be left out. Who? Should one person's feelings be deeply hurt so that the rest of the group can have a fine time at the Fair?

Introducing the Problem: Ask your group, "Has your family ever decided to go to a movie or on a picnic or on a trip, and then discovered that someone will have to stay home to take care of something—a sick person, or the pets, or to open the house to repairmen, or something of the sort? It happens in all families. Sometimes it happens when you have arranged to go someplace with friends. How do you decide what to do then? This is a story about such a problem. The story stops but is not finished. Try to think of ways in which the story might be finished."

When Mary realized what she had done, she felt just sick. It had been unintentional. She had no desire to slight anybody, to hurt anyone's feelings, but now she saw no way out of it.

"Mother, what shall I do?"

"About what, dear?"

"I've invited all the girls to my birthday party—and now there's one too many!"

Mrs. Neilsen laughed and said, "Is that all that's worrying you?" And then she understood, and she gasped, "Oh, my goodness!" And just stood there, stricken, trying to think what to advise Mary.

"I've got to talk to Beth and Nancy!" Mary said.

She ran out of the apartment, down the three long flights of stairs to the front areaway, and around to the back, to the laundry room where Beth was helping her mother. She found Beth moving clothes from the washer to the drier.

"Beth, listen!" She drew Beth into a corner. "Something awful has happened," she began, and explained.

Mary had invited her six closest friends to her birthday party—all girls in her sixth-grade class who lived in this apartment house. Mary and her mother had planned to hold the party in their apartment—to listen to records, play games, and have ice cream and cake. But her father had phoned home a half-hour ago and changed all that. Mr. Neilsen drove a taxicab for the Reynolds Company. He would take tomorrow afternoon off, he had phoned Mary. In his cab he would drive the whole birthday party out to the Fair Grounds. He had six books of tickets for the Fair, one for each girl in the group: Each book would admit one girl to the Fair Grounds and provide tickets for the rides, the big show, and a fine dinner. The public relations office of the Fair had given the ticket books to cab drivers who had been bringing people out to the Fair, and Mary's father had persuaded some of his friends to give him their tickets for Mary's party.

"Beth, I was so excited," Mary explained now, "I didn't stop to think. We've got six books of tickets, but there's seven of us girls. One too many!" And, as Beth just stared at her, Mary wailed, "Don't you *see*?"

"Well, I guess somebody can't go."

"But who?" Mary demanded. "I can't just un-invite somebody I asked to my party!"

Nancy arrived then, carrying a hamper of clothes to be laundered. Mary beckoned her to their corner and told her the exciting but upsetting news.

Nancy, at first, was too delighted with the treats in store to be worried. "You mean we all get into the Fair, and we get to ride that big ferris wheel and the rolly-coaster and eat in the revolving dining room on the tower and—everything?"

"And ride in the spaceship," Beth added, "and in the submarine gardens and . . ."

"But we can't all go!" Mary interrupted. "That's just it. We've got one too many people!"

"Let's chip in and buy another book of tickets . . ."

"They cost too much."

"Anyway, Dad says there's no more available. Besides, we couldn't get another passenger in the cab."

"Then we've got to leave somebody out."

"But *who*? Gosh, I—maybe we'd better have the party at home."

"And waste all six books of tickets? Oh, no!"

"But who can I leave out?"

They thought hard for a moment.

"Leave out Nora. She's new here. She's the girl you know the least, Mary. Tell her the party is called off."

"Then suppose she sees us all leaving together? Then I'm not only mean but a liar, too."

"Leave out Ruth," Nancy suggested. "She doesn't go to the same Sunday school we go to."

"Or Edith. She's black," Beth said.

"You've had a quarrel with Lucy," Nancy pointed out.

"Ruth's been sick so much, this past year," Beth then reminded them. "She hasn't been running around with us . . ."

"Or doing much of anything else," Mary said. "Don't forget: I *did* invite her."

"But, Mary, somebody has to be left out," Beth said, "or none of us can go!"

And Nancy added, "It's your party, Mary. You've got to decide. Who'll it be?"

Mary hesitated, and her voice trembled as she said:

Sacrifice Hit

The Problem: The issue in this story concerns the often difficult task of deciding when to cooperate with your close group of friends and when to stand against them. Should you do what your group wants you to do, although you would much prefer not to? The problem of this story deals with a youngster's difficulty in trying to make up his mind whether to cooperate in a group project when doing so will require a real sacrifice on his part, or to refuse and accept the penalty of being disliked and belittled.

Introducing the Problem: Ask the group, "Have you ever been a member of a bunch that voted to do something nice for somebody—something that was very difficult for you to take part in? Perhaps it required you to put in money you didn't have, or to do something forbidden by your parents. Whatever it was, remember what a spot you felt you were in? This story deals with such a problem. This story stops but is not finished. As I read, try to think of ways in which you would end the story."

Danny was having a nightmare—the same old nightmare. He was pitching for the sixth grade against the seventh-grade team. His side was one run ahead. It was the last half of the last inning. He had just tried his fast ball, and the batter had hit it—but the ball had soared almost straight up in an easy pop fly. So easy! All Danny had to do was stand there and wait for the ball to drop into his glove, and the game would be over with, his side as winner.

So he stood there, waiting for the falling ball to plop into his glove. But it didn't. Sunlight dazzled him. Sunlight was a blinding flare in his eyes. The ball slipped through his upstretched fingers and struck him on the forehead and glanced to the ground. Half-dazed with pain, he stood there a moment before realizing that the onlookers were shouting, that the batter was running toward first, that the man on third was streaking toward the home plate . . .

"Pick it up! Heave it—*heave it.*"

"Head for third, Pete!"

"What a butterfingers!"

Groggily he saw the ball on the ground where it had rolled. He bent to snatch it up and bumped headfirst into Pete Byers, his own shortstop, who had come running to get the ball. Pete fell flat on his face. Danny snatched up the ball and flung it toward home plate, but the ball went wild over the catcher's head; and the seventh grader got safely home for the winning run.

Danny woke up, heart pounding, his face damp with sweat.

This was just a nightmare, but the game had really happened just as he had dreamed it, a week ago. He had lost that game—and he would lose the next one, if he pitched for his team.

He ought to quit playing ball, he told himself dismally. He was still the best pitcher on his team, and he was a good batter. But he ought to quit because, no matter how hard he tried, his playing was going to get worse and worse. Unless . . .

"Danny, you all right?" his mother called.

"Sure," he answered.

"Time to get up."

Before dressing for breakfast, he opened the bottom drawer of his bureau and took out the old toy cash register that he used as a bank. He counted the coins it contained. He had exactly $39.50. He needed $21.50 more. How could he get so much money in time to be of real help?

Danny had this problem: He was a fine athlete, but his eyesight was defective. He needed glasses. He had reading glasses, but he did not have glasses for distance vision.

His eye doctor had suggested that, in time, he be given lenses that would not only correct his vision for distance but would be tinted to protect his eyes from sunglare, as well.

Wearing such glasses, he would easily snag a pop fly instead of letting it slip through his fingers to smack him on the head. With such glasses, he could recognize birds in a tree top, he could tell a DC10 from a 747 in the air. With such glasses, he could continue playing baseball.

He didn't want to ask his parents to buy the glasses just now; they couldn't spare the money. He figured that getting the distance glasses he wanted, but didn't absolutely *have* to have, was his own responsibility. He had been saving for them.

At lunch, that day, Pete Miller stopped him.

"Danny, I want the team to meet after school, at my place."

Pete was captain of their ball team; his folks' garage was the usual meeting place for the group.

"What for?" Danny asked.

"Something's come up."

That was all Pete would say, and Danny worried all afternoon.

After school, the group gathered in the Miller garage.

Pete explained why he had called them together.

"You know what happened at batting practice two weeks ago," he began.

Danny's worry sharpened. Their second-baseman, Tom Eads, had socked the ball clear out into the street. The ball had struck the windshield of a passing car, shattering it. The car belonged to Fred Turner, a young mailman. The boys had had to chip in to buy him a new windshield. It had cost them twenty dollars apiece. For Danny, taking that twenty dollars out of his carefully saved-up hoard of dimes and quarters earned by running errands and mowing lawns had been almost unbearably painful.

"Well," Pete said now, "I've discovered that Fred Turner paid more for a new windshield than he told us. They're expensive. But that's not all. He could have reported the accident to the insurance company and they would have replaced his windshield for nothing. But they would have reported the accident to the police and the park director."

"Oh, no!" Tommy Eads groaned.

"You know what the park people have told us. If playing ball in the park causes anybody to get hurt or any property to be damaged—off we go. No more ball diamond."

"And no more games," Tommy echoed.

"Darn nice of Mr. Turner not to squeal on us," Ed Norton said.

"That's right," Pete agreed. "I say we got to thank him. When people do you a favor you've got to show appreciation, or you're a slob."

"And they stop doing you favors," Ed said.

"Sure, we appreciate what Mr. Turner did for us," Danny said, uneasily. "So let's thank him."

"Here's what I think we should do," Pete said. "Mr. Turner's car is a hot rod. On weekends he runs it on the drag strip. So let's give him something he'd be darn tickled to get."

"Good idea!"

"Sure."

"But what, for instance?" Danny demanded.

"You know how drag racers dress up their engines. Let's give Mr. Turner a set of chrome air filters for the carburetors of his engine."

"He'd sure like that!" Tommy agreed.

"But what would it cost us?" Danny asked.

"Maybe fifteen bucks apiece would be enough."

"Wow!"

"We got to be *that* appreciative?"

"We can't be chintzy!" Pete insisted.

"But we paid twenty bucks apiece just two weeks ago," Danny protested, "and now you say . . ."

"Okay, okay, we'll buy cheaper chrome filters," Pete conceded. "That's the least we can do—ten bucks apiece."

"*You* get an allowance," Ed said. "Some of us earn our spending money."

"So earn it. Let's take a vote."

"Pete," Danny protested, "it takes a lot of mowing lawns to make ten bucks."

"Mr. Turner saved our ball park for us. Everybody in favor," Pete commanded, "raise your hand!"

Everyone but Danny and Ed raised his hand.

"Come on, Ed," Pete said. "I know you sold your bike last week."

"Yeah, but—okay, okay."

Now only Danny hadn't raised his hand. Everyone looked at him. He felt his face grow red and hot. Still, he did not raise his hand.

"Aw, come on, Danny," Pete insisted. "You know the club doesn't do anything important unless the vote is unanimous. You ain't a chintzy guy."

But Danny just sat there, mute, unmoving. All he could think of was those tinted eyeglasses he needed. He just couldn't spare another ten dollars!

"Doggonnit, Danny, you're not going to be the only guy holding out, are you?" Pete said angrily.

"You want it unanimous—you think it's really unanimous when you *make* everybody vote the way you want?"

"Never mind all the argument," Pete retorted. "You with us or ain't you?"

And Ed said, "If you're going to stay with a team, you got to cooperate, Danny!"

"Yeah. Yes or no? Give us your vote!" Pete insisted.

Danny said:

A Long Nose Has a Short Life

The Problem: Involvement or noninvolvement is the question. In this story, two boys are accused of cheating on an arithmetic test. One is guilty, the other is innocent. A third boy can clear the innocent person and expose the guilty one, but if he does so, he will be looked down upon by other boys as a tattle-tale and will have to take a licking from the cheater. He can escape both the beating and the stigma of "squealer" by simply remaining silent; he isn't supposed to know what's happening—he's eavesdropping; moreover, to some degree, he can salve his conscience by telling himself not to be a Judas who testifies against another boy.

The crux of this social imbroglio is, of course, the question of involvement. Is the innocent bystander really innocent? Bystanders who see someone being injured but do nothing to aid the victim and remain silent are themselves victims of our "epidemic of noninvolvement."

Newspapers have reported a series of incidents in which witnesses have been non-Samaritan in their behavior: In New York City, a young woman was repeatedly stabbed while thirty-eight neighbors heard her cries over a half-hour period. No one ventured out to help her; no one called the police; unaided, she died. A crowd watched, without interfering, as a gang of eight men tromped two men; and in another case, a student who had been stabbed by a gang of toughs asked watching motorists to take him to a hospital—but they rolled up their windows and drove away. In California, motorists saw a taxi driver being robbed and did not bother to stop or call police. These are just a few samples of many such incidents reported in the press.

In this story, "A Long Nose Has a Short Life," the issues are defined, and the alternatives delineated. The fact that when a bystander does interfere, some risk is involved, is not glossed over; the risk, sometimes, is very real. Nevertheless, the responsibility of the bystander exists. Again, you, as the teacher leading the role playing, must bear in mind that you do not put the answers into the pupils' mouths. They must respond to the issues of these stories as their own perceptions guide them.

Introducing the Problem: Ask the group how they feel when someone "squeals" on them. Also ask them how Raoul must have felt when accused of cheating, how Barney felt overhearing, and how Pete felt.

That morning when Barney Craig walked into the principal's outer office, he found Pete Haines and Raoul Marchant waiting there. Raoul nodded politely; Pete gave Barney a hard stare, which was all Pete ever gave anybody, unless it was an addition of lumps. Barney sat down, across from the other two.

Waiting, Barney sensed that the two boys were worried. Raoul sat stiff and straight, but his hands kept twisting together. Raoul was new here; he was French, and his English was very interesting but puzzling. In France, Barney had read, school was very strict; probably Raoul was in trouble and didn't know what to expect from Mr. Davis and feared the worst. Pete Haines was chewing gum, even here in the principal's office. Pete was big for his age, hard-muscled, and hard-headed. It wasn't just that he was a bully that made Barney leery of him, but the fact that Pete seemed to enjoy it. As far as Barney was concerned, if Pete had become extinct with the dinosaurs and sabre-toothed tiger, Barney would have been happy.

Mr. Davis opened his door.

"Come in, you two."

Pete and Raoul rose and walked into the other office. Barney sighed and settled down to wait. He was in charge of traffic patrol and wanted to suggest some changes to Mr. Davis.

Barney did not intend to eavesdrop, but the partition wall was thin, and Mr. Davis's words were distinct, especially when Barney leaned his ear against the wood.

"Boys," Mr. Davis was saying to Pete and Raoul, "Miss Duncan has brought me your arithmetic test papers. She is puzzled by them. So am I. Perhaps you can explain them to me?"

Raoul said, "Sir, I do not understand. Something is wrong?"

"Yes, Raoul. This test was a review of arithmetic covered by your class the past two months. You've made certain mistakes."

"I am sorry."

"Pete, the answers you gave to some questions also are wrong."

"Can't win 'em all," Pete said.

"Pete, you and Raoul sit next to each other, don't you?"

"I guess so. Miss Duncan put me there."

Raoul asked again, "Something is wrong, sir?"

"Yes, Raoul. You've made certain errors in answering the test questions. Pete, you've made the same errors. In fact, *exactly* the same errors."

"Oh, now, Mr. Davis," Pete protested.

Raoul said, "I do something not right, sir?"

Mr. Davis let out a long sigh; and Barney, overhearing through the partition, snorted to himself. *He* knew what had happened! Trust good old Pete Meathead Haines to be up to his usual tricks. When the muscle was passed out, Pete was out there with a washtub; but when the brains were being apportioned, Pete was standing there with an eyedropper.

"Boys," Mr. Davis said, "look at these arithmetic problems. This first one involves simple addition: just adding half a dozen numbers. The answer you got, Pete, is 387. And your answer, Raoul, is 387. You both put down 387. The right answer is 381.

"Another problem. This one involves dividing 4328 by 8. Your answer, Pete, is 547. Yours, Raoul, is 547. Again, you both have the same answer, and you're both wrong. The right answer is 541. Tell me, Pete, how did you happen to make such a mistake?"

"Beats me, Mr. Davis. I just don't know."

"Raoul, don't you think it's odd that the two of you made exactly the same mistake?"

"Sir, I do not understand."

"Can you explain your mistakes?"

"N-no, sir."

"It may seem to you that I'm making too big a thing of this. After all, anybody can make little mistakes in arithmetic. Even math geniuses sometimes can't add. That's not what has got me worried. It's something much more important. Boys, I repeat: You both made the same mistakes. I don't believe it was just an accident. Pete, I want the truth from you—and nothing but the truth. Did you copy from Raoul's paper?"

"Me, sir? Oh, no, sir! That would be cheating! I study hard. I don't need to copy from nobody!"

"Raoul, did you copy from Pete's paper?"

"No, sir."

"During the test, Raoul, did you notice Pete trying to get a look at your paper?"

"No, sir."

"Pete, did Raoul look at *your paper?*"

"Well, sir, you know how it is—I mean, for all I know. . . . Well, I was too busy writing to watch."

"Then neither of you has any explanation as to why your papers have mistakes that are exactly alike?"

Barney, listening in the outer office, jumped to his feet in a sudden excited rush of understanding. *He* knew what had happened! *He* knew that one boy had copied from the other, and he knew *which* boy had copied! *Pete had copied from Raoul.* What was more, Raoul had answered those questions *correctly*; but Pete, copying them, had copied them *incorrectly. And what's more,* Barney told himself excitedly, *he could prove it! Raoul is a good student, and he's honest; but Pete's a lazy dimwit and he's dishonest.* Those figures 387 and 547— they were incorrectly written on Pete's paper because *Pete had mistaken Raoul's figure* one *as a figure* seven. Barney's family had had a French student as a visitor; many French people wrote the figure *one* with a line slanting down from the top to the left. So it looked like our figure seven. The actual French seven had a crossbar in the middle, so that it looked sort of like an F. Raoul had written the right answers, 381 and 541.

Barney then heard Mr. Davis say, "I'm marking both these papers F. Raoul, starting school in a new country and a different language is hard, I know. But cheating is not an answer to your problem. You will get a reputation that will be difficult to change."

He's accusing Raoul, Barney realized—and impulsively moved to the door, telling himself, "*All I got to do is go in there and tell Raoul to show Mr. Davis how he writes the figure one. That'll prove he's honest and Pete's the cheater!*"

Barney grasped the door knob—and stopped. He would be getting himself into all kinds of trouble if he did this. He was running tattling to teacher, that's what he was doing. Pete would blab to everybody, Barney foresaw. The gang would call him a rat-fink squealer. And what would Pete Haines *do* to him? Just beat his ears off, that's all. Pete was the biggest roughneck in school. *It wouldn't be just one working-over he'd give me,* Barney foresaw. *Every day, going home after school, I have to pass the corner where Pete and his gang hang out. Every day, I'd have to run a gauntlet,* Barney realized. Every day, they'd jeer at him; they'd gang up on him. . . .

TEACHING HISTORY

History becomes a far more interesting subject to students when they become emotionally involved with the people they are reading about. Inevitably, history becomes more real as students learn that people in the past, just as today, faced problems for which they had no quick, easy solutions.

Young people grow in insight and sympathy as they discover that history is not just an elaborate time-line of explorations and coronations, of wars and elections and depressions, but a record of people who suffered all the familiar human ills—and more: of people who endured the hardships of creating new homes in raw wilderness, of many other people who got enslaved and died of despair, of others whose lives were wasted in futile wars, of talented individuals who benefited mankind, and of twisted individuals who harmed their fellow humans. Most definitions of history would agree that it is not only a bookkeeping of events, but also an examination of feelings—and that feelings counted in the past as now.

For feelings do count. Feelings impel action.

It was the moral indignation of the Abolitionists that did so much to create the climate of opinion that ended slavery. It was public outrage against the excesses of mobsters in the Prohibition era that helped to end it. It was widespread revulsion against the Vietnam War that finally terminated that crisis.

It is possible, through working with feelings in the study of history, that we can help young people develop more highly their capacities for compassion and responsibility.

How do we work with feelings in the classroom?

One effective method is role playing. The kind of role playing presented here is *sociodrama*—that is, decision making in a social crisis. The alternative ways of solving a problem are often harsh and once chosen, must be lived with.

Such dilemmas usually involve conflicts of value. For young people, the dilemma may involve a choice between a cherished personal goal and loyalty to the peer group, or a choice between parental wishes and the urgings of close friends. For the individuals we study in history, such choices were often crucially important to many people.

People in positions of great responsibility had to face issues that involved the welfare of tribes, religious sects, of whole countries, even of whole races. The king and queen of Spain had to decide whether to help a man named Columbus find a new route to the Indies—and possibly waste money, men, and ships. They also had to decide whether to allow the Indians to be made slaves, or risk failure of the plantations in New Spain. Separatist leaders had to choose between accepting religious persecution or facing the hazards of life in the New World. The early American colonists had to decide between accepting heavy taxes levied by the mother country or facing military retaliation. Abraham Lincoln had to decide whether or not to free the slaves and risk losing the Civil War. President Truman had to decide whether or not to drop the atomic bomb or risk losing many thousands of soldiers in an invasion of Japan. Such dilemmas involved an agonized searching of heart and soul, for the decisions had vast consequences for good and ill upon many future generations.

Role-playing such dilemmas enables students to identify with them. By standing in the place of people in crisis situations, students acquire an experience that is closer to actuality than what is available in print in a book. Students who role-play the making of critical decisions in history relive the drama of those times far more realistically than if they merely read about them. The process of reenacting crises makes such experiences so vivid and memorable that they can have a lasting effect upon young people's development as thinking, feeling individuals.

Ways of Using Sociodrama

Dilemma stories can be used in a variety of ways in teaching history. One history text presents a sociodrama at the beginning of each chapter in order to provide an empathy-arousing introduction to the crucial problem developed in the chapter.[1] The authors suggest that you, as the teacher, read the short dilemma story aloud to your class. The story might involve an issue such as freeing the slaves, migrating to the New World, or dropping the atom bomb.

After reading the story aloud, you might start your group discussing the problem. Or you might ask your students to write an ending to the unfinished story, revealing how they think the problem should have been solved. Or you might use the story as an impetus for role playing. After some discussion, you ask students to assume the roles in the story and act out a solution to the dilemma. You ask them to decide what they would do in this situation. You can ask questions that make them aware of their need for more information in order to make an intelligent decision. Further reading for facts will help them mesh data, make inferences, and draw informed and sensible conclusions.

After students have offered their solutions to a dilemma, you, as the teacher, will often have reason to say, "But this is not what really happened. There were other matters that you have not considered. Let's read this chapter and find out what choices these people really did make and why."

It may be worthwhile to make a tape recording of the role-playing

[1]George Shaftel, *Decisions in United States History* (Boston: Ginn & Co., 1972).

sessions. Then, when the work on the chapter is completed, the issue may be role-played again in the light of the new insights acquired. A comparison of the final role playing with the initial role playing may reveal dramatic differences or confirm valid viewpoints originally held.

Another way to use role playing in teaching history is to study an historical dilemma more deeply in a five- or six-week project. Harold Garvine reports such a project.[2] Garvine says that cause-and-effect teaching of history is apt to be dull—that students in such classes "miss the chaos and excitement" of history and "fail to grasp the full complexities of human motivation." Garvine works with twelfth graders. He chooses an area of study and assigns roles to students—roles that represent points of view in the historical problem to be studied. In a study of the American Revolution, for example, students are given the roles of patriots, loyalists, and ambivalent people caught in between. Garvine carefully assigns students to roles on the basis of personality, intellectual ability, and personal convictions. He points out, of course, that such matching requires that the instructor know the students well. In some cases, Garvine assigns students who are not deeply interested in the project to roles that will likely involve them so deeply that they will become enthusiastic partisans.

All students in the project are assigned common readings in both primary and secondary sources. In addition, each student is required to do additional reading on the viewpoint of the character whose role he or she is to portray and write a summary of it.

After this preparation, Garvine structures a problem situation with the group and starts them role-playing. He notes that the students will often spontaneously supplement the role playing with wall posters, placards, pamphlets, manifestos, letters, and other objects to press the cause they support. In some instances, they bring in copies of actual writings used at the time the historical event occurred.

Garvine is alert to intervene in the role playing at appropriate times. He slips notes to role players when he decides that they need pertinent arguments for the stand they are taking. He may also suggest next steps to take or courses of action to embark upon when the action is dragging. He may also intervene when the role playing is taking a course that distorts the facts of history or when the students omit critical factors that influenced the actual outcomes in the past.

Garvine requires participating students to keep journals of how they felt as they were involved in the role-playing sessions, their reactions to other participants, and their opinions on aspects of the role playing.

Garvine's role-playing project has a timetable of five or six weeks. The first two weeks are taken up with reading and preparation. Then two or three weeks are spent in the actual role playing. (To find the necessary time, the role-playing sessions are held after school on some days.) A final week is then devoted to evaluation of the project by the class. In this evaluation, students often discover a multitude of defects in their role playing. They sometimes let twentieth-century viewpoints distort their roles and realize

[2]Harold Garvine, "Teaching History Through Role Playing," *The History Teacher*, 3, no. 4 (May 1970).

anew that it is vital to portray attitudes appropriate to the period under study. They also let personal bias affect the way they behave in their parts. They further realize that inadequate preparation diminishes the quality of the role playing. Finally, they realize that they have gained new insight in discussing how the past influences the present.

Another history instructor, Wayne Dumas, finds role playing in the teaching of history an important asset.[3] He writes, "Through role playing, history is experienced more intimately and with greater personal meaning than is usually the case." He believes that historical role playing is most useful "in the replication of small group decision-making situations in history."

Dumas agrees with Garvine that role playing is most effective as a culminating activity in a unit of study. He also assigns preplanning and role research to his students and carefully structures the role-playing situation. Dumas considers a final evaluation to be indispensable. Students must have a chance to see their inaccuracies, their weakly supported arguments, and their faults in logic. Moreover, praise and appreciation for role playing that is well done should be given. Dumas, however, disagrees with Garvine in one respect. He believes that teacher interference or correction during the actual role playing enactments is a mistake. The instructor can help role players *before* and *after* the enactment but should not intervene during the action itself.

DECISION CRISES
IN UNITED STATES HISTORY

A broad sampling of dilemma stories for use in role playing episodes in United States history is included here. These dilemma stories are short and varied in type. They range from the agonized self-searching of a nation's leader who must make a decision that will determine the history of a great nation, to the troubled argument in groups striving to forge a clear line of political action, to individuals trying desperately to choose wisely for their own families.[4]

The Role-Playing Process

Recall that the role-playing process consists of these general steps:

1. Reading the sociodrama
2. Discussing the problem briefly
3. Delineating possible solutions

[3]Wayne Dumas, "Role Playing: Effective Technique in the Teaching of History," *The Clearing House*, 44 (April 1970).
[4]These stories are reprinted from *Decisions in United States History*, by George Shaftel, of the GINN SOCIAL SCIENCE SERIES, © Copyright 1975, 1972 by Ginn and Company (Xerox Corporation). All Rights Reserved. Used with permission.

4. Setting the stage and assigning roles
5. Enacting a solution of the problem
6. Discussing that solution and its likely consequences
7. Reenacting the situation for other solutions
8. Evaluation.

To elaborate on these steps:

1. You may begin work on a particular chapter or historical theme by having your group read the sociodrama that applies. You may ask for a volunteer to read the incident aloud or you may assign readers. It is most effective if the reading is done seriously and with a feeling for the drama involved.

2. After the reading is finished, you may ask, "What is happening here?" or "What is the problem?" and after some discussion, "What do you think will happen now?" If you feel that your group has grasped the situation and its dilemma quickly, you may skip these questions and ask, after the reading, "If you were ———— (the historical person involved), what would you do now?"

3. Encourage your group to suggest a variety of solutions to the problem. Do not betray, by your manner, which of them you consider best. Accept all offered solutions or alternatives as worthy of exploration.

4. Suggest to the class that they act out one of the offered solutions. Ask for volunteers to play the roles involved. Have them come forward. Ask the players what props they need, where they are, what time it is.

5. Invite the players to act out their solution. The role playing may be quite brief. On the other hand, if the students are deeply involved and full of ideas, it may be long. When they stop of themselves or falter, stop the role playing. Simply say, "All right, let's stop at this point." Then turning to the class, ask, "What has happened?"

6. After some discussion, it may be helpful to ask, "Could this have happened?" After the credibility of the solution has been assessed, ask, "What do you think would be the consequences of this way of solving the problem?"

7. Remind the group that someone has suggested still another way to solve the problem in your earlier discussion (or accept a proposed solution that is offered now). Proceed to role-play this alternative solution. Ask for volunteers to enact the roles. Set the stage. Start the new actors role playing. When the enactment ends, again ask if this solution could have happened and what the consequences would be. If the group has volunteered still a third solution to the problem, have it enacted too.

8. After this last enactment, move the class into discussion and evaluation. You may ask, "If you had to choose, which solution to the problem would you accept?" Then ask, "Why?" If the need is apparent, you may ask, "Do we know enough to make this kind of decision?" or "Do we need more information about the time, place, the people, customs, or the special circumstances involved?"

After the chapter has been studied, it may be worthwhile in some instances to return to the opening sociodrama. You may then ask the group, "In the light of what you know now, how would you solve this problem now?" You could have your group reenact a solution to the sociodrama. The solution they choose this time might be a direct result of the deeper knowledge they have acquired of the circumstances involved. They might, or might not, accept the course of action that was actually taken in history—for example, by Queen Isabella when she decided to back Columbus, or by the Separatists who chose to leave Europe and migrate to America.

King Ferdinand Decides

Use this sociodrama when your group begins to study the period of exploration and the discovery of America by Columbus.

The Dilemma: Should King Ferdinand and Queen Isabella provide ships and money for Columbus's effort to find a new passage to India? It's a wild scheme that can possibly result in a waste of money and the loss of lives and ships. But suppose Columbus *is* right? A new route to India would mean immense profits for Spain!

King Ferdinand and Queen Isabella of Spain faced a difficult decision. A sea captain from Genoa, Italy, had come to them with a daring plan. If it succeeded, it would bring great riches to Spain. If it failed, it would waste money, men, and ships. He wanted some ships to make a dangerous voyage of discovery. This sea captain's name was Christopher Columbus. He claimed that he could lead Spanish ships to the Indies in the east by sailing west over the unknown expanse of the Atlantic Ocean. We can imagine the conversation leading to their decision.

"I have no faith in this scheme," Ferdinand said.

"It's worth trying, isn't it?" Isabella questioned.

"Columbus will take our sailors to their death!"

"I don't think so."

"But this man is all wrong! Our geographers say that the Indies are much farther across the sea than he thinks."

"They don't really know. What if Columbus is right?"

"He can't be. Our royal counselors say it would take him three years to reach the Spice Islands."

"They may not be so far."

"But even if Columbus could sail to the far side of the world, he'd never come back! The winds are wrong. Ships could never sail back against them."

"Ferdinand, we don't really know that."

"It would be foolish to risk the lives of Spanish seamen on such a hopeless voyage!"

"Think of the new lands that Columbus may discover and claim for Spain."

"So many centuries after Creation, do you really believe that any worthwhile lands remain undiscovered?"

"Think of the people whom we may convert to the Christian faith."

Ferdinand's lips tightened stubbornly.

"Do you know what Columbus asks as a reward?"

"Wouldn't he deserve a great reward?"

"But he goes beyond all reason! He asks that we appoint him Admiral of the Ocean Sea—"

"Small payment for what he'd do for Spain."

"—and that the titles pass down to his sons and heirs forever."

"If he could find a new route to the Spice Islands, we would control the trade with the Indies."

"In addition he asks to be Governor-General of all islands and main-lands he discovers."

"That would be fitting."

"But are you willing to let him take one-tenth of all the gold, silver, pearls, gems, spices, and other merchandise that is obtained by barter or mining in such new domains? Free of all taxes, besides!"

Isabella's brows lifted. She sighed. "He does value his services highly."

"A mere sea captain! Yet with one voyage he intends to raise himself to the level of Admiral of Castile and to enrich himself with the ransoms of kings."

"But if he profits greatly, think how much more Spain profits."

"It's a foolish dream," Ferdinand insisted. "Our answer is the same answer we've given him twice before—no. No ships. No money."

"You are being cautious, I know . . ."

"Of course I am!"

"But are we being wise?"

"What do you mean?"

"Suppose," Isabella asked, "that Columbus goes to Portugal for help? Suppose he does find a new route to the Indies. Then Portugal would control all the trade with the Spice Islands."

"Isabella, I beg you to be sensible. We must say no to this man."

Queen Isabella did not respond. She sat there, absorbed in thought, visions of greatness passing before her mind's eye.

To say no would be sensible.

But would it be wise?

What similarities can you see between the arguments for and against Columbus's voyage of exploration and the arguments for and against the United States space program in recent times? What differences?

The Exiles Decide

Use this sociodrama when the class begins its study of the English colonies in America. This incident deals with the Separatists (later known as the Pilgrims) in the period just before they left the Netherlands.

The Dilemma: Should the Separatists risk the hazardous voyage to the New World and the hardships and dangers of starting a new colony in a strange land among hostile natives? Or should they remain in Europe—and continue to suffer poverty and persecution?

A sudden rapping on his door startled Pastor Robinson. When he opened the door, he recognized two of his poorest parishioners, John Kyle and his wife Martha. They looked very upset.

"Come in, come in," he urged.

They hurried inside. Martha Kyle demanded abruptly, "Is it true? Are we leaving the Netherlands?"

"Possibly . . ."

"But why? *Why*? We're safe here! Why leave?"

"Safe in some ways," Pastor Robinson said, "but not in others."

"I've tried to tell her," Kyle said. "She won't listen."

"We had to flee for our lives from England," she said. "Here we can worship God as we wish. Are you forgetting that?"

"True," the pastor agreed, and felt heavy of heart. He foresaw that others of his congregation would feel as Martha Kyle felt.

His modest parsonage, Green Gate, in the beautiful city of Leyden, was the center for a group of English exiles. They were devout Christian people. But a dozen years before they had fled from England, from law officers, and angry mobs. They were hated in England.

Why? Because they wished to separate from the Church of England. They had formed separate congregations that refused to practice the rituals of the established church. Called Separatists, and accused of blasphemy, even of treason, they had had to flee from England by secret ways.

John Kyle said, "Pastor, I've told Martha that life is too hard for us here in Leyden . . ."

"But in England we'd rot in prison. If we weren't hanged!" she insisted. "Here the Dutch are so kind to us."

"Here we're exiles," John Kyle said. "The language is strange, the people's ways are strange, the work we do is strange."

"Pastor, tell him he is out of his mind!"

But her husband argued, "We are farmers, but here we must work as button makers and drapers and hatters and barbers! Because we lack skill, we can earn only meager pay. So we live in poverty, in misery."

"We survive."

"We earn so little that our children die for lack of proper food."

"The weak ones."

"The strong ones we must put out to work. Some will soon lose their health and die in their youth. For their sakes, we must leave this land."

"Pastor, plead with him," she begged. "We cannot return to England."

"We do not think of returning to England."

She stared at him, puzzled, and then she guessed.

"No, you cannot mean it. To—to America?"

"That is what we consider."

"You would do that, knowing what our fate might be? That a storm might send our ship to the bottom, drowning us all? Knowing that even if we arrived safely, we might die of starvation? of lung fever? or that savages might slaughter us?"

"Calm her, Pastor," John Kyle begged. "We must go to America. It is the only thing left for us to do."

"Pastor, tell *him*," she demanded, "that he takes us into dangers he knows not of! Pastor, always before you have counseled us wisely. Do so now. Tell my husband that what he plans is so wrong!"

Pastor Robinson caught a sharp, unhappy breath.

"In what each of you say, there is much truth," he admitted. "But with what little wisdom I have, I can only urge that we . . ."

If you were Pastor Robinson, what would you advise? Why? How would you and your family feel if your father announced that you were all moving to a tiny colony in a faraway unsettled place? How would your situation be like that of the Separatists coming to America? How would it differ?

The Iroquois Dilemma

Use this sociodrama when beginning to study the period of the French and Indian Wars.

The Dilemma: Should the Iroquois people support the French against the British, although the French have long been enemies of the Iroquois? Or should they support the British—who are slowly but surely pushing them off their hunting grounds?

Listening intently, the old sachem (chief) sat silently by the camp fire. His face was calm and stern, giving no hint of his feelings. But the Onondago messenger, on the far side of the fire, gestured wildly as he spoke. And the Mohawk warriors, sitting respectfully behind their sachem, let their anger burn on their bronzed faces.

"You must choose," the messenger said urgently. "You cannot sit in the comfort of your longhouses while the French and the English go to war again!"

The sachem's son, Young Hawk, said, "We will fight the French."

"That is foolish," a warrior spoke out. "The French are our friends. It is the English who are our enemies!"

"We have always fought the French," Young Hawk insisted. "For more than a hundred years that has been so. Since Champlain killed our chiefs . . ."

It is time we make *peace* with the French," the messenger broke in urgently. "They buy furs from all the tribes. They bring us guns and knives and blankets. It is time we join with the white men who are our friends."

But Young Hawk retorted angrily, "You know our battle cry. *Let the French have no rest except in death!*"

"But the French marry Indian women. French traders live among us," the messenger went on. "They raise their children among us. Do the English traders marry Indian women?"

There was no answer. Then the old sachem spoke, "A few."

"Very few! The English despise Indians. They look upon us as animals that they must drive away."

"We do not run," Young Hawk said.

"But the French are like us—they live like Indians. The English are farmers, but the French are hunters and traders like us. The English cut down the forest to clear fields. They fence in their fields. They drive away the game that we must have to live."

From the warriors behind the old sachem came nods and murmurs of agreement. "Always the English increase their farms. Their cities swell in size. They push the Indian off the face of the earth!"

Again the warriors nodded assent, their murmurs louder.

But Young Hawk said firmly, "For every Frenchman, there are twenty Englishmen. You ask us to join the weaker side?"

"True. The English are many and the French are few. But that is good! The French live on posts that are many days' travel from each other, far in the wilderness. They do not cut down the forests to clear fields. They do not drive away the game. They do not push us from our hunting grounds!"

The warriors' words of agreement were loud and angry.

But abruptly the men became quiet as the old sachem lifted a hand and spoke. "When the Frenchmen first came, in the time of my grandfather's grandfather, they joined the Hurons against us. They killed Iroquois. Always, since that time, the Iroquois fight the French."

"It is true that in the past the French have been our enemies," the messenger broke in. "But we must look ahead! The English grow in number. It is they who will drive us from our lands. The English are farmers. Think what that means! As they raise sons, their sons will need land. Always more land! To get it, they will wipe the Iroquois from the face of the earth. Are we men without courage? Will we sit by our fires and wait for our doom? I say no! I say . . ."

But he stopped abruptly as the old sachem rose suddenly to his feet, his lined face harsh with purpose.

"All this," the old man said sternly, "to me is not new. I have long known that the French and English will fight again. To one, we must be friends; to the other we must be enemies. Of this I have long taken thought. I have made up my mind. We must fight. The foe we must fight is the . . ."

Judging from these arguments, whom do you think the Iroquois should fight, the English or the French? Why?

Redcoats against Minutemen

Use this sociodrama when your group begins its study of the colonies' struggle for independence from Britain.

The Dilemma: Should the colonists, who are British subjects, rebel or remain loyal to the mother country? Not to take arms and rebel means to continue to suffer abuses and "intolerable" acts of Parliament. However, fighting against the mother country is repugnant to many colonists who take pride in being English.

Jeffrey Groton and his son Alex were cutting firewood in the oaks beyond town when their black helper, Dan, came running to find them.

"Master! The Minutemen are gathering at the tavern!"

"The Redcoats are marching on us?"

"Yes, sir. Mister Haley says come quick."

As they ran homeward, Dan gave them more news. Seven hundred British soldiers had marched from Boston to Lexington last night. They had tried to leave Boston secretly. Patriots, however, had been watching every British move. Paul Revere and William Dawes had ridden to warn the people that the British were coming.

When the redcoated soldiers arrived in Lexington, they found a small band of Patriots waiting for them on the common. Shooting started. Eight Patriots were killed and ten others wounded. Then the British marched on to Concord to destroy gunpowder kept there by the Patriots. They intended also to seize Samuel Adams and John Hancock as traitors. However, Mr. Adams and Mr. Hancock had been warned and had already fled. The redcoated troops then destroyed what guns and powder they found. Now they were starting their march back to Boston. Patriots and Minutemen from all the counties around Concord and Lexington were gathering to pursue the king's men.

Martin Dundee, a neighbor, was waiting in front of the Groton house when the men arrived.

"Dan," Jeffrey Groton ordered, "fetch our rifles!"

"Wait, Jeffrey," Mr. Dundee begged. "Do you realize what you are doing?"

"We go to join the Minutemen."

"But don't you see what may happen? You go against trained troops!"

"We've got to show that we'll fight. Then maybe they'll make a reasonable agreement with us."

"No, they won't," young Alex protested. "Parliament hasn't once offered to meet us halfway. We've got to fight."

"You're too young to be sensible," Dundee said angrily. "But *you*, Jeffrey. From you I expect better judgment."

"The boy is right."

"Jeffrey, you forget that but for the protection of British troops, the French and Indians would have burned our villages and murdered our families."

"We fought 'em too."

"We'd be French-owned but for British help, and you know it."

"It's not help they're bringing now," Alex said bitterly. "Instead of French troops invading us, it's British Redcoats!"

"But you and other hotheads like you are bringing the British down on us! Jeffrey, look what happened in Boston. Men painted like Indians dumped valuable cargos of tea into the harbor. That is the behavior of wild savages, not of loyal subjects of the king."

"We *are* loyal Englishmen. We only demand the rights of Englishmen."

"But how can loyal Englishmen shoot at other loyal Englishmen?"

"We fight against tyranny," Alex said.

"Don't either of you see how it will end?" Dundee pleaded. "You commit treason. If you are not killed in the fighting, you will be hanged! Stay home."

"Is that what *you* will do?" young Alex demanded. "Hide while your neighbors fight your battles for you?"

"I hide behind no one," Mr. Dundee said harshly.

"Alex," Jeffrey Groton said, "Mr. Dundee must follow his conscience."

"Where does your conscience place you, Mr. Dundee?" Alex asked. "With your neighbors or with the British?"

"I say let us not resort to arms! Petition the king to right our wrongs."

"We have, again and again. We get no answer."

Dan had come out of the house, bearing rifles. Alex took one. Mr. Groton took one. Dan held a weapon out to Mr. Dundee.

"Coming with us?" Alex demanded, "or staying?"

Mr. Dundee said:

Judging from the arguments of these men, what do you think Mr. Dundee should do? Why?

Union—or No Union?

Use this sociodrama when your class begins to study the period after the Revolutionary War and the framing of the Constitution.

The Dilemma: Should the new nation have a strong central government, or should it remain a loose confederacy in which the major authority lies with the individual states?

They met in a tavern in Providence, on a cold March day. David Howells and Jonathan Hazard, entering, saw three friends seated near the fireplace, enjoying its warmth. They nodded and spoke greetings. General Varnum, Welcome Arnold, and Nicholas Brown nodded in answer. The newcomers ordered ale and sat down.

"Heard the news, General?"

"Of what, Mr. Howells?"

"Congress has called for a convention of delegates from all the states to meet in Philadelphia on the second Monday of May next."

"Expected it."

Welcome Arnold asked, "What for?"

"To revise the Articles of Confederation."

Arnold snorted. "I repeat. What for?"

"To put it simply—the nation needs a strong central government."

"Ridiculous!"

"General," Howells said, "you will probably be among the delegates elected to represent Rhode Island."

"If I am, I'll go."

Arnold said harshly, "Rhode Island will send no delegates."

"Come, sir, the welfare of the nation . . ."

"The welfare of Rhode Island concerns me. Nothing else."

"But you are a citizen of the United States, not just . . ."

"I'm a citizen of Rhode Island!"

Howells said reasonably, "But we do need a change. Times are hard . . ."

"And prices high. That I grant you."

"Civil disorders break out across the nation. Mobs jam the courts to get 'stays' on debt payment. People need relief, sir! Other states should follow our example in Rhode Island and issue more money."

"But paper money is almost worthless."

"Congress cannot issue more money. Congress cannot give back pay to our soldiers of the Revolution. Congress cannot even pay interest on our loans from the French and Dutch! Sir, our public credit is shameful. Congress needs power to tax the states and to coin money and . . ."

"Then we pay *double* taxes! To both state and federal governments. That, sir, is no solution."

"We'll have tax collectors everywhere," Brown grumbled.

"General," Howells asked, "surely you will agree that the country must support an army and navy? Pirates in the Mediterranean are looting and sinking our trading vessels. We have no navy to protect our trade."

"Right," Varnum said.

"Congress must tax to support an army and navy."

"So you'll give us a standing army again, living on our money! I say no. *Never.*"

"We need a new government," Howells insisted. "Otherwise, we are just a weak confederation of states."

"A strong central government will take all powers from the states."

General Varnum said, "Our foreign relations suffer."

"Of course," Howells said. "Other nations dare not make trade treaties with us. They do not know whether they deal with one central government or thirteen separate state governments. It's a situation that can only bring trouble. We need to establish a federal government with all necessary powers . . ."

"To tax," Arnold said. "Tax and tax and *tax!*"

"Otherwise it cannot operate."

"And that means a bunch of lawmakers in the capital who will become a set of high-and-mighty aristocrats, lording it over us while they exact the last dollar from our pockets!"

"But we have no choice, if we intend to survive as a nation."

"While I can speak and have friends to listen," Arnold retorted, "I will say and keep on saying—Rhode Island will send no delegates to this convention!"

"We *must* send delegates," Howells insisted. "Unless we work out a new plan of government, we have no nation. It boils down to this: Do we want a Union?—or no Union!"

"I disagree."

"I insist."

"General," Brown asked, "What is your opinion?"

General Varnum said:

If you were General Varnum, how would you answer? Why? Can a citizen be loyal to both his home state and to his nation at the same time? How? What do you think are the powers that a state should have? What powers should the national government have? What would happen if people consider themselves citizens of a state first, then citizens of the nation? What might have happened if the thirteen former colonies had split apart and had become three or four separate small nations?

What Shall Thomas Jefferson Decide?

Use this sociodrama when studying the period after the War for Independence.

The Dilemma: Should President Jefferson buy the Louisiana Territory? He has no legal authority to do so. Moreover, such a step might bring on a war with Spain. But *not* to buy Louisiana might mean losing the chance to add vast new territories to the new nation.

In 1801, Thomas Jefferson came into office as president of the United States. On July 4, 1803, President Jefferson received a letter from Paris. For long, anxious months he had been waiting for this message. But now, before opening it, he hesitated. Was it good news or bad? Had he got what he so badly wanted for the nation? Or was this letter a refusal that would create problems threatening the future of the United States?

The letter was from Robert Livingston, American minister to France. Jefferson had sent him there to make a treaty with Napoleon, the French ruler.

Jefferson opened the letter. As he started reading, he caught a sharp breath of surprise. He continued reading, with growing astonishment and delight. But as he finished the message, his first relief gave way to dismaying second thoughts.

This letter was not the answer he had expected. It went far beyond his greatest hopes. But if he let stand the arrangement that Livingston had made, the consequences might be alarming. Sadly he wondered—if he let this treaty stand, would he ever again know peace of mind?

By Livingston's treaty, Jefferson had bought what would be half a nation.

He had bought more land than any human being, before or since, had ever bought. He had bought one million square miles of North America. That had not been Jefferson's intention. He had asked Livingston to try to buy the port of New Orleans from Napoleon. Instead, as Jefferson's agent, Livingston had bought the entire French territory of Louisiana.

But I have no right to buy Louisiana, Jefferson realized. Even though he was president, under the Constitution of the United States he had no authority to buy foreign territory.

His political enemies would pounce on this action. They would accuse him of being a man who violated his most sacred principles. They would charge that Thomas Jefferson, who insisted so firmly that the Constitution must be upheld with extreme care to obey all its clauses exactly as they were written, now had shamelessly violated it!

Jefferson had maintained that the rights of the states must never be lessened by a strong central government. Now he had plotted to reduce the states' authority and to enormously strengthen the federal power.

Jefferson, who had preached stern economy with treasury funds, now was pouring out many millions of dollars to buy—what? A million square miles of harsh, barren lands of no use to anyone but wandering Indians! And that was not the worst.

In buying Louisiana, it might be that the United States had bought an enormous amount of trouble. With gloomy foreboding, Jefferson realized that perhaps he had started a quarrel with Spain that would lead to war. Moreover, it was likely that this purchase would arouse political problems that would cause strife and disunity in the nation for generations to come.

Sadly Jefferson tried to reassure himself. He was buying territory from France only to make sure that the growth and prosperity of the United States would be helped, not hindered.

Had he made a ghastly mistake?

There still was time. He could still cancel the purchase.

But should he?

What do you think Jefferson should do? Why?

Captain's Choice

Use this sociodrama when your class begins to study the foreign relations of the new United States. At this time, the young nation was facing a world in which the then great powers, France and Britain, were struggling for dominance.

The Dilemma: Should the United States side with France, which had helped it win independence from Britain, or side with Great Britain, to whom it sold three-fourths of its exports?

The lookout in the foremast called a warning. Captain Jonas Kirk peered forward and realized that the big British warship was steering to intercept him. He choked back an angry word. All too clearly he foresaw what was to happen. Aboard the warship, a cannon belched a dart of smoke and a ball sped across the bow of Kirk's little vessel. It was the command to stop. Resignedly, he ordered sails lowered. His crew moved with a reluctance he understood. They would rather fight. They knew what this meeting might mean for some of them. But how could he fight? His two small guns against a hundred-gun frigate!

Already the warship was lowering a longboat.

"Put over the ladder," Jonas commanded.

The boarding party climbed over the side—a snappy officer and a half dozen sailors leveling muskets.

"Ensign McCary," the British officer introduced himself.

"Jonas Kirk, master of the *Seabright*, bound from Savannah with rice, indigo, and tobacco for Liverpool."

"You have English deserters aboard. I want them."

Again, Jonas thought. Twice before it had happened to him, and a dozen times to masters he knew. *Impressment.* Britain lacked enough seamen to man her warships. Life aboard an English warship was so brutal that sailors jumped ship whenever possible and few would volunteer to serve in them. To make up this lack, "press gangs" prowled English cities, kidnapping men for the navy. And on the high seas, English warships stopped neutral vessels and inspected their crews. Finding Englishmen among them, the boarding party would take them by force to the English vessel.

Jonas said, "Ensign, I have no deserters aboard."

"Line up your crew!"

Jonas gave orders. His twenty men lined up on deck.

The British officer moved from man to man, giving each a sharp scrutiny, asking questions that demanded answers. Pointing, he ordered, "You—and you—and you, come with me."

Ruefully, Jonas realized that the Britisher had a keen ear for English turns of speech. He had spotted the two English seamen aboard, Conkey and Jaspers, and young Peter Harkness.

Conkey protested, "Sir, we're American citizens."

"You're English born and bred!"

"Not any more. We have our naturalization papers."

"Have they, Captain Kirk?"

"Aye, they have."

"And this lad?" the Ensign asked, pointing at Peter.

Peter said, "I don't need any. I'm American-born."

"You're English. Your speech is as English as fish and chips."

Jonas said, "The lad speaks the truth, Ensign. He was born in upper New York State. His father was once my skipper."

"He speaks English like a squire's son!"

"His mother is an English woman from Esher, in Surrey. When Peter was one year old, his father died and his mother returned to England, to her parents' home. She did not come back to America with Peter until two years ago. He learned his speech in England."

Ensign McCary moved to the rail, beckoning Jonas Kirk close. In a whisper, the officer said, "You don't want to see a youngster like that rot in a British ship—and I don't intend to return to my ship empty-handed. Those two seamen who claim they have United States citizenship papers . . ."

"I have their papers in my strongbox, sir," Jonas said.

"You have papers. But you know and I know and every halfwit between the Thames and Cape Cod knows that most such papers are *forged.* Now I ask you—think hard, Skipper! Do I take the two able seamen or the teen-aged lad? *Which, sir?"*

Big Jonas Kirk rubbed his chin, frowning. Send those two good seamen back to a British ship? No! But allow sixteen-year-old Peter to be taken? *No.* What then? . . . With a sweep of his arm, he could hurl Ensign McCary over the rail. One shout, and Jonas knew his men would rush the British sailors. Some would die before the muskets, no doubt, but the boarding party would be overwhelmed. He could clap on sail, then; the little *Seabright* would heel away under the light airs. Would the big frigate then shatter her with balls from those huge cannon? And would such a sinking go far to embroil the United States in war with Britain?

"Captain?" the Ensign demanded. "What have you decided?" Jonas Kirk said:

What would you do in Captain Kirk's place? Why?

Rivals for Empire

Use this sociodrama when the class begins to study the background conditions that resulted in the Monroe Doctrine. At this time, Russia warned all other nations to send no ships within 100 miles of the coast of territory she was claiming in northwestern North America.

The Dilemma: Should an American sea captain defy Russian orders against trading on the Oregon coast and risk causing a war between the United States and Russia? Or should he give up the valuable trade in order to maintain peace?

For months, now, Captain Doyle had thought this voyage would be a lucky one. But when he saw the Russian ship approach, he knew that trouble lay close ahead.

The little *Martha Deere* had set sail from Gloucester, in New England, five months before. This was young Michael Doyle's first trip as captain. It had been an easy journey, until now. Sailing down the Atlantic, around the Horn and up the west coast of South America, the little schooner put in finally at Yerba Buena, in San Francisco Bay. But there the captain learned that the sea otter and seal herds of the area had been thinned out by the Russian hunters from Fort Ross, close by. So Doyle had ordered sails up again, and the *Martha Deere* had continued north, to the Oregon Country.

Today, an hour before sunset, she had put into this sheltered cove. As Doyle and Barton, the first mate, peered at the tree-lined shore, they smiled at each other with relief. They saw the many bark huts of a large village of coast Indians. Trading, tomorrow, should be good.

The *Martha Deere* carried a generous cargo of beads, knives, gunpowder, cotton cloth, rum, and pottery. Bartered for furs, they should buy a rich haul of seal and other pelts. The *Martha Deere* would sail from village to village, adding to the store of furs.

It was then that a crewman suddenly yelled, "Sail!"

Glancing seaward, Captain Doyle saw a vessel just clearing the north headland, turning into the little bay. It was a Russian sailing bark, Doyle noticed. She carried a half-dozen cannon, twice his own fire power. He felt a cold touch of misgiving. Then he shrugged. Why should there be any trouble? Rivalry for trade, perhaps. That's all.

The Russian vessel anchored across the bay. But immediately a small boat was lowered. It approached the *Martha Deere*. As it came alongside, a tall man in officer's uniform hailed the deck. Captain Doyle helped the man come aboard.

"I am Lieutenant Rotcheff," the visitor said. His English was good, but unfriendly in tone. "Captain, I must give you a warning."

"About what?"

The warning was this: The Czar of Russia had just this year of 1821 issued a "keep out" proclamation to all other nations. No one but Russian citizens could sail or fish within 100 miles of the northwest coast of North America, from the Bering Straits south to the 51st parallel of latitude.

"Captain," Rotcheff said, "at sunrise you must sail due west until you are beyond our 100-mile limit."

As the Russian left, Captain Doyle, Barton, and Lloyd Thomas, the officer in charge of the cargo, looked at each other in dismay.

"But Russia's got no right to drive us off!" Lloyd Thomas exclaimed. "Oregon Country isn't theirs. Britain and the United States have a joint claim to it!"

"It seems," Doyle said, "that Russia has a different idea."

"What do we do?" Mr. Barton asked.

"We can obey. Or we can *pretend* to obey," the Captain said slowly. "Or we can refuse to obey."

"Go home," Mr. Barton said, "with nothing to show for a year's work? No!"

"We can out-sail that scow!" Lloyd Thomas said excitedly.

"Yes," Michael Doyle agreed. "But if the Russians have another vessel or two to join in a chase, they'd catch us."

"We can stand on our rights," Mr. Barton said, clenching a heavy fist. "We can put some goods ashore tonight and start trading with the Indians at sunrise. Meanwhile, we can load our cannons and have men ready, in case the Russians try to interfere."

"They'll blast us out of the water," Michael Doyle said.

"Then let's hit them first!" Thomas urged. "At midnight, I'll float a boat with a half dozen kegs of gunpowder under her stern. We'll sink her!"

"And with that treachery, start a war."

"We cannot let another nation seize Oregon. I'm thinking that if we try to trade tomorrow and the Russians drive us off by force, it will be an act of war. When word reaches home it will waken the government into taking action. A United States fleet will sail here . . ."

"Arriving a year or two late," Captain Doyle said. "Meanwhile, we are prisoners in a Russian dungeon or food for the fish at the bottom of this bay."

"Those seem to be our choices," Mr. Barton murmured. "Captain, what do you think we should do?"

Michael Doyle thought and said:

If you were the captain of the Martha Deere, what would you answer? Why?

Who Can Vote?

Use this sociodrama when your class begins to study the democratic process, including rights for women, ethnic minorities, the very young, the very old, and the handicapped.

The Dilemma: Should only responsible, competent, successful men have the right to vote in elections? Or should everyone have the right, no matter how poor, shiftless, uneducated, and incapable?

The men seated around the big table in the tavern were a committee. They were preparing the first draft of a constitution for their territory. In a few months, the territory would become a state and a member of the Union. At the moment they were writing an article for the new state's constitution that would say who could vote in elections.

The chairman asked, "Who shall we say can vote? All white men . . ."

"Twenty-one years of age."

"Who own one thousand dollars' worth of land."

"Too much," someone objected. "Make that five hundred dollars' worth."

"Mr. Chairman, I say that we ask for *no* property qualifications."

"Jem, be sensible. Land's cheap. If a man owns no property, that proves he's shiftless. No! I say we don't give the right to vote to riffraff like that."

"But maybe," another man protested, "a young fellow has just turned twenty-one and he's been studying to become a lawyer and hasn't had a chance to earn money yet?"

"Or he's just got out of the army?" someone else added.

"Ed, you wouldn't say such young fellows are shiftless!"

But Ed insisted, "I still say that a man who's built up a right nice farm is responsible. He doesn't vote for any hare-brained politician who promises him the world. That'd cost us ruinous taxes!"

"Mr. Chairman," another speaker put in. "I'm with Jem. No qualifications! Also, I say the age of eighteen is old enough to vote."

"Joel, you're daft."

"We'll take my nephew, for instance. Sure, he was lucky. He inherited a little money. He's got a four-hundred acre farm which he has put in fine shape. He's got a wife and son. But he isn't twenty-one. He'll be twenty next week. You figure he's not responsible enough to vote?"

The chairman demanded, "Can your nephew read and write?"

"Well, he started working so early . . ."

"He can't. So how can he vote for president, or governor, or even a congressman, if he doesn't know what they stand for?"

"He can ask and listen!"

But the chairman said, "I'll call for a motion that the vote be granted to white men, aged twenty-one or over, who own five hundred dollars' worth of . . ."

"No," objected a man who had been silent so far. "It makes me angry to think that any lout who has reached the ripe old age of twenty-one, and who has inherited or bought some cheap acreage can then cast a vote! He can lack all judgment and learning. He can be completely irresponsible. Yet his vote will count as much in electing a president for the nation as the vote of a county judge or a man who's been managing a thriving business. That is preposterous! A man of education and seasoned judgment should have a dozen votes for every vote of some untutored bumpkin of twenty-one!"

"Our idea is the universal franchise. Every man should have one vote."

"Ridiculous! Next you'll say that *women* should vote, or slaves."

"Order! Order!" The chairman pounded on the table. "The motion is that the vote be granted to all white males of twenty-one or over who own five hundred dollars' worth of land. All in favor, vote *Aye* . . ."

What do you think should be the qualifications for the right to vote? Why? What are the qualifications today?

Mr. Jensen Decides

Use this sociodrama when your class begins to study the westward movement.

The Dilemma: Should a family stay at home in Indiana, where its members feel secure among relatives and friends, although the family farm is inadequate for their future needs? Or should the family move west where opportunities are open, in spite of the dangers and hardships of travel across a wild continent?

It was thirteen-year-old Nora who refused. She said flatly, "No, I won't go!" There was a break in her voice that hinted she was close to tears. Mr. Jensen calmed her with a firm, quiet hand. "Easy, child. What do you think, Mary?"

Nora was the youngest of the four children. Mary, at twenty-two, was the oldest. John, twenty, and Seth, nineteen, were the other children.

Mary asked, "Why do you *want* to move to Oregon, Father?"

Mr. Jensen sighed. Why? Because it was in the air. All over Indiana, now, people were talking about Oregon. Stories were spreading swiftly of broad valleys with fertile land, waiting for the takers. Dense forests of fine timber were ready for the axe. Fish and game were plentiful. It was *new* country, where any man could find rich opportunity.

"Mary, this farm's too small. Oh, it'll still feed us. But it's really just big enough for one family. Nora's still a child, but the other three of you will soon need land for farms of your own. I can't buy farms for you. So the sensible thing is for us to move where we can take up rich farmland for almost nothing."

"How would we go?" John asked.

"By train to St. Louis. Then by boat to Independence. There we'd join a wagon train."

"How long will it take us to reach Oregon?"

"Oh, say four to—six months."

"Provided," Mary said, "we don't get scalped by Indians, or drown crossing a river, or starve to death in a mountain blizzard . . ."

"People die of snakebite right here at home," John cut in. "Father, I'm for going."

"I'm not!" Nora repeated. "I've got a lot of friends—I don't want to go off to nowhere and be all alone!"

"You'll make new friends, child," Mrs. Jensen said.

John said, "I'll ask Lucy to go with us. We'll get married as soon as I take up land and build a cabin in Oregon."

"Her mother will never let her go!" Mary said.

John shrugged. "Then she won't," he said mildly, but he lowered his eyes and firmed his lips to hide their quiver.

"Mary," Mr. Jensen asked, "how about you and young Reverend Norton?"

Mary caught a shaky breath. "I'm plain. Tom's started to court Matilda Carter. She's pretty."

"She owns nothing," Mr. Jensen said. "I plan to give you this farm, Mary. Tom Norton's a practical man."

Mary's eyes lit up. "Tom *is* practical," she agreed. But then she said, "That means I'd stay here. But I can't! Mother needs me."

Mrs. Jensen smiled. "Not that much, dear."

Mr. Jensen felt pangs of doubt. His wife was not strong. Would unforeseen hardship bring her to a lonely grave on the prairie?

Young Nora asked, "Why can't we go next year?"

John answered that. "The good land may be gone by then."

Mr. Jensen looked at his younger son. "Seth, what do you say?"

"Mr. Latham said I can read law in his office. I want to stay."

"We need you, lad."

"So?" John asked, looking at his father. "Do we go?"

Mr. Jensen did not answer at once. His glance moved around the table.

For each of them, there was reason to go—and reason to stay. The final decision was up to him.

Leave or stay?

Back in 1619, Separatist families in the Netherlands held such family conferences. In what ways was the problem faced by the Separatists (the Pilgrims) and Puritans similar to the dilemma later faced by people like Mr. Jensen? In what ways were their problems different?

Fugitive

Use this sociodrama when your group starts studying the slavery issue in United States history.

The Dilemma: Should two white men help a runaway slave and face a possible thousand-dollar fine, a prison term, and a slaveowner who demands heavy reimbursement, or do nothing and feel intense shame every time they remember the incident in the future?

The two men were fishing quietly at the edge of the broad river. Suddenly one called to his friend.

"Sam! Look. Out in the middle of the river. Ain't that a man swimming?"

"No, just a—Hey! By golly, you're right."

"Come on. We'll get a skiff and go haul 'im out."

They put down their fishing poles and started toward a little dock where rowboats were tied up.

"Never mind, Sam. Look. There's a man in a rowboat out there, now. Coming from the dock at Ripley."

"Sure enough. We can stop worryin'."

They started back toward their fishing poles.

"Sam!" The older man's voice held an odd note. "That man in the water . . . He's a black man!"

"Oh? Somebody's slave, I reckon."

"Don't you *see?*"

Sam caught a sharp breath of understanding.

"By golly, you're right!"

"The black man's a runaway."

"Of course."

"And the man in the boat is a white man who . . ."

"Owns him!"

"Right."

"And he ain't rowin' so hard just to rescue that black man . . ."

"No. He's going after him. To bring him back!"

Sam nodded, his sunburnt face grim.

"That's why he's swimmin' so strong. Breakin' his heart to get away."
"That white man chasin' him . . . He's sure bending his oars."
"The slave's goin' to make it, Tod. He'll get here first."
"But he'll be tuckered out. Sam, what we goin' to do?"
"Do? Why, nothin'. We ain't doin' nothin'."
"You mean you'll let that planter catch 'im?"
"The slave's his property, ain't he?"
"He may be black, but he's still a man!"
"You forgettin' the law?"
"It's a law I can't respect."
"It's still the law. Be sensible, Tod! You'll pay a thousand-dollar fine. You'll go to jail, too! You'll even have to pay for the slave if . . ."
"Come on! He needs help!"
The older man started running down the bank.
Sam hesitated, his feelings in a whirl. "Stay out of trouble!" he warned himself. But could he stand by and not help the slave escape?

Were there people who helped black runaways in spite of the possible penalties? Can you think of places in the world where situations like this existed forty years ago? Or even today?

A President on Trial

Use this sociodrama when your class begin to study the Reconstruction Period after the Civil War.

President Andrew Johnson was charged with a number of crimes, among them restoring citizenship and property to Southern rebels. When the Civil War ended, many Northerners felt extremely punitive toward the South.

The Dilemma: Should the Senate vote to impeach a president for acting in the light of his own best judgment? (This had never happened before and would set a very disturbing precedent.) Or did President Johnson *deserve* impeachment, since he had shirked his responsibilities to the country?

It was February 22, 1868. In Washington, D.C., the House of Representatives was meeting in special session. The question before the House was whether or not to impeach the president of the United States—that is, to accuse him of misconduct in office. If the decision of the House was *yes*, the president would be put on trial before the Senate.

The president was Andrew Johnson. As vice-president, he had become president when Abraham Lincoln had died from the assassin's bullet.

For two long days the issue of impeachment had been hotly debated. Now it was late afternoon of the second day. A hush fell over the crowded galleries. Many of the tense, watching faces were those of former slaves.

Slowly a thin figure struggled to his feet. He was Thaddeus Stevens, a life-long defender of blacks and an arch-enemy of slavery. He began to read the charges against the president.

Already Stevens was near death. The once commanding presence, bushy-browed and shaggy-haired, was now bent and shaken. His voice faltered. Unable to go on, he handed his speech to the clerk of the House to finish reading. He fell back weakly in his chair. But it was as though the cold indignation of his long-feared voice still rang like steel from the clerk's tongue.

The congressmen voted. The tally was 126 to 47 for impeachment.

A delegation from the House then moved to the Senate chamber. Somehow Thaddeus Stevens found the strength to speak again.

He told the Senate: "We appear before you in the name of the House and of the people of the United States.

"We do impeach Andrew Johnson, President of the United States, of high crimes and misdemeanors in office . . ."

A president of the United States was to go on trial. If convicted, he would be removed from office.

The trial in the Senate began. The arguments were bitter.

It was charged that Andrew Johnson was failing his trust as Lincoln's vice-president and successor. He was pardoning Southerners guilty of treason and restoring citizenship and property to them. He was undermining Congress's effort to give full rights of citizenship to the black freedmen of the South.

Ridiculous! said Johnson's defenders. He was rebuilding the South, just as Lincoln wanted. But transform ex-slaves into citizens? *Should* they become full-fledged citizens?

Each senator weighed the pros and cons. Each senator confronted the same dilemma. Should he judge Andrew Johnson guilty of high crimes or name him innocent? How should he sift the facts? How could he overlook heated emotions?

Each had to make his own decision. Each decision would add up to the final decision of the Senate—and the nation.

Unseat a president or keep him in office?

What would your decision be? Why?

Shall We Go on Strike?

Use this sociodrama when your class begins to study the labor movement in the United States.

The Dilemma: Should workers go on strike and lose desperately needed jobs, or should they passively continue to work for wages too meager to meet their basic needs?

Cornfield was just thirty miles west of Chicago Its main industry was the Forbes Wagon Factory, employing some sixty workers. A little over half of them had gathered here in Tom Williams's big barn. Tom knew that a lot more wanted to come. But they were afraid. The men here were also afraid. It was a hot summer night in 1890, but the sweat on the men's tense faces was not just from the heat. A strike vote was to be taken. Just to attend such a meeting might cost them their jobs.

Flickering lanterns hung from rafters overhead. In their stalls Tom's two horses stomped restlessly. A dusty smell of hay drifted down from the loft above. The men talked in low tones, almost furtively, sounding each other out. Finally Tom Williams shouldered his way through the crowd and stood on an upended box.

"Men, you know what this meeting's about," he said. "The factory's making money. We aren't. Leastways not enough to make ends meet. Hard times, they tell us. I say hard for *who*? Not for Mr. Forbes in his big house. We work twelve hours a day, six days a week. Now another wage cut. I say we should walk out."

"And lose our jobs?" asked Andy Dee.

"Now, Andy," Tom chided, "you know they can't make wagons without us to do the work."

"They'll get scabs to take our places," another man warned.

"We won't let the scabs in. We'll set up pickets to stop 'em."

"Just get our heads bloodied," Andy grumbled. "Like at the Plow Works in Chicago last year. They hired strongarm guards for the scabs. One picket got killed. The judge said the guards were just doing their duty. He said pickets are trespassers, and the guards were protecting company property."

From the back of the group, young Joe Lane called out, "It's all right for you, Tom, to say strike. You got a house and a patch of ground. Lose your job, you can still grow enough to eat. But, me, I have to pay rent. Got three kids and bills from here to there. Oh, what's the use. I just can't chance losing my job."

"If we get fired," Ed Barnett chimed in, "like as not we'll get blacklisted. We won't be able to get a new job anywhere."

Red Casey's booming voice joined in. "But which is worse? Getting knocked on the head? Or watching your wife and young'uns go hungry? Me, I say strike."

"Me, too," Tod Jones growled. "If we don't help ourselves, nobody else will."

The arguing went on. Finally Tom Williams called them to order. "We'll vote on it. Those in favor of striking, hold up your hand."

A few hands went up. Then several more, and more, then some lowered uncertainly. Tom couldn't tell if there was a strike majority. He began to count: "One, two—Sam, is your hand up or down?—three, four, five . . ."

Can you think of more reasons, not given above, why these workers should go on strike? Can you give more reasons why they should not go on strike?

Are there any other ways in which they might achieve their goals? Why does a man who owns his own house and land enough for a garden need an income?

The Battleship Maine

Use this sociodrama when your class begins to study American foreign policy at the turn of the century.

The Dilemma: Should a newspaper editorial writer in 1898 advocate that the United States go to war against Spain as a result of the sinking of the *U.S.S. Maine*, although there is no proof that Spain is responsible? Or should he urge that the United States investigate the incident thoroughly before taking any drastic action, even though this means the nation will be considered weak and cowardly?

Dan Carmer was chief editorial writer of one of the most influential newspapers in New York City. Usually he dashed off his editorials. But now he was in a quandary.

This editorial was to deal with the war in Cuba. The Cuban people were revolting against the Spanish government. The United States had sent a battleship, the *U.S.S. Maine*, to Havana to take on American citizens who might be in danger. There, at anchor, the *Maine* had been blown up. Two hundred and sixty crew members had been killed. Even before the sinking, feeling in the United States had been strong in sympathy for the Cuban rebels. Now the shocked public of the United States made a furious outcry for punishment of the men who had sunk the *Maine*.

Phil Russell, a news editor, paused at Dan's desk.

"What's your lead editorial going to be about, Dan?"

"Same as everybody else's today—the sinking of the *Maine*."

"Going to beat the drum for war?"

"Phil, this is a responsible newspaper."

"So?"

"If we say punish the criminals who sank the *Maine*, just that many more people will press Congress for a declaration of war."

"We're awfully near that point."

"Thanks to the *Journal* and the *World*," Dan said bitterly. "It's a sorry thing for this nation to be pushed to the brink of war because two sensation-mongering newspapers are fighting for circulation."

"Oh, come now, Dan, you know . . ."

"Hearst of the *Journal* and Pulitzer of the *World* have been deliberately exciting people into a frenzy of outrage against Spain. Atrocities have been committed by both the rebels and the army in Cuba. You know that! But the *World* and the *Journal* have been exaggerating brutalities by the army just to print sensational news that will sell papers. And on account of that cheap journalism this country'll go into a war that doesn't concern us."

"You think we shouldn't punish the men who blew up the *Maine*?"

"Who," Dan Carmer asked, "*did* blow up the Maine?"

"Why—the Spaniards, of course!"

"How do you know?"

"Why, everybody assumes . . ."

"But what's the proof?"

Phil stared a moment, then shrugged.

Dan pressed, "Does anybody know for sure that the explosion wasn't an accident?"

"Oh, be reasonable!"

"Or that maybe the Cuban rebels themselves blew up the *Maine*, just to drag the United States into the war on their side?"

A man spoke from the doorway. "What's the argument?"

They turned. Mr. McCrarie, the editor-in-chief, stood there.

"Boss, we need a top-level decision on this," Phil said.

"In my editorial," Dan asked, "do I accuse Spain of sinking the *Maine* and call for war? Or do I say let's not be anybody's dupe—let's hold off accusing anybody until we know for sure who really sank the *Maine*?"

Mr. McCrarie said:

What would you say? Why?

Pass a Literacy Test?

Use this sociodrama when your class begins to study immigration into the United States. As the nation grew, many people began to fear that so many immigrants entering the country would take jobs from native-born citizens. Others feared that we would be burdened with supporting many ill, incompetent, and handicapped foreigners.

The Dilemma: Should the United States enact a law requiring that immigrants who wish to become citizens pass a literacy test, thereby preventing many foreigners from becoming citizens? Or should it keep its door open to people from all over the world, no matter how many or how limited in capability?

The president looked up from his desk as his secretary ushered in a visitor.

"Good to see you, John! But what's so urgent?"

"I wouldn't have insisted on seeing you, sir, but . . ."

President Wilson gestured toward a document on his desk.

"You mean the new law setting up a literacy test for immigrants?"

"Yes. You haven't signed it yet, have you?"

The president said, "Do sit down." His face became thoughtful. This legislation on his desk, if signed by the president of the United States, would become law. If he did not sign it, his refusal would be a veto, killing the bill. "No, I haven't signed it yet."

"You mean you're not going to sign it?"

"I'm considering."

"But Congress passed it, sir."

"By a small majority."

"But we need this law. We must keep out a flood of new immigrants!"

"My friend, all Americans are immigrants, or their children."

"We don't *need* any more foreign newcomers."

"We needed and wanted them in the past. The fact is, we asked them to come. We offered big inducements to lure them into coming. Andrew Carnegie was a poor immigrant. Are you saying that we don't want or need any more great industrialists like him?"

"Of course not!"

"But how are you going to tell which immigrant will be a genius or an ordinary person?"

Flushing red, the visitor stammered, "B-But these foreigners who come today are so different. They don't know our ways."

"They'll learn. Their kids will be like our kids."

"We've got enough problems. Why add more?"

"That's what the English colonists said when the German immigrants started to arrive. That's what the German immigrants said when the Irish started coming over. That's what the Irish said when . . ."

"But if you leave the gates to immigration open, you'll let in sick people who can't work and lazy ones who won't. You'll let in criminals who'll rob us. You'll let in anarchists . . ."

"Every barrel of apples has a few rotten ones. Most are sound."

"You mean your mind's made up?"

"Well, no," the president admitted. "I'm—thinking out loud."

The visitor's face lit with hope.

"Then you'll sign this bill?"

"I haven't said that."

"You mean you'll *veto* it?"

Will I? the president asked himself. But aloud he said merely, "Tomorrow I'll announce my decision."

Tonight, he realized, *I must decide . . .*

Should immigration be limited by a literacy test? Why or why not?

Humankind's Most Powerful Weapon

Use this sociodrama when your group begins to study the post–World War II period, the era of the Cold War and nuclear deterrence.

The Dilemma: Should the United States drop the atomic bomb on Japan? To do so will end the war immediately and save the lives of many thousands of American soldiers. However, it will also result in the deaths of many thousands of Japanese civilians and introduce atomic warfare into the world, with the result that future wars will be enormously more costly in human lives.

(In March 1979, a classroom teacher used this historical dilemma for a group role-playing project. A television service videotaped the role playing, and parts of it were shown in television broadcasts all over the country. The news media obviously considered such a classroom activity worthy of nationwide attention.)

On May 9, 1944, a very special committee met in Washington, D.C. Called the Interim Committee, it consisted of some leading men in our government and a few top scientists. They had been asked to advise the president on one of the most important decisions ever faced by a human being. The question they were to consider was: *Should the United States drop the atomic bomb on Japan?*

Their opinion—*yes* or *no*—would affect world history. The committee members foresaw this. They met to debate the question in a mood of immense concern.

They were good, responsible, serious-minded men. But their opinions on dropping the atomic bomb on Japan were far from unanimous.

"Of course we must drop the bomb!" some insisted. "It will put an immediate end to the war. It means instant victory for us."

"But to use the bomb would be so brutal, so inhuman."

"It will wipe out an entire city in a single blast."

"Soldiers, women and children, old people and babies, animals—every living thing in the target area will be slaughtered."

"But what's the alternative? To let the war drag on for another year or two?"

"And lose hundreds of thousands more American soldiers? Who should we worry about? The Japanese who might die? Or our own young men who might die?"

"Let's not drop the bomb on a city. Drop it on an uninhabited island."

"You mean, just give a demonstration blast?"

"Right. Let the Japanese leaders see how awful it is. They'll surrender."

"But *will* they? The population may never even hear about the bomb. The leaders might suppress news of it. The Japanese army is tough—it will keep on fighting if ordered to."

"Right. We face a foe who doesn't quit easily. We've got to teach them a harsh lesson. We've got to paralyze the Japanese will to fight."

"I agree. Dropping the bomb will end the war immediately. That's what we all want."

"Yes, but do we want the consequences? How will other nations feel toward us? Especially if we drop the bomb on people of another race?"

"Look, we've got enough problems. We can't take time to look ahead . . ."

"We've *got* to look ahead! Don't you see that if we introduce this bomb we'll be changing warfare in the future? Fighting will be on a different scale. Instead of one-bullet-one-man fighting, we'll have one-bomb-one-city fighting. Nations will get wiped out."

"Nobody else has the bomb. No other nation can make it."

"That's true *now*. Other nations will develop it."

"Not likely. It requires a tremendous industrial capacity."

"But after we demonstrate how powerful the bomb is, other industrial nations won't rest until they have it, too. It will be considered a basic necessity of defense to build a stockpile of atomic bombs. Then do you see what danger we'll all be in?"

"True," someone else said. "We'd be dropping atomic bombs on each other. That could mean the end of civilization."

"No. There'll be no next world war. People will know that it means suicide."

"You hope! I don't have that much faith in everyone's good sense. There are too many fanatics and crazy people in the world. I say again—if we demonstrate this bomb's power to the world, in time other nations will have similar bombs. Do we want to live under a constant threat of annihilation? Is that the kind of world we want to pass on to our children?"

"Gentlemen," the chairman insisted, "we must deal with the immediate issue. How do we advise the president? Shall we drop the bomb on Japan? Yes or no? How do you vote?"

Suppose you had been on such a committee. Would you have voted to use the bomb immediately? Why? If not, why not? What other alternatives could you suggest?

TEAMING HISTORY AND LANGUAGE ARTS

History can't be dead to those who have a chance to live through it. This is the theme of a report by Sheryl Lee Hinman on a project in which an English teacher and a history teacher worked together to bring "dull" history to life for an eighth-grade class.[5] For the most part, in such a program, history provided the *content* and language arts provided *process* for the students' learning experience.

Such a program requires dedication, extra time, and energy from teachers, but the job of teaching becomes easier because the students get so involved that they *want* to learn. Teaching becomes exciting when students ask, "Can we write another play?" and "Will you read this revision of my essay?" Drama in the classroom can achieve such euphoric results. It brings history to life through the processes of research, writing, discussion, and informed role playing. Students enter the lives of the people who lived through crises of history and thereby relive those crises. The two teachers involved in this project were Cheryl Lee Hinman (language arts) and John Dolan (American history). Dolan took the eighth-grade class for history in the first period, and Hinman took the group for language arts in the second. At times, one of the teachers took the group for a double period.

[5]Sheryl Lee Hinman, "Dramatizing American History," *The English Journal* (September 1975), pp. 48–50.

How did this teaming of history and language arts work? The following section clarifies the procedure.

Drama as a Means of Reliving the American Heritage

HISTORY

Unit 1: A three-week unit on early American Indian culture. Material from a history textbook and other sources on life process.

LANGUAGE ARTS

Unit 1: A unit on the future. Students read short science-fiction stories by a variety of authors on a common theme such as problems of communication.

A. *Role Playing*

1. A contemporary individual goes back a century in a time machine. He visits an 1875 farm family and tries to explain life in 1975 to them.

2. Students prepare other role-playing incidents on the theme of difficulties of communication between people and between people and other species of life. Situations from their reading may be enacted by them, or they may originate new situations.

B. *Creative Writing*

1. The students are asked to draw (on paper with crayons) some device or machine they think might exist in the future.

2. Then they write an essay explaining the need that will stimulate the development of this mechanism and how it works.

C. *Role Playing*

(Unit continues.)

This unit ends with a structuring of an international crisis—for example, strange creatures living on a planet far out in space face the fact that their home sphere is going to explode (or that, through their own folly, they have made their environment uninhabitable for their species). Three different species of creatures are involved. They send emissaries out into space to find a hospitable planet to which they can bring their fellow creatures.

Three students play the roles of this trio of emissaries who reach Earth. These three are each provided with a strange mask and instructions to provide a description of an unusual creature. The three strange beings are quite different from each other. They all represent a far more "advanced" culture than man's stage of development on Earth. Each emissary is the representative of a population of 1 million on the home planet.

The rest of the class takes the roles of members of a World Congress, delegates from all the different countries, who have come together to listen to the three emissaries from space and to make a difficult decision: Which—if any—of these exotic creatures from outer space shall the people of Earth allow to migrate to our planet?

The Earth members of this Congress prepare questions to ask the emissaries from space: Will the space creatures and human beings be able to live side by side? If any of the three kinds of exotic creatures from space are compatible with human beings now, will they always remain so? Will the space creatures exert a good or destructive effect on earth environment? What is their rate of reproduction? Their culture is far more advanced than Earth's. What will be the effect on our culture? (And so on.)

The emissaries from space are invited to a meeting with the Earth officials. For two or three class sessions, the Earth men question the strange creatures from space.

(History unit continues.)

The Earth delegates then debate among themselves, using arguments pro and con for either welcoming or rejecting the in-migration of all or some of the aliens from outer space. The Earth people finally vote a decision on the dilemma.

Possible Two-Hour Sessions in Which History and English Units Mesh

Confrontation of Future with Past

The teacher asks the three students who played the three emissaries from outer space to change their roles: Now each is a delegate from a different Indian tribe or confederation (the Iroquois, for example).

The teacher divides the other members of the class into three groups: One group consists of Spanish explorers, the second group are now French trappers, and the third group are English pilgrims.

The teacher can either (1) assign readings to these groups on conditions in Europe from which they fled or (2) give them a reminding talk on conditions in Europe that make it no longer hospitable for them: famine, wars, poverty, great plagues, religious persecution, and oppressive social structure—all the reasons why Europeans sought a place in the New World.

These explorers, trappers, and would-be settlers meet with the Indian representatives. The Europeans tell the Indians why they have come to the New World, explaining the harsh conditions in their home lands from which they and their fellows are fleeing. They wish, and need, to find a better way of life in this new world of the Indians.

The Indians listen, but they are disturbed. To the Indians of America, these Spanish, French, and English newcomers are strange creatures from remote and exotic lands. These Europeans represent cultures that are far more advanced in many ways than Indian culture, especially in terms of technology and weaponry (for example, their use of ships, horses, and guns).

The Indians can appreciate many of the reasons why the Europeans seek a new home: They can understand the compelling need to flee from hunger, the cruel forays of enemies, and the waves of disease that depopulate villages.

But the Indians face a harsh dilemma that grows increasingly more acute as their awareness grows of the vast differences in technology and attitudes toward land and forest and wild life that exist between their own traditions and the needs and demands of the strange white invaders from far-off Europe. The question for the Indians grows ever more critical: Should they allow the Europeans to move onto the Indians lands of the New World? They debate the issue among themselves with great earnestness and dread.

Dolan and Hinman suggest some key questions that logically arise in such a debate:

Can the Indians prevent Europeans from migrating in vast numbers to the New World? How?

Does any culture have a real chance of defending itself against a more advanced culture?

The students grasp the analogy between (1) people of 1975 confronted with three different species of exotic creatures from outer space who have cultures far more advanced than those of Earth men, seeking to find a home on planet Earth and (2) the Indians of four centuries ago who had to confront the inroads of Europeans.

The class knows what happened to the Indians as a result of the coming of Europeans in vast numbers, with horses and guns, who came not merely to find food and space but who killed game for export and trade in furs, who felled timber to make fields, who built permanent towns and cities, who brought strange diseases to which Indians had no resistance, who respected no tribal boundaries.

Class discussion, then, can move back to the previous dilemma faced by earth people of 1981 when the three emissaries of strange, advanced cultures out in space arrive on Earth, seeking homes for their fellow creatures. The class discusses their reactions to the space creatures. The question arises: "Did their knowledge of how the Indians fared when Europeans migrated to America affect the decision they made about allowing creatures from a distant planet to migrate to Earth?"

The instructors can guide the students, then, to appreciate the generalization that knowledge of the past can help humankind make decisions about their future . . . and that the lack of such knowledge can cause the mistakes of the past to be repeated.

This unit requires students to employ a variety of language arts skills in obtaining data and using it: research, interviewing, writing, argumentation, role playing, and group decision making.

For an interval, then, the class meets with the history teacher the first period, taking routine assignments in their history texts, and in the second period, doing routine work in the English class.

Sheryl Hinman then involves the group in writing a play. In their history period, the class continues reading their text. But in the English period, Hinman assigns a book to be read—for example, a nonfiction account of the Salem witchcraft trials, *The Devil's Shadow*.[6] The events described in the book are to be used as the basis for the students' writing a play.

This exercise involves reading, discussion, and writing and revising a script. Improvisation is not involved. The students get valuable experience in research, in writing dialog, in correcting grammar and usage. Several weeks of preparation and one or two weeks of rehearsal are required for the project. The play is performed for other English and history classes and, sometimes, even on local television.

Hinman points out the benefits for students of doing such a play. They acquire in-depth knowledge of a segment of history. They derive vivid personal insights from the vicarious experience: The girl playing the woman being tried as a witch learns the frustration and helplessness of being unable to convince others of her innocence; the students realize how quickly and unfairly people sometimes judge others and that the more vehement and cruel a mob is the more likely it is that its members are trying to convince themselves that their abnormal behavior is justified.

---

[6]Clifford L. Alderman, *Devil's Shadow* (New York: Messner, 1967).

While improvisation and role playing were not used in this phase of the project, they could have been. Here we have a group of students who are going to use a nonfiction account of the Salem witchcraft trials as the basis for writing an original play. Hinman used reading and discussion as preparation for the collective writing and revision of the class script. It is possible that role playing could have been of value in this phase of the effort. The students could have role-played key situations of the play before moving into the writing phase. It is likely that the process of improvising vital aspects of the social conflicts involved would have helped the students gain even deeper insights into the emotional concomitants of the historical problem.

As the class moves ahead in its study of history, new units are worked into the problem. A unit on the Constitutional Convention has been a very popular role-playing topic.[7]

HISTORY	ENGLISH
(History class continues routine work, probably studying the post-Revolutionary War period.)	1. Each member of the class is assigned the role of a man who was present at the Convention. Each student gathers information on the historical person he's playing from reference books such as encyclopedias and the *Dictionary of American Biography*.

2. The class studies the issues which confronted the Convention:

   a. plans for state representation
   b. slavery
   c. foreign and interstate trade
   d. taxes
   e. branches of government
   f. amending the constitution etc.[8]

Each student makes an effort to learn the attitudes of the historical character he is portraying on these issues, so that the student can realistically portray that member's particular viewpoint in the Convention.

3. The class studies basic parliamentary procedure so that they can conduct the Convention meetings in an orderly, organized manner.

[7]Sheryl Hinman's report does not indicate whether the first-hour history session or her second-period English session concentrates on the research involved. Presumably either could. Let's assume that it was the second period English class.

[8]Of course, the group can be studying some of these topics when they meet as a history class in the first period.

Role Playing

When the preparations have been finished, the instructors start the group role playing the events of the Constitutional Convention. The meetings may take the full two-period sessions, running for two hours. (The history and English periods mesh.)

The group meets, and the Constitutional Convention opens.

Mr. Washington declares the Convention in session. He reads the first question and opens the discussion. (The students have no prepared and fixed script. They may have notes on specific topics from which to base their arguments pro or con.)

The delegates debate the issues (listed above), each speaking from the viewpoint and partisanship of the character each has assumed.

Small groups of the delegates can meet in caucuses, arguing how to vote on issues. Several may even pull out of the Convention. The issues on slavery, and on ways of amending the Constitution, may occasion sharp and recriminative debate.

Votes are taken on issues, and a final signing of the Constitution can climax the role playing.

The Constitutional Convention completed, the group moves on in its study of history to the westward movement. Dolan and Hinman start a unit on American Inventiveness.

HISTORY

Role playing: In the history period, the class begins a simulation game called *Pioneers* (Interact, 1974.)

1. The class members take on the roles of members of a wagon train bound for Oregon in 1840. They meet, elect a wagon master, and set a date for departure.

They debate on such issues as using mules, horses, or oxen. How much basic equipment for farming and building can they carry in their wagons, how much food and seed, guns and ammunition, cherished furniture and books that take room and are heavy but are not necessities?

2. En route, the wagon train faces emergencies, such as: Wagon master dies, and a new one must be elected.

Some refuse to travel on Sunday. Decision must be made.

Quarrels: Some families decide to turn back.

ENGLISH

1. In the English class period, the group starts studying a skill book entitled *How to Think Up Ideas* (Scholastic, 1971). It explains thinking techniques such as making lists and brainstorming.

2. Students do additional reading, as they wish, about American inventors and their inventions.

HISTORY	ENGLISH
The wagon trail branches: Which way should they go? Much debate.	*Writing:* The wagon train members develop a map on which they record their progress.
Prairie fire.	
Crossing a flooded river. Some freight must be jettisoned—much argument.	They keep individual diaries on their experiences and reactions.
Illness strikes: Children die and must be buried.	
Some mules stray, and some wagons have to be left behind. Their owners and goods have to be portioned out among other wagons: debate, and accusations and recriminations, with wagon master forced to act decisively in getting group decisions.	
Some crime occurs; wagon master must act as judge as group tries the law breakers.	
(The students volunteer crises they have learned about in their reading.)	
3. The unit may end with a field trip to some historical museum in the area. Such museums may provide guides to displays and show historical films.	

Sheryl Hinman concludes by pointing out that the two instructors plan and guide the development of most of the units. However, they also allow for individual and small group work. Students are encouraged to follow their own interests in doing small projects alone or with a partner or two. Two weeks of class time are set aside for this purpose. They can suggest a topic of their own or, lacking one, choose from topics the instructors may provide. The topics of course should be relevant to American history, such as

How did the introduction of the horse to America by the Spaniards provide a great technological breakthrough for the Indians?

What do we owe today to the Indians for the variety of fruits and vegetables we eat?

How did early immigrants to the New World—so many of them very poor people—get passage to America?

Tell the story of the Treasure Convoys—the link between Mexico and Spain.

What does our national Constitution owe to Indian precedents?

Tell the story of the New England whaling industry.

What was the importance of beaver furs in our history? Of the sea otter? Of buffalo?

Biographies: Benjamin Franklin, Sacajawea, Kit Carson, Abigail Adams, Dorothea Dix, Harriet Tubman, U. S. Grant, John Sutter, Sitting Bull, General Fremont, Albert Einstein, and so on.

Tell the story of the Chisholm Trail.

Tell the story of the Dust Bowl.

Describe social legislation that arose out of the Depression.

The students can write a report on their study and/or prepare an exhibit. At the end of the year, some junior high schools hold a project fair at which such exhibits are set up for all to see.

This program by Hinman and Dolan is presented here not as a rigid blueprint but as a fine example, an ingenious model rich in suggestions for activities to bring life to the study of history. Although two teachers cooperated in this particular project, meshing language arts activities with historical information, a single teacher can use many of the suggested units.

It is worth ending with the repetition of Sheryl Hinman's conclusions: ". . . the job of teaching becomes easier [when] students become interested enough to want to learn. . . .[H]istory can't be dead to those who have a chance to live through it."

14

Interpersonal
and Intergroup
Relations

SENSITIVITY TO OTHERS' FEELINGS

Many expressions common in our language reveal bias in our culture:

"That's real white of you."
"Don't be an Indian-giver!"
"I jewed him down."
"So that's the nigger-in-the-woodpile!"
"He's too Scotch."
"Nobody here but us chickens."
"White man speaks with forked tongue."
"Real clever, these Chinese."

Such sayings reveal stereotypes that belittle particular minority groups. These common expressions are often used with no intent to hurt the feelings of anyone within hearing. Nevertheless, they do imply a contempt for the minority group referred to, and they *do* hurt.

Young people who are sensitive to the feelings of others will not use such expressions. Children can be made aware that such stereotypes, even without the intent of offending anyone, do hurt other people's feelings and make them feel separate, inferior, and rejected. Role-playing stories using these "hurt words" can help build this kind of sensitivity to other people's feelings.

The Problem: Three stories follow: "But Names Will Never Hurt Me?," "Eeny-Meeny-Miney-Mo," and "Seed of Distrust." The first deals with direct name-calling; the second with the use of "hurt words" in expressions that are not deliberately used with intent to hurt anyone's feelings; the third with anticipated rejection because of race.

The teacher of a class that contains a large number of minority group children (black, Mexican, Native American, and so on) may find that there is considerable contention in the class, with name-calling. When using one of these stories, make the application indirect: change the minority group referred to. If the minority group children in the class are black, change the minority referred to in the story to Chicano, or Puerto Rican. The reason for this tactful measure is to avoid putting children so directly on the spot.

A problem should be considered at this point: Will the point of the story come home to the whole class? Will a "transfer" of meaning occur? Some children, of course, will immediately see the application of the principle and will come at once to a generalization: They will understand that using labels that belittle another group of people always hurts. Other children will fail to make this transfer; they will understand only the specific example shown.

Introducing the Problem: It is part of the teacher's role to give the class many applications of the general rule. Thus, the children will, on their own, achieve the "Aha!" experience of suddenly seeing the general application of the various instances. The teacher can help the class arrive at the generalization and insight by asking such questions as the following: "Can you think of other 'hurt words' that might offend children you know?" "What kinds of names make you mad?" "Why do you suppose some people use such words?" "How do you suppose people feel when they are called names or overhear name-calling talk?" "Have you ever been called such names? Or overheard expressions like 'He's too Scotch' that could refer to you? What started it? How did you feel? What happened? What did you do?"

Some groups may be quite unfamiliar with such language. In other groups, listing offensive words may cause tittering and embarrassment. The teacher should recognize this embarrassment, accept it without censure, and lead the group on to serious discussion.

When discussing "But Names Will Never Hurt Me?" the teacher may ask, "Why do you think these little girls were calling each other such names?" The group may or may not have a realistic appreciation of what often lies behind such behavior. They may say, "They don't like each other."

The individual's estimate of himself—his self-image—is in large part a reflection of the way people around him feel about him and respond to him. Minority group individuals are prone to have a self-estimate that reflects the opinions of them held by the dominant group. As a result, black and Puerto Rican and other minority group youngsters, when angry with one another, will use the insulting labels they have heard applied to them by members of the majority group. Such names, of course, may reflect their conditioned dislike of being minority group members.

But Names Will Never Hurt Me?

Lorna had just left the apartment and was walking onto the playground behind the housing project when she saw her sister, Ellie. *Heard* her, too. Ellie was crying loudly. Lorna hurried toward her and brushed Ellie's matted blond hair out of her eyes and put her arm about Ellie's shoulders.

"What happened?" Lorna demanded. "Why're you crying?"

Ellie, eight years old, was a third grader. Lorna, who was eleven and big for her age, was a sixth grader.

"They slapped me!" Ellie wailed. "They t-tore my dress!"

"Who did? Show me!"

Ellie turned, and led Lorna toward a group of three small black girls playing hopscotch in a corner of the playground. They looked up and grew silent as they saw Ellie approaching with her angry big sister.

"They did it!" Ellie shrilled. "They hit me and kicked me and tore my dress!"

They stood stiff and silent as Lorna's outraged glance swept their faces.

"Three of you," she said scornfully, "ganging up on one kid! I ought to slap your faces. Maybe I will."

"She called us names," one child said.

"Yeah," another said. "She called me a monkey. A black monkey."

Lorna caught a sharp breath. She looked at Ellie.

"*Did* you?"

Ellie nodded, her eyes filling with tears.

"B-but they were doing it too! I just said what they were saying. Lucille called Betty a—what they said."

Lorna looked at the three girls.

"Is that true?"

They nodded.

Lucille burst out, "But *she* can't call us that!"

Lorna turned.

"Come on, Ellie."

Ellie stood stubbornly in her tracks, her small face ugly with anger.

"Ain't you going to hit them back?" she demanded. "Go on—hit them!"

Eeny-Meeny-Miney-Mo

Martha asked, "You kids ever play Duck-on-a-Rock?"

"No."

"What's that?"

"Let's play, let's play!"

"Hold on. You can't play a game until you know what it is. Listen."

The faces of the third graders were respectful and eager. Martha, a big seventh grader, felt very grown-up and important. This was a new kind of arrangement being tried by the city schools—using some responsible seventh graders to help with primary grade children. The six- and seven-year-olds were delighted to have the big eleven- and twelve-year-olds thinking up games for them, playing with them, helping with their lessons.

Martha explained, "You take four of these wooden blocks and pile them up straight, like this," she said, building a straight column. She did not explain that when boys played Duck-on-a-Rock on a vacant lot or in a back alley, they did not use wooden blocks but half-bricks. "Then, everybody stands back here, back of a line, and takes turns throwing a block at the pile.

When the pile is hit and knocked down, everybody runs and hides—except the kid who is *It*. He has to run to the blocks and stack them up straight again—and count to thirty. Then he starts hunting the others. Everybody who can run past him and touch the pile without his tagging them is free. But if he tags someone, that person is It for the next game."

"That'll be fun!"

"Who's It?"

"John's It!"

"No, Lena's It!"

"No," Martha said. "We'll draw lots."

"Too many," Lucy said. "I know! Everybody stand in a circle. We'll find out who's It." And as the kids grouped around her, she started chanting, "Eeny, meeny, miney, mo . . ." and as she spoke each word, she pointed to a different child, moving around the circle, "catch a nigger by the toe. If he hollers, let him *go*! You're It, Sammy!"

But then something happened.

Toby Jones smacked Lucy's face.

For a startled moment, the group stood frozen in shock. Then Lucy burst out crying, and a chorus of angry words exploded from the rest.

"You crazy? Why'd you do that?"

"Why'd he hit her?"

"You can't play with us!"

"Martha, don't let him play with us!"

Toby had turned away from the group. He was leaving, his dark face set and defiant.

"Wait, Toby!" Martha called.

"Oh, let him go, Martha!"

"But why did he slap her?"

"We don't want him around."

"Wait," Martha called. "Toby, don't go!"

"What got into him?"

"Hitting a girl!"

Dora, the other black child in the group, had run after Toby and put her arm around his shoulder and was going off with him.

"Why did he hit me?" Lucy was wailing.

Martha said, "Wait here," to the group, and started to go after Toby and Dora.

The other children said, "Oh, let him go!"

"We don't care—we can play without him."

Martha said:

Seed of Distrust

Betty was all excited when she ran into the apartment.

"Mother, will you iron my green dress tonight?"

"I was planning to do it Saturday night, honey, so you'd have it for Sunday School."

"But I'll need it!"

"What's the rush?"

"Nora's invited me to a party tomorrow after school."

"Oh, I see," her mother said slowly, as if thinking hard. "Nora's the little girl who lives over on Linden Street."

"Yes. She's real nice."

Betty's sister Lucy, who was a sophomore in high school, asked, "Does her mother know?"

"Know what?" Betty asked.

"Nora's white, isn't she?"

"Sure!"

"Does her mother know she's invited you?"

"Of course! I m-mean, I guess so."

"Does her mother know you're black?"[1]

"Sure!"

"You mean—you *think* so?"

"Y-yes," Betty stammered.

"Better make sure," Lucy said, and turned back to the math she was studying.

"I'll iron your dress, honey," Betty's mother said reassuringly. "You'll look real nice."

"Uh-huh," Betty said dully. "Thanks, Mom."

And then, next day, after lunch, the thing happened. . .

Nora met Betty in the hall, outside the fifth-grade room.

"Betty, I've been hunting for you," Nora said urgently. "Listen. My aunt Dorothy phoned last night. She's arriving today for a visit. My grandma's coming over to see her, and mother's making a dinner for the whole family, cousins and all. You see? We've got to postpone my party. Until next week, maybe. I'll let you know!"

Betty looked at her, blank-faced.

"Don't bother," Betty said. "Don't bother at all." And Betty turned and walked away, her back very straight.

For an instant Nora just stood and stared. Then she ran. She caught Betty's arm and stopped her.

"Betty, what's the matter? Why're you talking like that?"

SURMOUNTING PREJUDICE

Second Prize

The Problem: Discrimination on the basis of color, creed, or nationality; this story deals with a subtle aspect of segregation.

Introducing the Problem: You may say to the group, "A great effort is being

[1]Or Chicano, Puerto Rican, or any other minority.

made today to rid ourselves of bias against people who are of a different race than we are. This is a story dealing with the problem of prejudice. The story stops but is not finished. As I read, think of ways in which the story might end."

Edith, Tom, and Lucia were puzzled and a little worried as they walked down the hall toward the principal's office. Edith was president of the sixth-grade class. Tom was secretary, and Lucia was treasurer.

"Why did Mr. Watson send for us?" Tom asked.

"You worry too much," Edith said. "Nobody's busted a window."

And Lucia said, "It doesn't have to be something *bad*."

"Mr. Watson doesn't call us in unless it's for something important."

As the students entered the office, Mr. Watson looked up from his desk and smiled at them. They relaxed; the principal was obviously pleased about something.

"Hello. Thanks for coming down so promptly. I've got an important job for you."

"What is that, sir?" Tom asked.

"I want you three to act as a special committee. I want you to select the boy or girl whom you believe to be the Best School Citizen of the Year.

"I'll explain. You remember, last month, when five-year-old Pete Doyle was lost in the park along Deer Creek? All you sixth-grade boys helped search for him. It got freezing cold that night, and if you boys hadn't found Pete he'd have probably died. His grandfather wants to show his appreciation by doing something for the sixth grade. I suggested that we could use a record player. He said sure, he'd give the school a good one. But he'd also like to give something nice to just one student. Something that would be his or hers to keep and yet, would give recognition to the school too. We decided to make it an award to the Best School Citizen of the Year."

"That's a good idea."

"What is the award, sir?"

"I can't tell you that; it's to be a big surprise. We're having Field Day on Friday, and Mr. Doyle will bring the present here and will give it to the winner himself. I'll tell you this much, though: It's a pretty wonderful surprise."

"Sir, can't you tell just the committee?"

"We'll be staying up nights, trying to guess . . ."

"Mr. Doyle wants it to be a surprise," the principal repeated firmly. "He says he wants to see everybody's eyes pop out when he unloads it. Well, I'll leave you now. You three are now in session as the selection committee. Pull your chairs up to the table and start balloting."

"It's not going to be easy, sir," Tom said.

Mr. Watson walked out. The students leaned their elbows on the table and frowned in concentration.

"Best School Citizen of the Year," Tom echoed. "Say, how about *you*, Edith?"

"Sure," Lucia said. "You got elected class president. You're our top citizen."

"I'm out. So're you two. We're the nominating committee."

"How about Sam Baker, then?" Lucia asked. "He ran the paper drive for his room last month, and they brought in the most paper."

"But that paper drive," Edith objected, "wasn't nearly as important as the milk drive!"

"That's right," Tom agreed. "Sending milk to refugee camps in Asia is more important."

"You think maybe it's a television set?" Edith asked.

"What is?"

"The prize, the prize!"

"Will you quit crying about the prize," Tom snapped, "and get to work?"

"But, gosh, Mr. Watson said it's something you'd enjoy for years. . ."

"How about Toby Anderson?" Lucia suggested. "Everybody likes him."

"But what's he ever *done*?" Tom demanded. "This isn't a contest for who's *liked* the most."

"Toby's good at baseball."

"So's Joey Stevens and Ralph Nix."

"Say, how about Joey Garcia?" Edith said excitedly.

"That's right."

"But what's Joey ever done?" Lucia asked.

"Well," Tom started to explain, "that day there was a fire on his block. . ."

"You missed it, Lucia," Edith put in, "you were absent that week."

"So what happened?"

"It was after school," Tom began, "and Joey was home . . ."

Joey saw the two small boys turn from the sidewalk into the weed-grown lot next door. At the time, it did not worry him. Kids often used that lot for a playground. A crop of weeds had grown over it. In spring the weeds were pleasantly green but now, after a hot summer, they were dead and dry. People who lived in the shabby tenement flats on each side of the lot often dumped rubbish in it.

Joey, sitting at the front window of his apartment, was busy doing his arithmetic homework. After looking up as the two small boys turned into the lot, he bent over his book and paper again.

He smelled smoke a minute or two before actually realizing what it was. Then he heard a crackling noise like strings of firecrackers popping. Faintly against that noise he heard a kid yelling.

Abruptly he jumped up, remembering. Those two small boys who had walked onto the lot. . . He ran out the front door and around the corner of the house onto the lot—and saw the fire.

Tall weeds at the back of the lot were tonguing flames a dozen feet into the air.

"Those kids! I bet they started it."

But where were they? He could not see them. He heard them, however. One was crying, the other yelling. Through his mind streaked an explanation of what had probably happened. They had brought matches from their mother's kitchen. Maybe a couple of wieners, too. They had come out here to play at camping; they were probably planning to put wieners on the ends of sticks to roast them. But, of course, the fire had got away from them. Once started in these dry weeds, it would spread like an explosion.

Where were they?

He saw them, as a gust of wind bent the smoke flat. They were on the other side of the fire, against the wall of the sheds behind them. They were trapped—and scared into senseless panic.

Joey didn't stop to think. He ran. He ran through the smoke over the charred ground and through the curtain of fire where it was thinnest. Reaching the two children, he lifted one six-year-old and hoisted him up onto the roof of the low shed.

"Run!"

He bent over and grabbed up the second boy. This youngster was heavier, but Joey somehow boosted up the boy onto the roof of the shed.

Smoke swirled around Joey's face; the smoke was scorching his throat, and he choked. Reaching up, he caught the edge of the roof. Heat struck his back like a slashing whip. He tried to climb, but his muscles lacked strength. A small hand grabbed his wrist. The fool kid was trying to help him! "Run!" Joey gasped. "These sheds'll burn too!"

Joey rested a half-second and made another hard try—and got his elbows over the roof edge. Heat licked at the backs of his legs, and drove him into frantic effort. He swung a knee up, got it onto the roof, and rolled over into safety on the roof top.

Both small boys were there, staring at him with big eyes.

"Come on!" he yelled angrily at them.

They climbed down the far side of the shed, ran through the hallway of the tenement in front to the far side of the block.

"Go on home," Joey told the two kids and ran home himself.

The backs of his shoes and jeans were scorched black. As he took them off, he heard the siren of a fire engine. He didn't run out to watch but stayed in the bedroom, hiding. His legs were red and the skin blistered. The blisters were beginning to hurt so much that he had to choke back whimpers of pain.

When his mother got home from work an hour later, she took one look, and said, "Come on, Joey! You can tell me what happened on the way." She took him by cab to a hospital emergency room three blocks away.

All that had happened over a month before; and the voices of the committee members were grave with respect as they discussed the incident.

"That was a pretty brave thing Joey did," Tom said.

"Sure was," Lucia agreed.

"I think," Tom decided, "that we ought to pick Joey for Best School Citizen of the Year.

"I agree."

"I vote for Joey too!"

Field Day came on a Friday. The whole school, from kindergarten through sixth grade, took part. Children were singing on the school lawn and doing folk dances to music from a loudspeaker. Parents and friends looked on.

The last event of the afternoon was the presentation, by the principal, of the surprise award. Mr. Watson was smiling as he picked up the microphone at the stand and faced the crowd of children and parents. Everybody became quiet.

"And now, friends," Mr. Watson said, "I'm going to make the presentation of the award for our Best School Citizen of the Year. First now, I'm going to let you see the prize, which has been kept a secret. Then I'll name the winner." He looked around, toward the corner of the building, and shouted, "All right, Mr. Doyle! Bring it on!"

A car came from around the corner of the school and down the driveway, towing a trailer. The rig stopped opposite the crowd. Mr. Doyle himself got out of the car, walked around to the rear of the trailer, opened its door, and carefully eased a pony out of it onto the ground.

The sight of that pony made the crowd gasp. Someone started clapping, and everybody applauded and whistled.

"What a beautiful pinto pony!" someone near Tom said. And that was what Tom—and practically everyone in the crowd—was thinking. The pinto pranced as Mr. Doyle led him around in front of the children. The pony wore bridle and saddle made of fine hand-tooled leather and studded with silver conchas that glistened in the sun.

Mr. Doyle led the pony to the stand.

"Here he is, Mr. Watson. Who does he belong to?"

Into the microphone, so that everyone would hear clearly, the principal said: "The youngster who has been chosen to receive this award as our Best School Citizen of the Year is—*Joey Garcia!*"

The crowd applauded heartily, some of the young people whooped until others shushed them. It was a popular choice.

Mr. Watson called: "Joey! Where are you? Step up here, son."

"I'm coming, Mr. Watson."

People made way for him, as he hurried forward; as he passed, friends patted him on the back and said, "Hurry, boy!" and "Nice going, Joey," and "Are you ever lucky!"

Mr. Watson shook hands with him and held out the reins.

"Here, take the reins, boy. He's all yours, Joey! Climb aboard and ride 'im!"

Joey swung into the saddle in a way that showed he knew something about horses. The pinto stepped out lightly into a trot. Joey rode back and forth before the crowd, beaming with delight as everyone applauded. Only Mr. Doyle stood dour and silent beside the principal, biting his lip as he stared.

"Mr. Watson," he said, his voice low but sharp, "I want to have a talk with you!"

On Monday morning Tom and Edith and Lucia were called to the principal's office again.

They found Mr. Watson looking very solemn and upset.

Tom said, "Good morning, sir. You sent for us?"

The principal nodded. "I'm sorry to have to tell the committee that Mr. Doyle isn't pleased with the way we awarded the prize for our Best School Citizen."

"Why not?" Tom asked. "It was a unanimous choice. We all three agreed on Joey Garcia."

"Mr. Doyle says that he never intended for the pony to be given to a Mexican boy."

"It wasn't given," Tom said angrily. "Joey won the pony—by being our best citizen!"

"I know." The principal sighed. "Mr. Doyle says Joey can keep the pony. However, Mr. Doyle says he has another pony just as fine as this one—a pinto, too. Mr. Doyle wants us to pick a *white* boy or girl who's our best school citizen and give him or her this second pony."

The students just looked at Mr. Watson for a moment.

"That's odd." Edith said.

But Tom demanded, "What did *you* say, sir?"

"I told Mr. Doyle that I'd leave it up to this committee. Shall we accept this second pony and choose another Best School Citizen?"

"But we've already picked him—it's Joey!" Tom insisted.

"But, Tom," Lucia said impulsively "what's the harm of having another pony to give away? No reason we can't have two Best School Citizens. It's just extra good luck. Let's choose another lucky winner!"

"No," Tom said. "We've made our choice—and it's a good choice, and I'm sticking with it!"

"But I don't see the harm . . ." Lucia insisted.

Mr. Watson looked from Tom's face, to Lucia, and turned to Edith.

"Well, Lucia votes Yes, and Tom votes No on choosing another Best Citizen. Edith, your vote will make a decisive two to one. How do you vote, Yes or No?"

Usually Edith was quick to make up her mind; but a long, breath-held moment passed before she came to her decision. She said:

Josefina

The Problem: The issue is that of discrimination on the basis of color, creed, or nationality. Josefina is Mexican-American. Her great-grandparents moved to Southern California long ago; her mother and father still speak Spanish in the home. In this story she meets a nice boy whose family has just moved to town from an eastern city. Josefina likes Ted, but he is an Anglo. When he asks her for a date, she is very troubled. If she goes out on a date with him, she foresees that the Anglo young people will snub him—and her Spanish-speaking friends will snub her. This story is for junior high or high school level.

Introducing the Problem: Say to the group, "Dating is a many-sided problem for most of us. Not only parents, but your friends, too, influence you in your choices of whom you'll ask to parties or whom you'll agree to go with. This story deals with one aspect of the matter. As I read, think of ways in which you might solve the problem of the story."

The big white rabbit hopped around the corner of the house onto the front lawn. He wasn't supposed to be there; he belonged in a hutch in the backyard. Josie Ruiz, seeing him from her bedroom window, sighed and realized that she'd have to go down and shoo the dumb brute back where he belonged. At dinner she'd tell her kid brother that he'd better put a lock on his hutches or he'd lose some of his pets. Josie pulled on a sweater and started brushing her hair.

Meanwhile, the rabbit hopped a little farther across the yard. He was a huge New Zealand buck with ears that looked big enough to catch baseballs in, a nose that wiggled constantly, hind feet that weren't really as big as snowshoes but were enormous, just the same, and a wide powderpuff of a tail. He sat down on that puff and looked around, his big ears swiveling to sample the breeze, like twin radar antennae. He heard nothing alarming, but he did see and smell a plot of pansies which Josie's mother had put out the day before, and he galumphed over to the bed and started putting down a square meal.

Josie saw, and thought, "Oh, gosh, mother'll have a fit!"

She delayed a moment, to finish brushing her hair—and then she heard the dog: the shrill, excited ki-yi-ing of a small dog that was chasing something. She glanced out of the window again and saw a small black and white dog starting across the street toward the rabbit.

"For goodness' sake!"

She slammed her brush down on the bureau and ran out of her room.

As she came out the front door, she heard somebody yell, "Spot! Spot! Come here!" She saw the big rabbit lift his head and look at the dog. She saw the dog, running across the lawn now—and a young fellow chasing after the dog.

She darted at the dog, crying "Git!"

The dog sat back on its haunches. The young man sprang at him and caught him. Holding on to the pooch, the young fellow looked at Josie.

"Hey, you oughtn't to let your rabbit run loose like that," he scolded. "Golly, I'd hate to have Spot kill it."

That little pooch kill Gargantua? Josie almost laughed out loud. The dog was a small terrier. Oh, he was probably full of fight, all right, and Gargantua was only a rabbit, but . . .

"You know, they use packs of terriers like this to hunt bears," the young fellow was saying. He smiled at Josie. "It's sure lucky I saw Spot start to cross the street."

Lucky for Spot! Josie thought. Oh, sure, Gargantua was just a big, fluffy-looking rabbit, but what he would have done to Spot would have been just plain murder, that's all. With those big hind feet, Gargantua could kick like a pile-driver—and those feet were armed with claws like sickles. Spot would have thought he had tangled with a combination tiger-and-mule that was kicking him to pieces and tearing him apart at the same time. Spot *was* lucky that he was still in one spot and not scattered all over the yard like confetti.

But Josie didn't say this to the young fellow; he was too nice. He was about her own age, fifteen or sixteen, and he had blue eyes and wavy brown hair and really was good-looking. And the way he smiled at her showed that he liked what he saw, too.

So Josie just said, "Thanks." And then she didn't know what to say; she was shy with new people, especially with Anglos.

"I'll help you catch the rabbit," he said.

They herded Gargantua into the backyard. He hopped up into his own hutch by himself; all they had to do was shut the door. Spot whined at sight of all the white rabbits, but the young fellow held the dog in his arms.

"My name's Ted Anderson," he said. "We moved in across the street just last week. I've seen you on the high school bus."

"I'm Josie Ruiz," she said. "We've always lived here."

"I'm a junior at high."

"I'm a soph."

"What's Liston High School like?"

She almost said, "Oh, I hate it!" but checked herself.

"Oh, it's all right, I guess—if you have friends."

"I've made a good start," he said, smiling. "Well, got to get home and practice. See you on the bus tomorrow, Josie."

Next morning, Josie put on a new plaid skirt and her favorite sweater, and tied a new nylon scarf about her dark hair.

When she came down to breakfast, her kid brother, Ramon, stared at her and said, "Gosh, Sis, you look neat!"

Josie flushed with pleasure. Ramon was usually far more apt to say, "Hey, what rock did you crawl out from under?" than to give compliments.

As she waited on the corner for the school bus, Ted Anderson walked up, carrying a musical instrument case. He smiled and said, "Hi." He wore tan slacks and a gray shirt, and he was just about the best-looking boy she had ever known, she realized.

There were plenty of vacant seats on the bus, but Ted sat down next to her.

"Got to finish a theme," he said. "I have band practice, first period, so I can't do it then."

He opened his instrument case. She saw the trumpet inside—and several books and some papers. He took paper out and started writing. In spite of the swaying of the bus, his handwriting was swift and readable.

"I'm writing a theme on the role of Spanish people in colonizing the Southwest," he explained. "I never knew how important a part they played!"

Josie thought a moment about how proud Mexican-Americans were of their past, but not their present.

Each time the bus stopped, other young people came aboard. Most were Anglos; some were Mexican-American. Many nodded hello to Josie. In grade school she had been close friends with many of the Anglo girls; but when they had moved up into high school, something had happened that cooled the friendship, that put a distance between her and the girls she had played with so often. At the same time—perhaps because of it—she had become closer to the young people of the same Spanish-speaking background as her own.

"Can you dance the Jarabe?" Ted asked her.

"Yes."

People across the aisle looked at them. Josie knew what they were thinking. The Anglo girls were wondering how she rated this good-looking new boy. The Mexican-American girls were wondering if she was busy social climbing. They were clannish, the Mexican-American kids. Very rarely did one of them go on a date with an Anglo boy or girl. If you did, the other Mexican-American students decided that you thought you were too good for them. They stayed away from you, then; among themselves, they said sarcastic things about you. You were an outcast from your own group. Josie had seen this happen several times.

And the Anglo group did not take you in. In fact, the Anglo kid who became chummy with a Mexican-American youngster would soon discover that he wasn't being invited to Anglo parties any more. . . .

Ted finished writing his theme as the bus drew up in front of the high school.

"I'll walk you to your class," he said, as they rose to leave the bus. "Say, isn't there a rally at noon today?"

"Yes," Josie said.

"Let's sit together, okay?"

"Why . . . yes," she said.

"Fine!" he said. And when they reached her classroom, he said, "I'll meet you here, Josie!" and hurried off toward the gym.

But as Josie sat down, her mind was very troubled. She had made a mistake, she told herself; she should not have made this date with Ted.

All morning she brooded over the matter. At noon, coming out of her English class, she realized she had to make a decision. She could wait here for Ted. Or she could avoid him by hurrying to the cafeteria to eat her lunch. Which should she do?

15

Guidance

SELF-ACCEPTANCE

Basic to good mental health is self-acceptance. How can we help young people realize that lack of self-acceptance creates an enormous inner conflict? Respect for one's own abilities and a calm acceptance of one's limitations free one from anxiety and help one become more venturesome and creative. It is said that before one can "accept" others, one must be at peace with oneself.

How can we help young people identify their strengths and limitations and cultivate their areas of competence? Role-playing specific problems of self-acceptance—with all the attendant discussion and discovery and enactment—opens the way.

Wishing You Were Bigger or Better

In the following stories, a problem of self-acceptance is brought to an acute focus in a dilemma. This is not an easy dilemma to construct; the area of concern is subjective and subtle. The method of these stories is to present a young person with a dilemma involving a chance to secure a longed-for role that is, actually, beyond his capacities. The coveted role is made accessible through a variety of means. The role is presented as a great kindness on the part of another person, or is made possible by mistake or an accident, or, although earned, will call for a performance that is beyond the individual's capabilities.

What are these coveted roles? Most of us yearn for strengths to compensate for our lacks. Shy, plain girls long to be beautiful and sought after. Boys are especially prone to wish they were fine athletes who are admired and respected by their peers. Such longings for status and achievement beyond their innate potential are especially keen in youngsters who are the least successful. The happier, more successful people are usually more reality-oriented individuals whose aspirations are not too far out of proportion to their abilities.

Troubled youngsters often intensely wish they were athletic or popular or very pretty or gifted in music or art or writing or acting or leadership ability. Such longing leads to much indulgence in fantasy, of course. For emotional balance, such individuals need help in frankly assessing what is a daydream and what is a real strength.

Most of us do have areas of strength. Even 50 percent of all mentally retarded individuals have some strengths. Identifying, refining, and reinforcing such capacities is a positive step forward. But with it must go a calm acceptance of limitations and handicaps.

The range of individual differences is, of course, infinite. And yet many types of disadvantages are common to vast numbers of people. So many of us are short and chubby; so many of us have a heritage and cultural background at variance with the coveted white–Anglo-Saxon–Protestant type that our culture values most. To be American also means to be black, Japanese, Catholic, Jewish, Seventh-Day Adventist, Menonite, and so on. Some of us are physically handicapped: We limp, we have bad eyesight, we have asthma or severe allergies. Some of us lack muscular coordination. Some of us find working with our hands far easier and more satisfying than coping with books.

To achieve a reasonable degree of happiness, we must all study our dissatisfactions and not let them upset our emotional stability or ruin our creative potentialities. We must identify our strengths and cultivate them to win a measure of confidence and pride.

In this group of stories the individual is given a chance to realize a highly coveted role. But at some point the individual becomes aware of how inappropriate this coveted role is for him (or her). The dilemma is whether to accept the long-desired role—in the light of possible consequences not only to oneself but to others—or to reject it and accept one's actual limitations. The more sensible goal is always to nurture and reinforce one's *actual* strengths.

What are the real dilemmas of self-acceptance? Most consist of either accepting one's shortcomings and reducing one's aspirations to a realistic level—or futilely struggling against them and living with resentment and disappointment.

Individuals who take the latter course become difficult people to live with. They try too hard and overcompensate. They compete furiously, brag obnoxiously, deride others out of envy, and sometimes even actively hamper and defeat others' efforts.

The more wholesome course for them is, naturally, to face up to their limitations and go on from there. Studies show that the most successful students are those who have set realistic goals for themselves. In practice, this means managing disappointment instead of withdrawing in hurt and anger. It means cooperating with the leader who got the job they wanted. It means relinquishing a task that is beyond their abilities to someone who does have the capacity to handle it well. Even more important, it means estimating their capacities as exactly as possible, finding the tasks that they can perform satisfactorily, and tasting to the full the rewards of competence that such tasks offer.

One caution is in order here: Individuals must estimate their capacities and potentials correctly and *fairly*—that is, they should not *underestimate* themselves. Teachers can perform a valuable counseling service by helping young people avoid the mistakes of underestimating or overestimating their capabilities.

Fast Ball

The Problem: Becoming reconciled to our limitations and focusing on improving our abilities. Learning to accept our deficiencies, nevertheless, is something that we all find difficult.

Introducing the Problem: Say, "All of us have strengths; all of us are good at something or other; and all of us have weaknesses and lacks. There are some activities for which we have no ability. Learning our strengths and weaknesses, and being sensible about them, is a problem we all must face. This is a story about a boy who faced this problem. This story stops but is not finished. As I read, try to think of ways in which you might end the story."

Eddie's team won the toss and was first at bat. Eddie led off; limping to the plate, he got ready for the pitch. He knew he wouldn't reach first, even if he got a hit, but of course he had to try.

The other team, warming up, tossed the ball around. And as Eddie watched, he felt a longing and envy more intense than he had ever felt before. This other team was good. The boys whipped that ball from first to second and home with a real snap. And they *looked* good. They wore brand new Little League uniforms and peaked caps and real baseball shoes with spikes. Eddie glanced down at his own faded jeans and torn sneakers. He felt like a tramp. His own team was just a scrub neighborhood gang. Compared to the Little Leaguers, they looked pretty sad.

"Play ball!" the umpire, Mr. Bonner, shouted.

The first ball was fast, but high. Eddie let it pass, and Mr. Bonner called "Ball one!" But the next pitch came straight for the plate, and Eddie swung. Bat met ball with a sharp crack and the ball went driving between second and third. Eddie started for first. He knew it was no use, but he lunged along as best he could.

The third baseman snagged the ball, straightened up, and took his time to snap it accurately to first. Eddie was not even halfway to first when Mr. Bonner shouted, "You're out!"

Eddie grinned as he limped back to his team. His right foot was twisted and underdeveloped; he had been in a bad car accident when he was four years old.

"That was a good hit, Eddie!"

"Gosh, Eddie, if somebody could just run for you!"

Eddie's next teammate was put out on strikes. The next batter hit a two-bagger, and the next man up drove him in. But the next batter fouled out, and the first half of the inning ended with a score of one to nothing, in favor of Eddie's team.

"We'll beat 'em, Eddie. Don't let a one of 'em get a hit!"

Eddie just nodded, and flashed his big smile as he walked out to the pitcher's mound. He was short, but strongly built, all except for his shrunken leg. In fact, he had had to use his arms so much, lifting himself around, that he was unusually well muscled in arms and shoulders. He was not muscle-bound, however; he was a skillful pitcher.

The opposing team came in from the field to take their turn at bat. Eddie studied their gray and blue-edged uniforms. Really neat, he thought. On the back of their shirts was printed the name of the donor: *Ames Shoes*, and a figure of a Tiger. The team called themselves The Tigers. They looked so smart and sharp! *I'd like to be on a team like that!* Eddie mused; but he knew how foolish such a wish was. A cripple like him? Why, he couldn't even run to get under a pop fly, let alone steal bases, or jump to snatch up a fast grounder. He couldn't make it to first when he hit a three-bagger. So he'd never be asked to join a *real* team.

"Batter up!" Mr. Bonner yelled.

The hard ball felt good in Eddie's clever fingers. He got his grip on it, wound up, and pitched. The ball sizzled straight and bullet swift across the plate, smacking into the catcher's mitt with a clear hard rap.

"Strike one!" Mr. Bonner called.

The batter blinked. He hadn't even swung. The ball had been too fast. He did swing at the next pitch—too late; the ball was already in the catcher's mitt. Tightening his lips, he swung more quickly at the next pitch; but Eddie had expected this, and sent over a teasing slow ball.

"Strike three. You're out," Mr. Bonner yelled.

The next batter was a bigger boy. He eyed Eddie with grim determination. Eddie grinned at him, and Eddie settled down to work. Again he whipped a very fast ball straight over the plate. The batter swung so late that the onlookers laughed. A second, and a third time, Eddie threw his fast ball.

"Batter out!" Mr. Bonner called.

The third batter up hit a foul on the first pitch; the catcher caught it and the batter was called out. With just seven pitches Eddie had retired the other side.

"Atta boy, Eddie!" his teammates yelled.

"You're going good, boy!"

The Little Leaguers walked out on the field, and looked at him very thoughtfully. Eddie just grinned; Eddie glowed with happiness. . . .

At bat again, Eddie's side got two men on base but never scored before their half of the inning ended.

Pitching again, Eddie fanned three batters, one after the other. They just could not hit his fast ball. He seemed absolutely invincible. He did not fool himself, however. His fast ball was his best pitch. Batters who practice against fast pitching would, after a while, start hitting him. To be a good all-around pitcher, he would have to develop different kinds of pitching. But, meanwhile, he had more speed than these Little Leaguers had any hope of handling.

Next inning, his side scored a second run. The Little Leaguers got one man on base but did not score.

The game finally ended, two to nothing, in favor of Eddie's scrub team. His teammates were so delighted that they threw their gloves into the air; they jumped up and down and whooped and hollered. They'd beat the snappy-looking Little Leaguers in their fancy uniforms. . . .

The boys began to scatter homeward; some of them were already late for chores. Eddie had to return his ball glove to Steve, a neighbor boy from whom he had borrowed it, so he started home.

"Eddie!"

The Little League team had gathered at the curb and were climbing into the truck in which they had come. Two of them, with Mr. Bonner, their coach, were hurrying after Eddie.

"We'd like to talk to you a minute, Eddie," Mr. Bonner said. "Go ahead, Pete."

"I—well, you see, Eddie," Pete began, stammering a little in earnestness, "the bunch of us just talked this over. You're a good pitcher. You're awfully good. We haven't got anybody that's in your class at all. What we'd like . . . Would you join our team?"

"Who, me?" Eddie gasped. "You mean—wear a uniform like you got, and everything?"

"That's right. What d'you say, Eddie?"

"And pitch for you?"

"You'd be our first-string pitcher."

Eddie stood there, his thoughts milling.

"How about it, Eddie?"

"B-but I can't run bases . . ."

"We want you just the same."

And I can't jump to grab a high throw. Even if I knocked a fly clear over the fence, a fast fielder could climb that fence and throw to home before I'd make it!

"What do you say, Eddie?"

There are real good teams in the Little League. This team needs good all-around players to compete. . . .

"Say yes, Eddie. We need your pitching!"

Eddie said, " 'I . . .'"

The Big Comic

The Problem: The issue is self-acceptance. Sometimes the difficulties of accepting oneself seem too great to surmount.

Introducing the Problem: Say to the group, "Many of us have private worries we don't like to have other people discover; or, if it's something that can't be hidden, we don't like to talk about it. If you stutter, you try not to talk at all when among strangers. If you have a birthmark on your neck, you wear something to hide it. In this story, a boy hides a handicap he has, although hiding it may cost him something he wants very much. As I read the story, which stops before it is finished, try to think of ways in which the story might end.

Every student in the class quit working when the stranger came into the room. Tom heard somebody whisper excitedly, "That's Eddie Morgan!" and Tom stared in sudden interest at the small, muscular man. Eddie Morgan was a movie comic, like Bob Hope and Woody Allen only not so important. Tom had heard him often on radio and also seen his television program a couple of times when he had been allowed to stay up later than usual.

Mr. Williams, the teacher, shook hands with Eddie Morgan and then turned to the class.

"I'm sure that you boys and girls have all heard Mr. Morgan's TV program. Most of you may know, too, that Mr. Morgan was once a student here at De Haven Junior High. He would like to talk to you a minute. Mr. Morgan."

Eddie Morgan grinned at them, and they couldn't help smiling back. He was a nice guy.

"I not only went to school here, I even graduated," he told them so proudly that they couldn't help laughing. But then he became serious. "Look, kids, I need your help. Your principal, Mr. Haines, has asked me to be the guest star this year on your annual Hi Jinks program. I'm proud and happy to be invited, and I want to put on a swell show. But to do that, I'll need your help. Can any of you kids sing or dance, or do any sort of stunt that I can spot in the show?"

"Tom Bailey can."

"Tom can do rope-spinning, Mr. Morgan!"

Tom felt his face grow red, and he slumped down in his seat. Just the thought of talking to Eddie Morgan in front of everybody scared him so that he wanted to sink through the floor.

"Rope-spinning?" Eddie Morgan said delightedly. "Wonderful! Tom? Where are you?"

The kids around Tom pointed at him and Mr. Williams said, "Tom, come up here, won't you?"

So Tom had to sit up, had to get to his feet, had to start to the front of the room, feeling like a Daniel in a cage of lions. But Eddie Morgan walked down the aisle to meet him, and put his arm about Tom's shoulders, and that made it all easier.

"Tommy, we can make up a good act. Both of us spinning yarns! You making with the rope, and me with the corny gags. Will you help me out?"

Tom managed to stammer, "S-sure."

"Great! Look, you meet me in the boys' gym in an hour."

He waved to the class and left the room. Tom walked back to his seat.

"Gosh, are you ever lucky!" he heard somebody say, and realized that the other boys envied him.

An hour later, Tom met with Mrs. Hale, the reading specialist, in her office. He explained about Eddie Morgan, and she excused him. He hurried to the gym.

Eddie Morgan was already there with a half-dozen other boys.

He explained: "We've got to work fast, boys. I'm so tied up with my radio and TV programs that two days were all I could take off. The Hi Jinks show is tomorrow night. Today is all the time we've got to rehearse, but it's enough! Now, the kind of show I want to whip up is this—lots of gags, lots of action. Corny, sure, but moving so fast that nobody's got time to stop laughing and throw rotten tomatoes." He looked at Tom. "Tommy, could you spin a big rope while you're standing on my shoulders?"

"I guess so."

"We'll try it. I got a swell act in mind. Al, and you, Pete—I'll want you boys standing on each side of me, inside the spinning rope. You'll juggle your Indian clubs—while we tell the gags. You see the act? Rope spinning, Indian clubs whirling—and all the time we're telling jokes. Tom," he demanded, "where did you learn to spin ropes?"

"My father showed me how."

"Where did he learn?"

"He used to travel with a Wild West Show."

"In show business, huh?"

"He runs a gas station, now."

"And eats regular! Okay, let's go. Tommy, hop up onto my shoulders!"

Mr. Morgan bent at the knees and took hold of Tom's hands; he stepped onto Mr. Morgan's knee, then onto his left shoulder and onto his right. Morgan straightened up, steadying Tom with his hands; and when Tom was upright, Morgan moved one hand and then the other to the back of Tom's calves, and held him securely in place. Tom had tucked his spinning rope into his belt. He shook out the rope into a loop, swung it, started it circling in a wide loop around him and Mr. Morgan.

"That's the stuff, Tommy. That's fine," Mr. Morgan said. "Ed and Pete, when Tommy makes the loop lift up into the air, you run inside it and stand beside me, Ed on the left and Pete on my right."

With extra force and a sudden lift, Tommy made the wide loop rise up as high as his own head, and that gave the two boys plenty of time to dart in to take their places beside Mr. Morgan. They carried their Indian clubs with them, and started juggling the clubs. One of them hit the lead of Tom's spinning rope, and that brought the rope to a snarled stop.

"That was just fine for the first time," Mr. Morgan said. "Ed, keep your Indian clubs lower . . ."

"I can keep the rope spinning higher," Tom said.

"Good. But not too high. We want the loop to be circling us. Boys, this is going to be a swell act! We'll smear the rope and the Indian clubs with luminous paint, and we'll have the stage lights turned off, so all that the audience will see will be the rope and the clubs spinning and twisting like gobs of fire! That'll be a swell finale for the act! We'll paint skulls and crossbones on our suits, too, to glow in the dark. It'll be great! Jump down now, Tommy. Let's read over the gags."

They sat down on chairs. He gave each one a sheet of paper filled with closely typed lines.

"I'll ask the questions. You'll take turns answering. We do this while Tommy is spinning the rope around us, and you boys are juggling the clubs. You'll have to memorize the lines today. Don't worry about not remembering—I'll have a teleprompter—we call it an 'idiot board'—that you can glance at when you feel uncertain. All right, let's read these through. I'll start by asking Tom, Why is the letter *F* like a cow's tail?"

Tom, staring at the sheet of paper before him, blinked and grew red, and did not answer.

"Because it comes at the end of beef," Mr. Morgan said. "It's there—the second line, Tommy. This has to be said fast, lad, so don't lose time coming in with the answer, any of you. Pete, the second gag. Why is a room full of married people empty?"

"Because there isn't a single person in it," Pete replied quickly.

"That's the speed! Al, your turn: What's the difference between a blind man and a sailor in prison?

"One can't see to go and the other can't go to sea."

"Good! Okay, Tom, line 10 for you, now . . .

Tom's face burned red with shame. No *use telling me the line*!

"Tommy, Why is a pretty girl like a hinge?"

Tommy's lips trembled; sweat beaded his forehead.

"Go ahead, Tommy, read it."

But Tommy did not answer.

"You got the right sheet of paper?" Mr. Morgan asked, and leaned over, and pointed with his finger.

"There it is. I ask, Why is a pretty girl like a hinge? And you say, Because she's something to adore. See it?"

Tommy nodded. *I can see it but I can't read it*!

"You come in real fast, next time, Tommy. Okay, Al, What's the difference between a husband and a guy who's been jilted?"

"One kisses the missus and the other misses the kisses."

"Fine! That's coming right back like I want it. Pete, Why do hens usually lay eggs in the daytime?"

"Because at night time they become roosters."

Sure, sure, I can see it but I can't read it! But Tommy didn't say this aloud; miserably, his head bent, he said, "Mr. Morgan, I—I can't be in your show."

Mr. Morgan blinked with shocked surprise.

"Tommy, lad, we *need* you. Don't you want to be in the show?"

More than I want anything in the world! Tom thought, but he said, "I'm sorry, Mr. Morgan, I—just remembered that tomorrow I got to go to my aunt's . . ."

"Tommy." Mr. Morgan was a bright, sensitive man. "What's wrong, son?"

I can't read, that's what's wrong. I never did learn to read like other people do! I've got to have special help to learn, and it's going slow, Tom thought, but said nothing.

"Tell me," Mr. Morgan insisted.

Tell him? In front of everybody? Say it out loud so that everyone will hear? I *can't read*! I'd just make myself look silly, and spoil the show for the rest of you . . .

"My aunt's giving a big . . ."

"What's wrong, lad? I wish you'd tell me," Mr. Morgan interrupted. "Maybe we can fix it up. Tell me."

Tom caught a shaky breath, and said:

Big Shot

The Problem: The issue is self-acceptance. Nora, a newcomer at school, is unknown to the other students. At her former school, she had been a leader; she wants desperately to become a "very important person" here. She gets a chance at a prestige position which, in her heart, she knows she really does not deserve.

Introducing the Problem: Say to the group, "Have you ever wished you were an important person at school? Someone that everybody looked up to? This is a story about a girl who wanted to be a leader, and who won a chance to become a 'big shot.' This story stops before it is finished. As you listen, think of ways you might end the story."

Nora Adams sat daydreaming at her study desk—daydreaming herself into trouble. Her family had moved to Westport just two months ago, so she was a newcomer to the Latham School. Back in Fresno, she had been a leader at school, but here she was still a nobody, and it hurt.

She was realizing that if she could get herself appointed to the editorial staff of the school paper, she'd be somebody. Take Mary Brooks, for example; Mary was pretty, and smart, and the most popular girl in the eighth grade. She would probably be made editor because she was so all-around capable. Because people liked and admired her so much, she could be very good at giving orders, at deciding which members of the editorial staff should go after stories, and who should do rewrites in the office, who should do lay-out, and so on. No doubt of it, Nora thought, Mary would be editor. Steve Cagle was a natural for sports editor. Sue Kearny should probably be art and drama reporter.

I should be a feature writer, Nora decided. I should be the kind of roving reporter who does her own column and has her name and picture at the top.

Nora could write tart, clever, little stories about such things as interesting signs, people with odd hobbies, interesting accidents, strange doings of animals. She really was clever; she could write verse and little sketches that made people laugh and say, "Golly, this kid's got a gift. She's smart!" But Nora wasn't disciplined, and she knew it. She couldn't write to order. She could write only when she was all excited about something.

"I better get busy," she scolded herself then.

Everyone who wanted to be on the paper staff was required to hand in a sample of his or her work tomorrow morning. A committee of three teachers and the principal would select the staff from these samples.

Nora decided to write a sample column. She wrote:

The Prowler

Overheard:

Pete Naylor went to the dentist yesterday. He gave the dentist a piece of advice: "Your office," Pete said, "should be called the drawing-room." Tch, tch.

Irene Mosely says that mosquitoes are religious insects. They sing and prey over you.

Yesterday, on the playground, Johnny Hoyle got into an argument with Mr. Bates, who was coaching the ball team. Finally Mr. Bates said, "Look, Johnny, are you coach of this team?" "No, sir." "Then don't talk like an idiot!" Mr. Bates said.

Daffy Definitions:

Hug: A roundabout way of expressing affection.

Hospital: A place where people who are run down wind up.

Usher: One who takes a leading part in the theater.

Conundrum:

Why is Ireland such a rich country?

Because its capital is always Dublin.

Nora flung down her pencil in exasperation.

"This stuff just isn't good enough!"

She almost cried in vexation. Abruptly, then, an idea came to her. Why not write a story about her great-grandmother who was captured by the Indians? Actually, she hadn't been kidnapped. She had run away and joined them. The Indians were not the fierce, bloodthirsty Plains Indians who burned settlements and scalped soldiers, but the peaceful Yokuts of California; and they did not harm her but took fine care of her and brought her home. The only harm she suffered was a spanking from her own father. But she *had* had a thrilling time with the Yokuts.

Nora wrote a title: *Captured by the Indians.*

She went on to write the story. Vivid details flowed swiftly from her pen. She told where the Yokuts lived—in the south end of the big Central Valley of California, which was desert but contained a huge, shallow, inland sea, Tulare Lake. The Indians had not lived in tepees but on big rafts made of bulrushes. Each raft held a small cabin made of reeds. A mud fireplace was located in the middle; and a blind set up in the pointed front of the raft from which the Yokut warrior shot at ducks and geese. The Indian women gathered clams and turtles. From a hole in the raft the men speared fish. Ashore, the men hunted antelope and held jackrabbit "surrounds." In details that were vividly real, Nora wrote the story swiftly, because it was all so familiar to her. When she had finished writing, Nora knew she had done a good job. The piece was better than anything she had ever written before.

Next morning, she turned the composition in as a sample of her work to the committee that would select the editorial board of the school paper.

The selections of the board were announced the following Friday morning by Miss Brameld, Nora's English teacher.

"Reporters will be: Tony Moore, Dan Leeds, Esther Bonner, and Tim Morris. You accept the assignments?"

The students nodded. Nora's heart sank. She wasn't considered good enough even to be a reporter!

"For sports editor, Steve Cagle. Okay, Steve?"

"Sure! I m-mean thank you, Miss Brameld."

"You're welcome. For art and drama reviewer, Sue Kearny."

"Hooray!" Sue exclaimed, clapping her hands. Everybody laughed.

I knew she'd get it, Nora thought. Sue deserved it. Maybe I can contribute pieces once in a while, she tried to reassure herself. Why wasn't I born bright?

"For student events editor, Mary Brooks. You accept, Mary?"

Mary nodded, smiling, "Yes, thank you."

Nora's stomach felt sick and hollow. She hadn't made the staff at all. If Mary, who was so very gifted, was just an assistant editor, Nora told herself, then I haven't a chance to be anything!

"And for editor-in-chief," Miss Brameld went on, "we have a person with far more ability than anyone on the committee expected to discover. Her writing shows so much maturity, so much awareness, such a vivid eye for detail and for story values that . . . Well, on the basis of the samples presented, there was just no question: the outstanding writer among the candidates, and the person selected to be our editor-in-chief, is—Nora Adams!"

Oh, no! Nora thought, almost gasping it aloud. But that should be Mary Brooks's job! She's so neat and orderly and punctual; I'm helter-skelter. Mary can get people to do things for her. Mary can write *everything*—and she can see the faults in things other people write, and she can help them correct things without making them sore. This job should be Mary's. Giving it to me's a mistake. Why, what I wrote was really my great-grand-mother's . . .

"Nora," Miss Brameld was saying, "this is a big job you'd be taking on. Do you accept the responsibility?"

Yes, it was a big job! She'd be important around school. She'd be going around with the best kids here, with Mary and Sue and Steve . . . But—but . . .

"Well, Nora?"

Nora gulped, and stammered, "Miss Brameld, I . . ."

Anticipation of Rejection

The Problem: The issue is an aspect of self-acceptance, of being comfortable with oneself. Specifically, these stories deal with the problem of an uneasy self-concept, of individuals who expect rejection, sometimes unnecessarily.

All of us have times when we feel unliked and unwanted, times when we think that people are treating us unfairly. Such moments are a natural and human reaction to difficulties we may encounter in our relations with others. Some people, however, feel this kind of doubt about themselves much more often than is necessary or justified.

Children need help in exploring such experience, and in confronting and analyzing their feelings. Were they too quick to judge the situation? Were all the facts in? Is it possible that they made a mistake? Often, when we act as though we expect mistreatment, we invite it by our behavior.

Introducing the Problem: You may say to the group, "All of us have times when we feel unliked and unwanted, when we think that people are treating us unfairly. Can you recall such times?" (Allow time for response.) "Sometimes when we have problems, it is easy to feel that someone is treating us in a way that is unfair. I am going to read you three short stories about people who felt that they were being treated unkindly. The first two stories are finished. When I read the third, I am going to stop, and ask you how that story might be ended."

Judy Miller

Something peculiar was going on. Judy noticed it as soon as she walked into the schoolyard that morning. First thing that happened was that she saw Marta and Nancy talking busily together. But when she turned toward them, when she called "Hi!" they shut up in a hurry. They glanced at her, and Nancy gasped and covered her mouth with her hand in a guilty way, and she and Marta both giggled oddly. Marta leaned close and whispered quickly to Nancy, and Nancy turned and hurried off as if she had something important to do on the far side of the yard. Marta did turn to meet Judy, then, and Marta said, "Hi!" in an ordinary way, pretending that nothing had happened.

But Judy told herself, "They've got a secret. They don't want me in on it. They're leaving me out." And Judy felt upset.

She and Marta had been best friends. But that had been two years ago, in the fourth grade. Then Judy's family had moved to Fresno. Judy had not liked going to school there. When the family moved back here, to Newton, Judy had been wildly happy, thinking that she would be back again with old friends whom she had missed so terribly. But things were not the same after these two years. Marta and Nancy and Edie and Nora and the others—they seemed to have changed. Almost a week of school had passed, and Judy still felt like a stranger with her former friends. She felt pushed out, set apart.

The bell rang, and the children in the schoolyard moved into the building. As the hours wore along into recess and lunch, the day proved to be rather odd. She felt a kind of electric tingle in the classroom. The boys were not part of it; they seemed unaware that anything unusual was going on. But the girls seemed to be making a hard effort to hide the excitement that was making them chatter in rushed whispers and choke back nervous giggles that bubbled from their lips. Not just Marta and Nancy were sharing secrets, Judy realized; most of the girls seemed to need to get together and make guarded, hurried talk.

But when *she* approached a pair whispering together, they glanced at her and turned quickly away. All the girls seemed to be in on the secret, whatever it was; she alone was left out. Her sense of being friendless grew steadily harder to bear.

She discovered the big secret as school let out. Unintentionally, she overhead Marta whisper to Della Ross: "I'll come by for you at seven. What dress are you going to wear?"

"My new white one."

"Like Dora's?"

"Yeah, but she isn't going to wear hers."

"See you later!"

A party! That was what everybody was so worked up about. And all the girls were going. Even Doris Gard, whom nobody liked very much. "Everybody's invited," Judy realized, "but me. They don't want me."

As she walked home, her thoughts were heavy with gloom. I don't have friends any more, she told herself. I'm not invited to that party because the girls don't like me. Why should they? I'm not pretty, not really, not like Alice and Nancy. I don't have nice clothes. My folks aren't important. And when you go to a church with an odd name and attend Sunday school on Saturday—why, you just can't be part of the crowd. You're treated like something was left out of the recipe when you were baked.

She tried to be sensible, then. She tried to get rid of her unhappy thoughts. She told herself that the girls of the class used to like her; before long she would be part of the group again. She should be patient.

But she could not shake off the disappointment and loneliness that put a sick, all-gone feeling in the pit of her stomach. . . . When she got home, she went to her room and lay down on her bed. For a minute or two she cried very quietly. Carefully, then, she washed her face; she didn't want her mother to guess that anything was wrong.

But at dinner her mother did seem to sense that she was miserable; her mother stared at her with a worried look on her face.

When Judy started to help with the dishes after dinner, her mother said, "Dear, I asked Mrs. Jeffers if she'd fix the hem on your red dress tonight. Would you take it over to her?"

Judy nodded. The red dress was fairly new, and she usually felt dressed up and gay in it; but, over the summer, she had grown and the dress needed to have the hem lowered. She put the dress on and walked two blocks down the street to Mrs. Jeffers' house.

An hour later, Judy returned home. The house was dark, she saw as she approached; and she guessed that her parents had either gone for a walk or to a movie.

Walking inside she switched the living room lights on—and gasped in sudden shock. The room was crowded with people. . . .

"Surprise! Surprise!" they were all shouting, and laughing at the amazed, wide-eyed look on her face. Marta was here, and Nancy, and Alice, and all the other girls in her class, even Dora. Everyone! All were crowding around her. All the girls who had been invited to that party she hadn't been asked to. But of course they hadn't invited her, she realized now, with a great lift of happiness. They couldn't invite her. But they hadn't left her out. They hadn't invited her because it was *her* surprise party—to welcome her back among her friends again.

Johnny Kotowski

Johnny wasn't eavesdropping; he didn't intend to overhear what Mr. Morton was telling the boys. Johnny's first thought as he realized that the Little League ball team was already assembled in Mr. Morton's yard was, "*Gosh, I'm late, and I thought I was arriving early.*" He started to hurry down the path beside the garage to the patio where the team was meeting. Then he heard Mr. Morton mention his name. The coach was talking about him. Then, as Johnny heard what Mr. Morton was saying about him, Johnny stopped short, frozen in his tracks. The boys couldn't see him, because of the high patio fence, and for this Johnny was suddenly grateful.

"Before we vote for either Johnny or Mike," Mr. Morton was saying, "we should take some thought about the candidates. Being captain of a team is an important job. Besides ability, it demands something that we call character. Now, Johnny Kotowski . . ."

So that was why the team was here, Johnny realized. Mr. Morton had asked him to come at 10 o'clock. So that he would arrive *after* the voting, Johnny decided. He knew that he and Mike Nolan were the two candidates for team captain.

"Well, Johnny's a little guy," Mr. Morton was saying. "Smallest boy on the team, I guess. He's not a natural athlete. Sometimes he's so awkward he trips over his own feet." This drew a laugh from some of the boys. Johnny, listening, felt shame and misery. "And sometimes Johnny's hay fever gets so bad he has to stay out of a game. Also, he's got a quick temper and loses it awfully easily. And he gets excited in a game. I guess that's why sometimes he stutters so badly you can hardly understand him . . ."

"B-Boys, let's g-g-g-get g-g-g-goin' . . ."

Pete Ames mocked Johnny's stutter, and some of the boys guffawed; but Mr. Morton said, "Pete, that's enough. To go on. Johnny's stubborn. He argues. He'll argue until you sometimes want to wring his neck, and . . ."

Johnny could not bear to hear more. He turned, blinking back tears and hurried out the way he had come—out of the yard, down the street toward home.

Talking that way about me! Mr. Morton! He's just like everybody else. If your mom and pop talk some language besides English, and if the food you eat has a lot of garlic—then you're different. You're somebody to laugh at and to play jokes on. Nobody gives you a fair break. You're the one who gets left out of parties. It's just not fair.

The more he thought about it, the deeper grew his misery. I haven't any friends, he told himself. I'm no good for the team. They put up with me when I tag along, but they don't really care what happens to me.

Reaching home, he walked around to the backyard. Here he had built rabbit hutches. He had six does with litters. He got busy cleaning out the hutches, working with a quiet fury in order to numb the hurt within him.

"Johnny!"

Pete McInness was calling him. Johnny's first impulse was to run indoors and not answer. He knew why Pete had come for him. It was almost time for the Little League game with the Centreville team. Jimmy's team had two pitchers—himself and Andy Roth. But Andy had just got out of bed after an attack of flu and was still pretty weak. If I don't pitch, Johnny realized, we'll lose the game for sure. What do I care, he thought angrily.

Just the same, he walked around to the front yard.

"For gosh sake, did you forget about the game?" Pete demanded, but his voice was relieved. "We thought you must be sick or something. Come on. Everybody's waiting for you."

"Let Andy pitch."

"He's too weak. Besides, we want you to pitch this one. You just got to, Johnny. Come on—run! Where you been, anyway? You missed the meeting."

"So what?"

"You should've heard what Mr. Morton said about you . . ."

"Yeah, I'm a little runt who falls all over his own feet and gets into fights and argues . . ."

"Yeah, but how'd you find out so quick? And he said you get rattled and you try to play ball sometimes when you've got hay fever so bad you ought to be home. You got all those handicaps, he said, but you rise above them!"

"Wh-what?"

"Yeah. He said you got handicaps that would make most guys quit, or make 'em impossible to get along with. But not you. He said you overcome your handicaps. He said that you study any sport you get interested in, until you know more about it than most guys. And he said you got real team spirit. You don't grandstand, you think about the team, and you're always working to give everybody else a chance to shine. He said you got what a team captain needs most, so that's why we elected you captain. Come on, it's time for the game to start!"

"Who g-got elected c-captain?" Johnny stuttered.

"For gosh sake, I *told* you. *You* did. Come on, we got to run!"

Johnny ran.

Jimmy Garrett

The sign in the drugstore window said: BOY WANTED. Jimmy, hurrying past, stopped short. A job. Just when he wanted one so badly! He read the small writing at the bottom of the sign: *To make deliveries after school. Must have bicycle.* As Jimmy read this, his heart sank. He had no bike. One big reason he wanted a job was to save up money to buy a bicycle.

But I do have a bike I can use, he reminded himself.

He turned to go inside the store, then hesitated. *You ought to look nice*, he warned himself. *Get washed and dressed up!*

So he went home, running most of the way. His mother, who worked—Jimmy's father was dead—wasn't home, but he found a clean shirt, and he washed, put on his best pants and the shirt and a sweater. Then he went out to the shed in back and brought out the bike. It wasn't a bike that would make anybody jealous, but it worked. He mounted and rode back downtown, hurrying.

As he dismounted in front of the drugstore, he discovered that he had a rival. Keith Lucas, who was in his class at school, was leaning his bike against the curb. He glanced up, saw Jimmy, and his mouth opened in surprise.

"What're you doing here?" he demanded.

Jimmy did not answer, pointedly ignoring him. Keith's freckled face reddened and he took a step toward Jimmy, but Jimmy didn't back away. Keith was two inches taller than Jimmy and a dozen pounds heavier. He had always taken advantage of his bigger size to push Jimmy around; but Jimmy, although he got the worst of it in a fight, always fought back. Keith decided that this was no time for a ruckus and stopped.

"Where'd you get that bike?" he demanded.

Jimmy retorted, "Where did you get yours?" and turned and started toward the door of the drugstore.

Keith darted past him. Jimmy did not run; neither of them would get the job if they scuffled here. He followed Keith inside.

Mr. Dormyer, the owner, smiled at them.

"So, two applicants for the job. What're your names?"

"Keith Lucas."

"Jimmy Garrett."

"Live near here?"

"I live at 43 Berenda Way," Keith said.

"Nice neighborhood. You, Jimmy?"

"At the end of Mulberry Lane."

"Pretty far from here. Well, I guess I'd better interview you separately. Who got here first?"

"I did," Keith said.

"Come into my office, Keith. Don't go away, Jimmy. I'll talk to you, too, presently."

The minutes passed, Jimmy fidgeted nervously. Finally Keith and Mr. Dormyer came out of the back office. Keith shot Jimmy a look of triumph and swaggered out.

Mr. Dormyer said, "Come in, Jimmy," but his face was thoughtful.

"Sit down, boy. Well, now . . . Jimmy, this isn't a big store, and the business isn't big, either. But I do need a boy after school to deliver stuff ordered by telephone. People pay for the stuff when it's delivered. Medicines can run to twenty dollars and over, so naturally, I—I need a boy I can rely on, who's responsible, and—honest."

So he just takes a look at me and decides I'm not honest, Jimmy told himself. Aloud, he said merely, "Yes, sir."

"You've got a bike?"

"Yes, sir."

"Brand new?"

"Second-hand."

"Where'd you get it?"

"I guess I—just borrowed it, sir."

"Who from?"

Jimmy felt hot all over; his throat was tight and his lips trembled. "I don't know his name, sir."

"Where does he live?"

"I don't know."

"Well! Does he know you—borrowed his bike?"

"I—don't know, sir. I . . ."

The bell over the front door tinkled as a customer entered the drugstore. Mr. Dormyer looked up through the open office door and got to his feet.

"Got to serve this customer. Jimmy, I'm sorry," Mr. Dormyer said, and his voice sounded sincere, "but I'm afraid I can't hire you."

He hurried forward to take care of the customer. Jimmy followed into the store, hesitated, then realized, *It's just no use!* and walked out of the store. Out of Mr. Dormyer's sight, he could not control his feelings; tears came to his eyes.

He mounted his bike and started home. His churning thoughts transmitted their troubled fury to his legs so that he bore down hard on the pedals.

I shouldn't have tried for that job, he told himself. I should've known what would happen. The minute he looked at me he was against me. Soon's he saw the color of my face, I lost any chance for that job. . . . But he did seem so nice to me at first. Then maybe Keith told him some lies about me? Oh, quit fooling yourself. You're crazy if you think people are going to be fair to you.

"Jimmy," young Mrs. Logan, who lived next door, called to him across the fence, as he was putting the bike into the shed. "I thought I'd better tell you. A policeman was driving around here today. He was asking people if any of them had seen a boy with a red-and-yellow-trimmed bicycle. It's an old bike, he said. It's got a siren that runs off the front wheel but no mudguards. Mrs. Akers told him she thought she'd seen a bike like that, but didn't remember just who had it. The policeman said he'd be back later. Just thought I'd mention it," she said worriedly, and turned away.

Jimmy swallowed hard. A policeman. Asking about his bike. It was the same bike, all right. No question of it. But a policeman. . . .

I shouldn't have taken the bike home, he told himself. *Now, I'm in trouble. . . .*

He went into the kitchen and sat down. He was shaking. He tried to reassure himself, to calm down, to think sensibly, to decide what to do next.

One thing he could do, he decided. He could take the bike back to McCrary Dam. He could let it roll down into deep water. Then, when the cop questioned him about it, he could say that he did not know anything about such a bike.

You'd be lying, he told himself. *You'd be just as bad as they think you are!*
So what if I am! he thought. *Look how they're treating me!*

[Here the teacher stops to have the group begin role playing. See Introducing
the Problem. After the role playing, the teacher reads the ending to the class.]

Jimmy's mother arrived home from work usually at five-fifteen. Jimmy
guessed that the policeman would be back looking for him just about that
time too.

He could just see the stricken look on his mother's face when a big
officer in uniform knocked on the door and asked, "Does Jimmy Garrett live
here?" And Jimmy couldn't bear to go through that ordeal. He left the
house. He'd hike out into the country, he decided, and come back late, when
he was sure the policeman had gone.

But first he went to the back shed and got the red-and-yellow trimmed
bike. He left it in front of the house, leaning against a tree near the curb,
where it could be seen instantly by anybody passing in a car.

Then he walked restlessly down the road, out into the country. He
went to McCrary Dam. There, he idled away time, skipping rocks across the
lake surface. He was scared and he was angry. Sensibly, he tried to argue
himself into a calm state of mind. He wasn't the only person who got treated
unfairly. If you had cross-eyes or a limp, you were the butt of a lot of stupid
jokes. So relax, he told himself. Don't be so touchy. Grin and bear it.

But jokes are one thing, he told himself; not getting a job he needed
was something else; and having a policeman hunting him for what he had
done—that made him so mad he wanted to break things.

At sunset he started home. It was dark by the time he arrived.

The old bike, he noticed, was no longer leaning against the tree near
the curb. This meant that the policeman had been back and had taken the
bike.

His mother was home. The aroma of frying chicken was a warm
invitation when he entered the kitchen. His mother, in the next room, heard
him come in and called worriedly to him.

"Jimmy, that you?" When he answered, she said: "Mrs. Davis from
across the street says a policeman was here, hunting for you. You in trouble,
son?" she demanded, coming into the kitchen.

Jimmy spilled the whole story, then. Day before yesterday, he told his
mother, he had hiked to McCrary Dam to go fishing. As he neared the dam,
a boy he didn't know passed him, going the same way. The boy was riding a
bike, and Jimmy had wished he had one.

Arriving at the dam, Jimmy climbed up onto the concrete arch. There
he saw a group of four boys, none of whom he knew, although he recognized
one as the boy who had passed him on the bike a little earlier. The other
three were bigger boys, thirteen or fourteen years old. They were teasing the
smaller boy on the bike.

"Why ain't you home practicing the piano?"
"Your momma know you're out?"
"Better not talk mean to him—he'll tell his daddy!"

The boy being teased did not talk back. He was scared. Swinging onto his bike, he started to leave. One of the bigger boys was carrying a stick. He threw it now as the younger boy rode past—threw the stick in the front wheel. It caught in the spokes and, as the wheel turned, came up against the fork, locking the wheel tight. The bike up-ended and somersaulted forward. The boy was flung face down onto the concrete.

He lay there prone, not moving, not talking. The boy who had thrown the stick muttered, "Aw, get up. You ain't hurt!" But the others ran to the fallen boy and bent over him.

"Blood on his face."

"I don't think he's breathing."

They stood up, and now *they* were scared. They looked at each other, then one of them ran to his own bike. The others followed. Straddling their bicycles, they fled away.

Jimmy called, "Hey! You can't just leave him lying there . . ."

The other three did not even look back. Reaching the end of the dam, they swerved down onto the highway and headed back to town, standing on the pedals to make speed.

"Of all the mean, dirty tricks!" Jimmy exclaimed.

He bent over the hurt boy. Blood was coming from his nose, which seemed twisted and flattened. His chin was laid open as if by a knife, and from it blood was streaming down his neck and over his shirt. He was breathing, however, catching short, choky gasps. His eyes were open and staring, though he did not seem to see Jimmy at all.

"You hurt?" Jimmy asked.

The boy did not answer; he moaned, and his chin quivered.

"You better go home and have your chin bandaged."

The boy did not answer, he did not seem to hear or see Jimmy at all. He was almost knocked out, Jimmy realized. He needed help—needed it right away.

Jimmy glanced around. No one else was fishing on the dam or swimming near the beaches beyond.

I can't just go off and leave him here, Jimmy told himself. Maybe nobody'll come along until tomorrow. He can't lie out here all night. He's bleeding; and it gets cold after dark. He'll be awfully scared. His only injury was the bad cut on his chin; it would be safe to move him.

Jimmy bent down. He picked up the hurt boy in a "fireman's carry"— by grasping one wrist, putting his other arm between the boy's legs and heaving him across his shoulder. Luckily, the boy was small.

Staggering, Jimmy started toward the highway. Almost at once he was gasping for breath; the boy's weight seemed to double with every dozen steps. Several times Jimmy almost dropped him. If I do, he warned himself, I won't be able to pick him up again.

Just as he reached the highway, a car came rolling past. It stopped with a sudden shriek of brakes, then backed abreast of Jimmy as he put the hurt boy down.

"Good heavens, what's happened?" the woman driver called to Jimmy.

"He—fell off his bike . . ."

"Look how he's bleeding! Quick! Let's get him into the car. He needs a doctor."

She got out, and together they lifted the boy onto the floor of the back of the car. The woman got in behind the wheel.

"Wait. His bike!" Jimmy said.

"Never mind! We've got to rush him to the doctor."

"But it'll be stolen!"

"Haven't room for it. We're wasting time!"

"Okay, I'll ride it to town."

Behind him, as he ran along the dam, Jimmy heard the car start off, motor roaring. He continued to the bike and picked it up. The stick was still in the front wheel and he had to pull it free. Three spokes were broken, but otherwise the bike was undamaged.

Not until he started riding back to town did he realize that he did not know where to take the bike. He did not know the injured boy, did not know his name, nor where he lived. He did not know where the woman was taking him, did not even know the woman's name.

There was just one thing for him to do, Jimmy decided: Ride the bike home. And this was what he had done. . . .

"So now," he told his mother angrily, "all the thanks I get is that everybody thinks I *stole* that bike! It isn't fair. If I were Eddie Gordon or Tom Allen, I wouldn't be treated like this!"

"I guess," his mother said worriedly, "I should've told you to take the bike to the police station. But it's such a junky bike. When you came home with it, I thought you'd found it on a rubbish heap somewhere. Guess I've been too tired to keep close track of what you're doing. Anyway," she said, and hugged Jimmy, "you just relax. We'll work this out."

"How can we, with that policeman hunting for me," Jimmy said hopelessly.

Jimmy's mother sent him to the market on Seventh Street for groceries. Returning home, then, he saw people in front of his house. Nearing, he saw that his mother was there—with Mr. Dormyer, the druggist, and a man in uniform, a policeman. Jimmy's throat choked up. *He's waiting to grab me,* Jimmy warned himself. He had a sudden wild impulse to run and hide; but he made himself walk straight on, although he could not help slowing his pace.

The policeman was leaning over the old bicycle, working the pedal action. *Checking to see if I ruined it! But that bike was junky when I brought it home.*

They heard him approaching. Then they turned and saw him. The policeman stepped forward and came toward Jim and reached out his hand. But the policeman was smiling, and he took Jimmy's hand to shake it. Mr. Dormyer was smiling too.

The policeman said, "I had a hard time tracking you down, Jimmy. After I'd been asking all around the neighborhood, Mr. Dormyer finally gave me a clue. He told me about a boy who had applied for a job and who had a borrowed bike but didn't know the name of the owner. I guessed that you were the boy I was hunting for. Jimmy, I owe you more thanks than I can say."

"Wh-what?" Jimmy stammered.

"That boy who got hurt on the dam Wednesday—the boy you carried to the highway—his name is Pete Jones. He's my son."

"He didn't die?"

"No, Jimmy. He might have, if he'd lain out on the dam, bleeding all night. He had double pneumonia a few weeks ago. In fact, Wednesday was the first time he'd really gone out by himself since he got sick."

"He had a bad fall," Jimmy said.

"Yes, his nose was broken and had to be set, and that cut in his chin needed a lot of stitches. But, thanks to you, he'll be back in school Monday."

"That's good," Jimmy murmured.

"Now, about this bike," the policeman said. *Now,* Jimmy thought. *Now he arrests me.*

"Sure needs a new saddle," Mr. Jones said. "I know where to get one for you. The way the paint's peeling off the frame sure makes it look crummy, but we can sand the paint off and put a couple of coats of fresh enamel on. I suspect that the coaster brake needs taking apart and oiling, but that's not hard. I'll show you how to do it. What you really need is a good luggage carrier for the handle bars, so you can deliver things on your bike."

"Wh-what?" Jimmy gasped, for the second time.

"Jimmy," Mr. Dormyer said, "my friend Mr. Kagle, who has a drug-store on First Street, decided that he could use a delivery boy after school, too. Now that you've got a good bike of your own, why don't you apply for the job?"

"But I haven't got any bike!"

"Jimmy," Mr. Jones said, "I talked it over with Pete, and we both want you to keep this bike. It isn't much, just a small way for us to begin to thank you. Believe me, if I had the money, I'd buy you a brand new one."

"But—you mean you ain't arresting me?"

"Gosh, no, boy, I'm trying to thank you."

"Jimmy," Mr. Dormyer said, "you going to ask for that job?"

Jimmy didn't jump up and down and yell with delight. He didn't kick up his heels and let out a warwhoop, but he sure felt like it. And all that he felt was in the happy way he said, "I sure will, Mr. Dormyer. I'll be there, tomorrow, right after school."

PRACTICE SESSIONS

The point of the preceding stories is just this: Often, in our relations with other people, things are not what they seem. People may seem to be slighting us when actually they have no intention of hurting our feelings. There may be a good reason for the way they are behaving which we do not know; and, until we do learn that reason, it is important for us not to jump to conclusions.

Just for practice in withholding judgment about behavior until we learn the actual reasons for it, answer the questions raised in the following problem situations.

1. Your best friend is away on a long visit to relatives. You have written a letter to him (or her). Several weeks have gone by, and you are upset because you have had no answer to your letter. You think that your friend is angry with you. Actually, your friend is *not* angry with you.

   List three reasons why your friend has not answered your letter. These must be good, sensible reasons. Remember, your friend is not angry with you. (For example, your friend has not answered because he (or she) has never received your letter; or you put the wrong address on it.)

2. You answered an ad in the paper and are applying for a job (such as boxing groceries in a market or baby sitting). You did not get the job; the people have not telephoned you.

   List three good reasons, that have nothing to do with you personally, why you have not been hired. (For example, you are too young to be employed in some grocery chains.)

3. Your aunt wrote to your parents, asking if you or your older sister could accompany her and her daughter on a vacation trip. Your parents decided to send your sister. You are very upset and resentful; your parents were partial to her, you think.

   List three good impartial reasons why they should have sent your sister and not you. (For example, your sister is three years older than you and is thus the same age as your cousin with whom she'll travel; moreover, they both dote on classical music, while you like popular music.)

4. Your classroom is putting on a play. You had hoped to be selected to play the lead, but you were not. You angrily wonder if the teacher has something against you.

   List three good reasons why she was right in not choosing you for the lead in the play even though she likes and admires you and thinks you have real talent. (For example, you are a star pitcher on the baseball team and are already getting a lot of attention and admiration. Your teacher wants to help other members of your class show their talents, too.)

5. Your Boy Scout group has selected a team to put on an exhibition of signaling (or gymnastics, or rescue work) at the county fair. You were left off the team. You are angry because you think you should have been on the team.

   List three reasons why not putting you on the team was wise. (For example, you've just recovered from a long bout of the flu and are not yet up to your usual strength.)

ACCEPTING OTHERS: THE DEVIANT

Bandit Cave

The Problem: The issue is accepting others—specifically, the responsibility of the group to accept and support the individual who is "different." Recent studies of child groups have increased our sensitivity to the sufferings of the youngster who is rejected by his age mates. Not only must teachers and parents help such children acquire behavior and skills that are acceptable to their peers, but the children's group itself needs to acquire more democratic attitudes toward children who are different. This is a story of a boy who stood on the fringe of play activities watching other children instead of participating with them.

Introducing the Problem: You may introduce the story by saying, "I'm sure you all know how it feels, once in a while, to be left out of activities your friends are taking part in. When they're starting up a game or are going on a trip and do not include you, you feel hurt and miserable. This is a story about such an incident. The story stops but is not finished. As I read, think of ways in which the story might end."

Johnny Whelan and Dick Barry sat on the grass, watching the other boys playing softball. Mr. McCann, on his way from the office to inspect the camp dormitories, stopped for a moment.

"Why aren't you boys playing ball?"

Johnny said quickly, "I turned my ankle yesterday and it still aches."

But Dick, more frankly, revealing the puzzled hurt he felt, said, "They wouldn't choose me, Mr. McCann. I can't play good enough."

The counselor understood, then. For a moment he studied the two boys. Johnny Whelan was red-headed and freckled and big for ten, but chubby and soft-looking; he was evidently too clumsy to play softball or tag football well. Dick Barry, on the other hand, was small for his age. He was dark haired and dark eyed; his skin had a paleness that two days at camp had not yet covered with sunburn. He looked frail, as if he had lived indoors too much.

Mr. McCann said, "I'm sure glad you aren't tied up just now. I need two boys to go into town on the supply truck and do some errands for me. Would you fellows help me out?"

"Oh sure," Johnny said. He was quick and bright enough. "Be glad to help you out."

Dick just sat there, letting Johnny do the talking.

So Mr. McCann sent them into Hampton in care of Mack, the driver, with a list of items to buy, and permission to see an afternoon movie while Mack had a new radiator mounted on the truck.

But then Mr. McCann, very troubled, reported to the camp director.

"Johnny and Dick have been left out of games so much that they're beginning to hate camp."

"Why?" Mr. Calhoun asked. "Are they unpopular?"

"No-o. I've asked around. The other boys don't dislike Johnny and Dick. But they can't play ball. Any side they play on is bound to take an awful licking. So, when the boys choose up sides, they leave Johnny and Dick out."

The director nodded. "Johnny's father is dead, and his mother's a concert violinist. She travels on tours, playing engagements. She has kept Johnny with her, and the result has been that he has lived in hotels and on trains and just never played with kids very much. He's had a tutor, so he's kept up his school work all right, but . . ."

"He's never had a chance to play games."

"That's it. And Dick hasn't either, though for a different reason. Dick had rheumatic fever when he was six, and he's had to take it easy for a long time. He's all right now, though."

"Steve, you question the two youngsters. There must be *some* sport that they would enjoy."

"Yes, sir."

Mr. McCann managed to have some casual talks with Johnny. He asked Johnny about himself—where he'd been, what he'd done. The camp counselor smiled to himself, pleased by what he learned, and hopeful. His talk with Dick Barry, however, brought him increasing worry.

"Johnny," Mr. McCann said the next evening, when the whole camp was sitting about the big outdoor fire for the evening sing and stunts, "show us how you make a spinning rope, will you?"

Johnny rose to his feet, flushing and self-conscious.

"Y-yes, sir," he stammered. "Only you need some spot cord . . ."

"Like this?" Mr. McCann held up a coil of cotton rope.

"Why, yes, that's right," Johnny said surprised. "And you need a hondo and string . . ."

"Like this, maybe?"

Everybody laughed. It was almost like a magic act, the way Mr. McCann whipped the stuff out from under his jacket. He had, of course, come prepared.

Johnny took the rope, and fitted it around the groove of the hondo— which was an "eye" of brass—and fastened the hondo snugly into the rope by wrapping twine around the three-eighth-inch cord. Then he coiled a snug layer of string around the far end of the rope, as well, to keep the threads from raveling.

Everybody watched, quiet and absorbed.

Johnny worked deftly, his gray eyes intent, forgetting his audience and his self-consciousness.

"The rope is twenty feet long, Johnny," Mr. McCann said.

"That's about right."

Johnny held up the long end of the loop and threaded it through the eye of the hondo. Then he took the loop in his right hand, and coiled the slack in the other hand. He held his hands up.

"To spin your rope, start by holding it like this," he said, "so that the loop will stay open and so's you can let go of it. And see that the slack will play out. Keep the far end tight under the last two fingers of your left hand."

He whipped the loop over his head, letting it down around him, and kept turning the rope with his right hand. The loop widened out as it spun in a steady, graceful ring around his body, suspended by the "lead" from his right hand held over his head.

Abruptly he lowered his right hand, then whipped it up, deftly timing it so as not to foul the "lead" around his body—and the hissing loop lifted high over his head, spinning flat out for a second or two before it lowered down around him again. He let it come almost down to the ground, then whoosh! he lifted the spinning loop up high over his head once more. Down, then up, down and up, he snapped the whirling circle. The onlookers burst out clapping and cheering.

Blushing with pleasure, Johnny worked on through a whole list of fancy tricks. He laid the spinning loop so low that it slapped the ground with reports like a lashing whip as it spun—and he danced over the turning spoke of the "lead" as he kept it revolving from his right hand.

He brought the flat loop up shoulder high, and spun it faster, faster, *faster*, until it was screaming as it whirled. Then, very gradually, he tilted the loop from its flat position and slanted it higher and higher, until finally it was spinning straight up and down like a giant wheel. Then, startlingly, he whipped the loop sideways and jumped clear through it. Then back he leaped. Back and forth through the vertical loop he sprang, whipping the spinning rope from side to side. The watching boys applauded.

He had to stop finally, sweating and gasping for breath. It was very hard work.

"How do you do it, Johnny?" they kept yelling at him.

"Where'd you learn, Johnny? Out on a ranch?"

"No," he said. They grew quiet, to hear. "Funny thing, but real cowboys don't know how to spin rope. When my mother was playing violin in a movie, a movie cowboy taught me how to spin. He used to spin rope in vaudeville. There's just one secret to it besides practicing a lot. That's to keep the rope, where you're holding it, twisting just as fast as the loop is spinning. You keep it twisting with your fingers, so that it never kinks up. Once it kinks, it's closing time."

"Show us how, Johnny!"

Mr. McCann grinned as Johnny showed them. Johnny was going to be popular. But Mr. McCann's face got serious again as he noticed that Dick Barry sat on the edge of the crowd of boys, saying nothing; he was not trying to push up close to see how Johnny kept the spinning rope from kinking, but just sitting, quiet as a mouse. . . .

Beside the swimming pool next morning, Mr. McCann started talking to Dick.

"Ever play tennis, Dick?"

"No, Mr. McCann."

"Call me Steve, Dick. Ever learn to play the mouth organ?"

"No, sir."

"Can you run pretty fast, Dick?"

"I don't think so . . ."

"Ever play basketball?"

Dick just shook his head, and swallowed hard.

"Or make model planes?"

Again Dick answered with an apologetic, hopeless shake of the head.

"Maybe you've collected stamps?"

Dick gave a shaky little laugh. "Guess I just never did anything."

"Dick, you're going on the hike with us, tomorrow, to Bandit Cave—aren't you?"

Dick nodded. "I'd like to go, sir."

"Better jump in, now, and have a swim, Dick."

"I—I ain't allowed to, Steve. I got bad sinuses."

"Oh, I see. Well . . ."

Mr. McCann stalked away, shaking his head and his lips compressed. In the recreation hall, during the rest period before dinner, Dick settled himself away from the other boys, in the library corner. He was halfway through a book that fascinated him. Its title was *Camels, Caves and Cavalry*, and it was a gossipy history of Southern California. During his long illness, he had whiled away endless tedious months in reading. There was a whole shelf of books about early California here, but most of them Dick had already read. His father, now dead, had been a travel writer. The book Dick held had been his father's first published work, and it had been out of print for twenty years. Dick actually had never seen it before. He pored over it now, remembering his father with painful vividness.

Twenty boys went along on the hike with Mr. McCann next morning. The tall, smiling counselor kept the pace easy, for Dick's sake. Time and again he had to caution the boys to slow up. They were excited at the thought of visiting Bandit Cave, and impatient to reach it. Mr. McCann became uneasy. The youngsters would be disappointed when they discovered that a hole in the ground was just a hole in the ground.

They found the cave on the left wall of a box canyon, at the base of a dry waterfall. The youngsters crowded up close and peered into it, silent and expectant and wondering.

"Shucks," Bill Callen said.

"Couldn't any bandits hide in *that* little old place."

"Bandit Cave. Huh! Gyp Cave."

"Mr. McCann, why is this place supposed to be something we ought to see?"

The counselor wiped sweat from his lean face with his bandana and frowned in thought. "Well, I guess horse thieves probably camped here. It's a famous spot, only I don't seem to recall all the details."

Bandit Cave? Dick Barry studied the hole in the cliff, his thoughts milling excitedly. Once it had been a deep cave. Flowing through it had been a clear stream of water and a current of cool air that told of a winding system of great dark caverns far within the mountain. That had been over a hundred and twenty years ago, when California was still part of Mexico, before Fremont and Sloat and Kearny had raised the United States flag over the territory. That had been back in the days of the missions and the big ranchos, when California was a sleepy paradise, troubled only by the occasional foray of thieves who came out of the desert to rob the missions and ranchos of fine mules and horses. "Chaguanosos," the Californians called these raiders, "thieves of all nations." They were Paiute Indians and a variety of white renegades. It was on moonlit nights that they swept down Cajon Pass, riding fast and hard, rounding up stock and driving the animals swiftly before them in a wild rush to whip through Cajon and into the Mojave before the rancheros could catch up with them. The Californios began to dread these "silver nights." They learned to keep vigilant guard. They armed themselves and slept lightly, alert for signals in the night that would summon them to seize lance and musket and mount their finest palominos to ride against the raiders.

Once they almost caught the leaders of the Chaguanosos, a white man called Pegleg Smith, and a Paiute known as Walkara, "Napoleon of the Desert." The raiders had split forces in an effort to shake off close pursuit.

Walkara and Pegleg Smith and several of their wounded men had finally taken refuge here in the cavern.

The rancheros had not dared to charge into the cave after the raiders, knowing they would enter an ambush. Instead, the Californios had built a fire in the cave mouth in an effort to smoke out the raiders and shoot them down as they popped out of the hole like rabbits out of a burrow. The trick didn't work.

For Walkara and Pegleg Smith and their men retreated far back into the cavern. The stream of clear water and the unceasing flow of cool, sweet air saved them.

In chagrin, the Californios used their gunpowder to blast down the roof of the entrance passageway, sealing it shut, locking the bandits inside it forever! Grimly satisfied, then, the Californios returned to their ranches.

That's why the cave now looks so shallow, Dick thought. *All we can see is just this end, where the roof was blasted down to shut the bandits up inside. The cave really extends 'way back. The hole inside of the mountain is just a honeycomb of tunnels and big, weird, ghostly rooms.*

Not that Pegleg Smith and Walkara were ghosts, now, haunting the cavern. For they had not died inside. By torchlight they had explored the winding limestone passages. They were worried, all right. They were scared and shaken. But the fact that the air flowed through the jagged tunnels, in a current that they could feel, gave them hope. They noticed, too, that there were many bats in the cavern. The bats seemed to leave the cave, and after a long interval, would return in large numbers. As if they were flying out of the cave at twilight and returning at dawn.

So they watched the bats. They followed the passages that the bats seemed to be flying through. And that way, climbing high to the top of the wall of a big room, they found a narrow outlet through which the wind sucked hungrily. It was a tight squeeze, but out of this coyote hole the bandits all escaped. Dick could imagine how they looked and felt when they stood in the glaring sunlight again. How they grinned at each other, and wiped their faces, and looked blinkingly at the sun and let its warmth beat upon their heads.

"To tell the truth, boys," Mr. McCann was confessing, "I don't really know why this cave is supposed to be anything special. Looks just like another hole in the ground."

"Mr. McCann," Dick began. "Steve . . ."

"Well, let's eat," Mr. McCann said. "Don't use all the water in your canteens. You'll want a drink on the way back."

"Steve, I know . . ."

"Mr. McCann!" Bill Lyle yelled. "Let's build a campfire in the cave. Just like the Indians! Let's fry some bacon!"

"Good idea. Scatter and look for firewood. Small stuff, for a cook fire."

"Steve," Dick said. "A long time a—"

"Mr. McCann," Peter Akers called. "Johnny Whelan brought his spinning rope. Can he show us some tricks while we eat?"

"That's a good idea. Feel like it, Johnny?"

"Soon's I eat one sandwich," Johnny agreed.

Dick turned away . . .

That night after the evening meal, Dick was called to the office. There was a phone call for him, from his mother.

"Are you enjoying camp, dear?" she asked.

"Well—no."

"Would you like to come home?"

He did not answer.

"Son," his mother repeated, "I can drive out to get you tomorrow. Shall I? Do you want to stay—or do you want to come home?"

Dick said . . .

The Squawk Box

The Problem: The issue is accepting others—specifically, the responsibility of a group to respect and support an individual who is different. Children can be cruel to one another, and a group can be especially cruel to a youngster who is different. Groups frequently tend to honor a child who does not merit specific recognition but is merely popular and a leader; meanwhile they ignore (and thereby reject) an individual who does merit an honor because he is not typical.

Introducing the Problem: You may say, "This is a story about a boy who is somewhat different from his playmates. Because he seems odd to them and lacks the abilities they respect, he is unpopular; and because he is not liked, he is not elected to offices he is really very able to fill. This story stops but is not finished. As I read, try to think of ways in which the story could end."

Andy Eaton remembers the day that the police cornered the mad dog out in front of the school gym. Andy has a good reason to remember it. . . .

The boys were choosing up sides for a ball game when Andy came to school that morning, early. He stood by as Neil and Jerry took turns naming the fellows each wanted. Neil got five on his side. Jerry just had four. Andy was the only boy not yet chosen.

"I don't want Andy," Jerry said. "He can't play ball."

"You've got to take him. There's nobody else."

"Ah, he couldn't catch a fly ball if it had handles on it."

Andy blushed. He knew that he was clumsy and slow. He wasn't very good at baseball or football, or any of the games the boys played. But he was a year older than most of the group, and bigger too.

"I beg your pardon," he said angrily, "but anybody could play ball if they practiced."

"Oh, I beg *your* pardon, but you couldn't bat your way out of a paper bag! Anyway, here comes Pete Neylor. Neil, I choose Pete!"

"I was here first," Andy insisted. "It's not very sporting to pass me up . . ."

"Sporting yet!" Neil hooted. "My word, Reginald, you'll get those sissy clothes mussed up if you play with us!"

"I mean it's not fair," Andy said. But he couldn't correct his clothes. His father had sent from England the gray flannel slacks and the smart blazer Andy was wearing.

"Aw, come on, let's play," Neil said. "We bat first!"

They all turned away from Andy, leaving him standing alone, ignoring him. Andy's fist clenched. He was mad enough to fight Neil and Jerry. Then he realized how upset his folks would be.

When the bell rang and the fifth graders all trooped into the classroom, their teacher had a surprise for them. Everybody crowded up front to look at the surprise on Mrs. Chandler's desk.

"What is all this stuff?" Neil asked.

"That's a record player," Andy said, "and an amplifier and loud-speaker and a microphone."

"What's it for, Mrs. Chandler?" Jerry inquired.

"For our program this afternoon. Children, the record player wouldn't be loud enough to use in the gym for our pageant, so I borrowed this equipment to use."

"Our music'll be plenty loud, now," Andy said. His brown eyes were shining with excitement. "That's a dandy Marvel-tone amplifier and a swell twelve-inch speaker. That set'll give a 60-watt output and that's plenty for our gym. Mrs. Chandler, the set's not hooked up. Please, can I hook it up for you?" he asked eagerly. "The loudspeaker has to be connected in back here with this round-pronged plug, and the mike line is screwed onto this connec-tion, here. Your turntable has two wires and they have to be put on at these terminals in back and the screws turned down tight."

"Oh, do you know how to run it, Andy?"

"Yes, ma'am, my Dad's taught me. This tone control here—you keep it set at ten for natural tone, unless you get feed-back. Then you can fiddle with the setting to cut it out . . ."

"Show-off!" Elsie Bates whispered.

Andy shut up, turning red.

"Thanks for explaining it, Andy," Mrs. Chandler said. "All right, children, back to your seats. We've got to plan."

That afternoon the class was to perform a pageant of the West in the gym. The other classes were invited to watch. The pageant would show a wagon train moving along the Santa Fe Trail. Then abruptly the scene would shift to a tribe of Indians holding a big medicine smoke. Chiefs would argue about the danger of the incoming white men and the loss of buffalo. Older chiefs would counsel peace; but young hotheads would make shrill demands for battle, and would start a war dance around their campfire.

"Remember, children," Mrs. Chandler reminded them, "we want to change from the wagon party to the Indian tribe very quickly. The shades will be drawn in the gym, and we'll have a spotlight on us. When the square dance ends, the light will go out. All of you pioneers run to the east doors and go outside. The children who are the Indians will then run in from the west hall. The light will come back on—and the Indians are to be sitting around a campfire in front of their wigwams. We want to make the change very quickly. So remember. Soon as the music ends, pioneers run for the exit door—and Indians come running in."

Andy put up his hand. Mrs. Chandler nodded.

"Excuse me, Mrs. Chandler, but you've got to have somebody at the turntable to start the records and to change them, and somebody to run the amplifier."

"You're right, Andy. I'll handle the records myself. We'll have to choose a sound engineer."

"Let Jerry be the sound engineer," Neil called out.

"Jerry, do you know how to handle the equipment?" she asked.

"Well, some," Jerry said hesitantly.

Andy waved his hand, trying to get permission to speak again, but Sam Balch spoke up, "Yes, Jerry'd make a good engineer!" and Susan Kyle said, "Let Jerry do it."

Jerry was very popular. He was good at sports, had a lot of ideas about games to play, and talked and laughed a lot.

"Please, Mrs. Chandler," Andy said, "if I may, I'd like to be engineer."

"Children," Mrs. Chandler said, "why not have Andy as engineer . . ."

"We want Jerry!"

"Let's have a vote!"

"All right," Mrs. Chandler said, "those in favor of Andy raise your hands."

Andy sat in front. He could see no raised hands. Two hands were raised behind him.

"Those in favor of Jerry," Mrs. Chandler said.

All but two of the children raised their hands.

"Jerry, you're elected. Andy, you'll help Jerry, if he needs it, won't you?" Mrs. Chandler said.

Andy wanted to say, "Sorry, but I certainly won't," but instead he swallowed hard and nodded.

"All right, now we'll have a rehearsal," Mrs. Chandler said.

The show was really a pantomime—that is, the children out on the gym floor would do their marching and dancing, while one person would explain everything through the microphone to the audience. Susan was the commentator.

She began, "It was the spring of the year 1846 . . ."

She stopped. Her voice wasn't coming from the loudspeaker.

Jerry was bent over the amplifier, turning the knobs.

Andy said, "I'm very sorry, but turning the phonograph knob doesn't turn on the microphone. Anyway, it's smart to wait until the tubes get warm before you turn up the juice."

"Sarcastic," somebody whispered.

Andy flushed. But he added, "Takes just a minute for the tubes to warm up."

"All right, Susan," Mrs. Chandler said, "start over."

Susan began again. The children settled back in pleased surprise as

Susan's voice came full and rich and loud from the speaker, carrying clearly to every corner of the room.

"And at St. Louis and Independence, wagons were being outfitted for the spring trip over the Trace to New Mexico and Cal . . ."

Squawk-howl-screech-meeow-rawr-wow!

Susan's voice was lost in the rumbling yowl that shrilled deafeningly from the loudspeaker, like the shriek of a giant panther wounded by an Apache arrow. Mrs. Chandler said something to Jerry, but the racket was so ear-filling that nobody could hear her words. Jerry looked at her, at Susan standing with her mouth open, at the amplifier, and didn't know what to do.

Andy reached over and gave the mike control a quick twist and the awful noise ended as if it had been chopped off with a hatchet.

By that time, the school principal, Mr. Bayley, had opened the door and was looking in, his face surprised and alarmed.

"What in the world was that?" he asked.

Mrs. Chandler pointed at the loudspeaker.

Andy said, "Feed-back."

"Feed-back. What's that?"

Andy didn't answer. He looked at Jerry. Jerry was the sound engineer.

"Whatever it is," Mrs. Chandler said, "it's awful. Jerry, what happened?"

Jerry looked at the amplifier, and edged away from it a little bit, as if expecting a dinohippopus to reach out of it and bite him.

Andy said, "If Jerry knew very much about a public address system he'd know that you get 'feed-back' inside a room, especially a small room."

"Andy," Mrs. Chandler asked, "will you please show Jerry what to do?"

"Yes, ma'am. Jerry, you had your volume control up too high. Turn it lower whenever she first starts to howl. Or turn your tone control down. Sometimes that'll head off a howl."

Mrs. Chandler said to Mr. Bayley, "I believe everything's under control now."

The principal shut the door, still looking doubtful.

"All right, Susan, start over," Mrs. Chandler said.

Susan wet her lips and lifted the microphone, shifting to a more comfortable position against the table.

But before she opened her mouth at all, from the loudspeaker came a whistle like a police siren screaming at the top of its voice. It was deafening, and growing shriller every instant.

The children clapped their hands to their ears. The room door was pushed open, and Mr. Bayley was there again, his mouth working as he yelled something which nobody could hear until Mrs. Chandler reached down and pulled the amplifier plug out of the wall connection. That wild whistle faded out like a rope jerked through a knot hole.

"—heavens, you'll blow the roof off this building!" Mr. Bayley was shouting.

"Jerry, did you turn the wrong switch?" Mrs. Chandler said.

"No. Susan hadn't even started talking," Jerry protested.

Everybody looked at Andy then.

Andy raised his hand and waited until Mrs. Chandler nodded. Then he said, "It's really very simple. If Susan will just be careful not to step right in front of the speaker with a hot mike in her hand, she won't cause that noise again."

Susan backed away from the speaker as far as the microphone cord would allow.

"We're learning," Mrs. Chandler said to the principal.

He nooded, his mouth tight.

"Trial and error. Or should I say 'trial and terror'?" he murmured, and shut the door.

"Jerry," Mrs. Chandler suggested, "don't you think we'd better let Andy run the sound system?"

"Oh, no. I know all the tricks, now," Jerry insisted.

The rest of the rehearsal went off all right, then. Jerry watchfully squeezed off every howl as it began by closing down on the volume or tone. Mrs. Chandler nodded, satisfied.

"Fine. Put the equipment away, Jerry. Let's finish the costumes now."

Jerry looked at Andy and whispered, "The big expert! It doesn't take any brains to run a P.A. system."

"You certainly proved that," Andy retorted.

"Wise guy!" Jerry said.

Mrs. Chandler said, smiling, "With your help, Andy, I'm sure that Jerry has that wild microphone tamed so it won't howl this afternoon."

"I'm sorry, Mrs. Chandler," Andy said, "but that microphone won't howl this afternoon—and it won't talk, either. It's going to be an awfully dead mike. We won't be able to use it."

"But why not, Andy?"

"Jerry's put it on that window shelf, over the radiator. That's a crystal mike, and the Rochelle Salt crystals in it can't stand heat. Leaving it over a radiator like that is a sure way to make junk out of it."

"Jerry . . ."

But Jerry was already moving the mike to a wall cupboard. "Wise guy!" he whispered at Andy. "Ain't you smart!"

The mad dog was a fine big Doberman Pinscher, a very well-mannered lady dog who came often to the school grounds. The children loved to pet her. However, she had not been inoculated; and somewhere, unluckily, she had picked up a rabies germ. The germ had grown, spreading itself, until today the dog was doomed. Mrs. Weaver, who lived across the street from the school, saw the Doberman coming down the street, her jaws flecked with foam. The dog carried her head at a funny angle, and turned into the school grounds. Mrs. Weaver, alarmed, phoned the police. Then Mrs. Weaver had a second thought and phoned the school principal's office.

But Mr. Bayley and all the teachers and children were in the gym, watching the fifth grade's pageant of the West.

From the loudspeaker was coming music from a record on the turntable which Mrs. Chandler was tending. To that music her children were performing a square dance. Mrs. Chandler was smiling; her class had done very well.

Mr. Bayley's secretary came through a side door and hurried to Mrs. Chandler's side.

"Mrs. Chandler!" the secretary whispered. "Tell everybody to stay in the gym. Nobody's to go outside. There's a mad dog on the school grounds. She's out on the east side of the play yard!"

Mrs. Chandler nodded. "When this record ends, I'll just announce it over the loudspeaker," she said. And then Mrs. Chandler had an awful thought.

This was the music for the dance now being played. When the record ended, the wagon train party was to run to the east doors and go outside—while from the west hallway, the Indians would come into the gym to take their places. When this record ended, her fifth graders would immediately go out those east doors!

"I can't stop the music!" she thought. "I don't dare shut off this music!" But the record was almost over. The needle was very close to the last grooves at the center of the disc.

"*Children!*" Mrs. Chandler shouted. "*Stay inside the gym! Don't go out those doors!*"

She hadn't been heard. The music was so loud that her voice hadn't a chance to carry over it.

Jerry, beside her, reached to turn down the volume of the music. Andy said, "No!" and stopped him. Andy seized the microphone, standing on the table before Susan. Andy turned up the mike volume control, but did not touch the phone volume control.

"Listen, Neil and Kenneth and rest of you kids!" Andy said—and though the music had not diminished at all, his voice soared loud and clear over the dance melody. It traveled through the microphone and amplifier and out the loudspeaker with the music, so that everyone in the gym heard it plainly. "This dance is almost over," Andy said. "When it ends, stay in the gym. You are not to go out, but stay right in the middle of the floor where you are!" And then his voice seemed twice as loud, for the music had come to the end of the record. "Ellen!" Andy called to Ellen Barnes. "Mike, Barry! *Stay—where—you—are! Don't anybody leave the room!*"

By now, Mrs. Chandler was running to the east doors to stop any children who tried to go out.

It wasn't necessary. They all stood where they were, surprised and wondering.

"Don't be frightened, children," Mrs. Chandler said. "We're to stay where we are for a while."

Now that the music had stopped, the Indians came rushing in, right on cue. They slowed up and stared, puzzled at seeing that the wagon train people were still on stage in the middle of the floor.

And then, outside, sounded the hard bang of a pistol shot.

Everybody's head jerked around to look at the east doors. Somebody cried out, as if scared. Mr. Bayley started toward the doors to see what was going on. Mrs. Chandler called to him.

"Wait, Mr. Bayley! Don't go outside!"

He hesitated; and while he paused, the door opened. It was pushed open from the outside. A tall policeman came in. He looked surprised when he saw so many people staring at him.

"We've got the dog," he said. "Mr. Bayley, it's all right to go outside now."

Later, Mrs. Chandler talked to Andy alone.

"Andy, I just can't thank you enough."

"Why, you're welcome, Mrs. Chandler. But it wasn't much," he said honestly. "I just knew how to use that mike, and I did, that's all."

Next day, Mr. Bayley sent word that he'd like to have the fifth grade put on their pageant for the Wilson Grade School, across town. The class voted to do it.

Mrs. Chandler said then, "Children, let's elect a sound engineer to serve for this performance."

"We've already elected Jerry."

"Sure, let Jerry keep on being engineer."

"But," Mrs. Chandler said, "Andy knows so much more about the job! Don't you think he'd make a good engineer?" she asked.

16

Role Playing
and Language Arts

Role playing can motivate children to use all the language arts skills: writing, listening, speaking, and reading.

For example, the teacher can read an unfinished dilemma story to the class and ask them to delineate the possible solutions; then, she can ask them to choose an alternative solution and write an ending to the unfinished story. (Some of the stories in this book have been used in this way by college classes in remedial writing.) A well-structured dilemma that touches upon young people's own concerns will involve them emotionally. Deeply interested, they are stimulated to respond. They will discuss the problem earnestly, read related materials, and write their responses with strong feeling. The dilemma story thus serves several purposes: It provides a topic, a take-off point, and a stimulus for discussion and writing.

Writing. In analyzing alternative solutions and writing endings to dilemma stories, students gain practice in using logical, analytical, and projective skills as well as writing skills. With guidance, they acquire a greater ability to reason from a premise realistically and coherently. Guided practice in composition further enhances their ability to put their feelings into words.

Speaking. In discussions that follow the reading and enactments, students will be motivated to argue, to express strong feelings for and against, and in the process, with guidance, to develop expository skills.

Listening. Their interest caught, children will listen attentively. They can be further guided to listen critically to a dramatic story—to watch for errors of fact and logic and for the deliberate use of devices that sway and mislead.

Reading. Confronted with problems that involve them deeply, students will be receptive to reading suggestions that will illuminate and broaden the issues involved.

In exploring the consequences of alternative solutions to a dilemma problem, students must use their imaginations. Some may tend to fantasize; others may be unable to envision consequences. The example and stimulus of interaction with their classmates will spark their imaginations and keep them reality-oriented. The role-playing experience, with its critical discussion and its opportunities for reevaluation, provides students with vital practice in extrapolating and modifying conclusions on the basis of new insights.

The consequences of a behavior come in sets. After they examine the sets of consequences that are likely to follow a decision, students can weigh one set against another and judge which outcome is most sensible and humane. Writing that involves such efforts provides important practice in developing good judgment. Teachers can help students keep their proposed solutions within the limits of reality and probability.

FEELINGS ARE IMPORTANT CONTENT

The most suitable area of the curriculum in which students can deal with their own feelings is the language arts sector. What better content for expression than young people's own lives? Feelings accompany every experience. Feelings cause behavior. Decisions are often made under the pressure of strong feelings; inevitably, decisions are followed by regret or satisfaction, by misgivings or euphoria.

As young people learn to read and write with increasing adequacy, they become more able to put emotion into vivid language. Their awareness sharpened, they become more responsible and compassionate.

In their reading, discussing, and writing, students learn to evaluate the dilemmas of daily life—dilemmas that involve such universal problems as fair play, responsibility, individual integrity, accepting others and surmounting prejudice, managing their own feelings, sensitivity to others' feelings, and the interactions between individuals and groups. Such abstract labels cover immense areas of human concern, of course. In the classroom, to involve young people in ethical problems, a dilemma must not be stated abstractly but presented in specific, factual terms. For example, young people are very vulnerable. They can very easily be made to feel put down, ignored, overlooked, and belittled. They often feel bypassed because they think others consider them inadequate or inferior. Even in the close, secure confines of family life they often feel jealous or rejected.

USING DILEMMA STORIES
TO MOTIVATE COMPOSITION

Writing Endings

Students can begin their writing either at the ending of a story or earlier. They can have the chief story character make a decision and act on that decision. More advanced students can be asked to write endings for *each* of the alternative ways they see to solve the dilemma.

Exploring Consequences

Solving a story by making a decision is just one step. It is important then to *explore the consequences of the decision that has been made*. This is a very important habit of thought to develop. Exploring the probable consequences of decisions under consideration is a crucial aspect of decision making, whether it's merely an exercise in classroom role playing or an event in actual human experience. Good judgment lies in being able to assess realistically the consequences of a decision, weigh one set of consequences against another, and choose the most sensible and acceptable. In weighing those consequences, moreover, the emotional concomitants must never be overlooked; one alternative may result in monetary benefits but with emotional conflicts and burdens. Sometimes it is actually more practical to choose an alternative that will mean a loss of luxuries but also peace of mind.

Such writing assignments provide practice in extrapolation, or projecting ahead the likely results of a course of action. This draws upon students' imagination, knowledge, and sense of fact. Young people who lack a firm reality orientation may foresee consequences that are mere fantasy; more practical individuals will foresee the consequences that are really likely to happen.

In the discussions and interactions of actual role playing, those who hold conflicting views influence each other. The more imaginative students will see some of the defects in their thinking, and the more practical students will have their limited views extended. This interchange between peers is a very strong influence on ideas, and both groups benefit. Similarly, if the written compositions are reviewed by the group, students of different viewpoints have a chance to share their thinking.

Changing a Basic Premise

To vary the writing assignments, suggest that students use the dilemma stories in still another way. Ask them to pick a point in the story where the main character can do something to prevent the dilemma from developing and to rewrite the story accordingly with a logical ending.

For example, in the story "Paper Drive," the teacher discovers that her pupils have been cheating by putting junk iron in their bales of paper to increase the weight. She is shocked. She orders them to stop. She considers whether to have them withdraw from the contest. That, however, would result in their conduct being revealed to the administration and to parents. She decides instead to do nothing. Her class probably will not win. She has scolded them; they know they've been doing wrong. She'll let it go at that. However, the class *does* win the paper drive. Now she has a difficult decision to make. If she had withdrawn them from the contest earlier, she would not be in this very troubling position now. There are points in every dilemma story at which, if the people involved had behaved differently, the final dilemma would have been avoided, and a different ending would have resulted.

New Dilemma Alternatives

Logicians refer to the alternative solutions of a dilemma as the "horns" of a dilemma, and of a person forced to choose between alternatives as being "hung on the horns of a dilemma." Sometimes a person facing a dilemma discovers that there is a third (or even a fourth) alternative solution to a problem. One of these new alternatives may be more acceptable than the alternatives faced originally.

It may happen that an individual, on analyzing a dilemma, discovers that he has misinterpreted one of the painful alternative solutions, that, actually, it is quite acceptable. For example, an airlines executive is very troubled when he hears reports that a certain type of plane has been grounded because one crashed when an engine fell off. Should he ground the one plane of the type that his little airline owns? He has not received official directives to do so—yet. If he does abort the flight, he'll lose passenger fares. But if he does not ground the flight, he might be cited by the authorities and fined. He decides to cancel the flight. Then, inspection of his plane reveals that the engine mountings *were* defective. If the plane had taken off heavily loaded with passengers and freight, it might have crashed. Many lives would have been lost. He would have gone bankrupt from the subsequent lawsuits. Choosing a painful alternative had proven to be the wiser course of action.

To sum up: You can give writing assignments to your class involving the use of any of the dilemma stories in this volume. You can ask your group to

1. Write an ending for one of the unfinished dilemma stories, focusing on one of the alternative decisions inherent in the situation and going on to explore the consequences of that particular course of action.
2. Write two endings to one of the unfinished stories—that is, follow each of two alternatives of choice to their logical consequences.
3. Rewrite one of the unfinished stories by changing a basic premise: Pick a point in the story where the main character can do something that will prevent the dilemma from ever developing. By changing the main character's actions, the whole course of the story can be changed.
4. Write an ending to one of the dilemma stories in which the main character

"escapes between the horns of the dilemma" by finding a new alternative to solve the problem.

5. Write an ending to one of the unfinished stories in which the main character discovers that he or she had misinterpreted one of the alternatives to solving the problem—that instead of a painful solution to the dilemma, it is an acceptable solution.

6. Suggest to your group that they each write a story with a dilemma that has actually happened in their own, or a friend's, experience.

The following sample analyses of dilemma stories show how a story can be taken apart in discussion and suggest ways in which the stories can be rewritten.

Analyzing Dilemma Stories

Money For Marty (p. 199)

The Problem: Bryan owes Marty a dollar which he borrowed but has not paid back. Marty now has a chance to get his money back in a dishonest way. Should he?

The Issue: Personal integrity. If someone has cheated you, is it fair for you to cheat him in return?

The Dilemma: By hiding the lost dollar with his foot, Marty can get back the money Bryan owes him. But Bryan is crying as he looks for the lost coin. It's a collector's item from his father's desk. If it's not found, Bryan will be in serious trouble with his father. Should Marty ignore Bryan's problem and get back his money? Or should he give the coin back to Bryan, knowing Bryan is lax about repaying his debts?

Possibilities for Writing: Ask your group to read the story to themselves. Ask them to write an ending that takes one of the alternatives to its logical conclusion.

  I. Develop the alternatives.
   A. Marty keeps the coin. Bryan's father is very angry and "takes steps" by coming to school and talking to the teacher. . . .
   B. Marty shows Bryan where the coin is, but days pass and Bryan does not repay his debt. What does Marty do?
 II. At some point in the story Marty could have done something differently, and the problem would never have arisen. Rewrite the story to develop this possibility.
III. Work up a parallel situation that you know about personally. Ask your students to develop it to the dilemma point, follow through on one of the possibilities that emerge.

Tell-Tale (p. 199)

The Problem: Ken and Jimmy play a prank: They put a harmless garden snake in a girl's lunchbox to frighten her. It works; she creates a commotion. Another girl, Dora, then reveals that Ken and Jimmy played the prank. The teacher punishes them. They resolve to get revenge on the girl who exposed them. Ken reveals his plan.

The Issue: Playing fair. The boys' revenge is far out of proportion to the crime.

The Dilemma: The trick Ken has thought up to get even with Dora for exposing them is, in Jimmy's mind, far too cruel. But Ken is his pal and is urging him to help. Ken will call him a gutless sissy if he reneges. Jimmy is agonized with indecision.

Possibilities for Writing: First, have your group read the story to themselves. Ask them to write an ending that takes one of the alternative endings to its logical conclusion.

I. Develop the alternatives.
   A. Jimmy puts the stolen lunch items into Dora's lunchbox. The child from whom the items have been stolen complains—and sees them in Dora's lunchbox.
   B. Jimmy refuses to go through with Ken's plan. What happens to their relationship?
II. At what point in the story could something have been done differently that would have prevented the final dilemma from arising?
III. From your own knowledge or experience, develop a similar account of an attempt to get even and write it as a story.

Frogman (p. 175)

The Problem: Older children's questionable behavior is being imitated by younger children.

The Issue: Accepting responsibility of setting an example for others.

The Dilemma: Should you allow others to imitate your own behavior if doing so may get them into serious trouble? However, if you refuse to let them do so, they will expose you.

Possibilities for Writing: Ask your group to read the story. Ask them to write an ending to the story that takes one of the alternatives to its logical conclusion.

I. Develop the alternatives.
   A. Let the younger boys have the gear, go spear-fishing in the forbidden area, and risk being caught. What might happen?
   B. Refuse to let the younger boys have the gear, even though they threaten to expose the older boys as the ones who had caught the big fish earlier.

II. At what point in the story could another decision have been made that would have prevented the present dilemma from arising?

III. Develop a similar dilemma story.

The Clubhouse Boat (p. 153)

The Problem: A group of boys have a chance to get an old houseboat as a meeting place for their club and are very excited at the prospect. However, they must collect enough money to pay for the repair of a leak in the hull before the boat will be turned over to them. Tommy has been unable to pay his share. The group has "borrowed" money from a lost purse. Now the owner is demanding his money back. Unless Tommy gets the money, the group will not only lose the houseboat but be in serious trouble.

The Issue: The situation develops into a conflict between peer-group demands and parental standards. Tommy is an honest boy, but he is caught between his father's standards of thrift and the pressures of his friends. His father says he must save his earnings. But he has promised to pay his share of the cost of the boat repair job. The only way he can get the money he needs is by conning people into giving him tips and by keeping money paid him by mistake.

The Dilemma: A customer inadvertently overpays Tommy (who delivers medicines for a drugstore). Tommy discovers the overpayment after he has delivered a package. Tommy hesitates: Should he keep the overpayment and use the money to pay his debt to his club? Or should he return the overpayment to the customer—and then be blamed by his group for failing to pay his share?

Possibilities for Writing: Have your group read the story for themselves. Ask them to write an ending to the story that takes one of the alternatives to its logical conclusion.

I. Develop the alternatives:
   A. Tommy knocks on the door and the old man opens it. Tommy explains how he was overpaid.
   B. Tommy does not tell the customer of the overpayment but takes the needed money to his group. They, in turn, replace the money they had taken from the lost purse. But matters come to a crisis next day when the customer, who overpaid for his medicine, comes to the drugstore and tells Tommy's boss that he (the customer) overpaid Tommy.

II. At some point in the story, Tommy could have done something differently, with the result that he would never have had to face the problem of getting enough money to pay his share. Rewrite the story to develop this possibility.

III. Develop a story with a similar dilemma: Should the group take advantage of an accident to benefit themselves at someone else's expense? For example: As a car speeds past their school, a bicycle is jolted off a rack on the car's bumper. The boys pick up the bike from the street. It has no registration plate, so no clue to the owner is on it. One boy says he could use the horn and light. Another boy says he needs a new tire. Another boy says he needs a good chain. The boys are tempted.

Use the parts on their own bikes? Or turn the bike over to the school principal so that he can report it to the police department?

Trick or Treat (p. 168)

The Problem: Older boys have induced some younger ones to play a Halloween trick that has resulted in serious damage to an old man's trailer home and injury to him.

The Issue: Fairness to others: Accepting blame when one could evade it because others are thought to be the culprits.

The Dilemma: Pete and Sandy have persuaded two smaller boys to attach a rope from a house trailer to the bumper of a car. The trailer is pulled off its foundation and the occupant hurt. The two smaller boys are blamed. Pete and Sandy, who were wearing Halloween costumes, cannot be identified. By saying nothing, they can escape punishment, and the two smaller boys will be blamed. By telling the truth, they can exonerate the smaller boys, but they will be in serious trouble.

Possibilities for Writing: Ask your group to read the story for themselves. Ask them to write an ending to the story that takes one of the alternatives to its logical conclusion.

  I. Develop the alternatives.
    A. The two older boys, Pete and Sandy, say nothing. What happens to the younger boys?
    B. Pete and Sandy come forward and exonerate the smaller boys, explaining how they induced the younger kids to play the Halloween trick. What happens to Pete and Sandy?
  II. At what point could Pete or Sandy have done something that would have prevented the serious consequences of their prank?
  III. Think of a situation similar to this—perhaps one in which you were involved—and write a narrative.

Paper Drive (p. 141)

The Problem: You, the teacher, want your pupils to win a contest. However, they have discovered that their rival class, runner-up to them in the contest, is likely to win because of cheating. Your students, following suit, are now cheating too.

The Issue: Rationalizing dishonesty: If your opponent cheats, is it therefore all right for you to do the same?

The Dilemma: Should you do nothing, and allow your pupils to win? Or should you be strictly ethical and withdraw your pupils from the contest, even though this means that the other class will win through cheating?

Possibilities for Writing: Have your group read the story for themselves. Ask them to write an ending to the story that takes one of the alternatives to its logical conclusion.

I. Develop the alternatives.
   A. The teacher decides that the class must withdraw from the contest because they have been cheating.
   B. The teacher says nothing and does nothing; the class wins the contest.
II. A dilemma arose for the children when they first learned that the other class was cheating in the paper drive. Should they have imitated their competitors and cheated even more so as to beat them at their own game? Should they have tried to win honestly? Should they have gone to their teacher and exposed the other side as cheaters?
III. Have any of your pupils ever been in a situation like this? Have them write an account of it.

The "Living Newspaper" Procedure

Current news incidents are a valuable source of real issues for role playing. Such real-life events often involve students more deeply and honestly than abstract, conventional school topics.[1] The "living newspaper" technique was perhaps first used by Moreno in Vienna.[2] Moreno used current newspaper stories as the basis for sociodramas. The basic human situation, the line of action implicit in that problem, and the kinds of characters involved are all taken from the newspaper accounts. This building up of an involved human situation requires exercise of analytical powers, imagination, background knowledge, and the ability to extrapolate — all of which is strenuous practice in communication skills.

For example: A news account in today's paper tells of a Halloween tragedy in Kansas City. A forty-year-old man was watching television in his own livingroom. Outside, a bunch of teen-agers were roaming the neighborhood, trick-or-treating. Some of these boys rang his doorbell. He went to the door and hastily told them not to bother him, shut the door, and returned to his television show. Some of those boys then threw rocks through the livingroom window, causing a shower of broken glass to burst in on him and his thirteen-month-old son. The man thrust the infant into his wife's hands, ran out into the front yard, and shouted angrily at the youths. One of them then threw a rock at him, and the whole group advanced on him. He reached into the front door of his house and grabbed a .22 calibre rifle and shot at the teen-agers.

A bullet narrowly missed one boy's head, and a second bullet struck another boy in the thigh. The teen-agers fled.

How could this news story be used for role playing?

One possibility is to set up a court scene, putting the man on trial for attempted murder. The *dilemma* set up for decision is whether to exonerate

[1]Harvey Tschirgi and John Stinson, "Sociodrama: A Learning Experience," *Improving College and University Teaching* (Winter 1972), p. 27.
[2]Jacob L. Moreno, *Psychodrama* (New York: Beacon House, 1946); *Who Shall Survive?* rev. ed. (New York: Beacon House, 1953).

the man of guilt on the basis that he was provoked beyond endurance by this attack on the peace and safety of his family or convict him of murderous assault on unarmed teen-agers.

The Scene: a court room.

The Characters: (1) the accused man, (2) the injured boy and his endangered companions, (3) judge, (4) prosecutor, (5) defense attorney, (6) witness for the defense (wife, neighbors), (7) witnesses for the prosecution (boys, neighbors), and (8) jury.

Line of Action: (1) The prosecution presents its case to the judge and jury. (2) The defense presents its case to the judge and jury. (3) The jury argues, arrives at a verdict, or fails to reach a verdict.

The Prosecution: The teen-agers' lawyer may say that the boys rang the man's doorbell, said "Trick or treat!" and he angrily told them to get lost. They called him a rotten sport, and he ordered them to get off his property or he'd beat their brains out. Angered, they threw rocks at his house. Some rocks broke his livingroom window. They had no intent to commit bodily harm: They just lost their tempers and wanted to teach him a lesson.

Witnesses for the Teen-agers: Neighbors and passersby may say that trick-or-treating in their neighborhood is an accepted Halloween custom and it is rare for a resident to refuse to give even a token treat and, instead, to order young people off his property.

The Defense: The man's lawyer may argue that the man was peacefully watching a favorite television program, his infant son on his lap, when rocks came crashing through his livingroom window, destroying expensive panes of glass, hurling shards of razor-sharp glass upon him and his small child that might have blinded them or been imbedded in their necks or bodies and left them bleeding to death.

Witnesses for the Man May State: After all, giving a treat was strictly a voluntary matter and that refusal to give a treat was usually accepted good-naturedly or by nothing more drastic by way of retaliation than soaping of windows. This rock-throwing was unusual, inexcusable, not to be tolerated.

The Role of the Jury Is to Decide on Questions Such As: (1) What was the intention of the teen-agers? (2) What was the result of their behavior? (3) What was the possible outcome of their behavior? (4) What was the man's intention? (5) What was the actual result of his behavior? (6) What was the possible result of his behavior? (7) Was the man provoked beyond endurance? (8) Was he justified in using as much force as he did in retaliation? (9) Is he guilty of murderous assault or is he innocent?

This case can be used in a language arts class in several ways.

Composition. The lawyers for the defense have to interview witnesses and the accused to gather data to write a coherent brief. Similarly, the prosecution side has to question witnesses and the accusers and prepare arguments to present to the judge and jury.

The class may be divided into two groups: One group prepares a case to prove that the man attacked the boys with a deadly weapon with murderous intent. The other group may prepare a case to prove that the boys unjustifiably attacked a man and child who were peacefully and innocently watching television in the privacy of their own home.

Reading. The class may be assigned to reading newspapers and magazines for similar cases, to find precedents for the defense or prosecution stands that they will take.

Speech. Lawyers for the defense and the prosecution will have an opportunity to present their arguments before the jury (and the remainder of the class who are observers). The judge may sum up.

In the jury room, members of the jury will argue their own opinions on the merits of the arguments presented to them by the adversary lawyers.

Dilemmas of Tact

The following two stories are short but complete dilemma situations. Assign students to work with one or the other story and have them list four or five alternatives for solving the dilemma. Then ask them to select two and write endings to the story. Stress the fact that whatever decision Jimmy makes and acts on, *it has consequences.* Students should develop these consequences in the endings they write. (For example, if Jimmy goes home without buying the bakery goods he was supposed to get, what happens at home? Or if he tells the young woman she has shoved in ahead of everybody else, how does she react? How do the other people in the line react?)

Your Turn Next

The Problem: Females will sometimes deliberately take advantage of the traditional "ladies first" privileges accorded them by considerate males. They will sometimes take these privileges for granted instead of waiting for them to be offered. Unthinking girls or women will even impose upon a young boy. (This is not to imply that men are never inconsiderate. For the moment, we are discussing the "ladies first" problem.)

Introducing the Problem: You might say to your class, "Have any of you, as a child, ever lost your turn waiting in line because an adult deliberately stepped in ahead of you? In some cases, perhaps, you were simply overlooked; in others you were imposed upon. This is a story about such an incident. As you listen to it, think back on your own experiences. How did you feel when some adult (a woman, if you were a boy) robbed you of your turn? Did you think it was unfair? Did you protest? Did you just gulp and say nothing?"

Jimmy Lee is in the corner bakery, impatiently waiting for his turn to buy the rolls and cake his mother sent him to get. It is late afternoon and the bakery is crowded with customers. Jimmy is in a hurry because he is due at the ball park to pitch for his Little League team. When he came in, he drew a number slip from the little machine on the counter. His number is 17. And the indicator on the wall behind the counter says *"NOW SERVING*: No. 16." He sighs with relief; he will be next.

A woman carrying a baby pushes past him to the counter. She doesn't notice the little number-dispensing machine—or else she deliberately ignores it. She calls out to the clerk who has just finished with the number-sixteen customer: "Please give me two loaves of whole wheat bread."

Jimmy feels a rush of red-hot anger. Why didn't the woman draw a number like everybody else and go to the end of the line? Behind him, Jimmy hears people mutter and stir; they've also noticed how the woman has crowded in ahead of him.

What should he do? Speak up? Say, "Ma'am, I think I'm ahead of you? I have slip number seventeen."

Will she—and the clerk and the other grown-ups—think he's a smart-aleck kid? Will she just ignore him? Will she say, sweetly, "Oh, a big strong boy like you won't mind doing me a favor, will you?" Maybe she never noticed the sign. Maybe she'll be very embarrassed. Maybe she'll blush and mumble, "Sorry," and hurry to the end of the line? She has a nice face, she does look tired, and she's holding a big heavy baby. Maybe she has to hurry home and fix dinner for a husband who'll come bursting in at six o'clock and yell, "All right, where's dinner?" or maybe she's one of those women who are always expecting males to step aside for them just because they are females.

What should he do?

Mind Your Own Business

The Problem: Andy sees Marta pick up a compact in a store and drop it into her purse. He also sees that the manager has noticed too. Andy knows that the manager will not do anything until Marta leaves the store, and then he will stop her. Marta is a pretty girl whom Andy would like to date. His impulse is to warn her to save her from being arrested. But he has misgivings. If he tells her to put the compact back because she's been seen stealing it, she'll always feel constrained with him afterward. She'll hate him for knowing she tried to steal, and she'll avoid him. There are other factors to consider. Maybe she's a spoiled, pretty girl who's in the habit of stealing. She should be stopped—now. Why is he so concerned about her, anyway? Just because she's a pretty girl he'd like to know? Would he care so much what happened to her if she were plain looking?

Introducing the Problem: You might ask your group, "Have you ever watched somebody you know steal something? Maybe it was just some apples off a tree, or a toy or bicycle. I'm sure you worried about your friend being caught. In this story I'm going to read you, Andy sees a girl steal something in a store. He also sees that she is going to be caught. His impulse is to warn her. Then he realizes that it might be a mistake. Maybe some of you have been in such a spot. As I read, think of ways in which you might end this story."

Andy, buying some socks in a department story, sees Marta pick up a compact from a counter and drop it into her purse. He is shocked. He is even more disturbed when, looking around to see if anyone else has noticed, he sees the manager staring at Marta. He obviously saw her taking the compact and is now watching her to see if she will take anything else.

Marta saunters down the aisle, like any browsing customer, and turns down another aisle to study the pretty scarves on display. The manager strolls after her, like a panther silently stalking an unsuspecting fawn. Just as quietly, Andy follows them. His pulse is pounding and his thoughts are churning. All too clearly he foresees what will happen: Marta will finally give up "browsing" and walk out the front door. And once she is outside, the manager will grab her. Until then, legally, she isn't guilty of shoplifting. A shoplifter has to actually leave the premises with a stolen article before the act is definitely a crime.

Why did she do it? Andy asks himself. She's a nice girl, a pretty girl. Why does she have to do such a stupid thing? Maybe she's sick. Maybe she's a . . . kleptomaniac. Maybe she's joining some girl's club and she has to steal something as part of her initiation. Maybe her folks are really poor and she desperately wants a nice compact to carry on a date. Or maybe she's just a spoiled, pretty girl who's used to pampering herself.

But *why* she did it isn't important just now, he realizes. She's in a jam. After the manager grabs her, he'll call a cop. And she'll wind up in Juvenile Hall, and there'll be stories in the paper about the daughter of a prominent local family caught shoplifting. Or maybe the manager will call her family. Her father and mother will rush down here, all weepy and heartsick; they'll pay for the compact and they'll apologize over and over to the manager and beg him not to prosecute. Everybody will be miserable.

What can I do? Andy asks himself.

He could catch up with Marta. He could whisper to her, "Look, go to the front window with that compact, look at it real close in the light, then shake your head as if it isn't really what you want, and take it back to the counter where you got it and leave it there. Thay way, you don't get arrested!"

But if he does this, she'll probably hate him. She'll always avoid him. He'll be somebody who knows something bad about her. She'll tell her friends he's a crude guy and should be avoided. *And what if I'm wrong about the manager? Maybe he didn't see her take that compact. Maybe he's just sauntering around the store keeping a general eye on things.* Possible. But not likely. She may be a habitual thief. If so, the best thing that could happen would be for her to be caught now, and a stop put to her stealing. If she needs help from doctors, she should get it early, before she does something too big to be overlooked.

But why are you so upset about her? he asks himself. She's not some cousin of yours. You don't really know her. Suppose she wasn't a pretty young girl but a man. Would you worry about him? No! You'd let things take their course. If he got nabbed, fine. He had it coming. Or if she were a frowsy old professional shoplifter? You wouldn't give her a second thought. Even if she were a girl but a plain or even homely girl you didn't know, would you butt in? No. You'd mind your own business. But just because she's a pretty girl, somebody you'd like to know, you're all bothered, you're beating your brains out to find a way to help. Is that really being fair?

What should he do?

Capsule Situations for Dilemma Stories

Ask your students to develop one of the following capsule situations into a dilemma story. The main character should make a decision and act on it. Then the consequences of that decision and the feelings of the people involved should be described.

1. Your friend Jerry, who lives next door, is a year older than you and has a driver's license and a car. It's not much of a car; in fact, it's a real junker. He leaves it parked at the curb of the dead-end street where you live. Your parents don't like having it parked there. It makes the neighborhood look junky, for one thing; and for another, it sets up a roadblock for any big truck or hook-and-ladder vehicle that might have to turn around at this end of the street. Your father decides to call your friend's father and ask him to have the old wreck parked elsewhere. This upsets you. Your friend will get mad at you. He'll make nasty remarks about you and your family at school. You ask your father not to call. You say you'll take care of the matter. You'll talk to Jerry yourself. "Okay, go ahead," says your father. "But if you can't get that kid to move that pile of junk, I'll handle it myself."

2. Your parents are having a Sunday afternoon party in the garden. The family next door is similarly having a party in their garden. But they are having a barbecue. The smoke from their barbecue is drifting over the fence into your garden, and your parents are getting livid with rage. Your mother asks you to go next door and tell the people that they are creating a nuisance with their barbecue smoke. You are reluctant to go. Your family is Japanese. You expect you'll get a very icy reception. You foresee a lot of neighborhood gossip about your family getting spread around—that they are stuck-up, touchy, and unfriendly.

3. A neighbor phones your parents indignantly, charging that while you were playing in the street, you hit a ball that smashed the picture window of their living room. You didn't do it; you weren't even at bat when it happened. But you know who did do it. If you squeal on your friend, however, you'll really be in trouble with him.

4. You come home early from school one day, and you discover that your ten-year-old brother and the twelve-year-old boy from next door are sitting behind the garage, smoking cigarettes. You realize, as you overhear from inside the garage, that the neighbor boy is egging your little brother on to smoke. What should you do? Rush out and make a big scene? Stop the smoking and send the neighbor kid home? You'd humiliate your brother. He'd say again, "You're not my Mom!" as he has said so many times before when you've tried to straighten him out. Although you're older than he, you're not much bigger. His friends would jeer at him for letting a bossy sister run his life. If you tell your parents, your brother will consider you a snitch. If you go to the other boy's parents and complain that he's setting a bad example for your brother, they'll perhaps be polite to you but they won't like you for it. They don't supervise their children very closely. What should you do?

"Getting Even" Situations

One of the strongest of all emotions is the outrage one feels when one has suffered an injustice. In the first wild heat of such a mood, one wants to pay back in kind for the wrong inflicted. Children are especially prone to feel burning desires to "get even." But behavior motivated by the urge for revenge is often unwise and far out of proportion to the cause. The wronged individual too often inflicts an even greater wrong than the one suffered. Moreover, when a so-called wrong is studied dispassionately, it often proves to have been something other than the vicious act it seemed at first.

The "Getting Even" stories in this volume can provide motivation for writing eloquently about such feelings. The stories (pp. 199–209) are: "Money for Marty," "Tell-Tale," "Eyewitness," and "You're Not Invited." All of them stop at the dilemma point. Students can therefore write endings in order to gain practice in exploring the feelings aroused by the need for revenge.

In writing extensions and endings for these stories, students should analyze

1. How a person feels who has suffered a wrong
2. Why the individual who committed the wrong behaved as he or she did
3. Why people try to get even
4. Whether the punishment fits the crime
5. The possible consequences of the act of revenge upon people other than the original wrongdoer.

USING ROLE PLAYING TO MOTIVATE READING

Role-playing situations have been ingeniously used to intrigue nonreaders into reading. Marcia Pitcole has developed a "previewing" technique that uses twenty dramatic scenes from Richard Wright's novel, *Black Boy*.[3] She briefly summarized each scene on a small card, describing the situation from the chief character's point of view. However, instead of naming the character, she substituted the pronoun "you." In effect, she placed the reader of the card in each critical situation. Then, at the bottom of the card, she added the question: "What would you do?" and gave further instructions.

Here is a sample scene.

You are in grade school and are accused of eating nuts in class and dropping shells on the floor. It was the boy in front of you, and you know it. The teacher is going to whip you with a switch. The boy in front of you says nothing. What would you say and do?

---

[3]Marcia Pitcole, "*Black Boy* and Role Playing: A Scenario for Reading Success," *The English Journal*, 57 (November 1968), 1140–42.

After writing down his or her decision, the student was then instructed to go to the novel (page numbers were given), read the scene in its original form, and summarize how the novel character actually solved the problem. The student could then compare his or her own decision with the one made by the hero of the novel.

After completing these papers, the students read their individual responses aloud in class. Discussion ensued. So much interest in the novel was generated that half the class signed out the book to read it in its entirety. Considering that this was a group of nonreaders, this "previewing" technique was heart-warmingly successful.

USING ROLE PLAYING
FOR SPEECH IMPROVEMENT

Young people who have acquired their speech habits in poverty-stricken homes often suffer a language deficit when they try to compete in the larger world. They can, of course, communicate in their own surroundings. But when they apply for jobs in offices and plants, too often their ability to earn a living at congenial work is limited by their language handicap.

English teachers in general believe that nonstandard speech has its rightful place in a student's life. Pidgin English, black English, Spanish, Tagalog, and Ilokano, all have their own validity. But a large percentage of our minority population who do not speak standard English are handicapped. Their speech is an obstacle to social acceptance and to upward mobility in the United States mainstream society. This handicap can be overcome. With help from sophisticated teachers, with strong motivation and determined effort, young people can acquire the language skills that will provide them with a broader choice of job and career alternatives, along with a greater ability to compete with members of the mainstream society.

Stimulating such students to make an effort to improve their speech is not simple or easy. Too many of them are not aware of the need to acquire better speech habits, nor are they motivated to make the continuing effort necessary to achieve them. For many such students, making better grades and winning teacher and parent approval is not a strong incentive. They fail to see that language skill is a basic survival tool. It is often difficult to induce them to work hard to develop abilities that do not result in an immediate payoff.

However many of these young people can be caught up in a drama which presents human problems that have a personal impact. Role playing can provide such a powerful stimulus for language use. Role playing can provide an opportunity for these young people to use English appropriate to the dramatic circumstances. Dramatic role playing creates a momentum of interest that sweeps participants along.

Highly charged situations evoke strong feelings, and feelings erupt into language—often into rapt, ardent discussions. Guiding such discussions, the teacher can gradually lift young people's responses to higher levels. The teacher can make students aware of distortions of perception and expression. The teacher can also make them aware that putting complicated feelings and reasons into words requires a greater refinement of meaning that can be achieved only by an ever-increasing range, flexibility, and accuracy of language.

Peer Group Support

Young people are often prevented from acquiring correct speech habits by their peer groups. If a boy uses better language than his friends, they are apt to jeer at him. The family too may be an obstacle; in some culture groups, the young person who tries to learn to speak well is seen as trying selfishly to rise above his family. Among groups that abhor competition, this is a grave sin.

Lee Salisbury sums up the problem: "It becomes the responsibility of the school to teach skills, attitudes, and concepts which the student has not been able to acquire at home (or situationally). Indeed, school can provide a sheltered environment in which the student can experiment with his language and behavior without the rejection and ridicule that he must encounter in daily life." In fact, as Salisbury emphasizes, ". . . *language change can take place only with peer group support.*"[4]

Role playing in school provides the setting in which young people can be motivated to use Standard English and receive the support of their peers while doing so. Salisbury uses games and improvisations in which young people act out problem situations. These impromptu dramas involve real concerns such as, *What do you do when you're sent to the principal's office for fighting on the playground?* Most young people are aware of the roles of the significant people in their lives. In enacting such roles in the classroom, they try to speak as the authority figures they know speak, they try to use Standard English. Their efforts receive the support and encouragement of their peers, who see the roles realistically. By playing the roles of educated people, the students try to use the speech of educated people. Such experiences will do much to help them acquire Standard English.

Salisbury sums up:

> We must not lose sight of the way that a human being learns new behaviors or makes them his own. He tries them on somewhat cautiously in a situation where he anticipates no criticism, and if they "work" he may use them again in another more threatening situation. As he develops confidence in their usefulness, they become a part of him. . . . As a natural human behavior, role playing can provide a bridge between classroom drill and real-life utilization of new language patterns. It can give zest and relevance to the process of language change.[5]

[4]Lee Salisbury, "Role Playing: Rehearsal for Language Change," *TESOL QUARTERLY*, 4, No. 4, 1970.
[5]Ibid.

English for the Foreigner

What is the most enjoyable way for a foreign student to learn English? (Or anyone else, for that matter?) Through drama, says Richard Via, language specialist for the United States Information Service. It is not only the most enjoyable way, it is also the most effective way, suggests Mr. Via, who has taught English to future teachers in various Asian countries. Drama, he says, transforms a language lesson into a "living experience . . . rather than another tedious class hour."⁶ Via's technique has been popular in a number of Asian countries.

Via has found that the teaching methods used in American acting courses and Broadway rehearsals are useful in teaching language. Over a two-year span he presented five full-length plays and fifteen one-act plays in Japanese colleges. The reaction of some 400 participating students and 14,000 observers, he notes, "was overwhelming." Students were not just studying English, he says, but using it and understanding it. They were not merely memorizing lines but *communicating*. Everything about the performances was done in English: make-up, sets, lighting, costumes, directing. Students were not merely practicing English vocabularly but *functioning* in English for necessary and important communication.

Salisbury and Via are just two of many instructors who urge the use of drama as a potent aid to language improvement.⁷ The literature of role playing reveals extensive support for this view. Black kindergarteners, Chicano children, even young people of such widely different groups as Eskimos and speakers of Hawaiian pidgin—individuals far removed from mainstream American culture—experience role playing as a vital rehearsal for language change. Role playing provides a bridge from formal classroom drill in better language to the spontaneous use, in life outside of school, of acceptable English. In projects that contrasted language growth between groups that did role playing and groups that were limited to discussion, the children who had the improvisation experience made markedly more progress in bettering their language than did the group that was confined to just discussing human problems. To sum up: Consistent use of dramatic activities in the classroom significantly improves both the oral and written English of children of widely different abilities and home backgrounds.

Reality Practice

Role playing need not always focus on dilemma situations. It can also provide excellent practice in coping with common, but difficult situations and using standard English. The teacher sets up situations such as the following in the classroom for the students to handle. (Students may help by volunteering situations they find awkward.)

⁶Richard Via, "Drama as Catalyst for Learning Another Language," *The Honolulu Advertiser* (May 28, 1976).
⁷Eloise Hays, "Drama, Big News in English," *The English Journal*, 47, No. 1 (January 1970), 15. See also Robin C. Scarcella, "Socio-Drama for Social Interaction," TESOL QUARTERLY, 12, No. 1 (March 1978), 41–45.

1. Applying for a job
2. Buying wisely something you want very much
3. Getting help in an emergency such as:
    a. A car accident
    b. A fire in the home
    c. When you're baby-sitting and:
        —A child suddenly gets frighteningly ill
        —The lights suddenly go off all through the house
        —A prowler tries to open a door very quietly
        —The kitchen suddenly starts flooding with water from a broken drainpipe under the sink.
        —The parents who hired you do not arrive at 11 P.M. as they promised and your parents have ordered you to be home by midnight at the latest—and it's past midnight now
4. Going home from school, you see a man breaking into a locked car
5. While you and your mother are driving home late at night, the car stalls and can't be started
6. You and friends need to take the bus home, but when you get on the bus you don't have the required exact change
7. You go to a beach and see a sign: THIS BEACH OFF-LIMITS TO MILITARY PERSONNEL: DANGEROUS RIPTIDES
8. You see small children who are playing with matches and are about to start a brush fire
9. Your father has bought a gasoline mower for your yard and it's your day to mow the lawn. But he's not home and you don't understand the directions for starting the mower.

Learning Languages Other than English

So far, we have focused on the need for children with a language deficit to learn to speak acceptable English. But there is also a great need for children who do speak good English to learn other languages. Role playing can also be of help in this process. It can help young people acquire enough skill in speaking useful, everyday foreign words and phrases to get along in a foreign country. Foreign-language role playing sets up situations in which students must use the new language for introductions, greetings, and fare-wells and numbers, dates, and time. As they gain greater proficiency, they learn how to handle weather inquiries, telephone conversations, ordering from menus, shopping, and asking directions. This is a basic minimum of language learning, of course, but it is so useful that most students demand to go on to more difficult tasks.

EXERCISES

The following story situations provide materials for both creative writing and speech improvement. The situations require the students to step into the roles of educated people who use English with variety and precision. The first story is fairly well developed and provides an easy entry into this kind of project; the others will require more fleshing out. Ask the students, as they enact (or write) the stories, to invent dialog to fit the roles and the circumstances in each case—that is, as they play a role, they should try to speak in the way they think the character would speak in real life. Realism of character portrayal should be the main subject of any discussion after role playing or writing.

The Wrong Mrs. Smith

Mary and Nora are high school sophomores. This afternoon, going home from school, they cut across the well-kept grounds of a big resort hotel. They feel a bit daring; their parents are working people, and they are trespassing in a place they would never visit as guests.

Then, under a bush, they find a woman's purse—a nice purse, so nice and simple it must be expensive. Somebody lost it and is probably awfully upset. They look inside for the name of the owner. There are only a few things, surprisingly—a clump of Kleenex, a ring of keys, a compact, a roll of Lifesavers, and a roll of Tums, but no wallet, and no money. However, there is a thick sheaf of fifty-dollar traveler's checks.

"No wallet, no credit cards, no driver's license, no letters, no bills. What happened?" Mary wonders aloud. "It's simple," Nora says. "Somebody snatched this purse from the owner, took the wallet with the money inside, and threw the rest away." "But how about the traveler's checks? They're money!" Mary says. "Purse-snatchers don't fool with credit cards and traveler's checks," Nora says. "Trying to use a stolen credit card, or forging a name on a traveler's check, is just asking for trouble. You really get thrown into the penitentiary for that! But cash—you can spend it anywhere with no questions asked. This batch of traveler's checks—gosh, it's a couple thousand dollars' worth, looks like. How do we find the owner?"

"She's probably a tourist staying in the hotel here," Mary reasons aloud. "But we don't know her name!" Nora says. "Say, it ought to be on the traveler's checks!"

There is a name on the traveler's checks: Smith—no first name, just an initial. But the owner has such poor handwriting that they can't tell whether that initial is a U, an A, or an N.

She is probably in the hotel, the girls decide. They go to the main entrance, walk into the lobby. A bellman frowns at them, but they march up to the registration desk.

"We want to talk to Mrs. Smith," they tell the clerk.

He stares down his nose at them, as if to say, What're you hoodlum kids doing in a ritzy joint like this? He says, impatiently: "Which Mrs. Smith? We have three Mrs. Smiths as guests this week."

Nora says, "Mrs. A. Smith. She's my aunt."

The haughty clerk doesn't believe her. He questions them. Are they sure their aunt is in this hotel? What do they want to see her about? Nora stalls him. Finally he says he can't let them go up to the Smith room unless he knows what their business is. A man has come up beside them; he is an army officer in uniform, and he has been listening. The man angrily bawls the clerk out. The clerk has no business prying into guests' affairs. Either the clerk accommodates the young women immediately or he, the guest, will take his complaint to the top management. The clerk mumbles something about scruffy kids always causing so much trouble, but then says curtly, "Mrs. Smith's in Room 406."

Mary and Nora go to Room 406 and knock on the door. It is opened by a kindly, middle-aged woman. She invites them in, asks their names, urges them to be seated. She senses their uneasiness and makes small-talk to ease their self-consciousness. Where do they go to school? She's a schoolteacher, she tells them; she and her husband are here on a wedding anniversary trip. Her husband is out, talking to the police. They had something stolen from their rented car.

"A purse?" Mary blurts. "No," Mrs. Smith says. "A camera." "Is that all?" Mary persists. Mrs. Smith goes to the bureau, picks up a purse, and shows it to them. She opens it, looks in, and finds everything intact. Then she asks, "Is that what you wanted to see me about?"

They tell her the story, then. When they finish, she says that maybe one of the other two Mrs. Smiths in the hotel lost a purse. They should go see the other women. But they don't know the room numbers, they tell her.

Mrs. Smith phones the desk; and when the room clerk gets inquisitive, she tells him in a tactful way that it's none of his business. It's a private matter but an important one. She gets the room numbers of the other two Mrs. Smiths.

The girls thank her. She praises them for trying to find the owner of the purse, and they leave.

Mary and Nora go to Room 810. They knock on the door. It is opened by a tall, beautifully dressed woman of forty or so. She has gorgeous blonde hair, fine features, and a shapely figure. She is obviously a woman who is used to the best things in life. She eyes them forbiddingly for a moment, then asks what she can do for them. Mary asks if she's Mrs. Smith. The woman nods and says, "So?"

Mary asks, "Have you lost a purse? Or had one stolen?"

The woman's eyes sharpen. "You found a purse on the hotel grounds?" she demands. Mary says nothing but Nora blurts a yes. The woman's manner changes. She becomes charming. "Yes," she says. She had gone shopping and, returning with her arms full of bundles, she had dropped her purse. Or maybe it was slipped from under her arm by a thief and she never noticed. Are her things still inside? Her traveler's checks?

Mary doesn't answer; Nora starts to nod but checks herself and looks away. "Have you got the purse with you?" she demands. "Oh, do come in," she urges.

They enter. The woman says she's so grateful to them for finding her purse. Mary says, "Would you please describe the purse?" The woman says that once she examines it, she can tell for sure whether it's actually hers or another one that resembles it, of which there must be many, it is such a common travel item! She sounds rather gushy and insincere.

Mary asks if there was a compact in her purse.

The woman hesitates a moment, then says yes. She has several compacts; probably it was her gold compact—gold-plated, that is. And, asks Mary, was there anything else in her purse? Oh, yes. Her wallet. She didn't remember how much cash, but not an awful lot. Then little things—a handkerchief, and probably her comb, and maybe she'd left some cigarettes in the bag. And some traveler's checks, of course. When you went on a trip you had to bring traveler's checks. The girls could keep the cash, whatever it was; she didn't mind. It was the traveler's checks she was worried about. Would they let her see the purse now? She could tell at a glance if it is hers.

But Nora tells her sweetly to just go down to the desk and ask the clerk for the purse. He'll be glad to return it to her. Mrs. Smith is so delighted that she wants to give the girls a reward; but they head for the door, and Mary says hurriedly that they're just doing their good deed for the day.

Out in the hall, the two girls look at each other and choke back their laughter. The compact in the purse, Mary says, isn't gold at all but *blue cloisonné*! What a phoney that woman is! Wait till she tries to claim that purse from the desk clerk! She's a mean one, Nora says. Is she going to be mad when she finds out we played a trick on her! We better get out of here. No, Mary says, they've got to try the third Mrs. Smith. Maybe she's the right one.

They find Room 1212. Mary lifts her hand to knock, but Nora grabs her hand and stops her. Nora's face is suddenly very troubled. Mary asks what's wrong. Nora says she just had an awful thought. So tell me, Mary insists. Nora pulls her away from the door and whispers to her. Maybe this third Mrs. Smith really *is* the one who lost the purse. That'll be wonderful. Oh, yeah? Nora says. Listen. Suppose this third Mrs. Smith looks in the purse and says, "Hey, where's my wallet? Where's the hundred dollars cash I had?" And she glares at them and says, "You give me back that money!"

"Oh, no," Mary protests. They're bringing the purse back. That proves they're honest. "No," Nora says. "Suppose she's the kind of sneaky person who thinks some smart-aleck kids would steal her money then have the gall to bring the purse back and try to work her for a reward! Maybe we're just asking for real trouble. Let's get out of here!"

Mary nods; but she feels very troubled and hesitates. "But," she says, "suppose she's a nice person like the first Mrs. Smith? Maybe she needs these traveler's checks real bad? I'd hate to be mean to a person like that!"

"Come on!" Nora insists. "We can't take a chance!"

Mary says . . .

The Accuser

Janet has just gotten a job in a department store, clerking in women's wear. She sees a woman slip a scarf off the counter into her handbag. As the woman turns away, Janet grabs her arm and calls to the older clerk behind the counter. And Janet blurts out to the older clerk that she saw this woman steal a scarf.

The woman is middle-aged, well-dressed, and is obviously a person of education and background. She is outraged. She did not steal a scarf. She has not stolen anything, she insists very angrily and very haughtily. The young lady, she says scornfully of Janet, has made a bad mistake.

"Let go of her arm," the older clerk whispers urgently to Janet. "You'll be in real trouble if the boss finds out!" Janet lets go of the woman's arm but demands that the woman show the contents of her purse. That, says the woman, is an indignity to which she will not submit. And to the older clerk, the woman says that if she (the older clerk) prefers to accept the word of "this ignorant child to mine," she will hand over her purse to be searched. But if she is forced to tolerate such an affront, she will immediately thereafter go to the front office, ask to see her friend the general manager, and tell him how she has been treated in this store. "Now what do you want to do?" the customer demands of the older clerk and Janet. "Are you going to get out of my way and permit me to proceed about my business—or do you want to search my purse?"

The older clerk apologizes to the customer and says that her assistant is new to the job and is of course mistaken and that, of course, they won't search the customer's purse. She is free to go.

When the customer stalks away, Janet turns furiously to the older clerk and says that she saw the woman steal the scarf. She *saw* her do it! But, the older clerk tells her, until a customer actually walks out of a store with a stolen item, she cannot be legally stopped and accused. And, says the older clerk, suppose Janet *is* mistaken? Then that customer would sue the store! What does Janet think would happen to her job?

Janet says she'll follow the thief outside and yell for a cop. Otherwise they're just letting her get away with her theft! The older clerk says to forget it—and go back to work. She turns to wait on a customer, gesturing for Janet to wait on the person who has just come to her side of the counter. Janet hesitates, peering after the thief who is hurrying toward the front door. . . .

Hijacker

1. You are a teacher, and on your way to school one morning you discover two of your eighth-grade boys "hijacking" a fifth grader: They are taking his lunch money. One of the eighth-grade boys is the son of a close friend of yours. What do you say and do?

2. You are a policeman and you come upon this hijacking.

3. You are a local minister, and you witness this incident. The boys all go to your Sunday school. (You may be a Protestant clergyman, or a Catholic cleric, or a rabbi.)

Where There's Smoke

You get a job as a receptionist in a dentist's office. A couple of teen-age boys come in and sit down. While waiting for their turn, they start smoking. You point to the sign on the wall over your desk: THANK YOU FOR NOT SMOKING. Sullenly they put out their cigarettes. Presently a woman patient comes in, gives you her name, and takes a chair. She's a fine-looking, gray-haired woman, well-dressed, charming, and confident of manner. The dentist comes in from his lab for a moment, nods to everybody, but is especially cordial to the gray-haired woman, holding her hand and asking about her husband. He tells her to make herself comfortable, and that he won't keep her waiting long.

The dentist goes back to work. The gray-haired woman takes a pack of cigarettes from her purse, selects one, and lights up, sighing with gusto as she exhales.

The two boys glare at you. Presently they take out their cigarettes and, deliberately, watching you, they start to light up.

And you . . .

Bus Fare

You are a retired librarian. You now work as a clerk, part-time, in a bookstore to add to your pension. You have just finished an ice-cream soda in a drug store, and you are waiting in line at the cash register to pay your bill. You're impatient because you'll have to hurry to catch your bus to go to work.

Two twelve-year-olds are ahead of you at the cash register. The owner of the shop is giving them a bad time. They don't have enough money to pay their bill. The furious owner is telling them that he is sick and tired of being ripped off by no-good kids like them. They've done this to him before—walking out without paying their bill. They protest that they've never done that. Well, if it wasn't them, he charges, it was kids like them. Once and for all, he's going to make an example of them!

You interrupt. You offer the kids change to phone their mother to come pay their bill. She can't, they say; she's at work. The owner then says their mother can come after work to pick them up at the station house—because he's calling a cop.

You look into your wallet. You have just enough money with you to pay your bill and take the bus—or pay your bill and the kids' bill, but no more. You'll have to walk to work. And it's a new job. You don't want to come in late.

You say . . .

IMPROVISATION FOR UNDERSTANDING LITERATURE

Many teachers use role playing as an aid in teaching literature. Gene Stanford writes:

> Role playing can make a special contribution to learning that sit-and-talk approaches cannot accomplish. It can help students develop empathy for characters in literature as well as insight into their behavior faster than any other method, and until modern science develops a better way to exchange places with another person, role playing is the nearest we can come to *being* another person. In role playing, a student can try to see things from another person's point of view and to respond as he would respond. By consciously trying to be the other person, the student gains an understanding of him and a deeper sensitivity to his feelings.[8]

Dan Donlan also considers improvisation to be very effective in enabling students to grasp the human subtleties of literary works.[9] Donlan uses drama in a three-stage teaching procedure which he calls (1) *warm-up*, (2) *improvisation* (role-playing), and (3) *evaluative assessment*. Donlan recommends an elaborate warm-up sequence that becomes progressively more demanding. (It must, of course, be suited to the maturity level of the students involved.) Then he moves the group into improvisation; he begins with nonverbal exercises and pantomime that grow into impromptu dialog skits involving dilemma conflicts. This experience culminates with a group analysis of the choices made in resolving the dilemmas and in evaluating the level of moral sophistication evidenced by these choices.

Warm-Up Activities

The purpose of the warm-up exercises is, of course, to reduce self-consciousness as young children and teen-agers start to do role playing before their peers and to provide practice in impromptu acting. Donlan suggests a variety of warm-up activities, such as:

1. Pairing off and pretending to play catch. Students pantomime throwing a ball back and forth. Variety and interest is gained by pretending that the ball changes from a pingpong ball to a tennis ball to a hard baseball, and finally to a heavy medicine ball. The miming should be realistic and requires that the players constantly adjust to the physical aspects of the different balls being thrown.

---

[8]Gene Stanford, "Why Role Playing Fails," *The English Journal* (December 1974), p. 50. Despite the title, this article strongly supports role playing; it discusses mistakes made by novices.

[9]Dan Donlan, "Drama and the Three Stages of Teaching Literature," *The English Journal* (February 1977), p. 74.

2. Imitating animal behavior. Young people can mime such animal events as a prairie dog popping up out of his hole, peering around, shrilling an alarm, and dodging back into his lair; a cat stalking a bird; a monkey grooming himself; a buzzard soaring on a thermal current; a dog hiding a bone; a kitten trying to make friends with an indifferent human; a dog chasing a ball being thrown by a small boy in a crowded apartment; or a duck leading a brood of ducklings across a road busy with traffic.

3. Forming geometric patterns. In small groups, the young people form circles, squares, triangles, and rectangles. This can be an easy, informal horizontal exercise or a strenuous, acrobatic, hilarious vertical one.

4. Pantomiming human activities. After doing some of the simpler activities, the group can move into more advanced pantomiming, either individually or in small groups. Such activities might include striking out a batter; winning at a slot machine and scrambling to gather the small avalanche of coins; flipping pancakes in a skillet; ironing a shirt; tossing a victim in a blanket, catching him as he comes down, tossing him even higher and higher. Another amusing skit is to have a boy, who speaks only English, try to make a date with a willing girl who speaks no English; he might through pantomime suggest such activities as skiing, swimming, clam digging, and so on. These activities are continued until onlookers guess the nature of the activity being improvised.

Such warm-ups are usually fun for the students. But they also have a serious purpose: They create an atmosphere in which concentration on the activity helps reduce inhibiting self-consciousness. If the preparation has been thorough enough, the group is ready to go on to improvisation.

Improvisation

Donlan opens the session by giving each student an envelope containing a card on which is written a brief description of a character trait, such as the following:

> This person is an awkward bumbler who fouls up everything he or she tries to do.
> This person is touchy, irritable, and sees an insult in every effort to give him directions or suggestions on how to do something.
> This person is very slow and lazy.
> This person cannot do anything in front of other people without trying to get a laugh out of them.
> This person is so insecure and cautious that he or she cannot do anything without checking and rechecking constantly.
> This person is a flatterer; in every relationship he or she praises and overpraises, trying to be liked and accepted.
> This person is so self-absorbed in whatever he or she is doing that it is almost impossible to get him or her to cooperate in any group activity.
> This person is angrily impatient in everything he or she does.

This person is compulsively helpful; he butts in on everything another person is doing, trying to show him or her how to do it better.

This person is uncooperative; his favorite reaction to anything someone else asks him to do is "That's stupid!"

After giving all the members of the class a chance to read their cards, the teacher sets up a simple story situation. Students then volunteer or are selected at random to play the roles in the story and carry the story problem to a logical solution. (The story may or may not produce a dilemma.) The teacher may help the group set the stage, decide on the time, and tell them to begin. The enactment is entirely unrehearsed and spontaneous. In acting out the skit, each person plays the role in accordance with the character trait on the card he or she has received. (Of course, the story situation must lend itself to the creation of individual roles.) The best skit situations are those involving simple dilemmas—for example:

A boy has found a half-dollar. Another boy claims that it fell out of his pocket and is his. Both appeal to a witness.

A girl has picked a scarf off a counter in a women's shop. A clerk accuses her of stealing it. She insists that she walked toward the front door only to look at the scarf in clear daylight. The manager questions both of them, trying to decide what to do. Other customers intervene on both sides.

It's the school lunch hour, and Toby is biting into a big wedge of cherry pie when the teacher in charge and an angry girl come up to him. The girl accuses him of stealing her lunchbox. He denies it. The teacher asks where he got the pie. A friend gave it to him, he says. Who is the friend, the teacher asks. He hesitates . . .

Two boys have taken a friend's Moped for a ride, have had a spill, and have damaged it. They need money to get it repaired. One of the boys, who works as a bag boy in a supermarket, sees a customer drop a ten-dollar bill. He picks it up and looks around. No one has noticed. The woman is still in the parking lot. If he runs, he can catch her. But his friend has insisted he bring some money to him that evening . . .

A girl has promised to baby-sit for a friend of her mother's. The girl gets invited to a basketball game by a boy she very much wants to date. She thinks of a plausible lie to get out of the baby-sitting job. Her friend urges her to tell it.

A boy has promised to help his kid brother build a box kite. They are working on it together when friends stop by and invite the older boy to go water-skiing, which he very much wants to do.

A small girl, crying, tells the teacher supervising the play yard that two older girls hijacked her, taking a bracelet and some money. They deny it hotly. Search them, the younger girl insists. They refuse to be searched.

After each skit is enacted, the observing group is asked to identify the character trait each role player was working to portray.

Finally, when all the skits have been presented, the casts of characters are changed and the skits enacted a second time. This time, of course, the individuals playing the different roles are each portraying a *different* character trait; this produces varied reactions to the same problem and to each other, and possibly a different solution. With this second enactment (or third or fourth if time permits), the group is ready for the third stage of the project, the assessment.

Evaluation of the Dilemma Choices Made

Donlan then requires the students to discuss how the dilemma situations were solved. He presents a set of *guide questions* by which to judge these solutions. These guide questions are paraphrased from Lawrence Kohlberg's stages of children's moral development.[10]

With certain classes, Donlan believes that the formal Kohlberg terminology can be used. Kohlberg's classification, as listed by Donlan, reads:

  I. Preventional Level
    Stage 1: The punishment and obedience orientation
    Stage 2: The instrumental relativist orientation
 II. Conventional Level
    Stage 3: The interpersonal concordance, or "good boy-nice girl"
         orientation
    Stage 4: The "law-and-order" orientation
III. Postconventional, Autonomous, or Principled Level
    Stage 5: The social-contract legalistic orientation
    Stage 6: The universal ethical principle orientation

From these formal stages of moral development, Donlan abstracted a set of informal questions in language that young teen-agers could more readily understand:

1. Was the problem solved because the characters feared they would be punished in some way if they didn't agree?
2. Was the problem solved by some compromise where one character said, "I'll be good to you if you'll be good to me?"
3. Was the problem solved because the characters wanted to be "good guys" or "nice ladies"?
4. Was the problem solved because the characters felt law and order should be enforced?
5. Was the problem solved because people felt it was the civilized thing to do?
6. Was the problem solved because the characters acted out of a high and noble sense of what was right?[11]

In other words, did the person base his or her decision upon (1) fear of punishment? (2) horse-trading expediency? (3) a desire to win liking and approval? (4) a belief that it was necessary to enforce law and order? (5) a

[10]Lawrence Kohlberg, "The Child as Moral Philosopher," *Psychology Today* (September 1968), pp. 28–30.
[11]Donlan, op. cit., p. 75.

belief that the choice was the decent, civilized decision to make? or (6) a high and noble sense of what was right and just?

Donlan has had his students use Kohlberg's stages of moral development and his own guide questions in their reading. These stages and guidelines give them an "orientation by which to judge the ways in which the characters in [a literary work] make choices."[12] Donlan first requires the students to become familiar with the guide questions by applying them in discussions after the skits. Thus they are prepared to use them in assessing decision making in literature.

Donlan assigns the reading of a literary work such as a short story. One story Donlan uses is Jack Cady's "The Burning." It deals with a mercy killing. A truck driver, Gates, is forced to swing his rig into the ditch to avoid a head-on collision with two young women in a speeding car. The truck crashes and catches on fire. Gates, injured, is unable to extricate himself from the crumpled cab. Some passing truck drivers see the wreck, halt their rigs, and run to help him. Gates, however, is trapped. The flames are gradually engulfing the wreckage. He yells for help, then screams in agony as the heat reaches him. One of the other truck drivers shoots him. The "killer" is arrested. The young woman driver who caused the accident is let off with no penalty, except for the burden on her conscience.

After the students have read the story, Donlan suggests that they discuss it according to the guide questions. What dilemmas were confronted by the driver of the car which caused the accident and the truck drivers who stopped to try to help? Donlan asks the class to assess the morality of mercy killing and on which of Kohlberg's stages of moral development this decision falls.

Students usually eliminate the first four stages quickly. At the fifth stage, they must ask, "Did the killer believe that shooting the trapped man was the decent, civilized thing to do?" Students can make a good case for this motivation. The man who shot Gates acted out of empathy; he was trying to put an end to the victim's useless agony. This was an immensely decent motivation. Of course, killing (in the abstract) is not a "civilized" act. It is a heinous crime in every civilized society. But a doctor who operates in an effort to save a terminal cancer patient and loses the patient is not called a murderer. Yet the man who commits a mercy killing is arrested as a criminal.

Some students may urge that the decision was motivated by the sixth stage in the Kohlberg moral formulation, a "high and noble sense of what is right and just." A strong case could be made for this assessment, of course; but there may be some dissension. Someone may argue: Do we wish to set a categorical imperative for euthanasia? In such a situation, is immediate death the only method of preventing suffering? Suppose we don't have all the information? How would we feel if, in some cases, we discover we've made a mistake? No, some students may argue, we cannot make a general rule; we must always consider particular circumstances.

After working with the story "The Burning," Donlan assigns other literary works for study. Meanwhile, he helps the students refine their

[12]Ibid., p. 75.

improvisation, discussion, and writing skills by means of several group projects.

In one project, for example, the instructor reads the first part of a dilemma story to the group. The class divides into small groups of five or six. Each group then briefly discusses the situation that has been read to them, selects people to play the roles, and enacts a solution to the dilemma. Several of these improvisations are enacted before the whole class. The class discusses the stages of moral development that the actors use to solve the dilemma.

The enactments are short, for the class then convenes to listen to the end of the story, to see how close their improvisations came to the actual resolution.

In another exercise, the class is again divided into several groups. Each group then selects one of the guide questions and develops an improvisation around a problem situation such as one of the following.

Some Problem Situations

1. Johnny and Luke, hurrying to the airport to catch a plane, see a chipmunk at the edge of the road. It has been run over and its hind quarters are crushed on the concrete, but its front legs are scraping frantically. It is trying to drag itself off the road.

Johnny starts to slow the car and bring it to a stop. "We've got to put that poor thing out of its misery."

"We're late!" Luke protests. "We can't take the time!"

2. A party of fishermen has flown to a remote mountain lake. They've arranged for the bush pilot to return in three days to take them out. The fishing has been wonderful. On the third day, now, they start hiking out to the landing site where the pilot will pick them up. Resting on a rise, they look back—and see smoke. In their rush to break camp, they had not fully doused their campfire. It has flared up and started a fire in the brush.

"We've got to rush back and put it out before it runs clear out of control!"

"But if we're not at the rendezvous, the plane won't wait for us."

"Maybe it's not from our campfire but somebody else's. . ."

"Doesn't matter *who* started it! We've got to put it out."

"Gosh, man, be sensible. Look at the sky. It's clouding over. A storm'll hit us, and that pilot won't be able to come pick us up for days!"

"That storm'll put out the fire. . ."

"It may not hit till night, and by that time, the fire will have covered miles of timber. Come on!"

"But we're out of grub. Rain can turn to snow, and we're not outfitted for real cold. . ."

"You don't go off and leave a fire in the woods!"

3. Alan, sixteen years old, has had his driver's license suspended because of a speeding violation. His parents, just before going on a trip, had ordered him not to use the family car. He disobeys. One afternoon, he takes some friends to the beach. Next day, his younger brother asks for the car keys. He refuses. "You can't drive—you haven't got a driver's license." The younger brother insists he can drive as well as the older. And the younger brother threatens: "You don't give me the key, I'll tell Dad you took the car when he told you not to. You know how mad he'll be!" The older boy ponders. His younger brother can't drive as well as he thinks he can. He'll be a danger to himself and others on the highway. But the younger boy insists, "Aw, come on. There ain't much traffic on the road to the beach on week-days. No problem! If you don't, you're going to be in real trouble with Dad!"

Maybe he's right, the older boy thinks. But . . .

4. A young woman lies in a coma; she is being kept alive by sophisti-cated hospital machinery that keeps her lungs, heart, and kidneys function-ing. The doctors hold out no hope for recovery. Yet, they say that they must make every effort to prolong her life. They do not have all the answers; sometimes a patient in this condition does revive. The relatives are in great doubt. Are they merely prolonging a kind of pointless vegetable existence? The medical expenses are impoverishing the family. The patient may have already suffered brain death. Should they, as an act of mercy and of good sense, now "pull the plug"? But suppose there is still a chance that the patient will regain consciousness?

Appendix

Materials for Role Playing

In this book we have emphasized the basic process of role playing and the use of the problem story. However, other strategies and materials are useful in role playing. In working with young children (four to eight years of age), the use of large dilemma pictures is very successful.[1] There are many picture kits on the market that provide the teacher with resources for this approach.

Dilemma photographs are especially effective in stimulating young children to respond spontaneously in gesture and language. They also serve a very important function in the process of socialization; they can help children learn how to negotiate with one another to solve interpersonal problems. These pictures also provide rich opportunities to use language-in-action and practice behavior under controlled conditions.

The method of using such photos consists of three major steps:

1. Showing the photo and asking the child, "What is happening here?"
2. After discussion, inviting the children to play out the event and then asking: "What will happen now?"
3. Playing out the possible endings.

With very young children, the purpose is simply to stimulate language in action and to work for a positive conclusion. Six- to eight-year-olds can handle more elaborate role playing, depending upon their level of maturity.

Another medium that lends itself well to the classroom is the filmstrip that presents a dilemma situation.[2] Some are structured as problem situa-

[1] Fannie Shaftel and George Shaftel, *Words and Action: Role-Playing Photo-Problems for Young Children* (New York: Holt, Rinehart & Winston, Inc., 1967).

[2] Fannie Shaftel and George Shaftel, *Values in Action* (Minneapolis: Winston House, 1976).

tions; others can be stopped at the critical point, and the class can be invited to finish the story. The virtue of the filmstrip at the upper elementary and secondary levels is that it provides a brief (usually six minutes), dramatic presentation that is especially effective with children who are habitual TV watchers.

Films can be very dramatic; they focus the class's attention with little effort from the teacher. However, they do require equipment and *time* and should be reserved for special uses. Some films are especially designed as problem situations and, like the stories in this book, stop at the dilemma point.[3] Others can be adapted to such use by being stopped at the critical point.

Some simpler techniques use sets of cards that describe a problem situation and then delineate individual roles. Thus, for example, you might develop for your class a set of cards like this:

> Pete, a fifth grader, came to class with a brand-new holster belt and an elaborate toy gun. After lunch, when he returned to his desk, the holster and gun were gone. And absent from class was Alan, who had been there in the morning.

1. You are the teacher of this class. You've had problems with things disappearing.
2. You are John, a friend of Pete's. You and Pete have had fights with Alan.
3. You are Alan. No one will let you play on his team.
4. You are Greg. You've never had a nice toy like Pete's gun.

There are many ways to use role cards. They can be handed out privately to each player. After initial enactments, the cards can be exchanged so that each player gets another version of the situation.

---

[3]Fannie Shaftel and George Shaftel, *Values Films*, Dimension Films, (Los Angeles: Churchill Films, 1969–1970). Titles now available include *Paper Drive*, *Trick or Treat*, and *The Clubhouse Boat*.

Bibliography

AXLINE, VIRGINIA, *Play Therapy*. Boston: Houghton Mifflin Co., 1947.

BANDURA, ALBERT, and RICHARD H. WATERS, *Social Learning and Personality Development*. New York: Holt, Rinehart and Winston, Inc., 1964.

BARTLING, DEBRA, and BARRY P. JOHNSON, "Future Games," *Man/Society/Technology*, 38, no. 5 (February 1979). Reprint: UMI

BEALE, ANDREW V., "Working with Parents: A Guidance Drama," *Elementary School Guidance and Counseling*, 8, no. 3 (March 1974), 182–88.

BENNE, KENNETH, *Education in the Quest for Identity and Community*. Columbus, Ohio: Ohio State University Press, 1961.

——, "The Uses of Fraternity," in *Ethnic Groups in American Life, Daedalus*, Spring 1961, pp. 233–46.

BRONFENBRENNER, URIE, *Two Worlds of Childhood*. New York: Russell Sage Foundation, 1970. 190 pp.

BRUNER, JEROME S., *The Process of Education*. Cambridge, Mass.: Harvard University Press, 1960. 97 pp.

BRUNER, JEROME S., JACQUELINE J. GOODNOW, and GEORGE A. AUSTIN, *A Study of Thinking*. New York: Science Editions, Inc., 1962.

BURNHAM, BRIAN, and JOSEPH MURPHY, *Measuring the Moral Reasoning Power of Elementary School Students: A Report of a Two-Year Study*. Aurora (Ontario, Canada): York County Board of Education, September, 1976. Available from York County Board of Education, Box 40, Aurora, Ontario, Canada. EDRS   ED   138   485[1]

CALIFORNIA STATE BAR, *A Critical Review of Curriculum Materials in Civic and Legal*

[1]EDRS refers to the ERIC Document Reproduction Service, P.O. Box 190, Arlington, Virginia 22210. ED   000   000 refers to the microfiche number, for example: ED   138   485.

Education. Law in a Free Society. Santa Monica, Calif.: Law in a Free Society, 1973. 21 pp. Available from Law in a Free Society, 606 Wilshire Boulevard, Suite 600, Santa Monica, CA. 90401. Also available from EDRS   ED   139   682.

CALLIOTTE, JAMES A., *Initial Attempts at Developing Appropriate Human Relations Experiences for Potential Teachers.* Paper presented at American Personnel and Guidance Association Convention, Atlantic City, N.J., March 1971. EDRS   ED   056   004

CHESLER, M., and ROBERT FOX, *Role Playing Methods in the Classroom.* Chicago: Science Research Associates, 1966.

CICIRELLI, V. G. "Use of Multiple Role Teaching in Teacher Education," *Education,* 98 (Winter 1977), 232–36.

COMPRONE, JOSEPH, "Role-Playing and the Short Film: A Creative Approach to Composition," *Journal of English Teaching Techniques,* 4, No. 3 (February 1971), 1–7.

CONOLEY, COLLEEN, and BETTY J. MOORE, *The Counselor as Consultant to Teachers: Improving Communication Through Role Playing.* Paper presented at the Annual Convention of the Texas Personnel and Guidance Association, Brownsville, Texas, October 1975. EDRS   ED   141   712

CROSBY, MURIEL (ed.), *Reading Ladders for Human Relations* (4th ed.). Washington, D.C.: American Council on Education, 1963.

DALY, FLORA, and LEO CAIN, "Mentally Retarded Students in California Secondary Schools," in *California State Department of Education Bulletin,* 20, no. 7 (October 1953).

DEKOCK, PAUL, "Simulations and Changes in Racial Attitudes," *Social Education,* 33, no. 2 (February 1969), 181–83.

DENNIS, JACK, et al. *A Pilot Experiment in Early Childhood Political Learning.* Report from the Project on Concepts in Political Science. Madison: University of Wisconsin, Research and Development Center for Cognitive Learning. Sponsoring Agency: Office of Education (DHEW), Washington, D.C. Cooperative Research Program, 1968. EDRS   ED   043   368

DONLAN, DAN, "Drama and the Three Stages in the Teaching of Literature," *English Journal,* 66, no. 2 (February 1977), 74–76.

ETTKIN, LARRY, and LESTER SNYDER, "A Model for Peer Group Counseling Based on Role Playing," *School Counselor,* 19, no. 3 (January 1972), 215–16.

FLAVELL, JOHN H., *The Developmental Psychology of Jean Piaget.* Princeton, N.J.: Van Nostrand, 1963.

——, *The Development of Role Taking and Communication Skills in Children.* New York: John Wiley & Sons, Inc., 1968.

GOLDBECKER, SHERALYN S., *Value Teaching: What Research Says to the Teacher.* Washington, D.C.: National Education Association, 1976.

GREENE, RICHARD, "Role Playing for Effective Learning," *Pointer,* 20, no. 3 (Spring 1976) 32–34. (Role playing as a technique to accelerate learning of the mentally handicapped.)

GUMAER, JIM, ROBERT BLECK, and LARRY C. LOESCH, "Affective Education through Role Playing: The Feelings Class," *Personnel and Guidance Journal,* 53, no. 8 (April 1975), 604–608.

HAAS, ROBERT B. (ed.), *Psychodrama and Sociodrama in American Education.* New York: Beacon House, 1949. Many examples of classroom practices using these techniques.

HAYES, ELOISE, "Drama, Big News in English," *Elementary English,"* 67, no. 1 (January 1970), 13–16.

HENDRY, CHARLES E., RONALD LIPPITT, and ALVIN ZANDER, "Reality Practice As Educational Method," Psychodrama Monograph No. 9. Beacon, New York: Beacon House, 1947.

HINES, M. E., "Role Playing in Language Learning," Chapter 13 in Light, Richard L., and Alice H. Osman (eds.), *Collected Papers in Teaching English as a Second Language and Bilingual Education: Themes, Practices, Viewpoints*. New York: New York State ESOL and Bilingual Educators Association, Teachers College, Columbia University, 1978.

HINMAN, SHERYL LEE, "Dramatizing American History," *English Journal*, 64, no. 6 (September 1975), 48–50.

HOHN, ROBERT L., and EVELYN M. SWARTZ, *Development of Attitudes Toward Others in Young Children: Final Report*. Washington, D.C.: Bureau of Research, Bureau No-BR-O-F-008, 1971. Sponsoring Agency: Office of Education (DHEW). EDRS   ED   051   304.

HOPKINS, CHARLES R., "Role Playing and Sociodrama Provide Student Involvement," *Business Education Forum*, 25, no. 3 (December 1970), 54–55.

HURST, JOE B., and DANIEL L. MERRITT, "Pre-Structured and Semi-Structured Role Playing," *The Social Studies*, 67, no. 1 (January/February 1976), 14–18.

IOZZI, LOUIS A., and JANEY CHEU, *Preparing for Tomorrow's World: An Alternative Curriculum Model for the Secondary Schools*. Paper presented at the First Annual Conference of the Education Section of the World Future Society, Clear Lake City, Texas, October 22, 1978. EDRS   ED   162   936

JENNINGS, HELEN HALL, "Sociodrama as Educative Process," pp. 260–85 in *Fostering Mental Health in Our Schools, 1950 Yearbook*. Washington, D.C.: Association for Supervision and Curriculum Development, 1950.

KENWORTHY, LEONARD S., "Role Playing in Teacher Education," *The Social Studies*, 64, no. 6 (November 1973), 243–46.

KOHLBERG, L. "Moral and Religious Education in Public Schools: A Developmental View," in T. Sizer (ed.), *Religion and Public Education*. Boston: Houghton Mifflin Co., 1967.

———, "Stages of Moral Development as a Basis for Moral Education," in C. Beck, B. S. Crittenden, and E. Sullivan (eds.), *Moral Education*. Toronto: University of Toronto Press, 1971.

LEHMAN, DAVID L., *Role Playing and Teacher Education: A Manual For Developing Innovative Teachers*. Washington, D.C.: Commission on Undergraduate Education in the Biological Sciences, 1971. Supported by a grant from the National Science Foundation to the American Institute of Biological Sciences, 3900 Wisconsin Avenue, N.W., Washington, D.C. 20016. Library of Congress Catalogue No. 76–145578.

LEYSER, YONA, "Role Playing: Path to Social Acceptability?" *Elementary School Journal*, 79, no. 3 (January 1979), 156–66.

LIPPITT, RONALD, and MARTIN GOLD, "Classroom Social Structures as a Mental Health Problem," *Journal of Social Issues*, 55, no. 1 (1959), 40–49.

LIPPITT, ROSEMARY, and ANNE HUBBELL, "Role Playing for Personnel and Guidance Workers," *Group Psychotherapy* 9 (1956), 89–114.

MACCOBY, MICHAEL, *The Gamesman*. New York: Simon & Schuster, Inc., 1976.

MARBACH, ELLEN S., and THOMAS DANIELS YAWKEY, *Role Play in Nutrition Education for the Young Child*. 1978. 13 pp. EDRS   ED   164   124

MARCUS, SHELDON, and JOYCE MARCUS, "Utilizing Sociodrama in the Social Studies Curriculum," *The Clearing House*, 50 (February 1977), 272–73.

MCALPINE, JULIE CARLSON, "Original Sociodrama," *Instructor*, 82 (January 1973), 66.

MEAD, GEORGE H., *Mind, Self and Society*. Chicago: University of Chicago Press, 1934.

MOORE, BETTY JEAN, *Living History: Using Role Playing in the Classroom*. Paper presented at the Annual Meeting of the National Conference on Language Arts in the Elementary School, Atlanta, Georgia, March 5–7, 1976. 14 pp. EDRS   ED 120   698

MORENO, JACOB L., *Psychodrama*. Beacon, N.Y.: Beacon House, 1946.

———, *Sociometry*. Beacon, N.Y.: Beacon House, 1951.

———, *Who Shall Survive?* (rev. ed.). Beacon, N.Y.: Beacon House, 1953.

———, "Role," in *The Sociometry Reader*. New York: Free Press of Glencoe, 1960, pp. 80–86. A short essay on the meaning and origin of the terms *role* and *role playing* by the originator of the sociodrama method.

MORENO, JACOB L., and LESLIE D. ZELENY, "Role Theory and Sociodrama," in Joseph S. Roncek, ed., *Contemporary Sociology*. New York: Philosophical Library, 1958, pp. 642–54.

MORTON, BEATRICE, "Listening: First Steps in Developmental Drama," *English Journal*, 66, no. 5 (May 1977) 68–73.

MULLEN, T. PATRICK, *Simulation, Role Playing and Games in Preservice and Inservice Education*. Paper presented at the Plains Regional Conference of the International Reading Association, St. Louis, Missouri, February 20–22, 1975. EDRS   ED 163   806   CS   001653

NARDI, PETER M., "Moral Socialization: An Empirical Analysis of the Hogan Model," *Moral Education Forum*, 9, no. 1 (New York: Hunter College, City University of New York, 1979), 10–16.

NICHOLS, HILDRED, and LOIS WILLIAMS, *Learning about Role Playing for Children and Teachers*. Washington, D.C.: Association for Childhood Education International, 1960. 40 pp.

NIELSEN, KEITH E., *Scenario Role Playing as a Means to Inter-Ethnic Communication*. 18 pp. Paper presented at the Annual Meeting of the International Communication Association, New Orleans, April 17–20, 1974. EDRS   ED   101   387

OLSEN, TUREE, "Values Education in the Junior High School," *English Journal*, 66, no. 4 (April 1977), 88–91.

OTERO, GEORGE G. *Police. An Experimental Unit*. Denver: Denver University, Colorado Center for Teaching International Relations, 1975. Sponsoring Agency: Office of Education (DHEW), Washington, D.C. EDRS   ED   128   268

PITCOLE, MARCIA, "Black Boy and Role Playing: A Scenario for Reading Success," *English Journal*, 57, no. 8 (November 1968), 1140–42.

PRATT, CAROLINE, *I Learn from Children*. New York: Simon & Schuster, Inc., 1948.

PRATT, FRAN, and CHRIS CASTENDYK, "Perspectives on Aging," *How To Do It Series*, Series 2, No. 6. Washington, D.C.: National Council for the Social Studies, 1978.

SALISBURY, LEE, "Role Playing: Rehearsal for Language Change," *TESOL QUARTERLY*, 4, no. 4 (1970), 331–36.

SCARCELLA, ROBIN C., "Socio-Drama for Social Interaction," *TESOL QUARTERLY*, 12, no. 1 (March 1978), 41–46.

SCHAFF, J. F., and H. E. RANDLES, "Simulated Interviews for Teaching Positions Conducted by Student Teachers and Administrative Interns," *Science Education*, 56 (April 1972), 227–30.

SCHUNKE, GEORGE M., "Action Approaches to Learning," *Social Studies*, 69, no. 5 (September/October 1978), 212–17.

SCHWARTZ, SHEILA, "Involving Students in the Drama Process K–12," *English Journal*, 64, no. 5 (May 1975), 32–38.

SEARS, PAULINE, and VIVIAN SHERMAN, *In Pursuit of Self Esteem*. Belmont, Calif.: Wadsworth Publishing Co., 1964.

SEEDS, CORRINE A., "Newer Practices Involving Dramatic Play," *Newer Instructional Practices of Promise. 12th Yearbook*, Washington, D.C.: National Education Association, Department of Supervision and Directors of Instruction, 1939.

SELMAN, R., "Relationship of Role-taking to the Development of Moral Judgement in Children," *Child Development*, 42 (1974), 79–91.

SHAFTEL, FANNIE R. "Role Playing: An Approach to Meaningful Social Learning," *Social Education*, 34, no. 5 (May 1970), 556–59.

SHAFTEL, FANNIE R., CHARLOTTE CRABTREE, and VIVIAN SHERMAN, "Problems Resolution in the Elementary School." Chapter 2 in Richard Gross and Raymond Muessig, (eds.), *Problem-Centered Social Studies Instruction*, Curriculum Series, No. 14. Washington, D.C.: National Council for the Social Studies, 1971.

SHAFTEL, FANNIE, and GEORGE SHAFTEL, *Role Playing for Social Values: Decision Making in the Social Studies*, 1st ed. Englewood Cliffs, N.J.: Prentice-Hall, Inc., 1967.

———, *Values in Action*. Filmstrips for Middle Grades. Minneapolis, Minn.: Winston House, 1970.

———, "Values Films: *Paper Drive. Clubhouse Boat. Trick or Treat.*" Los Angeles, Calif.: Dimension Films, 1970. Distributed by Churchill Films, 662 N. Robertson Blvd., Los Angeles, CA.

———, *Words and Action*. Photo pictures for *Role Playing with Young Children*. New York: Holt, Rinehart & Winston, 1967.

———, *People in Action*. Photo pictures for *Role Playing*, Grades K–4. New York: Holt, Rinehart & Winston, 1970.

SMILANSKY, SARA, *The Effects of Sociodramatic Play on Disadvantaged Preschool Children*. New York: John Wiley & Sons, 1968.

STAUB, ERVIN, *Determinants of Children's Attempts to Help Another Child in Distress*. Paper presented at the meetings of the American Psychological Association, Washington, D.C., Sept. 1969. 18 pp. EDRS price 25¢   ED   039   023

TORRANCE, E. PAUL, *Guiding Creative Talent*. Englewood Cliffs, N.J.: Prentice-Hall, Inc., 1962.

———, "Sociodrama as a Creative Problem Solving Approach to Studying the Future," *Journal of Creative Behavior*, 9, no. 3 (1975), 182–95.

TRAVISS, SISTER MARY PETER, *The Growth of Moral Judgment of Fifth Grade Children through Role Playing*. Unpublished dissertation, Stanford University, May 1974, 103 pp.

TSCHIRGI, HARVEY, and JOHN STINSON, "Sociodrama—A Learning Experience," *Improving College and University Teaching*. 25, no. 1 (Winter 1977) 27–28.

VAIL, W. J., "Dramatization and Role Playing for ITV Productions," *Educational Broadcasting*, 9, no. 1 (January/February 1976), 13–18.

WILKINS, ROBERT, "The Use of Role Playing to Induce 'Plus One' Dissonance in Moral Education," *Social Studies Journal*, 5, no. 2 (Spring 1976), 11–15.

WILSON, JOHN, "Moral Education: Retrospect and Prospect," *Journal of Moral Education*, 9, no. 1 (October 1979), 3–9.

YAWKEY, THOMAS, *Role Playing and the Young Child*, 1977. 34 pp. EDRS   ED 142   298

ZELENY, LESLIE D., and RICHARD E. GROSS, "Dyadic Role Playing of Controversial Issues," *Social Education*, 24 (December 1960), 354–58, 364.

ZELENY, LESLIE D., *How to Use Sociodrama (Practical Exercises in Role Interaction)*. Washington, D.C.: National Council for the Social Studies, 1964. 8 pp. EDRS   ED 083   054

Index

Abuse
  physical, 40
  verbal, 40
Academic achievement, 25−26, 36, 39, 98
Acceptance
  of feelings, 15
  of others, examples, 304−16
  by peers, 21, 24−25
    examples, 36−38, 43
  of self, examples, 283−303
  social, 332
Advice, 139−41
Aging, attitudes toward, 9
Alcohol use, effect of peer pressure on, 4
Alderman, Clifford L., 265
Ambiguity, 31
American history, curriculum materials for,
    237−69
American Indians, curriculum materials re-
    lating to, 90−91, 240−41
Analogies, 76,86
Animal behavior, imitating, 342
Antisocial attitudes, 31, 70
Antisocial behavior, 33, 153−57
  examples, 49−56, 153−57
Attention span, 44
Attitude changes, 10, 99, 101
Attitudes
  antisocial, 31, 70
  provincial, 80
  of teacher, 35, 63, 70
  toward aging, 9
  toward authority, 25

Audience, in role playing, 60, 109, 110
Audiovisual materials, 348−49
Austin, George A., 97
Authority
  attitudes toward, 25
  of peers, 63
  of teacher, 31, 98
Automation, 19
Autonomy, 8
Axline, Virginia, 68

Bad example setting
  examples, 175−83
  themes, 103−4, 322-23
Beginners, in role playing, 72−74
Behavior
  animal, 342
  antisocial, 33, 49−56, 153−57
  causal aspects of, 22−23, 65−66
  contradictory expectations, 28
  cultural aspects, 26, 29
  of disadvantaged children, 49
  ethical, 5−8, 83−84, 101−4, 148−50,
    344−47
  group dynamics, 29
  perceptions of, 17
  physical, 69
  verbal, 69
Benne, Kenneth, 14, 18
Betrayal, 101
Bias, in language, 270
Biber, Barbara, 85
Biological sciences, 3, 145

Black Boy, 331
Blame taking
    examples, 159−63, 168−71, 181−86
    themes, 103, 324
Bleck, Robert, 40−41
Bossiness, 40
Bruner, Jerome, 86, 97

Cady, Jack, 345
Capabilities, estimation of, 283−85
Casual play, 87
Catharsis, 23
Challenges, of contemporary society, 3−4
Character traits, 342−44
Cheating, 31
    examples, 141−43, 199, 229−32
    themes, 103, 321, 324−25
Chesler, Mark, 113
Children
    culture of, 21
    disadvantaged, 49
    handicapped, 41−45, 284
    mentally-retarded, 44−45, 284
Chi-Wee, 90
Citizenship, definition, 18
Citizenship education, 9, 17−34, 213−69
Civil rights, themes, 113−15
Classroom dissension, 35, 39−41, 47, 97−101
Classwork, improvements in, 25−26, 36
Cliques, 30, 35, 39, 69, 101
Codes, of conduct, 5−6, 21, 49−56, 63,
    164−68, 323-24
Coercion, 69
Cognitive learning, 85
Cohesive group, 20, 30. *See also* Group
    cohesiveness
Communication
    cross-cultural, 20
    teacher-pupil, 4, 10, 117
Communication process, role playing as, 5,
    117
Competition, 14, 98
Conditioning, cultural, 26, 27
Conduct
    codes of, 5−6, 21, 49−56, 63, 164−68,
    323-24
    parental, 164−68
Conflicts, 4
    of conduct codes, 49−56, 186−87, 323−24
    group, 30, 80, 97−101, 323−24
    school-student, 9
Conformity, 21, 25, 83−84
Consequences, considering, 33. *See also*
    Consequential thinking
Consequential thinking, 15−16, 19, 31, 33,
    69, 82−83, 97, 318, 319
Constructive work, 92
Controversial issues, themes, 113−15
Cooperation, 73, 83, 213
    examples, 215−32

Counseling, 10, 21−22, 35, 39, 47
Courses, in role-playing leadership, 112−13
Creative thinking, 26, 32, 86
Creative writing, 262, 335−40
Creativity, 32, 283, 284
Criticism, 74, 89
    effect on attitude changes, 31
Cross-cultural perceptions, 20
Cross-cultural values, 20, 29
Culture
    American values, 20−22, 27, 284
    and behavior patterns, 26, 29
    of children, 21
    core values, 27
    relation to self-concept, 24, 271, 284
    and values development, 20−22
Curiosity, 87
Curriculum, role playing in, 3−11
Curriculum materials, for role playing,
    118−347
    English, 261−69, 332−47
    guidance, 283−316
    history, 232−69
    interpersonal and intergroup relations,
    270−82
    in language arts, 261−69, 317−47
    moral development, 153−212
    social studies, 213−69
Curriculum planning, innovations, 3

Decision-making process, 4−5, 10, 11, 13, 15,
    28−29, 64, 214−15, 319
    in social crises, 232−61
Delinquency, 25
Demonstration, as learning technique, 86
Denial, 23
Developmental considerations, 20−22
Deviance. *See* Individual differences
Devil's Shadow, The, 265
Diagnosis, of children's needs, 23−24, 35, 47,
    79, 99
Dignity, personal, 137−38
Dilemma choices, evaluation of, 344−46
Dilemma point, 57, 99, 319−20
Dilemmas
    alternative solutions, 320−25
    clarification of, 68
    ethical, 148−50, 344−47
Dilemma stories. *See* Problem stories
Directedness, inner, 19, 25
Disadvantaged children, behavior, 49
Disappointment, managing, 284
Discipline, maintenance of, 98, 147
Discrimination, racial, examples, 114−15,
    149−50, 270−82
Discussions, guiding of, 30, 39, 58, 61−62, 63,
    73, 75, 76−78, 91, 109−10
Dishonesty, 82
    examples, 141−43
    themes, 103, 321, 324−25

Disrupters, 39, 42, 96
Dissensions, in classroom, 35, 39–41, 47, 97–101
Dolan, John, 261, 269
Donlan, Dan, 341, 344–45
Drama
    and language skills, 9, 334
    spontaneous, 10
Dramatic play, 56, 85–96
    arranged environment of, 90
    beginning of, 90–91
    follow-up, 92–93
    goals, 88–89
    organization and procedures, 89–96
    participation in, 93, 96
    and sociodrama, 85, 96
Drug use, effect of peer pressure on, 4, 15
Dumas, Wayne, 235

Education, for citizenship, 17–34
Egocentricity, 5, 23
Ego expression, 87
Ego strength, 25
Emotional climate, of classroom, 39–41
Emotional involvement, in role playing, 57, 62, 101
Emotional pressures, 85
Empathy, 5, 8, 9, 10, 15, 20, 69, 81, 97, 100, 104
Enactment levels, 78
Enactments, patterns of, 75–76
English
    curriculum materials for, 261–69, 332–47
    nonstandard, 332
    as second language, 9, 334
    standard, 333
Erikson, Erik, 85
Ethical behavior
    examples, 148–50
    themes, 101–4, 344–47
Ethical development, 5–8, 83–84, 318
Ethnic studies, 3
Euthanasia, 345
Evaluative assessment, 341
Example setting
    examples, 175–83
    themes, 103–4, 321–23
Exclusion, effect on self-concept, 29–30
Expectations, of teacher, 66
Expediency, moral, 34, 344
Experience, sharing of, 63, 110
Experiences, personal
    and self-concept development, 19
    and value development, 16
Exploration, 85, 86
    individual, 32
    of roles, 26–27, 32, 71
    subject matter, 72
Expository skills, 317

Expression
    of ego, 87
    of feelings, 23, 67, 68, 69, 70, 74, 79, 317, 318

Fantasy, 318
Feelings
    expression of, 23, 67, 68, 69, 70, 74, 79, 317, 318
    of guilt, 80
Fighting, 150
Films, 348, 349
Flavell, John, 5
Foreign languages, 335
Fox, Robert S., 98, 113
Friendship, integrity in, 183–212
Futures studies, 10

Gaming, 85–86
Garvine, Harold, 234–35
Generalization, 29, 63, 73, 78, 82, 110
Goals, personal, 214, 222–24
Goodnow, Jacqueline J., 97
Group acceptance, 21, 24–25, 36–38, 43
Group behavior, dynamics, 29, 32
Group cohesiveness, 14, 21, 30, 31, 39–40, 80, 101
Group counseling, 21–22, 39, 47
Group life, 18
Group responsibility, 18, 35, 83–84
    examples, 304–16
    themes, 103–4
Group status, changes in, 25–26, 36, 79
Group structure, 29–30
Group support, 21–22, 24, 27, 31, 33, 66, 214–15, 333
    examples, 304–16
Group work, organization of, 146
Guidance, 10
    curriculum materials for, 283–316
    of groups, 21–22, 35, 39, 47, 57–84, 91, 95
Guilt feelings, 80, 82
Gumaer, Jim, 40–41

Handicapped children, role playing for, 41–45
Hartshorne, H., 6
Hays, Eloise, 334
Heaton, Margaret, 67
Hinman, Sheryl Lee, 261, 265, 266, 268–69
History study
    curriculum materials for, 232–69
    role-playing in, 9–10, 72, 232–62
    sociodrama in, 232–69
Hogan, Robert, 8
Home influence, 6
Honesty
    examples, 49–56, 153–86, 193–99, 297–301

themes, 102−3, 141−43, 323−24
Hostility, 25, 31, 39
How to Do It Series of National Council for the
    Social Studies, 9
Huebner, Dwayne, 70−71
Human relations, 9, 23−24, 28
Humor, in problem stories, 118−41

Imagination, 23, 86, 318, 319
Impressing others, 120−22, 123−25
Improvisation, 266, 341−47
Impulsiveness, 16, 33, 34, 70
Independence, 25
Independent thinking, 26
Individual, and group, 21, 29, 30, 35, 39−40,
    66, 69−70, 99−101, 213−15
    examples, 215−32, 304−16
    integrity, 18, 25, 83−84, 213−14
Individual differences, 30, 39−40, 69−70,
    80, 99, 214−15
    examples, 304−16
Individuality, 14−16, 17, 21
Individual needs, 79, 80
Individual rights, 30
Inferiority, 82
Inhibition release, 71
Inner directedness, 19, 25
Inner security, 18−19
Insecurity, 25
Insensitivity, 79
Integrity, 22
    examples, 183−212, 215-32
    in friendship, 183−212
    individual versus group, 18, 25, 83−84,
        213−14
    personal, 25, 83−84
    themes, 102−4, 321
Intellectual authority of teacher, 31
Intellectual capacity, 86
Intellectual development, 86, 87
Intellectual interaction, 117
Interpersonal relations, 9, 24
    curriculum materials for, 270−82
    and self-concept, 19
Involvement, examples, 229−32

Janis, Irving L., 61
Judgment, moral, 6−7, 8, 83−84

Kenworthy, Leonard S., 146
King, Bert T., 61
Kohlberg, Lawrence, 6−7, 344

Language
    bias in, 270
    unacceptable, 79
Language arts
    curriculum materials for, 261−69, 317−47
    role playing in, 8−9, 261−69, 317−47

Language deficit, 332
Law in Society programs, 3
Leader, of role playing, 107−50
Leadership, 21, 29, 30
    of teacher, 63
Learning
    achievement, 25−26, 36, 39, 98
    cognitive, 85
    through play, 86−96
Learning process, dramatic play in, 86−96
Learning situations, 31−32
Lehman, David L., 145
Life changes, 19−20
Lifestyles, 3
Limitations
    acceptance of, 283−303
    maturity, 86
Lippitt, Ronald, 21, 98
Listening, 60, 70−71, 77, 78, 317−18
Literature, understanding, 341−47
Loesch, Larry C., 40−41
Loyalty, 30
Lying, 31
    to escape punishment, 80, 193−97
    examples, 159−63
    themes, 103

Maturation, 97
Maturity limitations, 86
May, M., 6
Mentally-retarded children, 44−45, 284
Minority groups, 270−82, 332−35
Mistakes, 125−27
    correction of, 138−39
    learning from, 48, 65
Mobility
    in contemporary life, 19
    upward, 332
Modeling, and moral development, 6
Moon, Grace, 90
Moral development, 5−8
    curriculum materials for, 153−212
    examples, 153−212
    parental influence in, 6
    stages of, 344−45
Moral education, 5−8
    research in, 7−8
Moral expediency, 34, 344
Moral judgment, 6−7, 8, 83−84
Moral knowledge, 8
Moreno, Jacob, 64, 85, 113, 325
Motivations, of youth, 3

Naas, Normal H., 157
Name calling, 40, 270−74
Nardi, Peter M., 8
National Council for the Social Studies, 9
National Education Association, 6
National Religious Education Association, 6

Needs
   children's, diagnosis of, 23–24, 35, 47, 69, 99
   in human relations, 23–24
   of individual, 79, 80
News incidents, use in role playing, 325–27
Nichols, Hildred, 41–43, 79
Nonevaluation position, of teacher, 16, 70, 95, 110, 117
Noninvolvement, examples, 229–32

Observer
   tasks of, 60, 61–62, 73, 109, 110
   teacher as, 95
Openness, 18–19, 20, 69
Operational thinking, 73–74
Opportunism, 127–36
Organization, of group work, 146
Overeating, 119–20

Pantomime, 341–42
Parental conduct, 164–68
Parental goals, 147–48
Parental influence, in moral development, 6
Parental standards, 49–56, 153–57, 323–24
Peer acceptance, 24–25
   examples, 36–38, 43
Peer culture
   improvement of, 29–30
   influence, 4, 15, 21, 25–26, 31, 63, 69–70, 82, 84, 333
      examples, 49–56, 153–57, 215–32
      themes, 323–24
   resistance, 25, 213
Peer interaction, 5
Perceptions
   cross-cultural, 20
   individual, 13–14, 72
   in problem-solving, 32–33
   of self, 24
Personal dignity, 137–38
Personal goals, 214, 222–24
Personal integrity, 25, 83–84
   examples, 183–212
   themes, 321
Personal interest, 83
Personality, conflicts, 97
Physical abuse, 40
Physical behavior, 69
Piaget, Jean, 5, 6, 8, 86
Pitcole, Marcia, 331
Play
   dramatic, 85–96
   casual, 87
   function of, 85–87
   as learning technique, 86–96
   spontaneous, 86–87
Play centers, in classroom, 87
Pranks, 218–22, 321–22

Prejudice, 101, 114–15, 149–50, 271–82
Preservice training, of teachers, 145–50
Pretending, 87
Problem confrontation, 16, 33, 34, 48, 57–58, 67, 81
Problems
   of contemporary society, 3–4
   out-of-school, examples, 45–47
Problem solving
   on action level, 32
   creative aspects of, 26
   effect of school environment on, 31–32
   feeling-thinking-acting sequence, 34
   group, 12, 32–33, 64
   in human relations, 28–29
   orientation, 19, 34
   procedures, 4–5, 11, 32–33
   teaching strategies, 31–32, 57–84
   transactional aspects, 32
Problem stories, 8–9, 12, 15, 26, 29–30
   acceptance of others, 304–16
   advice giving, 139–41
   analysis of, 321–25, 331
   antisocial behavior, 49–57, 153–57
   bad example setting, 175–83
   blame-taking, 103, 159–63, 181–86, 324
   cheating, 103, 141–43, 199, 229–32, 321, 324–25
   correcting others' mistakes, 125–27
   dishonesty, 141–43, 324–25
   ethical behavior, 101–4, 148–50, 344–47
   function in role playing, 57–58
   group acceptance, 36–38, 43
   handicapped children, 41–43
   in history teaching, 233–69
   honesty,   49–56,   141–43,   153–86, 193–99, 297–301
   humor in, 118–41
   impressing others, 120–22, 123–25
   individual versus group, 215–32, 304–16
   integrity, 183–232
   moral development, 153–212
   opportunism, 127–36
   out-of-school problems, 45–47
   overeating, 119–20
   peer influence, 49–56, 153–57, 215–32
   racial   discrimination,   114–15,   149–50, 270–82
   rejection, 293–303, 304–16
   resisting temptations, 119–20
   responses to, 78
   responsibility to others, 168–87, 304–16
   revenge, 83, 199–212, 321–22, 331,
   rules observed, 122–23, 171–81
   self-acceptance, 283–304
   tact, 136–41, 327–30
   writing of, 115–17, 233, 317, 319–31
Productive thinking, 48
Provincialism, 80

Psychotherapy, 64
Punishment, 83
  lying to avoid, 80, 159–63, 193–95

Racial discrimination, 114–15, 149–50, 270–82
Reading Ladders for Human Relations, 49, 67
Reading skills, 327, 331–32
Reality interpretation, 13
Reality orientation, 33, 284, 318
Reality practice, 48, 61, 69, 147–50, 334–35
Reality testing, 60
Rebelliousness, 25
Re-education, vocational, 19–20
Re-enactments, 62–63, 75, 110
Rejection, 81, 82, 99–101
  examples, 293–303, 304–16
  themes, 98–101, 303–4
Remy, Richard C., 18
Responsibility
  and decision making, 232–33
  development of, 34
  of group, 18, 35, 83–84
    examples, 304–16
    themes, 103–4
  for others, 22
    examples, 168–87
Retaliation, 28
Revenge
  examples, 83, 199–212, 331
  themes, 321–22, 331
Ridicule, 29
Rogers, Carl, 68
Role(s)
  attributes, 5
  behavior, 19–20
  exploration, 26–27, 32, 71
  identification, 58–59, 69
  interpretations, 62
Role playing. *See also* Problem solving
  beginners in, 72–74
  in citizenship education, 17–34, 213–69
  climate established in, 66–71, 109
  as communication process, 5
  curriculum functions of, 10–11
  curriculum materials for, 118–347
    English, 261–69, 332–47
    guidance, 283–316
    history, 232–69
    interpersonal and intergroup relations, 270–82
    language arts, 261–69, 317–47
    moral development, 153–212
    social studies, 213–69
  in decision-making process, 4–5
  defined, 12, 64
  developmental considerations, 20–22
  discussion and evaluation, 30, 39, 58, 61–62, 63, 109–10

  emotional involvement, 57, 61, 101
  in ethical development, 6–8
  extended, 97–104
  feeling-thinking-acting sequence, 34
  feelings class, 40–41
  and group cohesiveness, 30
  and group status changes, 25–26
  guidance functions of, 35–47
  guilding of, 21–22, 35, 39, 47, 57–84, 107–17
  for handicapped children, 41–45
  in human relations problems, 9
  in language arts, 8–9
  leader of, 71–80, 107–17
  observers' tasks, 60, 61–62, 109, 110
  outcomes, 80–84
  participant selection, 58–59, 74, 109
  patterns, 75–76
  preparations for, 57–60, 66–67, 109, 341–42
  process of, 4–5, 11, 12–16, 32–33, 48–64, 235–37
  thematic sequence of, 97–104
  theory and methodology, 3–104
  training to lead, 107–50
  as transactional process, 11, 13
Role theory, 12–16
  cohesive group structure, 14–16, 30
  individual and group, 17–22
Rosenberg, Pearl P., 61, 99
Rules observed
  examples, 122–23, 171–81
  themes, 103–4

Salisbury, Lee, 333, 334
Sarcasm, 99
School environment
  effect on problem-solving behavior, 31–32, 72–73
  and language skills, 333
School guidance services, 35
Sears, Pauline, 25–26
Security, inner, 18–19
Seeds, Corinne A., 86
Segregation, 274–79
Self-acceptance
  examples, 283–303
  themes, 303–4
Self-concept, 29
  development, 19, 20–21
  effect of culture on, 24, 271, 284
  improvement of, 24–26, 36–38, 47
  of minority groups, 271
Self-confidence, 25, 35
Self-consciousness, 73, 79, 90, 110, 341, 342
Self-esteem, 26, 36, 80, 137–38
Self-examination, 30
Self-indulgence, 83
Selfishness, 15, 214

Self-preservation, 186–87
Self-realization, 17, 29
Self-respect, 25, 68, 213
Sensitivity, to others' feelings, 19, 20, 23, 29, 36, 48, 72, 79, 81, 82, 84, 86, 101
   examples, 137–41, 270–74
Shaftel, Fannie, 111, 114, 348, 349
Shaftel, George, 111, 233, 348, 349
Shyness, 39, 79
Silliness, 73, 90
Simulation, 85–86
Sincerity, 66
Skills training, 5, 19–20, 31, 67–68, 71, 79
   for teachers, 145–46
Social acceptance, 332
Social crises, decision making in, 232–61
Social interaction, 5
Social problems, 3–4, 9
Social studies
   curriculum materials for, 213–69
   program innovations, 3
   techniques, 9–10, 72, 87–88, 90–96, 146
Socialization, 8, 23, 25, 87, 348
Sociodrama, 56, 64, 113
   and dramatic play, 85, 96
   in history teaching, 232–69
Solt, Marie Zimmerman, 79
Solutions, alternative, 320–25
Speech skills, 317, 327, 332–40
   examples, 335–40
Spontaneity, 13, 32, 33, 57, 60, 64, 66, 73
   training, 44, 71, 85, 86, 89
Spontaneous drama, 10
Spontaneous play, 86–87
Standards, parental, 49–56, 323–24
Stanford, Gene, 341
Status, in group, 25–26, 36, 79
Stealing, 328–30
Stereotypes, racial, 270
Stinson, John, 325
Student-school conflict, 9
Studies in the Nature of Character, 6
Subcultures, 20, 21, 26, 27, 80
Subject-matter exploration, 72
Supportive attitude, of teacher, 35, 62, 70
Sympathy, 82, 100

Tact, 119
   examples, 136–41, 327–30
Tasks, in role playing, 60–62, 109, 110
Teacher
   authority of, 31, 98
   ethical dilemmas, 148–50
   expectations of, 66
   guidance of groups, 21–22, 35, 39, 47, 57–84, 91, 95
   influence, 25–26
   nonevaluative position, 16, 70, 95, 110, 117
   preservice training, 145–50

   role of, 4, 11, 14, 20, 24, 35, 66, 70, 77, 92–93, 95, 110, 271, 285
   as supportive adult, 35, 63, 70
   training for role-playing leadership, 107–50
Teacher education programs, 145
Teacher-parent relationships, 146
Teacher-pupil relationships, 4, 10, 24, 68
Teaching, philosophy of, 147
Teaching-learning process, 65
Teaching strategies, 11, 31–32, 57–84
Team teaching, 261–69
Temptations, 119–20
Tensions, 23, 35, 47, 70, 97
Thematic sequence, of role playing, 97–104
Therapeutic relationship, 68
Torrance, E. Paul, 69
Training
   to lead role playing, 107–17
   preservice, 145–50
Transactional aspects, of problem solving, 32
Traviss, Sister Mary Peter, 7
Treanor, John H., 157
Tschirgi, Harvey, 325

Unacceptable language, 79
United States history
   curriculum materials for, 237–69
   decision crises in, 235–61
Upward mobility, 332
Urban living, 34
Urban studies, program innovations, 3

Value orientation, 17
Values
   American cultural, 3, 17, 20–22, 27, 284
   clarification, 19, 28–29
   conflicts of, 25, 28–29, 33, 49–56, 186–87, 232–33, 323–24
   cross-cultural, 20, 29
   development, 22
   discrimination of, 84
   subcultural, 20, 21, 26, 27
Vandalism, 15
Verbal abuse, 40
Verbal behavior, 69, 79
Via, Richard, 334
Vocational re-education, 19–20

Warborough Trust, 8
Warriner, John E., 157
Wilson, John, 7–8
Work, constructive, 92
Workshops, in role-playing training, 111–12
Wright, Richard, 331
Writing
   creative, 10, 262, 335–40
   problem stories, 115–17, 233, 265, 317, 319–31